# RISE
# AND
# FALL

# MILOVAN DJILAS

# RISE AND FALL

Harcourt Brace Jovanovich, Publishers

San Diego   New York   London

*Published in Serbo-Croatian under the title* Vlast.

LIBRARY OF CONGRESS CATALOGING IN PUBLICATION DATA

*Djilas, Milovan, 1911–*
*Rise and fall.*

*Translation of: Vlast.*
*1. Djilas, Milovan, 1911–    . 2. Yugoslavia—*
*History—1945–    . 3. Statesmen—Yugoslavia—*
*Biography. I. Title.*
*DR1305.D56A3813   1985      949.7′023′0924      84–12972*
*ISBN 0–15–177572–9*

Designed by Mark Likgalter

*Printed in the United States of America*

*First edition*

A B C D E

# Contents

# Part One

# POWER

# 1

If memory serves, it was in the spring of 1946. At the initiative of Minister of Internal Affairs Aleksandar-Leka Ranković and his aides from State Security, a meeting had been called to discuss building a new jail in Belgrade. Those we had inherited—scattered all over the city—were unsuitable in every respect. Wartime destruction was not the reason, however, since the occupation authorities had adapted to prison use structures far bigger than the ones demolished. When we convened and took a look around, it was apparent that to the last man we were all former convicts. Politburo member Moša Pijade and I, though not responsible for arrests and imprisonment, were included for that very reason.

That we had to have a new jail was obvious, and no one argued the point. There were appeals to hygiene and humanity, but if the meeting had one keynote, it was this: on the outside, the new prison should resemble anything but a prison; on the inside, it should have none of those imperfections or "conveniences" that Communists had turned to advantage in their illegal prison communication back in the days of the Yugoslav monarchy. We would preclude any exchange of tapped messages by doubling the walls, and prevent notes or food from being pushed through the sewage pipes by building them with twists and bends. By providing for deep, insulated cellars, we would ensure that the light of day would not penetrate to the cells, and that no human voice calling from down there would ever be heard above. We would have windows of insulated glass set in concrete, which would look out on passageways, not on the outside world or the inner exercise courts. Finally, we envisioned a clean, wholesome prison, from the water supply and the toilets in every room to blankets and food preparation.

A vast assortment of political prisoners was to be put to work on this large, new jail: Chetniks, followers of Draža Mihailović; followers of the fascist leader Dimitrije Ljotić; Croatian Ustashi; Balists, Albanian minority fascists; White Guards; spies and collaborators with the occupation forces and the Western powers; and war profiteers, speculators, slanderers, and writers of anonymous letters. The need for a new jail would have arisen with any government; our distinction consisted in our planning for complete control over the prisoners, whose isolation had to be certain.

The jail was to be spacious, with many autonomous units. Otherwise, total isolation could not be secured, nor could we guarantee that preliminary investigations would be flawless. Ironic remarks were heard in this connection, to the effect that real masters of prison building had at last been found, instead of Austrian bureaucrats and brutally primitive royal police.

When asked what purpose was to be served by a jail of such massive dimensions, the comrades from Security replied that it would house political culprits from all of Yugoslavia. Common crime, and political crime if insignificant, would be dealt with by the republican and local authorities. Hence the new jail was dubbed "Central," though the title did not stick, because political circumstances took an unexpected turn. When someone observed that the number of political prisoners might be reduced, the experience of the Soviet Union was cited, and, naturally, Comrade Stalin's doctrine whereby an ever-sharpening class struggle must accompany the building of socialism. The main advocate in all

4

these arguments, both practical and theoretical, was Svetislav Stefanović-Ćeća, Ranković's first assistant, a graduate of the party school in Moscow who had had some experience working with the NKVD (the Soviet secret police).

Work on the Central Jail was quickly begun. For speed and efficiency, German prisoners were used, too. They had already earned such a reputation for diligence that tradesmen competed for their services all over Yugoslavia. As far as we were concerned, though, the Germans were simply laborers carrying out our construction projects.

In our cities, including the biggest, life was now safe and secure even for the highest officials, although there were still all kinds of hidden fascists, collaborators, and counterrevolutionaries. Members of the Politburo and the federal government moved around with a single escort and, in most cases, kept only a guard or two in front of their villas. The exception, as in all else, was Tito; comprehensive measures were put into effect for him, with the help of advisers from Soviet Security. Indeed, he himself insisted on it, as he did on an impressive and numerous entourage.

No attempt was made on the life of any leader except Miladin Popović, the secretary of a regional committee, who was killed in Priština by a fanatic young Albanian. Surely what contributed most to public order was the fact that the party and the organs of Security were organized, resourceful, and rooted in the people —conditions that were not God-given but had evolved from war and revolution, from divisions among the people that the occupation had planted and distorted. It was known what side, if any, everyone was on.

In all the little towns and settlements, security had been established automatically as the occupation forces withdrew and the new regime took over. Collaborators had no place to hide; so if they did not retreat with the occupying forces, they turned themselves in. There were virtually none in Macedonia and only a few in Slovenia and Vojvodina. But elsewhere the forests were teeming with renegades from pro-fascist and counterrevolutionary units that had been routed. The Security leadership estimated that there were 40,000 of them in 1945, though their numbers diminished rapidly. These groups were made up mostly of peasants, who, if not entirely sunk in criminality, returned to their homes as soon as the authorities offered them amnesty and humane treatment. The minority, whether for crime's sake or out of ideological hatred, held out in smaller groups in the forests, but were quickly crushed. In 1945 and 1946 the roads in Montenegro were still unsafe, but by the following year even high officials could drive them with only minimum Security detachments.

Renegades soon found themselves in a hopeless situation. Popular support had suddenly waned, illusions of Western intervention flickered out, and the victory of us Communists and the Soviets was fast becoming an indisputable fact. Above all, the outlaws had no program and no heroic leaders—nothing to attract people.

In Yugoslavia, right from the war's end the government was well organized and firmly in the hands of the Communists. It had sprung from the grass roots, from the gradual development of party and guerrilla formations. Despite the upheavals and hatreds of war and revolution, after two or three years of peace Yugoslavia became a secure country. Secure, but hardly well ordered. Administrations were quickly set up and a cultural life emerged, but all within a framework of party ideology. It was still wartime when old theaters reopened and new ones started up, and many magazines and newspapers made their appearance. Their content, however, was controlled. Yet though the nation's younger generation was fired with enthusiasm, its working class loyal, and its party strong and self-confident, Yugoslavia remained a divided, grief-stricken land, materially and spiritually ravaged.

We had embarked on that course characteristic of every revolution: inspired fervor directing a reckoning of accounts. The more exalted the fervor, the more merciless the reckoning.

Though implacable toward the enemy—remnants of counter-revolutionary units and occupation agencies—the leadership at the same time endeavored to expand its authority on the basis of a new People's Front. When the cities and towns of Serbia were suddenly liberated in the autumn of 1944, and those of Croatia and Slovenia in May 1945, the Communist party quickly found itself in new difficulties, enmeshed as it was in administrative, national, social, and economic problems for the solution of which it had neither sufficient staff nor adequate experience. We were strong and self-reliant enough to handle military and police affairs, but our support among the people, particularly the middle classes, was limited. The revolution could not be stopped—no one in the party wanted that—but the transition to a new state of affairs could be made easier for Communists and non-Communists alike, or at least for a significant portion of non-Communists.

Most of this work fell to Vice-Premier Edvard Kardelj. My job was to frame a common platform with adherents of the People's Front: Republicans and Agrarians. Our discussions of the program drafts—mainly at night—were lengthy, but we ran into no problems of any significance. Jaša Prodanović, leader of the Republicans, was the most stubborn, not because he was a man in his eighties, but because he insisted on matters of "form." In one such discussion he said to me—and I will never forget it, though at the time it seemed ridiculous, even childish—"For me, it's the form that counts, not the content! You can proclaim Communism tomorrow, as long as it's done democratically!"

The leader of the left-wing Agrarians, Dragoljub Jovanović, was more easygoing, but, when it came to substance, also more obstinate. On the whole, however, these discussions and hairsplittings were respectful, even friendly, The only incident was caused by the representative of a rather insignificant group of intellectuals. Something provoked him into shouting irritably, "We're not equal! We demand equality!" That provoked me to shoot back: "You're not equal and you can't be! Behind us Communists stand fifty divisions and a terrible war. You're only one little group. You have the wrong idea of equality. What's needed here isn't equality but understanding!" They all fell silent, and Dragoljub Jovanović smiled with self-assured irony.

Essentially, these groups were remnants of former parties that had now joined the Communists—the majority for patriotic and social reasons, but some out of a concern for career and privilege. We Communists were very careful and correct toward our domestic allies. Even in dire wartime need, officials and headquarters people had given priority to non-Communist "patriots." But we allowed no individuals or groups to create or enlarge their own independent organizations. If the question ever came up, we would stress that the People's Front was broad enough to accommodate everyone, a position that won general approval. Most so-called war patriots were even taken into the party. Among the People's Front politicians in Serbia, the single exception was Dragoljub Jovanović, who neither renounced autonomy nor tried to renew and broaden his party. He was also incorruptible, impervious to honors and privileges. Open conflict with him was only a matter of time.

Such nonparty groups stood in the way of full, formal recognition of the Communist party. But there was another consideration as well: relations with the West. We must not be too visible while striving for international recognition and economic aid. Yet it was common knowledge that the Communists controlled everything, that anything of importance was in their hands. But no one knew—except those whose business it was to know—just who in the administration exercised control, and in what way. The Central Committee's headquarters were located in the former Hotel Madeira, which bore no sign outside to this effect.

Our quasi-legality did have its subjective cause. An invisible authority suited Tito and the group around him—an authority controlled by no elected assembly. Even in this narrowest of circles there was talk of holding a party congress; I think Ranković mentioned it most often. But Tito and Kardelj kept putting it off, partly because they were overburdened with current affairs, and partly from the habit of absolute power.

Nor was the federal government convened, because of that same easygoing attitude so typical of absolutism and Tito's own brand of autocracy. Though head of the government, Tito did not call a single session, other than to mark some formal occasion. It was Kardelj who called the government into session, albeit rarely—a practice that continued even after 1948. The issue of full, open party legality and legitimacy sharpened, and ultimately forced the confrontation with the Soviet Union in 1948. One result of this sudden, stormy process of legalizing the party—and of powerful, deep-seated impulses toward national independence—was a tendency for member groups of the People's Front to dissolve themselves. The party leadership did not encourage this tendency. It was unnecessary to do so, and it would only have created a damaging impression of Communists as narrow-minded and exclusive.

Among the higher ranks of the party there were no essential differences, least of all as regards consolidating power, strengthening the party, and extending its domination. Nor were there any differences over hunting down counterrevolutionaries and collaborators. Yet differences were felt, as always, at the very top. They reflected varying degrees of dogmatism and idealism, the diversity of responsibilities, and differences of temperament. Thus Tito's positions, because of his national and autocratic role, appeared now milder, now sharper, when compared with those of other officials. There were also differences among state agencies, but these were not basic either. The ministries—especially economic and cultural—struggled day after day with hardships, disorganization, and lack of staff; hence they were as a rule more moderate and less dogmatic.

On the other hand the Agitation and Propaganda Section—Agitprop—which I directed, was one of the harsher, more radical institutions. It was driven to this by its very function: to disseminate ideology and agitate against an ever-active enemy. A distinct, if accessory, role was played by an inner core of Agitprop intellectuals, smart, well indoctrinated, and steeped in ideology. That accounted for our harshness and inflexibility when we theorized about Marxism-Leninism in the public media, and our manner of popularizing revolution and the revolutionary heritage, then exclusively termed the "War of National Liberation." Generally, Agitprop followed and popularized official positions, and so contributed not only to revolutionary fervor but also to persecutions and acts of vengeance. Agitprop's work was an obligatory component of revolutionary-autocratic power, and the most intellectual one.

Still, Agitprop interfered in the affairs of other agencies only to "straighten out" some line or "correct" some position. Its influence was not felt in the everyday work of the news media unless there was something exceptional at stake or an issue that was either vague or debatable. About once a week, conferences were held at Agitprop with the comrades from the papers to discuss problems and changes in the "line." The greatest care was devoted to the party newspaper, *Borba*, and to the Yugoslav news agency, Tanjug, our link with the outside world. Agitprop was not an executive but an advisory agency: on all important or unclear matters I would consult with Kardelj or Ranković, and in unusual cases even with Tito. Each would make suggestions and proposals, and Tito would also issue orders. There were differences and misunderstandings, but never the kind of discord that stems from larger principles.

Agitprop never had any connection, except propagandistic, with arrests and trials. Furthermore, in the big trials, like those of Chetnik leader Draža Mihailović and Archbishop Alojz Stepinac of Zagreb, Agitprop was not even directly in charge of propaganda. Then, Agitprop was under State Security and developed according to its instructions.

But of course the leading members of Agitprop—"old," prewar Communists with connections and friends in State Security (then called OZNA)—were able to exert influence or intervene, even with Ranković. They did so especially in the first months after Belgrade was liberated, when extralegal wartime arrests were still going on.

The right to pronounce death sentences was taken away from State Security at the end of 1945. Thereafter, these as well as all other political sentences were submitted to the presidium, which more or less automatically confirmed them. In some cases they were changed, mainly on the initiative of Vice-President Moša Pijade and after consultation with Security or with Ranković. Let me recall what Central Committee member Vladimir Dedijer, citing no documents apart from his own memory, writes about this: "I came to know Moša [Pijade] intimately; he was a good man but very hasty. After the war, when he was Vice-President . . .

he sometimes tried to get people out of prison, but kept encountering the strong arm of Aleksandar Ranković, and also that of Milovan Djilas."* Insofar as it concerns me, Dedijer's assertion is inaccurate and ill-intentioned. I had nothing to do with arrests—that was not my business—and no one could have encountered my "arm," gentle or strong. I think Dedijer's remark is also inaccurate with respect to Ranković, who carried out his distasteful duty only after informing himself as fully as possible, and in accordance with Politburo positions, which is to say, Tito's: indeed, he consulted Tito on even the most trifling matters. Ranković's arm was Tito's arm extended—now strong, now gentle, according to calculation or need. This, Dedijer should have known, if only because we worked together daily on the same tasks at Agitprop, with whose jurisdictional limits he was familiar.

I worked very closely and harmoniously with Ranković, the party's organizational secretary. But neither Kardelj nor I involved ourselves in the affairs of Security except on the rare occasions when some problem affected us. Moreover, though there was no rule about it, written or spoken, it would have been rather awkward for anybody to get deeply embroiled, or even take an interest, in Ranković's jurisdiction. One simply cannot whitewash Tito by denigrating his closest colleagues from the prewar, wartime, and postwar (anti-Soviet) periods. They—we—all came out of the same litter (though naturally there were individual differences) and were as one in carrying out the revolutionary mission. When the Croatians—and in their wake the Albanian nationalists —claim that Ranković introduced in Crotia—or in the Kosovo Region—a regime of his own, they not only distort facts but also exploit Ranković's Serbian origins for propaganda purposes. There was no such "Ranković regime," at least not while I was in power. It was all Tito's regime, run by him and the group that had consolidated around him since before the war.

The allegation is even more inaccurate with regard to Croatia.

---

* Vladimir Dedijer, *Novi prilozi za biografiju Josipa Broza Tita* (New Contributions for a Biography of Joseph Broz Tito), Zagreb: Mladost, 1981, p. 722.

Internal conditions there were under Tito's direct control, through the Croatian minister of internal affairs, Stevo Krajačić. Krajačić was only formally and administratively under Ranković—that is, under the federal ministry; he was in fact directly under Tito, for whom he performed all sorts of deluxe "official" services, such as obtaining the choicest villas, paintings, or sculptures. When in Zagreb, I was frequently present at informal meetings where Krajačić would make his reports to Tito, sometimes in the presence of Ranković; the close tie between Krajačić and Tito was obvious and indisputable. In 1952 or 1953, in Zagreb, I met with Krajačić on business. My earlier impression of his incompetence was confirmed at that time. I said as much to Ranković upon returning to Belgrade, to which he replied: "That's the way it is!" In other words, he could not do a thing about it.

The consolidation of the new regime and new land and property laws—the continuation of the revolutionary process—found expression more in Tito's prominence than in that of the Communist party itself. This did not come about simply because Tito was the head of the new regime, whereas the Communist party still operated semilegally. No, a "cult of Tito" had begun during the war. The aroused masses needed a leader and the party was "Bolshevized"—that is, Stalinized. Those demands and needs, emotional and practical, were built into the military and other hierarchies step by step. Actually, the cult of Tito was made official and institutionalized at the second session of AVNOJ (Antifascist Council for the National Liberation of Yugoslavia) in Jajce on November 29, 1943. Tito, an agent of the Comintern since 1937 with veto rights over the Central Committee, was confirmed—thanks to the Bolshevization of the party, his own resourcefulness, and, above all, the revolutionary process—as an autocratic leader. He had conducted himself as such from the start, in 1937; after Jajce he enthroned himself through his own sheer will, the will of a revolutionary leader.

That confirmation became clearly visible soon after Jajce: dazzling uniforms, pomp, unrestrained applause, wild cheering. With his entrance into liberated Belgrade in October 1944, Tito took the final, crowning step toward personal, autocratic power.

To be sure, none of it happened as simply and naturally as it might seem from today's perspective or from my description, whereby a perceptive, adroit "outsider" took advantage of circumstances and "manipulated" everyone, even his closest comrades. Tito was not just the creator but also the instrument of certain aspirations, certain groups, and a specific system. The comrades surrounding him were not merely his submissive servants. They, too, had a role to play in his reign, and were entirely persuaded that both hierarchy and system were the unavoidable "transitional" form of an ideal future state of affairs. Simply put, the glorification of Tito renewed and sustained the revolutionary process itself.

Even before the war had ended, the Communist youth secretary, Rato Dugonjić, suggested organizing a relay race in honor of Tito's birthday. Tito had nothing to do with this idea, apart from agreeing when told about it. We other Politburo members also agreed. Who could have disagreed—or, rather, dared to disagree—with an expression of love and consideration for the leader of a war of liberation and the coming renaissance? At the outset, the relay seemed only an open-handed, unforced gift; Tito did not even accept the relay baton at the palace in Belgrade, but in Zagreb, where he happened to be at the time. Pijade wrote an editorial for *Borba*, which was not like the litanies of later years; in context, it expressed the hidden, illusory desire that such litanies would never come to be: "In the absence of a formal celebration which might offend the modesty of a great man of the people . . . on the day that marks his birth the whole country is filled with sentiments of the highest gratitude and unbounded love, trust, and devotion toward its great leader." In addition, Arso Jovanović, chief of the General Staff, wrote (as was his duty) a little column for Tito's birthday. But only a year later, in 1946, a consecrated, national character would be conferred on the relay—at Tito's insistence, in fact—and the government and Central Committee members would pay a visit to wish him a collective happy birthday and be present when the relay baton arrived at the White Palace.

The royal palaces at Dedinje had been neglected and were

run-down. Under Tito's supervision they were put in order before the war was over, and he settled into them even though, technically, they should have gone to the regent, as head of state. The regency, however, was now composed of former politicians sympathetic to Communism rather than to King Peter, and none of them objected. He also took over the remaining royal properties, except for Topola. Topola passed to the Serbian leadership, probably because of its remoteness, but perhaps also because it would have been extremely awkward for Tito to move into the dynasty's necropolis.

So a new ruler mounted the old throne and began to introduce his own "revolutionary" novelties alongside the old, threadbare customs. Servants and employees of the top leaders started referring to Tito's office as "the court." Only later were these terms replaced by more appropriate phrases like "the Marshal's headquarters." I spoke of this at some length in my book *Tito: The Story from Inside*. Here I shall recapitulate briefly and add a little more.

In royal times it had been the custom for the ruler to become the godfather of a family's ninth son. Tito took up the custom, all the more willingly because the wish sprang from below, from the people. Simple people instinctively grasped that Tito's function did not differ essentially from that of earlier monarchs, while we at the top kept telling ourselves that these were "human" weaknesses and needs, to be indulged during the "transition to Communism."

His monarchical godfathering rapidly began to assume grotesque forms. After all, men and women being equal, why not be godfather to the ninth daughter, too, and why just the ninth child and not the tenth or eleventh? The godchild received a gift and enjoyed favorable lifetime prospects. There were objections, even at the top, to this godfathering of Tito's, but they were silenced by the opportunistic appeal to tradition.

Besides the royal palaces at Dedinje and royal properties throughout Yugoslavia, Tito took over the best hunting preserves for himself and the top leaders, and also certain estates—one belonging to the large landowner Mosek specifically to provision the Security forces, and others to satisfy arbitrary, absolutist conceptions regarding the needs of state leaders. Peasants referred to Mosek's property as "Tito's homestead." I laughed when I heard about it, as did Tito when I passed it on.

The founding of a Guards unit directly responsible to Tito entailed the resettlement of the officers' families—most of them from villages in rebel areas. It was decided to put them in evacuated German villages near Zemun, across the river from Belgrade. There was nothing noteworthy in this except for Tito's reasoning, characteristic of victorious Communists: "Why, of course," he said, "install them outside Belgrade! We'll have a reliable populace of our own. The Russian czars used to resettle Cossacks along their borders." Such rationalization sounded strange to a few people, including me, but no one—again including me—ventured to oppose him. Our unanimity was total when it came to consolidating power.

Enjoying his role as leader, Tito would distribute cash gifts when making visits, most often to a children's home. Sreten Žujović, his frugal and energetic minister of finance, would grumble and mutter as he handed out fresh bank notes, and even Ranković privately criticized this practice.

Along with other sports, horse racing was resumed, and horses "from Marshal Tito's stable" made their appearance. Newspapers began to mention this stable in their racing sections. It was, in reality, a military stud farm belonging to the Guards. We had many troubles on that account, and many awkward questions: What if the horse from the Marshal's stable does not win? How come a Communist leader owns a stable anyway? And where do the earnings from this stable go? I brought this nonsense to Kardelj's attention. How he straightened it out with Tito I do not recall, but news items about the stable stopped appearing.

The train Tito used had formerly belonged to the palace and was kept in a special station (which had likewise once served the palace) in the park at Topčider. High officials used to meet Tito there whenever he returned from a trip. Later the train was given

15

more luxurious fittings, and two other cars—one for Security and one for the entourage—were attached to it. When top officials traveled with Tito, there was a compartment for them in his car as well.

Everywhere, a noisy mass welcome would be organized for him. Even when his train stopped briefly at some station, he would be greeted by a crowd notified in advance. Flowers, children, honor guards. Organized spontaneity, spontaneous organization. Banquets, toasts. Every step, every little word that the Leader uttered, was reported on the front pages of the papers. Once, in 1945 or 1946, we were at Tito's, either in the White Palace or his villa at 15 Užička Street, watching Chaplin's film *The Great Dictator*. Along came the scene where the train engineer keeps trying to align the door of the car, from which the dictator is about to emerge, with the carpet spread out in his honor. We all felt ill at ease and grew sober and subdued. The scene was identical with what happened whenever Tito got out at a station, except that his engineer was more adroit. Tito noticed the similarity and turned around to us, left and right, laughing with mischievous irony, as if to say: "That's the way it goes—now he's got no way out!"

The cult of Tito was not just Tito's doing, but also the result of organized political action. It was the product of a Tito faction, which gradually emerged within the leadership. It was the product, too, of a certain mood among the people, a people led by a single totalitarian party and accustomed to charismatic monarchs.

It goes without saying that Tito was not the only one ensconced in luxury, privilege, and exclusiveness, though in such matters no one could match him. The rest of the top leaders, federal, republican, and more than likely at the municipal and district levels too, behaved similarly, indeed identically. A new ruling class was materializing spontaneously, systematically, and along with it the inevitable envy and greed. The top leaders not only failed to halt the process but, themselves wallowing in privilege, corrected only the worst excesses.

In those first postwar years all the best hotels, especially in the summer season at tourist resorts, were, for all practical purposes, taken over by agencies of the federal government and the various republics, and by recipients of the Certificate of Service (veterans from 1941, the start of the Yugoslav uprising), who had the right to a free one-month vacation in whatever hotel they liked. As for villas and rooming houses, they were simply grabbed up, and the lack of them only reinforced the envy, jealousy, and backbiting among families. Of course there were also modest, unselfish leaders who were glad to take what was offered them by the agencies providing institutions and officials with lodging, furniture, pictures, and so forth. But even they could not entirely avoid the scramble, since it was awkward not to be in step with one's circle and social level. I do not think that any of it could have been stopped, or that Tito and the Politburo were to blame for it all. Total power was consolidating itself through privileges to a far greater extent than the top leaders realized, while they themselves were dissipating their energies in the reconstruction of the country and in theorizing. Even if we at the top had been less ostentatious, the very nature of power and the system, plus the fact that we were emulating the Soviet system, would have pushed us into compromises and brought us to similar practices.

The top echelons, predictably enough, censured only "irregularities"—sloppy work, speculation, negligence, and dishonesty; the system itself was beyond discussion. In those days I, too, was one of the agile critics of "irregularities." In the journal *Komunist*, which started to come out in 1946 and which I edited, I published an article quoting the proverb "From the spring clear water flows, but what the people get to drink is muddy." Meanwhile, in *Borba*—was it in 1945 or 1946?—I attacked the courts for delivering too lenient a verdict against some small-time swindler. I highlighted Lenin's thesis that ours are class courts, ideological courts. The article was published, I think, on the eve of May Day; when Tito and I met on the reviewing stand the next day, he congratulated me on it. That article was the ultimate, if not the proximate, cause of our consolidating party-police control over the judiciary. The wretched swindler was given a death sentence; fortunately, he was not executed, I heard. From the standpoint of

17

ideology and revolutionary morality, I was right, but the consequences for order and legality were catastrophic.

In all that grasping for privileges, the most extreme and arrogant institution was the one in charge of the special stores that provided the leading party and government bureaucrats with food, clothing, and other necessities. These stores were set up on the Soviet pattern and were therefore hierarchical: on the highest level was the diplomatic store, supplying foreign diplomats, Central Committee members, and the highest federal officials; next came the one for generals and higher officers, then the one for leaders of the republics, then an officers' store, and so on. Prices in these stores were nominal. There was instant abuse. One high official ordered forty quilts for his relatives!

The Central Committee reaction to such abuses took the form of mild pressure from Ranković and myself. But the special stores were unpopular from the start and gave rise to much detraction and protest. These stores spread with the growth of the government bureaucracy. As commerce improved, they became a source of speculation. When Politburo member Boris Kidrič and I proposed getting rid of them (I think it was in the summer of 1951), we at first ran into resistance from Tito and Kardelj. But Kidrič was determined: the stores were a glaring anomaly in the economy and in the developing system of financial accounting. When approval finally came from Tito, Kidrič and I wrote the decree abolishing the special stores.

In the fall of that year, at a meeting at Tito's, the conversation touched on another aspect of our incomes—salary. While agreeing that one could live quite decently as things were, we held that Tito could not and should not keep a tight rein on himself, in view of his exceptional position. Yet in those days he lived on his salary just like everyone else and was fond of saying, "Once can get along very well like this; it's incredible how much money they've squandered on me." Jovanka—soon to be his wife—had by then taken his household affairs into her own hands and divided personal from state expenditures. Even the salaries of ministers were still relatively modest. Of all the leaders, Ranković was the worst off, because he had large family obligations and received no out-side income.

Even after the special stores were abolished, members of the Politburo and a lesser number of top officials continued to have privileged sources of supply. They were fed by Tito's farms and, through his staff, were provided with first-class merchandise at advantageous prices.

# 2

Although I had nothing to do with economics and understood little of the subject, something I once wrote may serve to illustrate the unrealistic but potent desires characteristic of our economic leadership. In my statement—published, I believe, in 1948 in the Cominform organ *For a Lasting Peace, for a People's Democracy*—I declared that in ten years Yugoslavia would catch up with Great Britain in per-capita production. That may sound like naïve boasting today, but at the time of my prediction it was something much worse. I was actually voicing what I heard from our "economic experts"—Andrija Hebrang, Boris Kidrič, Sreten Žujović, and others. Such were their views and such were our plans, five-year plans and all the rest. Even a year or two after the 1948 confrontation with the Soviet Union, we were still caught up in that "industrial" and "socialist" euphoria.

The first five-year plan was drawn up by Hebrang, who right after the liberation of Belgrade was put in charge of the economy, and to all intents and purposes was taken into the Politburo. One reason he was given so much responsibility was to assuage his resentment at having been dismissed as secretary of the Communist party in Croatia. But that was not the only reason. Basically, we had confidence, Communist grounds: Hebrang really did have a bent for economics and had mastered Marxist economic theory more than adequately for practical as well as ideological purposes.

From all I could observe, Hebrang worked hard. Whatever differences arose among us were fleeting variations in viewpoint. Only later, when political relations with him became strained, would these "economic" differences be perceived and treated as "not accidental" but, rather, political in origin. As I now see it, our own lack of realism—as well as his—went much deeper: Marxist economic theory, however significant historically and ideologically, was useless in its application and caused confusion and unprecedented troubles. Besides, Tito and those immediately under him had plans for the economy that were overambitious, and political rather than economic in nature: to transform Yugoslavia from the very start into a strong, independent industrial power. Hence the neglect of agriculture, which was approached in ideological rather than practical terms.

Hebrang submitted his five-year plan to the Politburo in the winter of 1946–47. We were all enthusiastic over the high projected achievement and prosperity. There were no prolonged, substantive discussions. How could there be? Ranković, Pijade, and I understood little about it, and we did not care much either. Besides, Tito and Kardelj were responsible for government and the economy. Everyone else was isolated in his own bailiwick.

Hebrang unquestionably had Soviet plans before him as a model and probably consulted their specialists as well. At the time no one faulted him for it, given our faith that the Russians had discovered basic laws and efficient structures. Criticism of Hebrang for "copying Russia" came later, after open conflict with the Soviet Union and with him as the "Soviets' man."

Yugoslavia was backward and devastated, and this, too, spurred us toward an overly rigid, unrealistic, radical plan. Yet those very judgments of backwardness and devastation contained emotional and propagandistic exaggeration.

It is true that in the kingdom of Yugoslavia 75 percent of the population lived on farms, that 44.6 percent of the young went to school, and that industrial production constituted 26.8 percent of the national income. But it is also true that the northern parts of the country—Slovenia, northern Croatia, and Vojvodina—were hardly below European averages, having passed through the Industrial Revolution earlier. Thus Yugoslavia already possessed the technical and trained manpower base for smooth industrial development. The revolutionary movement, however, craved an accelerated, forced, independent industrialization and felt strong enough to achieve it. It would, unfortunately, be quickly demonstrated that we had no resources other than agriculture to draw upon—and at the cost of a lowered standard of living.

It was the most backward parts of the country—Montenegro, Bosnia, southern Croatia, and southern and western Serbia—that were most thoroughly destroyed. Of the larger cities, Belgrade had suffered heavily; in the economic sector, rail transport was hardest hit. But in spite of whole regions laid waste and millions homeless, an industrial and cultural base had been preserved. Of course the country had to industrialize, had to renew itself. But our helter-skelter scramble and distorted economic development can be explained only by a doctrinaire, Stalinist, mythological obsession with heavy industry and by the yearning of a new, revolutionary social power to build a happy, "perfect" society at once. Where my own domain was concerned, Agitprop's responsibility for the economy was discharged routinely by popularizing the government's measures and achievements, and by criticizing sloppy work and disorganization.

Reconstruction and renewal called for extraordinary measures. Arising out of wartime necessity, spontaneous workers' efforts rapidly became important and even imperative for anything involving heavy, unmechanized work. Soon, renewal and reconstruction were no longer regulated by their own economic and human laws, but originated more and more with the state bureaucracy and its directors. As industrialization proceeded, labor shortages became the most critical problem. In propaganda and in official consciousness, therefore, renewal and reconstruction came to be understood as sacred, patriotic, socialist duty, in the wake of which came mobilization into "voluntary mass labor brigades"—a mobilization more and more forced. The police began to play a part of their own in the economy by supplying these bridges to agricultural co-operatives. They were composed mainly of peasants, though they also included convicts of all kinds. At that time convicts numbered in the tens of thousands. The whole system multiplied and spread, and who knows where it might have led had it not become more costly than it was worth—had we not found ourselves in a dead end of inefficiency and Soviet manipulation. We got no help from anywhere except from UNRRA—the United Nations Relief and Rehabilitation Administration.

There was disagreement with the Americans regarding aid distribution. We resisted broad local control, but reached a compromise by naming a Russian as director, Mikhail Sergeichuk, whereupon collaboration with his team, which included Americans, proceeded smoothly. Our economic and political leaders put this aid to wise and objective use so as to bring relief to our population and set industry in motion; transportation was given priority. UNRRA aid was distributed evenhandedly, without regard for political or other convictions. When the question came up in Montenegro whether to share the aid with Chetnik families, the decision was categorically affirmative long before our comrades there were informed that the federal government had obligated itself to a nondiscriminatory distribution. This was the first consistent step toward stilling the hatreds left over from the civil war.

Compulsory sale of agricultural products at low or nominal prices had always been hard on the peasants, even though they understood the need for such measures in wartime and immediately following the war. But after a year or two their resistance suddenly hardened, and coercive measures were resorted to— raids, mistreatment, mass arrests. Overhasty, inefficient industrialization contributed to this resistance and the consequent use of force. Accompanying such industrialization were a shrinkage of the market, shortages, and, later on, collectivization. Requisitions were unavoidably harsh, which only provoked more cunning and fraud on the part of the peasantry. I do not recall that there was serious mass peasant opposition anywhere, as there had been in the Soviet Union. The new Yugoslav regime's power grew in the villages and little towns and became consolidated, but it was not so arrogant and totalitarian that desperation replaced hope.

Side by side with the ideological monopoly, executions, and coercion, cultural life rapidly revived and developed, and the school system was broadened and improved. Along with the compulsory volunteer labor brigades, brigades of eager youths who were true volunteers set to work on key transportation projects. The biggest such project involving young people was the construction of the Brčko-Banovići rail line in 1946, sponsored by the Central Committee of the Communist Youth League. At the end of September, Tito paid a visit to this railroad built by the young; Ranković and I went with him. Boys and girls by the thousands dropped whatever they were doing and thronged to welcome their leader. Spontaneous enthusiasm, the unquenchable fire of youth! We, too, were carried away by ecstasy—an ecstasy as strong as in war, as pure as in children. A few days later I was moved to write an article for *Borba* on the heroism of the young. It was imbued with self-confidence and with indignation against the West, whose press was savagely attacking us for having shot down several American aircraft and for having arrested Archbishop Stepinac.

# 3

The formation of a coalition government at the beginning of March 1945, composed of representatives from the Partisan assembly (AVNOJ) and from the royal government-in-exile, conformed to the Allied agreement made at Yalta. But that agreement was interpreted and carried out by the party and AVNOJ leaders in their own way, through the initiative of Tito and Kardelj. Despite Great Britain's efforts, we did not accept the king, but a regency consisting of people disposed in our favor. No one, whether in the top ranks or only on the periphery of party leadership, could have failed to grasp that the fate of the monarchy was thereby sealed, though quite a few were unhappy with the form the solution took.

The most prominent wartime exiles who entered the government were Milan Grol, leader of the Serbian Democratic party, and Ivan Šubašić, who represented the Croatian Agrarian party. Šubašić had already been president of the royal government and, as such, agent for the crown, though he did not care much about either the crown or the king. Behind him stood the British government and, to a lesser degree, the Americans. We had to accept Šubašić along with the decisions made at Yalta and elsewhere by the Big Three (the U.S.S.R., the United States, and Great Britain). But Grol we ourselves wanted, realizing that Serbia ought to be more broadly represented. No one forced us into it; indeed, the Soviet diplomatic representatives voiced objections. Doubtless we looked on Grol's participation in the government as a move that would be well received in the West, but so far as I know, the West had no share in it. Nor was he the direct advocate of Britain, which could not have been said of Šubašić.

I did not get to know Grol well, either personally or as a politician. I had no opportunity to do so, since that government never really convened. We had no fondness for each other: I viewed him as a "bourgeois reactionary," and he saw in me a "revolutionary ideologue." When I attacked him for calling in question the way the Macedonian issue had been resolved, it only reinforced our mutual antipathy.

Unlike Tito and Kardelj, I was not directly involved in day-to-day relations with Grol, Šubašić, and other representatives of the old order. Still, one way or another, I formed certain impressions of Grol.

Milan Grol was a European intellectual of a high order, and as such was more inclined to literary and political writing than to pure politics. He measured his words like a miser, and was impervious to corruption and human weaknesses. He had reached the top of the Democratic party just before the war, after the death of Ljuba Davidović, who represented Serbian liberalism. Amid the decadence and corruption of prewar political life, Davidović, too, had enjoyed the rare reputation of an honest man.

Differences and misunderstandings with Grol began soon after the government was formed, while he was still one of its members. He set conditions for his participation in the People's Front, insisting on his independence and the renewal of his party. That party was indeed formally approved, but was not permitted any organized activity other than the publication of its weekly organ, *Demokratija* (Democracy). Around Grol there began to collect not only adherents of his own party but also fanatical anti-Communists and nationalists. An underground campaign against him as the agent of reaction—even of the Chetnik collaborators—grew hotter from one day to the next, with every issue of *Demokratija*, until the paper was banned and Communist youth, with the knowledge of the party leadership, burned it in public. Grol protested against the arrests and executions which the Security people were carrying out in 1945, mostly without trial. Security kept an eye on all that he did, very likely even while he was still in the government. His comment on one occasion, "This isn't a state—it's a slaughterhouse!" went the rounds of our leadership.

Relations with Grol were strained for two reasons: first, the terror, which kept striking his real and potential followers; and, second, the restricted rights of the Constituent Assembly and the way elections to it were carried out. The election law had been framed by Kardelj in the Politburo in such a way as to block the participation of any opposition. Slates of candidates in the districts and republics were linked with the federal ones. Since all political groups except the Communists were national, not Yugoslav,* it was the electoral committees—controlled by the Communists and the Peoples Front—that decided whether candidates could participate in the elections. In addition, the election law provided a priori that the decisions of AVNOJ could not be changed by the Constituent Assembly. Moreover, the constitution of old Yugoslavia (the kingdom of the Serbs, Croats, and Slovenes) had contained a prejudicial clause guaranteeing the acceptance of the Karadjordjević dynasty, and thereby a dominant role for the Serbian monarchical parties.

Based on the decisions of the Big Three at Yalta, AVNOJ had been broadened to include prominent "uncompromised" prewar politicians. Then, early in August 1945, it was transformed into the Provisional National Assembly. When the Constituent Assembly election law was debated in this body, Tripko Žugić, Grol's close colleague and an old member of the Democratic party leadership, diplomatically but decisively expressed his reservations, indicating that Grol would leave the government and move to open

---

* Territorial and religious, as opposed to federal. —Trans.

opposition. And that was what happened: Grol resigned on August 18, 1945. There ensued a series of attacks against him—first by Pijade, then Kardelj. A little later Kardelj attacked him in an article, contending that reactionary elements from the Yugoslav National party (JNS) and the Yugoslav Association of Radicals (JRZ)—prewar reactionary parties associated with the old regime—had rallied around him. He was also attacked by Dragoljub Jovanović, the left-wing Agrarian, from both Jovanović's own standpoint and that of the People's Front, but in solidarity with the Communists. Savko Dukanac, of the Democratic party, maintained that the Democrats were not opposed to federation, but that the Constituent Assembly could not prescribe in advance that it would be bicameral—that is, that the various republics would also be represented in it. Grol and the Democrats were doubtless willing to recognize Croatia and Slovenia as federal units, but not Macedonia and Montenegro—at least not to the same degree—and they must also have had reservations about the creation of autonomous regions and of the federal units of Bosnia and Hercegovina.

Grol's resignation surprised us in the top echelon only in one sense, in its dignity and in his serious, unruffled analysis of the political scene. The government did not convene for the occasion, nor was it even formally notified, though Grol was its vice-president. I was informed of the resignation by Kardelj, who was impressed by the moderation and serious tone of its text. Tito felt the same way. Grol was prepared to offer loyal opposition, but was not willing to sacrifice personal and party integrity. The Communist leadership respected him to the end.

That could not be said of Dr. Ivan Šubašić. From what we knew and could judge, he did not resign for the same reasons as Grol. He had attached himself to the People's Front but was not very active in it; his position was special. Survivors from the official Croatian Peasant party, led by Vlatko Maček, of which Šubašić had been one of the prewar leaders, had not joined the Front. Former followers of that party who had joined the Front—including such prominent peasant leaders as Gaži, Lakuš, and

Krce—did not like Šubašić and did not support him. It was the Western powers who supported him, especially Britain. First Šubašić "took sick" for a short time, then resigned soon after. His timing, like Grol's, was connected with the scheduling of elections and the fact that non-Front groups were disqualified. Certain politicians—Savica Kosanović, for instance, who had come back with Šubašić from exile in 1944 to work with Tito (or, more precisely, with the National Committee of Liberation)—tried to dissuade him from resigning, but to no avail. The British overestimated the importance of his resignation. Certainly his presence in the government represented the continuity of old Yugoslavia, and also the West in its accommodations with the Soviet Union. With his resignation, even the form of old Yugoslavia was being snuffed out, and the understandings between the Soviet Union and the major Western powers would soon be undermined.

Šubašić had no clear, steady concepts; he was too flexible and ready to change his mind. He was not stupid or disagreeable— far from it. Though superficial and irresolute, he was lively, resourceful and adaptable. An intellectual, he had the manners and good breeding of a man of the upper classes. Yet there was nothing in him of the leader, least of all the type of folk leader the Croatian Peasant party used to have in such abundance. He was doubtless most adroit and useful in concluding agreements and in negotiating, but a revolution was in full swing: already it had achieved legitimate authority. Conditions that might have favored the talents of a Dr. Šubašić had evaporated.

While he was preparing to resign, Šubašić's villa was sealed off. He was not arrested, however, and after the resignation he resettled in Croatia, where he was not active in any way and was reluctant to see even his close friends. No campaign was conducted against him, as there had been against Grol. But his resignation was ignored by our press.

Elections for the Constituent Assembly imposed their own brand of legislative stabilization in political affairs, less because of opposition from Grol and Šubašić than out of a need for tactical maneuvering vis-à-vis the West, whose press was attacking us for establishing a dictatorship, and for being an outpost of the Soviet Union, which was nothing new. In this context, a press law and a collectivization decree, defended by Kardelj, were passed.

The press law was vague: there was no censorship and the press was to be free; yet there was nothing that could not be prohibited. In regard to this law Kardelj attacked the Assembly "minority," but in defending the law on collective farms he attacked Grol directly, for not grasping the changes taking place and not believing in the masses. A law on crimes against the people and the state occasioned a public appearance on my part. I, too, attacked Grol, but rather mildly: he did not understand the course of events.

Preparations for the elections moved ahead amid tension and polemics, but without serious problems. Jaša Prodanović, the leader of the Republicans, suggested that a "box without candidates" be provided, into which those who wanted to vote "no" could drop their ballot; the people dubbed it a "blind box." In this way, formal democracy was satisfied. The night before the elections, Ranković spoke in Slavija Square. To my surprise, I did too—"by general request of the masses," as *Borba* put it. Of course I had delivered my major speech in my native Montenegro.

On election day I drove out with a few comrades to Topčider and Kragujevac to see how things were going. In the latter I met foreign journalists, including, as I recall, some Americans. They had no criticism of the balloting as such, but made no effort to conceal their view of the elections themselves: a farce, they said, because it was known in advance that all candidates would be elected, there being no opposition. In those days the British prime minister, Clement Attlee, was calling this kind of election in Eastern Europe a "race with one horse."

Demonstrations, parades, and banners attended these Constituent Assembly elections. We had scarcely any experience as yet in conducting such "one-horse" elections, but everything went off smoothly and without the usual Balkan hullabaloo.

In *Tito: The Story from Inside* I mentioned the party leadership's assumption that the Front—that is, the Yugoslav Communist party—would attain an absolute majority. We were not threatened with defeat, but naturally wanted no opposition at all, and were a little fearful that, if any materialized, it might become institutionalized. Prospects had been discussed in the Politburo, as well as ways of forestalling any opposition by manipulating the electoral legislation.

As confirmation of both our maneuvering and our intentions, I quote Tito, speaking to members of the British Parliament and British journalists (published in *Borba*, November 13, 1945): "In the Front, as you know, there are many parties [in actuality there were only groups, the remnants of parties], and in a parliament within the Front an opposition will probably crystallize. I am confident that there will be an opposition, a strong one at that, but not the kind there used to be." (He was thinking of Grol and Šubašić.)

November 29 was chosen for convening the Constituent Assembly, in order to link it with the second session of AVNOJ, held on November 29, 1943, in Jajce. At this first meeting a republic was proclaimed. Before the session got under way in the Assembly building, however, Vladimir Velebit told the leadership the British ambassador had expressed confidence that we would not be so unreasonable as to proclaim a republic. His intervention was taken as a belated shot in the dark, and merely strengthened our resolve.

The new constitution had already been prepared and was now submitted for "public discussion." Our model was the Soviet "Stalinist" constitution and the Soviets' own "public discussion" of it. Kardelj was responsible for drafting it, as he did subsequent constitutions, but he was assisted by Professor Jovan Djordjević and others. Soviet representatives did not participate, though Ambassador Sadchikov was consulted about the draft. I remember his suggesting that it was too early to introduce social security for the peasants, since not even the Soviet Union had that—a suggestion that was adopted, along with some minor ones.

Kardelj had to go to London, so I took over his work on the constitution, including its interpretation before the Assembly. During the government's private discussion of the draft, Tito had objected to our formulation of the right of Yugoslav peoples to self-determination, including secession. He was energetically against it. "We're not in the same situation as the Russians," he said to me. "We just can't do it. If something changes in one of the republics, say Macedonia, and they ask to secede, then what do we do?" After racking our brains and tackling the matter with Djordjević, we hit upon the following formulation: the Federal People's Republic of Yugoslavia (FNRJ) "is composed of people equal in rights, who on the basis of the right to self-determination, including the right to secede, have expressed their will to live together in a federated unit." Once more I went to see Tito, who accepted this formulation, but not until after I had argued that we could not omit the principle of self-determination, to which all socialist movements subscribed.

The name "Democratic Federated Yugoslavia" had attained wide currency through propaganda and the conversations and writings of officials after Jajce in 1943, and especially after the liberation of Belgrade in 1944. Democratic Republic of Vietnam and German Democratic Republic were thought up much later—with no thanks to us, their ideological forerunner. Never inclined to change any term in common use, Tito was for keeping this name in the new constitution. But Kardelj talked him out of it, with my help. "A programmatic designation," argued Kardelj, "cannot designate a country, a state." Tito grasped this at once and agreed. Hence the state was called a "people's" republic—a term borrowed from Leninism, meaning that it is in a transitional stage of becoming "socialist."

With the adoption of the constitution on February 1, 1946, the government was reorganized. The most important change, I think, was that Ranković assumed the post of minister of internal affairs, which had been held by the priest Vlada Zečević. Until then Ranković had been director of the Bureau for the People's Protection (OZNA) in the ministry of the armed forces. This bureau —in fact, the secret police—was directly under Tito as supreme commander and minister of the armed forces. A little more than a month later came the reorganization of OZNA itself, whose name was changed to UDBA (Administration of State Security).

It might or might not have had something to do with our parting of the ways with the opposition—Grol and Šubašić—but at this point the Soviet government chose to bestow more medals on the Yugoslav leadership. At the beginning of September, Tito was awarded the Order of Victory, and at the end of October a few of our top officials were given orders: Peko Dapčević was awarded the Order of Kutuzov, and the generals of his rank, Koča Popović and Arso Jovanović, were given the Order of Suvorov, which was considered the higher of the two.

The Soviet armed services had been unhappy with Dapčević ever since he had collaborated with them on the Srem battlefront. Ranković and I noticed the way the Soviets thus belittled and made an exception of him, and suggested to Tito that he at once decorate Dapčević with our highest order, National Hero. Tito agreed. And I made sure that Dapčević's decoration, which he would otherwise have been given at a later time, was featured in *Borba* more prominently than the Soviet medals. Our relations with the Soviet ambassador and his government were not abrasive at that time, but we were sensitive even on this level. The Soviet representatives did not make an issue of it, but they could not fail to take note.

# 4

Many political trials took place in Yugoslavia in the first years after the war. So large was their number—especially in the provinces—that they could not possibly all have been publicized. Nor had we the slightest desire to do so, wishing instead to play down any impression of persecution. So what was brought to public attention were only the most important trials—those of the leaders of particular groups, or of conspicuous representatives of the occupation terror.

As I have said before, my role in these trials was secondary, since they soon became the responsibility of the Security apparatus. My assignment amounted to general oversight of the media. State Security had its own direct links with the papers and radio; I was consulted only if disagreement arose. In any case, Security largely determined the thrust of a trial—the way it was conducted in court, and the points emphasized by the prosecuting attorney. I thought then, as I do now, that Security and the courts were prone to exaggerate, often inflating those sensational minor details with which political life is swamped under any circumstances, but especially in time of war or revolution.

I do not mean to imply that I was in no position to influence the course of a trial. On the contrary, very often my suggestions were accepted. But at times they were doomed in advance, the course having already been set by either Tito or the Politburo. Afterward I simply carried out the decision as a disciplined Communist.

Here I shall take up only the great trials, stressing details that are not known or have been wrongly interpreted.

How Draža Mihailović was captured is no secret. One of his most "devoted" commanders, Nikola Kalabić, was enticed to Belgrade, where he was arrested and recruited by Security. Then, with a group of OZNA agents, Kalabić penetrated Mihailović's hiding place and drew him into a trap. This dramatic story is of special interest because it illustrates the superiority and cleverness of revolution over the naïveté and disarray of counterrevolution.

No sooner had Mihailović been caught, in mid-March 1946, than preparations began for his trial. We had no control over its significance or the direction it would take, still less so because most of the Western press lined up in his defense. To be sure, hymns of praise to Mihailović as the heroic resistance fighter had long since subsided. But now the West glorified him even more for fighting Communists. What is more, the U.S. government delivered a note at the beginning of April in which it tried to show that Mihailović was not a traitor and expressed a desire that American fliers he had saved participate in the trial as witnesses. Domestically, especially in Serbia, the trial was important for similar, if not precisely the same, reasons. In underground propaganda emanating from the nationalists, as in the minds of many peasants, he was considered a good man whose struggle against the occupation on behalf of the nation and the Serbian people had been hampered by Communist rebellion and the Communists' evil cunning.

The allegations converging from the West and the distortions welling up from within, among the Serbs, had to be dispelled and eradicated. Obviously the situation called for public trial and due process, and required that judges and prosecutor alike be not simply lawyers, but Serbs from Serbia. It was decided that the press should give extensive coverage to the trial and that it should be broadcast over the radio.

What had to be proved was that Mihailović collaborated with the German occupation against the Communists. But that was not all. Not only did his collaboration differ in no respect from that of other Quislings—the Serbian nationalist Milan Nedić and the Serbian fascist Dimitrije Ljotić—but also he was in league with them. For this reason, both fascists and collaborators were tried alongside him. And since units under his command as armed forces minister for the royal government-in-exile—especially units from ethnically mixed regions—had exterminated Moslems and Croats, we obviously had to expose his chauvinistic Greater Serb operations.

Ranković was in Tito's entourage on a trip to Moscow at the time the Mihailović trial was being prepared, so I, as a government minister, was appointed his deputy. Miloš Minić, the prosecuting attorney, consulted with me. As we talked it over, I felt he was putting too great an emphasis on Mihailović's struggle against the movement for national liberation, and not enough on his commanders' collaboration with the occupation. I pointed out that abroad, in the West, Mihailović's fight against the Communists would not be held against him, but would actually work in his favor. Minić quickly took this in.

The Security chiefs had closely studied Mihailović long before he was captured, so once they had him they knew how to handle him. From all I heard and later read, Draža Mihailović was a brave man, but extraordinarily unstable in his views and in decision-making. He had no talent except as an intelligence officer. A traditionalist, he was incapable of grasping stormy times, let alone navigating through them. For him the common people, especially Serbs, were deeply religious, patriotic, and in their good-natured way devoted to king and country. While he tended toward military authoritarianism—and those around him even more so—he was inclined to bourgeois liberalism rather than to dictatorship. His loyalty to the king and the monarchy stemmed more from loyalty to his oath and to tradition than from any well-founded political or philosophic doctrine. In any case, he had no strong or clear ideas. Even his identity as a Yugoslav was inconsistent and shifting, not simply from allegiance to a Greater Serbia but because he was fundamentally unsure of anything. Although his units—sometimes at his direct orders—carried out mass crimes against the non-Serbian population, wantonly executing Communists and their sympathizers, Draža himself was not considered harsh or fanatic.

Security sought to make Mihailović admit his collaboration with the occupation, in order to undermine his prestige. That would confirm the Communist charge that he was a servant of the occupation and in no way different from all other collaborators.

From the beginning of the investigation he proved mild and receptive, the more so because he was being treated properly. The man in charge was Josif Malović, a high Security officer, patient, intuitive, and enterprising. Draža wanted to shave off his beard, but Malović and the other top Security people graciously denied his request on the grounds that he and his beard were inseparable. In effect, they believed that he would project a more menacing image if he kept that beard—the mark of a Chetnik.

I do not think that Draža was drugged at the time of the trial, though I have no direct knowledge of this. He was permitted brandy, otherwise forbidden to prisoners, but I never heard of him getting drunk. Malović, undoubtedly in league with Ranković and his aides, insinuated to him that his life might be spared if he acknowledged collaborating with the occupation. Draža took the bait—whether tacitly or explicitly, I don't know—and admitted to collaboration when Minić pressed him with documents. It was the decisive moment. Foreign correspondents rushed out of the courtroom to their telephones to announce the confession, whereupon Western interest in Mihailović suddenly dissipated.

Defense attorneys from abroad had offered Mihailović their services—Morris Ernst, for example, from the United States. We probably would not have permitted them to take part, but Draža spared us any embarrassment by rejecting them himself, proclaiming his confidence in the court and the official defense counsel. He actually had good reason to be confident of his defense attorneys, publicly appointed though they were. Both of them defended him conscientiously and devotedly. Nikola Djonović was a respected lawyer and leading member of the Democratic party; Dragić Joksimović carried out his duty with such zeal that he was attacked in our press for not helping the court. I had known Djonović before the war, renewed the acquaintance after leaving prison in 1961, and renewed it again in 1966. He told me that he had tried to persuade Mihailović to defend himself as the leader of the other side in a civil war, and not to get involved in the issue of collaboration. Everyone, so Djonović told him, who loses a civil war is charged by the opposite side with treason, but such a charge is meaningless, especially in the light of history. However, these arguments fell on deaf ears. Credulously, Draža yielded to the fate that had befallen him. Later, the Security people, resentful of Joksimović's stand at the trial, found him guilty of something or other—it was not hard to do then—and sent him into forced labor, from which he never returned.

When we met with Tito, Ranković reported on the trial and on Malović's agreement with Draža—the agreement that could allegedly save Draža's life. Tito remarked, with a roguish, ambiguous smile, "Well, that's not out of the question; it's a political trial." Whereupon everybody present—I don't recall exactly who was there, but certainly the "leading threesome"—argued that not only would our fighting men find such a verdict incomprehensible, but also the relatives of countless victims would be outraged. Tito bowed silently to the arguments, more readily because he himself at heart was not opposed.

Mihailović was given a death sentence and executed shortly thereafter. I heard that a high official in Security witnessed the execution, but I am not familiar with the details.

With the trial of Archbishop Alojz Stepinac I was even less involved than with that of Mihailović, but I know some details that led up to it. At the beginning of June 1945, soon after the liberation, Tito received a delegation in Zagreb of Catholic prelates headed by Bishop Salis-Sevis. Tito chose this opportunity to state that he was dissatisfied with the wartime conduct of "some of the Catholic clergy." This was when he let slip the phrase "I, as a Catholic . . ." Enthralled at the time by the victory that had installed him as absolute ruler, Tito would blurt out remarks that were sometimes tactless. When the text of his statement reached Belgrade, several people called me, including Radovan Zogović, who was in a quandary as to what to do about it. I had no way of getting in touch with Tito, so I telephoned Kardelj, who instantly agreed: "Delete it! The secretary-general of the party a Catholic? Nonsense!" So Tito's slip never saw the light of day. During the conflict with the Soviet Union after 1948, I once recalled that incident, and Kardelj and I laughed at the thought of what ample use Molotov and Stalin would have made of Tito's "Catholicism" had we not purged it from the text.

Tito later received Stepinac—twice, as I recall. I do not know what they talked about, but I do remember that the top echelons were taken by the idea of developing and strengthening a "national Catholic church"—a church that would break away from the Vatican. There was even mention of an undercurrent of sentiment and certain priests leaning in that direction, though within the church itself there were no appreciable aspirations to break away. If Tito steered the conversation with Stepinac in that direction, it could only have angered and alarmed the archbishop. Stepinac, in my judgment, had always been a loyal shepherd of the Vatican and remained so.

He would certainly not have been brought to trial for his conduct in the war and his collaboration with the Croatian fascist leader Ante Pavelić had he not continued to oppose the new Communist regime. I was not especially concerned about Stepinac and his trial, but I have no doubt that he collaborated with Pavelić, supported him, and urged him to force conversion on the Serbs. At the same time, however, he dissociated himself from Pavelić, remaining independent and loyal to Vatican policy. This does not mean there were no grounds for a charge against him, or for an investigation immediately after the liberation.

Quite a few other high clergymen—and not only Catholics—
merited censure, even by standards more tolerant than Communist and revolutionary ones.

But a triumphant leadership—in essence, Tito—had in mind
expediency and consolidation. At first he tried to make some
accommodation with the church and Stepinac, which they may
have seen as weakness. Already in the autmn of 1945 the
Catholic bishops, led by Stepinac, had come out against the new
regime in a pastoral letter. Our press reacted sharply, probing
wounds that were still fresh, citing the crimes of priests who were
Ustashi or pro-Ustashi and were now in the Široki Brijeg camp.
Tito himself wrote an article, published in *Borba* on October 25,
1945, in answer to the pastoral letter.

I can draw only one conclusion from the statement of Archbishop
Stepinac and certain other high dignitaries of the church: they are
prepared to persist in their struggle at the cost of personal sacrifice.
My conclusion is that they acquiesced in conditions under Pavelić, not
out of fear but for ideological reasons. My conclusion is that they have
now declared war in the new, democratic, federated Yugoslavia according to a set plan, in partnership with the remaining forces of
reaction in Yugoslavia. . . . I don't want this to be interpreted as a
threat, but I must warn that there are laws which forbid fomenting
chauvinism and discord, forbid jeopardizing the hard-won legacy of
this great war of national liberation. Those laws should be obeyed by
everyone who desires the good of his country.

At that time, or a few months later, whenever the conversation
turned to Stepinac at Tito's, he would stubbornly exclaim: "The
church cannot be above the state—the state must be above the
church!"

Tito's article and his remarks in the inner circle were early warnings—but not the only ones—of a fixed position. In December
1945 the Croatian Communist leader Vladimir Bakarić issued a
statement about the visits of Erih Lisak, an Ustashi emissary to
the archbishop's residence, and about the arrest of priests from

the residence. And in January 1946 the Croatian press began to publish documents on Stepinac's collaboration with Pavelić.

The conflict with Stepinac then subsided, but after a period of watchful waiting it broke out again at the end of 1946. In the People's Front, meanwhile, we had come into conflict with Agrarian leader Dragoljub Jovanović. And, accidentally, around the same time the downing of two American planes over Yugoslavia on August 9 and 19 had put our relations with the United States under the severest strain. The *New York Daily News* urged that an atom bomb be dropped on Belgrade, and Secretary of State James F. Byrnes summoned Kardelj (both were attending a peace conference in Paris) and threatened him in no uncertain terms. On September 19, 1946, Public Prosecutor Jakov Blažević suggested that proceedings be started against Stepinac, who was soon arrested.

I do not know the nature or extent of the American government's role, but from what I recall and from the course events were taking, there is no doubt that U.S. intelligence was much involved in causing our relations to deteriorate. American military personnel simply took no account of our national sovereignty, and despite our many notes of protest and warning to the U.S. government, its planes overflew our country from their bases in Italy and Austria as if it belonged to no one in particular. This became intolerable, unless we were prepared to acknowledge our impotence and shame publicly. Tito gave orders to direct the American planes to land at certain of our airports, and if these orders were ignored, to open fire. At first there was some hesitation among our air command—the planes were unarmed transports—but Tito was scathingly emphatic, and so the inevitable happened. The first plane landed only when peppered by machine-gun fire. A Turkish officer who was aboard was wounded and some of his personal possessions were stolen when he was transferred to a hospital. The other plane, with four crew members, was shot down. At the same time, the American authorities refused to hand over river vessels of ours that the Nazis had removed to Austria.

After Secretary of State Byrnes rebuked Kardelj in Paris about the downing of the aircraft, Kardelj relayed their exchange to Tito, who then issued a conciliatory statement that planes would not be shot down in the future but that their markings would be recorded. Upon his return, Kardelj told us that the members of the Soviet delegation were enraptured by our shooting down American planes, but that they had some advice to offer: "Don't shoot down a third!" The Americans suspended hostile over-flights, but relations failed to improve.

The United States embassy in Belgrade played a substantial role in this affair. Its employees were arrogant and provocative, even going so far as to promise certain individuals—our enemies and some leaders of former parties—that parachute troops would take over Belgrade and the navy would seize the Adriatic coast. I remember how in June 1946 the Americans scornfully refused to let our officials participate in consecrating the cemetery for their fliers in Košutnjak, yet they let two or three hundred of our bitter adversaries attend. The American embassy even published a leaflet inviting our citizens to attend the consecration and so "give vent to your feelings against the oppressor." On top of all that, an American officer shouted, "Tito—Heil Hitler!" Of course there were affronts from our side as well, but the Americans undoubtedly took the initiative, if only because they overlooked or underrated the change in Yugoslavia and treated our leadership as "Satellite Number One."

The trial of Stepinac began soon after his arrest, since the bulk of evidence had already been gathered. The trial proceeded according to plan. Quite a bit of convincing material was published and the testimony of numerous credible witnesses was heard—witnesses who confirmed Stepinac's collaboration with the Ustashi regime. But the prosecution strategy and tactics were misconceived and bound to fail. Stepinac was attacked mainly for his conduct in the war, whereas the real reason for the trial was his postwar opposition. This could not be hidden, for Stepinac had been arrested fifteen months after the war's end, after having had discussions with both Tito and Bakarić. No, it could not be hidden, regardless of his wartime conduct, regardless of all our evidence and documentation against him. Needless to say, the Western press discovered that flaw in the argument, that element of "staging" in the trial. Stepinac himself contributed to the failure of the trial by his firm and dignified bearing. He was sentenced to sixteen years in prison.

While the trial was still in progress, we recognized that it was ill-timed, that it had not been thought through to the end. There were even discussions about it at the top. But there was not a hint of criticism from anyone, so the trial proceeded exactly as directed by the "sovereign will." The poor timing and lack of forethought, however, caused the matter to remain a lively issue in the West. It became a serious problem for us after the break with the Soviets, when we began to obtain aid from the West. Meanwhile, Stepinac was given privileged treatment in prison. A few years later we found a way out that appeased the West while satisfying both our prestige and our insistence that he not return to the archbishop's residence: he was interned in his native village without having his sentence revoked.

I do not recall exactly when the leader of the left-wing Agrarians, Dragoljub Jovanović, was taken into custody, but I think it was in the fall of 1946; he came to trial in early October 1947. Our press had begun a fierce, high-handed attack on him in August. Some of the details of his arrest and trial come back to me now. The case can be understood only in the context of our embittered relations with the West, the United States in particular, and the measures taken by the various East European governments against the leaders of agrarian parties.

Yet I cannot say that relations with Jovanović became strained simply because he had been influenced by Western intelligence services. I believe that he acted in the light of his convictions and of his own accord, but that he counted on support from the West, support that at the time seemed both possible and logical. Dragoljub was bound to come into conflict with us Communists. Relationships within the Front and within the People's Agrarian party, which the Communists had gradually been infiltrating, were such that he had either to confront us or to renounce any independent role. And because he was the party's founder and the creator of its program he could not give up his independence without accepting political death and the shame of cowardice and corruption. Thus Dragoljub Jovanović's fate resembles that of the Social Revolutionaries in Russia, except that he was not a revolutionary, while we Yugoslav Communists were, if possible, more Bolshevist than the Bolsheviks.

The Soviet representatives had no direct role, so far as I know, in Jovanović's arrest. But it was no accident that the arrest took place at a time when the leaders of other East European agrarian parties were being attacked and persecuted—Nikola Petkov-Gemet in Bulgaria and Stanislaw Mikolajczyk in Poland. At the end of the war and in the months following, Soviet representatives in unofficial conversations had criticized our restraint toward Jovanović; yet relations between him and the Soviet representatives had been good, even friendly, though of course without that conspiratorial closeness that prevailed between the Soviets and us. Thereafter the tendency of Communists to monopolize power grew stronger; relations with the West deteriorated; and all at once the Soviet representatives began to slander Jovanović, even to criticize us— unofficially, of course—for not taking more initiative against him. This poisoned the atmosphere between the Communists and Dragoljub. But the decision to arrest him—like most other decisions—was taken independently by our leadership.

Its immediate cause was a speech he made in the Assembly on July 17, 1946, in connection with the law on the collective-farm movement. It was at a midday session; Dragoljub requested the floor. He was expected to come out against the law because it deprived co-operatives of their autonomy. No sooner did he begin speaking than the ministers, and along with them the representatives, started to file out of the chamber. He ended up holding forth before a virtually empty Assembly—the only people left were four or five of his followers. I also stayed, on my own initiative, in order to respond in the name of the government. And respond I did, with earnest and soul-stirring emotion. As I statred in, the chamber quickly filled up again.

I don't recall whether a message was handed to me in the

chamber or whether I reported to Tito after returning to my apartment, but at suppertime I found myself at his villa. Ranković was also there. I began reporting on the encounter with Jovanović. Tito and Ranković already had some information about it and were obviously pleased with my performance. I had barely concluded my report when Tito, who did not like to see his daily routine interrupted, invited us to supper, where the conversation continued. In a somewhat angry but decisive voice, Tito said, "Dragoljub must be arrested!" To which Ranković responded, "It'll be hard to get anything on him." Tito: "Then make him guilty of something!" I listened in silence. For me, and I think for Ranković too, that was new, something novel in methods of persecution. Up to that time we had indeed exaggerated guilt, but the guilt itself—at least by our own ideological, revolutionary criteria—had always existed. Now it had to be created.

Indeed, Dragoljub Jovanović's guilt would not have existed at all had he not made so firm a defense of his own and his party's political integrity. In court the evidence against him was weak: by associating with Vlatko Maček, the leader of the Croatian Agrarian party in exile, he had been taken advantage of; by making statements to a foreign journalist, he had passed information to a foreign intelligence service; he had links with the Slovenian opposition members Nagoda and Sirc; and the like. He was sentenced to nine years. The lawyer Veljko Kovačević, who defended Jovanović, and later defended me three times, once told of seeing him in prison. Overjoyed by this visit after many months of isolation, Dragoljub insisted, "You know, I haven't betrayed my country and my people." In 1952, Anthony Eden interevned on his behalf while visiting Yugoslavia and so played a part—a small one—in getting him released a few months ahead of time. Rankovic, in proposing his release, recalled that it would soon be nine years since his arrest, at which Tito observed with conscious cynicism: "How quickly the time passes!" Ranković was bothered by the way accounts had been settled with Dragoljub, as if to say, "We barely brought off that trial." As for me, I did not have second thoughts about the Jovanović trial until I myself fell from power.

Sentences handed down at the most important trials were presented by Ranković to the Politburo—that is, to the top leaders—for review. There was never much discussion. Proposed sentences were most often "for information only," but each could make his comment. The majority of verdicts—an enormous number—were treated in like fashion by the republics and the local administrations. State Security had rights of review and regulation but did not make decisions directly. This procedure closely resembled that of the old kingdom of Yugoslavia, where the state security court submitted proposed sentences to the palace for approval. In that old court the procedure itself had been proper; nothing was concealed. There were also differences, however: in the old kingdom, as a rule, only one court—the state security court—had pronounced political verdicts, whereas under our regime every district court has been given such responsibility. Thus in the old kingdom, except for the state security court, the judiciary was not at the mercy of political considerations; it was more independent than it is today. Over and above that, most judges today are members of the party, and so are inevitably subject to political pressure. I used to think that after 1950 Security and the party committees had stopped collaborating in handing down sentences for criminal offenses. But while in prison I became convinced, both from conversations and from reading verdicts, that plenty of this kind of meddling continued. For the same deed, the compliant and the noncompliant got very different sentences.

Political trials are inseparably linked to political circumstances and to the power structure of a revolution. The way verdicts are determined is a part of that power structure, as is every other aspect of judicial policy. Yet the relationship is not mechanical, since political factors continue to carry weight, often with undiminished potency, even after the power structure is firmly established. With time, power becomes not only a force but also a world in its own right.

# 5

By virtue of my special party function, I had the opportunity to meet some of our more important artists and scholars, even to get to know them well. The writer Miroslav Krleža was without question the most important and interesting. We were close friends, especially after 1948.

In the decade following World War I, Krleža was the foremost figure of the intellectual Left. With his poetic and polemic gifts and his incredible activity, he overshadowed not only Communism's literary epigones but also writers of other, opposed, ideologies. Then, too, he was an active member of the party until 1929. After that his participation declined, partly because the party was disintegrating, partly because he himself drifted away. He was never expelled, however. After 1929, in the years of the royal dictatorship, party officials who unlawfully returned to the country would drop in to see him from time to time, even though he was not engaged in any illegal activity. Those were the very years when his literary pursuits expanded—the years when he published his most important works and edited a number of periodicals. His influence on rising generations and on public opinion was unparalleled and inestimable.

Though in the mainstream and certainly at the forefront of the leftist intelligentsia, Krleža remained outside the party ferment of those years. He was therefore unprepared to accept the Moscow trials and the Stalinization of the Yugoslav party; his reaction, in fact, was one of aversion. He belonged to the first postwar, postrevolutionary generation for whom Lenin was more a visionary than the creator of a specific regime, and for whom Russia was only the beginning of a world-wide movement that would do away with wars and exploitation. He experienced the rise of fascism, and the victory of National Socialism in Germany, as a prolonged, uncontrollable surge of dark forces across Europe, hostile to humanity and civilization. Though not a strong doctrinaire Marxist, he never disowned Marxism. He recognized other factors—biological and not just economic—as being important in art and human behavior. Although his skepticism and pessimism grew with the darkness descending over Europe from Germany and Russia, his combativeness did not weaken. At the outbreak of the war, he came into conflict with the party leadership, for whom the Soviet Union and Stalin were indisputable ideals, and for whom victory over fascism was not only indispensable, but a means to power. Krleža once told me that his wife, Bela, often tried to dissuade him from taking public issue with the party and the party line, but that he would not and could not acquiesce.

The party's settling of accounts with Krleža, in which I participated, had enormous significance for both sides. As Krleža's influence on the Left and on the party itself dwindled, the party completed its Bolshevization and prepared itself inwardly, spiritually, to lead a revolution. Breaking with him, as I see it, meant breaking on the issue of revolution.

Yet the party leaders kept him in mind when war and revolution did come. They asked him to leave Zagreb and join the Partisans in free territory. He refused. When he finally came to Belgrade in the late summer of 1945, to meet Tito and make his peace with the party, he first dropped in on me at the Central Committee. I was asked to attend the meeting because Tito did not want to meet with Krleža alone. As we chatted while waiting to see Tito, I asked Krleža why he had not joined the Partisans. "At first I was afraid I might be shot because of my disagreements with the party," he replied. "Later, with victory in the cards, I was ashamed to." Slavko Goldstein, Krleža's friend and a Zagreb publisher, told me a few years ago that Krleža recalled that meeting in his memoirs: he described me as wearing boots—all of us still wore boots!—and quoted me as saying that he might indeed have been shot. To which Krleža added: "And everyone knew that the arm of Agitprop was a long one." No "long arm" of Agitprop existed, because during the war there was no Agitprop in the Central Committee. Besides, it never occurred to any of the leaders to get rid of Krleža; on the contrary, we desperately hoped that he would join us. I believe that his resistance had deeper and far more complex roots.

Unlike us Communists, who idealize revolutions—especially the one we are responsible for ourselves—Krleža did not look upon them as ideal acts bringing happiness in their wake. Not that he denied their impact on the life and development of nations: both are changed by revolutions, he maintained, but not necessarily for the better. The fact is that instinctively, intellectually, and politically Krleža had a horror of war and violence.

Yet in Zagreb he lived in constant danger from the Ustashi. At the beginning of the war he was arrested, only to be released a few days later through the intervention of Mile Budak, a writer and high-ranking Ustashi official. As it turned out, during the royal dictatorship Krleža had publicly protested an attack by the police on Budak, which surely played a role in his release. His quarrel with the party also contributed to his being spared by the Ustashi. But most instrumental, I believe, was the great name of Miroslav Krleža.

He published nothing while the Ustashi were in power, and made no public appearances. For a time he took refuge in the sanatorium run by a Dr. Vranešić, who was ideologically involved with the Ustashi regime. Otherwise Krleža spent the entire war in Zagreb, keeping a diary and writing a study of neuroses. When I asked him why he, as a writer, had selected such a topic, he replied that being a writer was itself a kind of neurosis, and that this had inspired his preoccupation with its history.

Dr. Vranešić was shot soon after the war. I don't know how guilty he was, but the dissatisfaction of the Croatian Communists with Krleža's wartime aloofness contributed to the doctor's death, though it was not the major cause. At the time, Krleža's relations with the party had not yet been completely normalized. Nevertheless, he mustered enough courage to intervene on behalf of his protector. But it was too late: his appeal never reached Tito and the Politburo.

As I have already mentioned, Krleža himself moved to restore his relationship with the party in the summer of 1945. But it was not until 1947 that he was taken back into the party. I was asked to tell him that his membership had been approved. "It doesn't make sense. I've had so many arguments with him," I objected. "No, no," my comrades clamored. "All the more reason you should do it."

Krleža came often to Belgrade, always on business of some kind, always promoting some idea or other, and always by the morning train. He would stay at the Majestic, where a room was reserved for him. After making himself comfortable, he would come to see me at the Central Committee. I arranged an appointment for him, if possible that same morning. Frequently I drove him to my house for dinner, especially in the later years. We used the formal form of address with each other until, at his suggestion, in 1949 or 1950, we switched to the familiar. This was not just Communist informality, but a step toward intimacy. Krleža called on Tito, of course, and sometimes on Kardelj. His relationship with Ranković was an interesting one: Ranković treated Krleža with a deference blending idolatry with caution; Krleža was likewise most considerate of Ranković, but with a touch of fearful compassion, as if to say: Look at this good, conscientious comrade —saddled with such a grim, thankless job! They had little contact other than at dinners or receptions to which both had been invited.

Krleža enjoyed great respect among the party leaders. Old quarrels and discords were forgotten. But that would not have come about so quickly and easily had he not been an exceptional person, witty and amiable, his wisdom vivid and expressive. Stocky and bald, with a businesslike manner, he neither attracted nor proimsed anything pleasant or unusual at first glance. But no sooner did a conversation start than his unbridled eloquence—poetic, meditative, rich in associations—overwhelmed one. His plump, fleshy face would come to life with a smile now wild, now tender, his eyes gleaming from under short, overhanging brows.

It is commonly assumed that Krleža shone among artists and political leaders but had no feeling for simple people. That's not true. The Central Committee employees, including my secretary, were always delighted to see him. He had a kind word for everyone. For example, he had a natural, unassuming friendship with my mother, a clear-headed woman who hadn't learned to read until the war. She would say, "I don't know what you all quarreled about with Krleža, but I've never seen such a fine man."

Indeed, looking back on my life and the famous people I have met, I can think of no one more honest, more humane, or more intelligent than Miroslav Krleža. Yet many today regard him as a coward and a conformist, a view that is simplistic and wrong. He accepted the new order as something which he himself had sought, but was well aware of its drawbacks. Only rarely, and for the sake of form, would he discuss socialism and Communism. He worked to ennoble the world through culture and to advance and transform the South Slavs, whom he regarded as rough and provincial. Ultimately, he believed that the victory of the revolution offered great possibilities for cultural transformation.

As early as 1945 or 1946 Krleža brought me a sweeping proposal for cultural reforms and new cultural projects. I presented it to the chief members of the Politburo, but we all considered it unrealistic, or, at the least, premature. How I managed to tell him in so many words that his proposal had been turned down I don't recall, but it did not damage our relationship, perhaps because many of his other recommendations on culture and scholarship were adopted. It was his idea to create a Lexicographic Institute and publish a Yugoslav encyclopedia—projects he was put in charge of in 1950. The concept and organization of the Exhibit of Medieval Yugoslav Art in Paris, in 1950, were also his. The exhibit may have cost too much, but it changed the image of the South Slavs as primitives beyond the pale of European culture—which was Krleža's intention. It need hardly be said that in these and other undertakings he consulted with Politburo members or the Croatian Central Committee—with Vladimir Bakarić in particular. Only by going through the top echelons was it possible to get anything done.

Krleža looked on Communist power as his own, as the only one possible, and in his way he contributed to its consolidation. He allied himself with this regime, or, rather, with its top ranks, without sentiment or false enthusiasm, as a historical necessity that marked the beginning of a new, perhaps more humane epoch. But he never entertained any illusions about the regime; he in fact had a very low opinion of it, though he rarely expressed it. He once told me, "It's really awkward being subject to a district committee." When we abolished the special stores for officials and bureaucrats, I asked him his reaction. He replied, "To be a Pompadour for a slab of bacon, ashamed when your comrades peek into your pot—that's not exactly pleasant." At the time of "debureaucratization," of the ideological turmoil in the top party ranks and among the intellectuals—I think it was the summer of 1953—he remarked to me more than once: "What am I? A poet at the Weimar court!"

The range of Krleža's knowledge and memory was astounding, as one could gather from conversations with him, not to speak of his writings. How can anyone deal so easily with such an abundance of facts? Krleža was at home in any area. It was as if he simply could not forget anything he had read, heard, or seen, as if he possessed a brain apart from and beyond the one belonging to most of us, as if he was burdened by a memory acutely alive, one that had no limits.

His opinion of himself as a writer was extremely high, and it was in the circle that gathered around him (such as gathers around every great person) that he felt most at ease. But he never boasted, and even avoided conversations about his works. What I rate most highly are his war stories and novellas, his novel *The Return of*

*Filip Latinović* (1932), and his essays, especially those concerning our history and the tragic fate of the South Slavs.

While writing these lines I read and then heard that Krleža had been paralyzed and was taken to the hospital. Now the radio is announcing his death, composed and tranquil. What I have written, then, is my personal farewell to Miroslav Krleža, a man worn out by violence but whose spirit and art did not surrender to it. In him, human weaknesses were overcome by the writer.

*Andrić and Krleža as Antipodes,* a book by Nikola Milošević, was published not long ago. I have not read it, but the title alone has such a ring of authenticity that it begins to sound like the most commonplace, undeniable truth. For the two were poles apart, not only as writers but also as individuals.

Krleža was wild, ungovernable, irresistible, whereas Andrić was restrained, steady, and unobtrusive. Physically, too, they differed, Krleža being compact and corpulent, Andrić lanky and bony. Both achieved fame as young men, practically novices, soon after World War I. Yet just as they were different as writers, so their lives sharply diverged: Krleža the revolutionary, the free writer; Andrić the career diplomat—and a 1961 Nobel Prize winner—fettered by convention and tact.

Like most intellectuals, I had read Andrić's stories. In 1932, as a young man, I had reviewed one of his collections for a Cetinje literary magazine. Andrić, who had come across my piece, once said to me: "It's interesting that you discovered way back then that, in their form, my stories have a novelistic structure."

I first met him early in 1945 at a dinner given by the writer Radovan Zogović. At the time, Radovan and Vera Zogović and Mitra and I shared a villa on Lacković Street—they lived on the ground floor, we on the second. Zogović and I admired Andrić's steadfast refusal to deal on any terms with Nedić's Quisling regime, and we knew that he had written two or three novels during the occupation which were to be published soon.

We brought him to dinner in a used car. Andrić was dressed in an elegant suit, we in uniform. The occasion was not memorable, apart from the reserve and balance so characteristic of Andrić, and his height, noticeably greater than mine when we stood side by side. He came once again to dinner at Zogović's. Not long ago, Zogović recalled how that time Andrić brought with him two pamphlets, one written by Zogović, one by me, and asked us to autograph them. Zogović declined, but I signed.

I had less contact with Andrić than with Krleža. Andrić liked living and working in peace. His participation in public affairs, whether local Bosnian or federal assemblies, or, for that matter, appearances at celebrations, always came at the urging of party officials. The guardians of culture, too, were happy to hang on to Andrić's coattails. His greetings and toasts were far more flattering than Krleža's, precisely because Andrić was an alien fitting himself into a new situation, whereas Krleža, for all his criticism, strove to improve a situation with which he identified. Andrić was simply an opportunist—but not a simple opportunist. With the collapse of the old Yugoslavia he had lost faith in the state and its renewal, but since he viewed all regimes as essentially the same, he met officials halfway whenever they desired his participation. In reality, politics needed him, not he it. Disillusionment in one brand of politics had finally made it possible for him to devote himself entirely to writing.

Andrić asked to see me only a few times. Once, I recall, it was on a private matter—he asked that the authorities not move someone else into the apartment of a woman acquaintance of his. Another was of a political nature. In 1951, the army arranged an exhibit of the 1941 uprising on the Kalemegdan terrace, with models, sketches of the offensives, and blown-up photographs. One of these huge photographs showed Yugoslavia signing the Tripartite Pact. Cvetković and Ribbentrop were seen affixing their signatures, while Andrić—then royal envoy and minister pleni-potentiary to Berlin—was standing in the background straight and tall in full dress, in all his majesty. Several days after the opening —was it early summer?—he phoned me to ask if I would see him. It was early in the morning, before business had jammed my schedule, so I said he could come at once. Obviously upset—it was the one time I saw him excited and frightened—he said on entering: "You know that exhibit on Kalemegdan? I'm in one of the pictures—people will recognize me, they'll begin to wonder, they won't understand. . . ." I begged him to sit down and ordered coffee. Recovering slightly, but still with a bitter, even savage, twist to his lips, he asked if I would please have him cut out of the picture. In his presence I phoned the army's political administration and conveyed his request as my own. Said General Otmar Kreačić, "We'll remove the whole picture!" Andrić calmed down and we changed the subject; he stayed twenty minutes more. As we said good-by, he radiated gratitude.*

But Andrić and I never became close. He was so withdrawn that I doubt if he was close to anyone, though he was correct and considerate toward all. As far as I know, he never harmed a soul, though I cannot boast of his having done anyone any good either, over and above the conventional courtesies. He lived for himself and literature, giving little heed to his place in life—or in history, for that matter. For Andrić, to live meant to exist in more or less continuous pain and tragedy, punctuated by only a few bright moments of artistic creation. As for history, I believe he regarded it as a chain of errors and evils, which culture only mitigates. For Krleža, the tragic was the tragedy of history; for Andrić, it was the tragedy of life.

In his personal life, Andrić detested every form of violence. Yet at the same time he actively sought out drastic forms of evil and violence, as if these extremes most fully embodied human beings and their institutions. No doubt he considered violence and evil to be special features of the Balkan climate and history. I once tried to explain to him how the party leadership endeavored to put behind them those frightful events they could not avoid during the war and revolution. I told him how, in the mountains of eastern Bosnia during the first years after the war, Security agents had killed an infamous renegade, a Chetnik. It was a long way for

---

* In September 1940, Germany, Italy, and Japan signed the Tripartite Pact, which various Balkan nations were thereafter inveigled into joining. Pressured by Hitler and Mussolini, the Yugoslav government signed on March 25, 1941. —Trans.

them to carry his body to the city, but they wanted to put it on public display. So they cut off his head and exposed it in the marketplace at Tuzla. When Belgrade was informed, I was talking with Ranković in his office at the Central Committee. He received the report over the phone with a look of revulsion and gave immediate orders to remove the head and to avoid such displays in the future. Andrić's response was one of wise resignation: "You people took it too much to heart—in Bosnia that's normal."

In Andrić's cautious and quiet reserve there was something hard and unyielding, even bitter, which any threat to the deeper currents of his life would have encountered.

Andrić was a man of exceptional delicacy. Never did I hear him speak ill of anyone. Even about writers, he would either have something agreeable to say or be evasive. "No book is all bad," he said on one occasion. "Once a writer has put so much of himself into his work, something can always be found there." Nor did he ever disparage his former superiors, the king's ministers and politicians, though he deferred to the new regime and even joined the party. He displayed no interest in Marxism; his temperament was indifferent to a thinker like Marx or an event like revolution. In his youth he had taken part in the anti-Austrian Young Bosnia movement, but even that was cultural and idealistic, not activist or revolutionary. But Andrić was still young then, and Yugoslavia something yearned for and to be realized in the future. I once asked him, "What do you feel like, a Croat or a Serb?" "You know," he replied, "I couldn't tell you that myself. I've always felt Yugoslav."

In his deepest and most creative self, Andrić tried to live outside finite time. Though adjusting to present circumstances, he faced the past, orienting himself to its events as sources of knowledge and inspiration. Somehow everyone must pay his debt to his times, but the wise man thinks his own thoughts and does things his own way.

I had met Desanka Maksimović in my youth, while on the editorial board of the monthly review *Misao* (Thought). She was already a famous poetess, I a beginning writer, and she had now forgotten our acquaintance of those days. But her sister Mara, once my schoolmate, remembered me.

Mara's husband had been executed, which was why Desanka looked me up soon after Belgrade had been freed, early in 1945. She told me what had happened. Desanka's brother-in-law, a Serb from Croatia, was a royal army officer who had gone to Belgrade during the occupation and been taken into Nedić's Home Guard to perform some administrative function. No sooner was Belgrade liberated than a neighbor denounced him to the Partisans, who dragged him off and shot him without investigating—our standing procedure for all officers and policemen of the collaborationist regime. Desanka didn't even have a chance to intervene on behalf of her brother-in-law. She implored me to see her sister and reassure her with regard to her children, since Mara feared for them. This I did; the children were under no threat, but I was sorry for Mara.

From that time on, my friendship with Desanka was never interrupted, in spite of long periods when we did not see each other and despite our different views and divergent destinies. She would come to see me at intervals, always with some trifling request. Once, she arrived with Smilja Djoković, the former publisher of *Misao*, who had invested her inheritance in the review. I was asked to make some arrangement with regard to her apartment or pension.

As in her poetry, Desanka in her person and everyday life combined high intellectuality and the simplicity of the common people. Whenever we were together, I felt I was back in the village of my childhood, yet simultaneously in the well-tended surroundings of philosophers and poets. We always discovered common interests and a common language as well, even though we differed in everything—mentality, ideology, politics. There was nothing she could not understand swiftly, whether intellectually or intuitively. The eyes of this woman, who had never been beautiful, were extremely intelligent, youthful, and alert. Her words were at once warm and generous, firm and self-confident.

A person of marvelous, unfathomable range, she could ac-

commodate the most varied and dubious human beings—renegades of all kinds, people from the power structure, and that
innumerable majority, neutrals and conformists. Even so, she remained her own self. Never did I hear her speak out in praise of
Communism, yet countless times she expressed sympathy for
individual Communists. Having herself suffered, she sympathized
with the bereaved and deprived, yet felt no rancor toward the
rich. Though very nationalistic, she made friends with cultural
workers of other nations, even those who had oppressed and disparaged her Serbian people under the occupation. She never
approved of force and was incensed by those who employed it.

Many, perhaps most, people think of Desanka Maksimović as a
tender, sickly person—an impression fostered by her youthful
love poetry. This impression is incomplete and also incorrect.
Though she does have such qualities, at heart she is tough, self-
reliant, impregnable. In her poetry she has remained consistently
pure and true to herself. In politics, too, she has remained true to
some principle of her own. She did not break with the banished
Zogović, when he was forced to live in a tiny apartment with a
police informer as roommate, and she visited me as well soon
after my own fall from power. Nor did she cease to be friends
with Russian writers and to love Russia, even when the feud between the Soviet government and our own raged most fiercely.

Her personal life has not been happy, though this is not readily
seen. Desanka got along well with her Russian husband, Sergei.
When he fell ill, she cared for him with a motherly concern.
Deaths in the family have been hard on her, especially that of
her sister Mara, with whom she lived. Mara was her inseparable
friend and companion. When she died a few years ago, Desanka
felt measureless sorrow and despair. Among the first to gather at
her house then were Zogović and I, and, later, Matija Bećković
and I. The whole room seemed to be engulfed by grief. Probably
because I knew and loved her, I believed that, fortified by her
indestructible core, she would recover. I met her in the fall of 1981
at the funeral of a mutual friend, the lawyer Veljko Kovačević.
Bećković, Borislav Mihailović-Mihiz, and I gathered under her
umbrella, one rain-sheltered third of each of us finding added

shelter in her unquenchable wisdom and vitality. Mihiz recalled lines from one of her poems: a funeral, with peasants speaking of death as a natural event and God as the head of the village. The verses seemed to rise from Desanka's imperishable, unchanging roots, which are as much her people's as her own.


Perhaps less than two weeks after the liberation of Belgrade, I received a letter at the Hotel Majestic—where I had been put up along with other high officials of the new regime—from the writer Marko Ristić. Conciliatory and dignified, he pointed out that it was futile for the Left to split into factions, and that whatever differences others might once have had with the Communists made no sense now, in view of the war and the party's decisive role in it. Though not a party member, Ristić had been among the most active participants in Miroslav Krleža's "revisionist" journal *Pečat* (The Seal). Taking the letter as Ristić's bid to put his relations with the party in order, and considering an exchange of such letters to be cold and official, I asked him to call on me. We in the party were trying to rally intellectuals on a broad, non-doctrinal basis, but I also had a personal wish to forget old quarrels.

I had never met Ristić except to shake hands with him once before the war, in Aleksandar Vučo's apartment. But I knew a good deal about him, from conversations with his Surrealist friends and from his literary activities, and a little, too, from factional exaggerations. Ristić knew quite a bit about me, of course, through similar channels and also through mutual acquaintances.

Whether because of this background knowledge, or perhaps because of our mutual desire to understand each other, Ristić and I had a heart-to-heart talk at that meeting, and even became friends. Soon after, in the spring of 1945, when we needed to name an ambassador to Paris, I proposed his name, and Ranković and Kardelj concurred. Ristić had no political experience, but his fluency in the language and his knowledge of French culture, plus his contacts in Parisian intellectual circles, made him the perfect choice. Once at his post, he relied too much on himself and made no accommodation to the embassy staff. Irreconcilable disagreements between them led to his recall. Even so, I do not think my choice was bad, since he fulfilled his duties scrupulously, and no one faulted him for lack of probity or diligence. Upon his return in 1952 or 1953, it was proposed to give him a pension. But he complained to me and others, "I'm not old yet; I can still work." A Committee for Cultural Ties Abroad was being formed at that time, so I proposed that he head it; with relief, he accepted.

Ristić came from the highest circles of old Serbia, an aristocracy of bureaucrats. His grandfather was the celebrated statesman Jovan Ristić. Something of that aristocratic temperament survived in him. In culture and manners he was more a Parisian than a man of Belgrade. Not by accident had he been the creator and spiritual leader of Belgrade Surrealism.

Yet it would have been hard to find anyone who so loathed his own class, and whatever smacked of it, as did Ristić. At heart a dogmatist and purist, an intellectual moralist, he had a good nose for all that was bourgeois, especially in Belgrade, and hated it, as a sinful and incorrigible part of his own past. His demeanor was that of a decadent but dissenting offshoot of those obsolete social classes, and his appearance only fortified this impression: silky, thinning hair, damaged teeth, delicate bones, a narrow, sunken chest. He was half blind but had the powerful fists of a peasant. Doubtless he was of nervous disposition and hypersensitive. But if he had not been Surrealism's ideologue, and had not set himself up as a decadent, no one would have seen him as such. Ristić's decadence was part of his self-critical coquettishness, egoistic and doctrinaire.

My relations with Ristić—as with almost everyone with whom I had been on close terms—were broken off after my expulsion from the party leadership in January 1954. About ten days later, I encountered him in front of the Majestic with Čolaković. Ristić scrutinized me with ironic curiosity but did not give me a greeting. This did not sit well with me. At the main post office a few months later, when I ran into his wife, Ševa, an unusually nice person, considerate and unassuming, who greeted me kindly, I turned and hurried away. Even today I smart at the memory, although my gesture expressed, above all, the impulse to be done with everything connected with my previous life.

Zogović could not stand Surrealism or Surrealists. "Nursery-schoolers," I heard him call them a few years ago, because of their greedy, conformist behavior. That is too simple, too caustic and purist a view. They accepted the new Communist order with sincerity as the repudiation of a brutal, primitive Balkan bourgeoisie made up of big shots and parvenus. They most likely viewed joining the party and adapting to the new regime as a matter of accepting party discipline. For them this involved more than it did for the older generation Communists, for whom discipline combined action and ideology. Individuals differed, of course. Even the "party-minded" Ristić remained by and large his own man.

By contrast, Aleksandar Vučo was the most devoted and disciplined, not to say the most obedient, of the Surrealists who joined the party. I had known him well before the war, and had even hidden in his apartment. His wife, Lula, had served the party significantly and had done it quietly and cheerfully. At one time she had been a courier to Paris, when the Central Committee was located there. Though not a party member, Vučo, too, had served in important ways, and he and his apartment had formed a center for leftist activity.

Vučo had not joined the Partisans. That bothered him. He used to try to explain it away by saying there was confusion over passwords. My own belief is that he did not take to the woods because he was reluctant to expose himself to risk. And his position, after all, was difficult: arrested, held in a camp and interrogated, under constant police surveillance. Then there was his older son, not political at all, who had his throat cut by the Chetniks in Valjevo, where his parents had hidden him.

Yet after Belgrade's liberation, the Vučos, husband and wife, accepted assignments with great zeal. Lula organized and managed the Kultura bookstore; Aleksandar produced films and built the film town "Košutnjak," a difficult, exhausting job in that postwar time. Vučo spared no effort. Yet three or four years later, fiscal inspectors began poking about in everybody's books—as if there could be tidy bookkeeping for what had sprung from chaos! I stepped in to stop these investigations, but by then Vučo was fed up with bureaucratic intrusion. He asked to be released from his film obligations to devote himself to literature.

In both official collaboration and our personal contacts, Vučo was exceptionally agreeable, good-natured, and flexible. That has its bad side, too, when resistance is called for. It was he who, as secretary of the Yugoslav Association of Writers, introduced the resolutions against me when I was thrown off the Central Committee. And in a recent interview, taking credit (not without grounds) for his prewar services to the party, he spoke of my using his apartment with my "entourage"—Radovan Zogović and Stefan Mitrović. We did indeed often use his apartment, and if the party group happened to be in need, Vučo borrowed money to help out. But Mitrović could not have been part of my "entourage" before the war, since he was then in prison. And I would have been the first illegal operative to have had an entourage, assuming I wanted one. Moreover, the proud, willful Zogović would be the most unlikely and impatient of candidates for the role of courtier in anyone's retinue.

The critic Milan Bogdanović I had known superficially before the war. As a student, in 1932, I had used a typewriter belonging to a monthly review for which he was an editor, to type a leaflet, ostensibly without his knowledge.

Bogdanović was not in the Communist movement then, but in the insignificant leftist Republican party. When the war broke out, he was an adjutant to the commander-in-chief, Bojović. Sent to a POW camp in Germany, Bogdanović, who knew German well, worked with the Communists and represented the officers in negotiations with the German authorities.

As a cavalry officer in World War I, he had been badly wounded. Later he was awarded the highest honor, the Star, only to turn it down in favor of one of the soldiers, so he said, but also because he was an antimonarchist even in those days. After the 1915 retreat, he was sent to France to convalesce and complete his education.

Following World War II, Bogdanović did not return to the Republican party, but joined the Communists instead. Surprisingly, this writer, by then around sixty, who neither temperamentally nor intellectually had anything in common with Communism, collaborated with ardor, not to say discipline. Like us, he had been dissatisfied with the old order—a dissatisfaction that came to a head with the confused and shameful capitulation. In addition, he had been impressed by the way Communists behaved in his POW camp, and still more so when they raised the banner of revolt. For him this meant that the warlike, rebel tradition of the Balkan peoples—especially the Serbs—had not died.

Bogdanović was a bon vivant. It went with his eloquent and lively nature and his strong, thickset body. Careless in money matters, always in debt though he had a good income—that was Milan Bogdanović, both before the war and after. In Paris once, while delegate to UNESCO, he appealed to me for a loan, pleading a need of medicines for his son Bogdan, who had been wounded on the Srem front (today he is a well-known architect, a designer of memorials).

Once one got to know Bogdanović and became friends with him, he was extraordinarily charming, inexhaustibly resourceful and witty. In the summer of 1952, Jennie Lee, wife of British Labour party leader Aneurin Bevan and herself a member of Parliament, who was staying with us at Lake Biograd, went to Kolašin to buy groceries. There she ran into Bogdanović, who at once put himself at her service. She returned bubbling with enthusiasm over his charming manner. "Do you know what he said to me," she told us, "when I came out with something against decadence? 'A little decadence is a good thing—life is sweeter and more interesting'!"

I had seen little of the former Surrealist writer Oskar Davičo before our conflict with the Soviet Union erupted. Then, both being critics of Stalinism, we renewed our former intimacy of prison days. In the first postwar years he called frequently on Zogović, and the two of them would have heated but friendly discussions of Davičo's poetry. Only in passing was there any discussion of Surrealism, which Davičo now viewed as outgrown and—even for him—belonging to the long ago and far away.

Davičo at that time thought of Zogović not only as a fine poet and respected official, but also as a good critic. Their relations were correct, even comradely, but not warm. Every so often Zogović would draw me into their talks. On such occasions, I wavered between indulgence toward modern forms of expression and adherence to what was comprehensible and simple.

The well-known Zagreb architect Drago Ibler appeared in Belgrade in 1946, if not earlier. He quickly made contact with Tito (how or through whom I do not know), and took the job of planning a magnificent opera house. In the air also was the idea of constructing a beautiful palace at Dedinje.

In those first months after the war, everything seemed possible to us at the top. We had no idea what anything cost, still less what our priorities were at any given moment. Ideology— omniscient, omnipotent ideology—played a substantial role in dazzling and blinding our reason. It was power that had the deciding role, however: the power of the victor over the vanquished (especially our internal foes), raw power, independent of institutions or of any external control, even though we felt it to be the people's power.

With Ibler, we dreamed of a beautiful modern Belgrade situated on its two great rivers, and we were confident that we would realize our designs with speed and ease. Soon we began the construction of a federal hall and a hotel, the Yugoslavia. For years to come, their bare skeletons would elicit curiosity and astonishment.

Whose idea it was to build the palace at Dedinje I don't know. It could have been Ibler's, but in any case Tito embraced it with open arms. I remember one conversation when I opposed it— ostensibly because such a palace would spoil the space, but really because I was put off by the luxury and megalomania of royal proportions. Tito stood firm, however, as he did in all things touching his prestige and role in history. To the best of my recollection, the palace went no further than its initial concept, and was dropped altogether once we took a closer look, especially after the 1948 confrontation with the Soviets and their ensuing blockade. But Ibler's work on designing an opera house moved ahead; I remember that the plans were completed.

In the Politburo, I was entrusted with general supervision of the New Belgrade construction. This was not because I knew more than the others but because, as head of Agitprop, I was less preoccupied with matters of state. Tito and the other leaders were present at the important meetings, such as the one that decided on an urban plan for Belgrade, to be administered by the architect Nikola Dobrović, and the one where a design for the Central Committee building was adopted. My role was soon reduced to being kept informed, or to intervening to eliminate stumbling blocks and resolve disagreements.

Such, too, was my work with Ibler on the opera house, at the beginning. But he was finicky and inaccessible. Every two or three months he would arrive from Switzerland to show me his sketches, and to pick up a foreign-currency installment of the fee he had negotiated with Tito. For several years work continued along these lines while people on the federal level grumbled over Ibler's extended foreign-currency compensation, which was too high to boot, they said.

I felt uncomfortable working with Ibler and may have behaved a little stiffly, though on each occasion I did learn something from him. I did not regard myself as competent in a job that seemed to demand my actual supervision, and wondered if I was his cover for dragging out the work and thus assuring an income for an unlimited period of time.

Ibler himself gave no grounds for such doubts. He was a polished, broadly educated man. His theories about opera under socialism—presented in a written introduction to his original project—seemed to be easy intellectual formulations, but they diminished neither the breadth of his professional knowledge nor the depth of his gift. He was flexible in his thinking, but persistent and self-confident.

Our collaboration lasted until 1948, when further work on an opera house became impossible. It was much too expensive and had to give way to higher-priority buildings. By then, Ibler had completed his plan. When I read in prison that he had been killed in an auto accident, I recalled our work together with a pang and was sorry that his creation had never been realized.

I had met the sculptor Antun Avgustinčić at Jajce in 1943, but we didn't get to know each other really well until we went to Moscow in March 1944—he as a member of the military mission and I as its head. I warned him not to be condescending and derogatory, as he sometimes was, in Moscow—it could be dangerous. He himself saw how the Soviet atmosphere instilled apprehension in newcomers.

He was lively, voluble, mildly sarcastic, and professionally enterprising. His best-known sculptures were those commissioned by kings and dictators whom he didn't like. He had been sympathetic to the Communists before the war, though active only in intellectual discussions. During the occupation he sculpted a bust of the Ustashi leader Pavelić and, after coming over to free territory, busts of Tito and members of the Politburo. The move from the Ustashi to the Communist leader did not seem that dramatic at the time, least of all to him. The first job had been a matter of necessity, the second came about of his own free will.

Because of his lack of party involvement and his reputation as an artist, he was chosen to be vice-president of the Partisan assembly (AVNOJ) in Jajce on November 29, 1943. He was loyal to Tito, perhaps more as a power center than as a person, if the two can be kept separate. He felt the same about Tito's colleagues, as long as they were in power themselves and reflected Tito's own might and brilliance.

It was Avgustinčić's idea to create "master studios," ateliers organized around reputable artists that would be talent schools and carry out the biggest and most important state commissions.

He convinced those who mattered—Tito, Kardelj, and me, and Krleža, of course—that his idea was valid. The concept was entirely in harmony with his understanding of power and the artist-power relationship.

The master studios did not justify themselves and soon ran into hidden resistance from artists and other creative intellectuals—resistance that blazed up openly after 1948.

As soon as the painter Peter Lubarda returned in 1945 from a prisoner-of-war camp in Germany he attached himself to the new revolutionary movement wholeheartedly. He joined the party, too. Before the war he had not been known as a leftist, but then, he had been no great monarchist either. I had met him superficially in 1932. In my opinion, he did not become a Communist without reason. What Communism meant to him in the beginning was fairness and justice, and the chance to participate in a cultural renaissance. In the end, it left him isolated, a sick and disenchanted conformist.

His accent had remained that of his birthplace—Ljubotina, in Montenegro. His native region was his greatest inspiration as well. In 1946, if not the previous year, he was talked into leaving Belgrade for a remote spot in Montenegro, to help found a painting academy; I supported the Montenegrin government's initiative in this and saw him off. Milo Milunović, another well-known painter, went with him.

Lubarda was modest, simple in all things, indifferent to the way he dressed and to everyday life in general. Little interested him apart from painting. His earnings were good, but you would not have known it from his appearance or life style; money ran through his fingers. And when he tried to explain his art, he did it in a strange way: either he was too complicated and not lucid, or else he was much too simple.

Upon his return from Montenegro—I think, in 1950—he came to see me at the Central Committee, seeking some larger painting commission. The purchase of paintings was then restricted to state agencies. I remembered that in the mansion that housed the offices of the president of Serbia, formerly Prince Paul's palace and now restored, Andrejević-Kun was to paint a "Battle of Kosovo," depicting the famous encounter between Serbs and Turks in 1389. Kun was a slow, sluggish painter, and was generally thought inferior to Lubarda—an opinion I shared. Also, the theme was more suitable to Lubarda. So I intervened with the Central Committee of Serbia. There was some resistance, especially from my wife, Mitra, since Kun had already accepted the commission. It was also awkward to criticize Kun, a well-deserving prewar Communist. But Kun magnanimously agreed to give his commission to Lubarda. Perhaps he was more considerate because he was at work on some other painting and busy running one of those master studios.

Lubarda also took a long time over his "Battle of Kosovo"— about three months. When it was ready, he called me in to see it. I liked the painting very much. As we talked, he spoke of how important the Serbian and Turkish banners were to him because of the way their folds showed up in the picture. A few days later he burst into my office to make me a gift of one of his paintings of Lake Scutari.

Once, he dropped in to announce that he wished to do my portrait. He worked a few days at my house on a sketch for it. In 1968, he remembered the sketch and gave it to me. I don't think it resembles me, but he captured something far more important— the whetted keenness of a Montenegrin, his asceticism and self-assurance.

When I was expelled from the Central Committee, I heard that Lubarda took it very hard. But I did not see him until my last discharge from prison, when we met at his exhibit at the Academy of Sciences. Our obvious mutual liking was tinged with sadness: he was a party member and I an outcast. Nevertheless, we talked as if nothing had happened, as if years had not passed since we last met.

# 6

Looking back on my life, I know that I would have become critical of Communism even without the Soviet-Yugoslav conflict and my later rift with Tito. My views, actions, and ideas have changed, but my essential self has remained the same. Even before the 1948 confrontation—from our very first contact with Soviet officials and the Red Army in 1944—I had entertained doubts about Stalin and the Soviet system and wondered whether action can ever really coincide with principle. All that was needed for similar reservations to surface regarding the Yugoslav system was to stay true to my thoughts. It required but a short step, one all the easier to take because Tito was, for me, neither an infallible leader nor the embodiment of an ideology.

My relationship to the Soviet Union was one thing, to Yugoslavia, another. I was aware of being unable to adapt to the new postwar order in my country. Apathetic, alienated, I felt a certain restlessness. I was estranged from my work, from the duties of my office. Not that these ceased to be a concern—earnest and conscientious, I strove to let nothing slip by me. Nor did I draw away from my comrades. On the contrary, I yearned to be close to them with all our wartime intimacy. But I was no longer content with my work and responsibility, whereas they seemed to be immersed in theirs. I was troubled, on edge. Yet "class enemies" and "imperialists" were still at large. Easing the struggle against them I saw as conscious weakness, almost betrayal. But to be resolute and inflexible was sheer torment, shackling my thoughts and thwarting my efforts to set out along my own critical path.

This obscure discontent took the form of an aching, insatiable longing to be creative in literature. It was not just an escape from politics and political activity, I think, but a genuine desire to bear witness to myself, regardless of where my real talent lay. No doubt another factor was also at work: a subconscious impulse, vague and embryonic, to break free and stand on my own two feet.

I tried to imagine what this "breaking free" would be like, what concrete form it should take. Withdrawing from the party never so much as crossed my mind. I thought of avoiding party forums and time-consuming positions, of taking on some kind of minor, "intellectual," duties. I even approached Tito. Remonstrating, he asserted that it was premature, that I was still needed, that I could somehow arrange my time to include both the Politburo and literature.

If I had succeeded in shaking off party work and the Politburo and devoted myself to literature, I would have rushed, guns ablaze, into the 1948 confrontation with the Soviet Union with all the vigor and intellectual power at my command. All else being equal, that encounter of itself would have rocked the foundations of my faith and induced the same critical perception to which I came after 1948, and after the Central Committee and I had parted company.

Obviously, I was already dissatisfied. But why, and with what?

Not with my function, though I spurned the honors and privileges that came my way far more than I enjoyed them. I might add in passing that they could not easily be ignored, once you belonged to a certain privileged circle and hierarchy. You found yourself beset with reproaches: "You're setting yourself apart from the other comrades." "It complicates Security's job." "You'll be a living reminder of how alien we've all become to our own people, that our life style is wrong, that we're a bunch of parvenus. . . ." I was given a taste of such reproaches in 1949. On the pretext of wartime bomb damage to my villa, I moved into an apartment in town. But once the renovation was completed, I had to move back out there to save the party leaders embarrassment.

I recognized that our regime could not, or "not yet," be anything other than what it was: a dictatorship of the party, or—in the Leninist variant—a "dictatorship of the proletariat." For power had not suddenly sprung into being as if from the head of Zeus; it had grown out of a revolution, out of conditions created by a civil war. What I did not like was the way power was functioning. Still less did I like its alienation from the people, its transformation into the brute weight of hierarchy sitting on their heads. This had been flagrantly apparent from the moment Belgrade was freed. We had seen privilege and hierarchy before. Politics and political operations can no more exist without them than in a vacuum, and least of all in wartime. But I liked to think that now, after the war, privilege and hierarchy would be streamlined and even curtailed, that they would be subject to popular supervision and decision. But it had turned out the other way. Then, too, that brotherhood of ideological revolutionary movements that I had thought so special to Communism had now melted away. Officials scrambled for villas and cars and shut themselves up in their own lives, without moral discomfort or the need for any pretext.

I most disliked our new regime's banality and vulgarity. It was like power anywhere else; if anything, more arbitrary and unscrupulous. Though I saw it all and was inwardly repelled, I tried to justify it as temporary and appealed to the classless society just around the corner. I became split between being an emotional malcontent and, paradoxically, all the more stubborn a prisoner of such an idealized future.

This ambivalence, both intimate and public, crystallized in my relationship to Tito. While I accepted him as a leader and loved him as a man, my revolutionary puritanism and indigenous nationalism made me fret at his transformation into an autocrat. Not only did this autocrat enjoy too much brilliance and luxury, but he used it to turn the party into an instrument of idolatry, and its leadership—including the Politburo—into obedient and faceless aides.

But—a *but* always turns up when one has not thought things through to the bitter end—I accepted those little weaknesses of Tito's as minor in the movement toward an ideal—an ideal of which the greatest spirits of the past had had intimations and which now—still in its infancy—was ours to develop and fulfill.

I will not dwell on Tito and my relationship to him, having already written comprehensively on the subject elsewhere. I want only to point out that my ambivalence toward him and toward political realities took its toll on both my personal and my public life. Restless in the one, I was cool to my first wife, Mitra; moralistic in the other, I was critical of minor negative features, which were a legacy of the past, and fiercely apologetic on behalf of the established order.

I have never been a "village politician," was never enthralled by romantic notions of "the land," but it bothered me when we Communists abruptly turned our backs on the peasants and subjected them to economic and police pressures. I understood compulsory food sales—the cities had to be fed, raw materials provided. But we requisitioned foodstuffs as if pushing strangers around, not our own people. Maybe this reaction was a throwback to my peasant childhood in Montenegro, with its youthful rural fantasies. But it also stemmed from my revolutionary disposition and experience. Overnight, it was forgotten that all of us leaders were from villages, no further removed than the second generation, if not the first. It was forgotten that without the peasant—who lived in poverty and backwardness, suffering and sacrifice—we Communists could not have overthrown the old order and seized power. All of a sudden, interest in the peasants was reduced to herding them together for meetings; pressuring them into selling to the state at set prices and donating their "voluntary" labor; or, at best, sympathizing with individual cases of hardship and talking with peasant relatives and former village neighbors on holiday visits home.

Soon after, it dawned on me that we were behaving the same way toward our industrial workers, except for our propaganda and daily activity among them. Actually, there was not a great deal that could be done in such an impoverished, backward, and ravaged country. But we could have behaved differently. I did not realize at the time that this sudden distancing of those in power from the common people, the peasantry and the workers, stemmed less from negligence and preoccupation than from the transformation of Communists themselves into a special category, alien and privileged.

Hunting preserves and hunting were mandatory privileges. I was among the first to get interested in the sport, though I didn't contribute to the hunting "craze" that spread along with the rise of the "new class." I was drawn to the sport by my own restless, stifled protests, by the need to quell my inner conflict.

Usually I would hunt wild duck in the great swamps bordering the Sava, or if I found a promising spot along the way, I would fish for trout. The swamps had no wardens and no guides. Exploring them for myself was a new, unfathomable experience. And the trout fishing? A return to childhood, with its dreams and fears.

I don't know how a man arrives at ideas and themes in art. They fit together out of his memories and observations, conversations and fantasies. I do know that with me it happened most often when I was out hunting or fishing—most spontaneously and abundantly when I was fishing for trout—and that it had something to do with the intense vigilance combined with half-conscious dreaming so characteristic of those moments. Dreaming, returning to some immemorial state of being, was more attractive to me than the sport itself and any success it might bring. But retreating into my inner solitude, I became inadvertently alienated from my comrades and from the reality they and I were creating.

73

# Part Two

# CONFRONTATION

# 7

With considerable help from Soviet troops as the war drew toward its end, the new regime found, in Belgrade, a permanent home at last. Our exhausted political leaders, famished for creature comforts, rushed to take advantage of the blessings conferred by a villa of one's own. Yet throughout the country Yugoslav blood was still being spilled—heroically, ruthlessly—in settling accounts with our conquerors or with each other. That was the moment—early 1945—chosen by Moscow to send a film crew to Belgrade to make a movie about the struggle of a "Yugoslav patriot." Its arrival was like a Mongol invasion—violent and irresistible.

Because he was to be the film's main hero, Tito was involved in the project early. But all the support work fell to Zogović and others in Agitprop: stage sets, staff, food and lodging. Even though we were continually surprised by new demands from these Soviet film makers, organizational and material difficulties were overcome. There was no chance of our influencing the film's political or artistic content, in spite of all our ideological identity and Slavic brotherhood with the Soviets. Yet such kinship would be affirmed with special fervor at parties, for which the Soviet representatives displayed matchless talent and zeal. Nor could we manage to change the film's title—"In the Mountains of Yugoslavia"—to something more pithy and historically apt. The portals of the Soviet art bunker would swing ajar only to admit our knowledge of folklore. The result was a thoroughly commonplace, cliché-ridden peasant rebellion with virtuoso effects. Tito had a poor role—unenterprising, static. Mikhail Romm, the director, and Georgi Mdivani, the scriptwriter, found themselves in quite a different dilemma. How should they realize "artistically" the mandate they had been given, to show that in the Yugoslav uprising the Russians played a crucial role? For right up to the end of the war the Russians had been so far away that their agents could not even be brought in by plane. So a Russian escapee from German forced labor was invented, who had somehow become Tito's "good angel" adviser. That "creative" little joke was more Mdivani's than Romm's. Romm was jaded and withdrawn, while Mdivani—touted to us as a famous writer—was a vulgar, always tipsy chatterbox who in the wink of an eye could contrive whatever artistic solution was needed.

Recognizing the film's shallowness and derogatory nature, I made my feelings known to Tito and others. Our Soviet "experts," however, had ingratiated themselves by assigning Tito the hero's role. The actor impersonating him—famous, of course—fussed around Tito learning his gestures and mannerisms. Even Tito got fed up. Later, upon seeing the film, he raged with shame when he realized how subordinate his role had turned out to be, both in the plot and in history. Zogović, too, regarded it as a dead loss, especially artistically. Most other leading party comrades took the pragmatic view: our struggle was finally on film, which was better than nothing. It was no hit at the box office, and no *succès d'estime* either, despite our critics' sincere ideological and political identification with the Soviets.

But that was only the beginning. The Russian film crew was at work for several months poking here, there, and everywhere in Yugoslavia, mostly at our expense. Our own people were engaged to play the secondary roles and to provide technical services. The banquets that the crew arranged everywhere often turned into orgies. We all knew it, but looked the other way. Why, these were artists—Soviet comrades! Our own artists, not to mention party members, would never have dared do such things, not in their wildest fantasies. I was present at one such banquet, in the villa at Dedinje assigned to the film crew, and only my restraint and Zogović's puritanism curbed the debauchery.

Both the carousing and the wandering around Yugoslavia, like the film itself—as our secret police discovered after the "bubble burst" in 1948—were designed to recruit Yugoslavs into Soviet intelligence and to infiltrate the art world. The revolution was still at a boil then and its doctrinaire asceticism still prevailed. Yielding to debauchery brought in its wake conflict with the reigning party morals and authority, thus creating a basis for recruitment. Large numbers of us were repelled by this "immorality" and "dissoluteness," but no one—not a soul—saw through the film's duplicity or discovered the ulterior motive of the orgies.

Ideological unity and brotherhood made us leaders trusting and indulgent, despite our hard-won experience at the cost of so many lives, despite our power forged in fire and tempered in blood. We tried to understand those little "weaknesses," which we stifled in ourselves, tried to justify Soviet "deviations," which had been uprooted in ourselves.

Stalin had long since dealt with the likes of us in the U.S.S.R. He may not have been exactly dazzled by the ingenuity of his agents, but he surely must have had a good laugh at our revolutionary gullibility. Under the pretext of verisimilitude, the film makers assigned a part to Tigar, Tito's dog. To be sure, this was not the original animal—that one had met his end at the height of the Fifth Offensive. But he was the same breed, a German shepherd, and had even been captured from the Germans. Naturally, his master could hardly accompany the dog all over Yugoslavia just for the purpose of shooting a film. A most suitable man was picked to do this, Tito's personal bodyguard, whom Tigar knew perhaps even better than his master, since they spent most of the day together in front of Tito's living quarters. Thus it happened that B. and Tigar were attached to the film crew—B. as a kind of consultant into the bargain.

Tigar, luckily for him, was just a dog and unable to get embroiled in human and ideological difficulties. But B., who only yesterday had been a soldier and was now lapping up the sweets of victory, B., whose party puritanism and responsible position still kept those sweets from going to his head, was lured by three con artists into some orgy and then recruited into their intelligence service. An unprepossessing, myopic peasant, B. had made himself indispensable as Tito's bodyguard by virtue of his diligence. True, Tito's remorse and compassion for the sufferings of the Valjevo unit whose remnants, including B., had found refuge in Bosnia possibly played a part in the relationship. Moreover, Tito always resisted change, both in his personal habits and in the personnel around him, so after the war B. continued to tend Tito's anterooms; he was a good coffee maker and dutiful in all things.

Professionally, B. lagged behind his comrades in arms except in rank: overnight, he had been jumped to major. He remained directly under Tito and constantly by his side, if I recall, for about two years after the feud with the Soviets broke out. Upon his discovery and arrest, it became clear that B. had been depressed throughout that period. Everyone was shocked at the dangers to which Tito had been exposed, and Tito himself was exasperated—at the Soviets, at his own negligence, and at the disloyalty of a fellow soldier whom he himself had promoted. Why was no attempt made on Tito's life by Moscow, acting through B.? One can only guess. I imagine they were checked by B.'s own hesitancy, as he vacillated between his past and a present under the spell of pro-Soviet dogma.

The motivation for those who joined the Soviet secret service—including B.—was the safeguarding of Communism in Yugoslavia. Their more experienced control was needed. No doubt this is where the moral disintegration of the personality began. But the conscience was locked in a dilemma, especially for participants in the war; for the "younger" and less "evolved," Yugoslav Communism was identical with Soviet Communism. B.'s conscience—like that of the vast majority (but not all) of the Partisans who declared for Stalin—was not, at least in the beginning, so alienated and hate-filled that Soviet intelligence could induce him to commit murder.

The Soviet film makers had added more than B. to their "cast." They had been preceded by a Yugoslav emigrant named S., who had arrived from the U.S.S.R. and forced himself on the director of a new film enterprise in the capacity of "expert." Meddlesome, greedy, and dissolute, he was removed before the confrontation began, at which point he came out for Stalin. Later he was exposed as a spy. S. served mainly as an intermediary between Moscow and us on film questions. In 1946, he submitted the draft of a Soviet-Yugoslav agreement for film collaboration to Vladislav Ribnikar, who directed cultural affairs for the federal government. Mild and co-operative though he was, Ribnikar noticed something inappropriate in the agreement and, since it touched on ideology, consulted with me in Agitprop. The agreement would have crippled our Yugoslav film industry, which our film makers were developing from scratch. According to the terms, Soviet films were to monopolize the Yugoslav market, and the most unfavorable, most humiliating conditions for us were set. I consulted with Kardelj and notified Tito. Both agreed with my assessment but argued that a rift had to be avoided and compromise solutions sought. I dictated those solutions, in negotiations with Soviet embassy employees and S., who quickly backed down, obviously annoyed. But enough subservience remained in the revised agreement, approved by Tito and Kardelj and accepted by the Soviets, to make us feel the sting of shame, until our later resistance rendered that agreement obsolete.

# 8

It is very difficult—impossible, in my opinion—to date the outbreak and list the causes of the Soviet-Yugoslav confrontation. Divergences began during the war. But our sense of intimate association with Moscow also stemmed from that period, and those feelings grew even more intense after the war. Differences would surface, accumulate, and fade away, but there was no change in the basic relationship right down to the beginning of 1948. On the eve of the war, the Yugoslav party had considered itself Bolshevized and thereby one of the most loyal to the Comintern—in other words, to Moscow. During the war, unanimity with the Soviet Union had been a demonstrable tradition, a living awareness. The war's end had brought changes in conditions and tactics, but not in leaders and orientation. Our party remained the most militant, the most doctrinaire, and the most pro-Soviet, to the point that, as I mentioned, the Western press called Yugoslavia "Satellite Number One." I resisted such a label; we really did not feel like a satellite. This only confirmed our delusion that the Soviet Union had no control over us and could not re-duce us to a vassal. I conclude that the roots of the conflict lay in our feeling, spawned by the revolution, of being an independent power. As we consolidated our authority and became more aware of ourselves as a distinct political entity—as we came to know our own possibilities—conflict with the Soviet Union was preordained.

My conclusion can be disputed, and it certainly is not the last word, but the fact is that not a single party leader was anti-Soviet —not before the war, not during, not after. Tito and Kardelj, having had a taste of the Soviet system, were cautious and realistic, without the rapture and idealization of Ranković, myself, and others not schooled in the Soviet Union. Yet there were no differences in point of view or loyalty. Leaders and ordinary party members could not have been as united or as imbued with ideology had they not been devoted to the "leading power of socialism." Stalin and the Soviet Union were our cornerstone and point of spiritual origin; we even felt ourselves to be a part of their body politic, until we founded our own regime and political differences began to emerge.

It was between our two secret services and our two propaganda services that frictions first arose. National conflicts over power and self-image are inevitable, and given the undemocratic, doctrinaire nature of both our states, they were focused initially in these two areas, where Soviet impatience and boorishness first became apparent.

No sooner did Soviet military missions arrive in our liberated territory than they began making the kinds of contacts with our administrative personnel that, however customary among larger nations, were incomprehensible and unacceptable to us. They kept hinting at danger from the West, especially from the British; they were "earnestly concerned" for our party unity, citing their painful experience with Trotskyites and other deviationist "spies." The Pan-Slavist, pro-Russian toasts offered by fellow travelers from the bourgeois parties delighted them. With the Western missions, they were courteous and tolerant. But Communists were almost the only people they cultivated, though they were not put off if one's party past was not the deepest red.

The Red Army's breakthrough into northeast Yugoslavia had been accompanied by the proliferation of Soviet intelligence services. The recruiting of Yugoslavs, especially Communists in sensitive positions, became aggressive and systematic. At first they arrested our citizens as well, but this stopped after our intervention, which gave them "rights" only over their compatriots, White Russian émigrés. Formally, these were citizens of Yugoslavia, but we, being just as red as the Soviets, supported their policy. We took an interest only in our own people, whereas they were after both theirs and ours.

By early 1945, disclosures were pouring in to the Central Committee from Communists everywhere whom the Soviets had tried to recruit in the name of Revolution, Brotherhood, and Communism. In the prewar period it would never have presented a dilemma to any good Communist to be asked to work with Soviet intelligence; he or she would have felt honored. But now that we Communists were in power—a power obtained through revolution—such a practice looked excessive, even absurd. Was our party not tested, not reliable? To the teachings handed down from Lenin our revolution, whether deliberately or not, was adding its own empirical innovations. No one was wholly aware of the strength and dimensions of this contribution, though we were already openly affirming that war and revolution had introduced much new experience requiring theoretical analysis. Soviet officials could not—dared not—take note of our innovations, our enrichment of the teachings of Lenin. Molded to the exact contours of their stuffy ideology and terrorized by Stalin, they were blind to anything new.

Failing to grasp that our revolutionary perception had been changed and enriched, the Soviets ignored it, explaining away the dilemmas of Yugoslav Communists serving Soviet intelligence as eccentric nationalism and ideological immaturity. Our resistance, however, drew sustenance from change, in spite of our adherence to Leninism and the Soviet Union. That is why, precisely when they dealt with Communists, the Soviet agents' plans most often miscarried.

The case of Dušica Perović inaugurated these frictions in a

dramatic and alarming way. A young girl from a Communist family—five sisters, all Partisans and party members—she had been put in charge of cryptography when the Central Committee staff was organized. In those days, Communists in our intelligence service felt easy about fraternizing with Soviet agents, were even eager to do so. Dušica attended a party of Soviets and Yugoslavs, during which a Soviet major tried both to seduce her and to recruit her. The story lost nothing in the telling; more than facts inspired the racier versions. The major's flirtation, so went the rumor, had enjoyed some initial success. But one fact was undeniable: Dušica at once told Ranković about the major's attempt to recruit her for the secret service. She was confused. Why were they doing this? In the name of what? Against whom?

Dušica's case was not the only one, but Ranković chose it for detailed disclosure in a meeting at Tito's. He presented it methodically, especially the events in which he had been involved, with substantive details. Tito's response to this was unabashed outrage: "A spy network is something we will not tolerate! We've got to let them know right away." The inner circle agreed. I, too, agreed, though I could not imagine what need the Soviets had of recruiting us. Were we not all part of the same movement, wedded to the same ideal? I do not know what Tito said to the chief of the military mission and Ambassador Sadchikov about these activities; third parties have no place at such conversations. Still, from Tito's comments to his closest associates and what we told one another, I can guess that he said something like this: "This shows you don't trust the leadership; it sows discord in the party; it demoralizes the cadres; it even creates doubt about the Soviet Union's intentions." In politics, the most telling arguments are the most legitimate and the least varnished.

The representative of the Soviet intelligence service was a lieutenant colonel named Timofeyev, I believe, whom I encountered many times, always in the Central Committee building. He would go there to see Ranković, either on matters of intelligence or because Ranković was "putting him on notice" concerning the further machinations of Soviet agents.

Timofeyev looked more like a man from the Caucasus than a

Russian, and he did not display those sudden onslaughts of friendliness so characteristic of Russians. Though reticent by nature as well as occupation, he drew close to Ranković. Yet he remained subordinate in the relationship, not because Ranković knew more, but, rather, because Ranković played a more open and independent role. Timofeyev would arrive at Ranković's office looking serious and anxious. He would leave either refreshed and invigorated or with his tail between his legs, depending on whether they had discussed mutual collaboration or Ranković had confronted him with indisputable facts about Soviet recruitment of Yugoslav citizens. They would always talk things out as if unimpeded by Ranković's scanty Russian and Timofeyev's even scantier Serbian. Then some flagrant case of recruitment would again be uncovered, Ranković would again press Timofeyev, and the same excuses would be made: this was the work of individual agents; it was not official policy, and certainly not his own. I once remarked, half in jest, that Timofeyev himself was behind it all. Ranković replied confidently that Timofeyev didn't approve of it and didn't even know what was going on. As liaison officer with our secret service, Timofeyev found himself uncomfortably wedged between official denial and covert recruitment, between our Communist candor with Moscow and the hypocrisy of the Soviet system.

Eventually he was recalled, probably in 1947. When I traveled to Budapest in March 1948 as head of a delegation to commemorate the hundredth anniversary of the revolution in Hungary, there to greet me was Timofeyev. The Soviet leadership had by then sent us their first letters of accusation and recalled their specialists. Still, I shook him warmly by the hand, as an old acquaintance. He was uncommunicative, as if we did not know each other, and made a point of pronouncing his surname, different from the one he had gone by in Belgrade. He quickly informed me in a whisper that he had just been appointed Soviet ambassador to Budapest, that I was to pretend not to know and was not to call him by his Belgrade name.

Frictions with the Soviets also began early in Agitprop—in tandem, so to speak, with those in intelligence, though at first the incidents in Agitprop were not as irritating. Although our propaganda resembled Soviet propaganda and in all respects reflected Soviet influence, there were differences. Our tone was brighter and more aggressive. Behind this external and, at first glance, inconsequential difference lay divergent efforts of which we were at first unaware. The Soviets had long since become accustomed to ideological clichés, bureaucratic limitations, and change from the top down. Thus the greatest and most significant revolution of our era had got stuck in the ruts of bureaucracy and, unlike the earlier "bourgeois" revolutions, had thereby become more intolerant and aggressive. But our leaders, fresh from the fire, administered directly; the limitations they felt stemmed mostly from ideological conviction. And so the second revolution, Yugoslavia's —small, vulnerable, ideologically dependent—was freeing itself to pursue its own course and to work out its own living forms.

Not for a moment did our propaganda lose its independence, either organizationally or politically. Because we believed that we belonged to the same universal socialist camp, we freely publicized the Soviet position on any issue at hand and published their materials. But they could not force anything on us. Our editors and propaganda apparatus were strongly linked to the Central Committee, or, more precisely, to Agitprop, its political propaganda core, of which I was the head. Anything Soviet that differed with us in method or tone was thoroughly discussed, but without the slightest anti-Soviet intent.

The Soviets were aware of this. The one determined attempt they made to alter things met with such a rebuff that they beat a retreat. Representatives of the Soviet Information Agency (SIB), set up in wartime to provide press coverage, repeatedly tried to flood our press with pieces about the Soviet Union. They were more zealous than astute, more meddlesome than resourceful. They made their connections directly with editorial offices—with our knowledge, of course—and immediately showered them with articles on all aspects of Soviet life. At first the editors took the material, partly from good will toward the U.S.S.R., partly in the belief that the leadership approved. But opposition built up, from both Agitprop and the editorial staffs themselves. Our journalists were given general directives—the "line"—in weekly meetings at Agitprop. Otherwise Agitprop did not get involved in the internal operations of these offices or in the writing and editing processes, except to answer a call for help or when some sudden change made it mandatory.

Thus, within given limits, every newspaper took on a look of its own. *Politika,* for example, was considered a more informative, less prescriptive paper than *Borba,* and the same was perhaps even truer of the Zagreb papers. Such newspapers, controlled and managed as they were, would have lost their *raison d'être,* had they submitted to SIB's inundation; they would have become Soviet newspapers in the Yugoslav languages. Relations were also strained because SIB's materials were of poor quality, the products of routine mass production, to say nothing of the agency's unpleasant, offensive, clumsy representative.

I raised the SIB issue—perhaps in 1946—with Tito and my Politburo comrades. Tito wanted no conflict but was opposed to "Sovietizing" the press. We agreed to suggest to SIB that it come to an agreement with our editorial staffs about the selection of texts to be printed. Only confusion resulted: what SIB considered important our editors thought insignificant; further, our people now claimed the right to edit the agency's material or eliminate it entirely. Matters grew tangled and strained. Even the ambassador intervened, through the cultural attaché Sakharov. Sakharov was an official in the first postwar embassy and a major in the first military mission; he knew Serbo-Croatian, and had come to know our leaders and our conditions well. Above all, he was courteous, adaptable, and intelligent. During a talk with me at the Central Committee, he understood our reasons for being upset but insisted on his own. So we simply decided that SIB and our editorial staffs should try to get on better. More confusion, strain, intervention. At last, at a meeting with the editorial staffs— approved, of course, by the Politburo—I announced that they could publish only what was consistent with their editorial policies.

For some time after, SIB rained materials on our editors and the editors kept on editing them, but finally both SIB and the embassy gave up. Resentment still rankled, even though our press continued to feature significant statements issued by the Soviet leadership and to carry broad coverage of the Soviet Union. As for the helpful, clever Sakharov, after 1948 he, too, was discovered to be a secret agent, one who subsequently supervised the publications of the Yugoslav émigrés in Moscow. The Soviet system admits of no more enviable a role than the one for which this diligent bureaucrat was cast.

# 9

It was around Tito that the conflict with the Soviet Union first began to crystallize. This was not only because of Tito's leading and central role, but because of the peremptory, authoritarian characteristics of Yugoslav Communism, which were essentially no different from those of Soviet Communism.

Yet we Yugoslavs did not absorb those characteristics mechanically from Leninism and the Soviet party: the Soviet experience simply provided the most expedient and accessible mold for certain aspects of the Yugoslav movement. An ideology that fuses a world view with a political movement inevitably generates despots and oligarchies. Even during the war there were muffled complaints from the Soviets about our glorifying Tito on the same level as Stalin. But they had no way out of this trap of their own making. Tito, too, was a Communist, and it suited Moscow to see Communist power in Yugoslavia strengthened through his exaltation. We conceded to Stalin historical supremacy on a world-wide scale, but in Yugoslavia Tito was lauded right along with him.

In the first official attack on Tito, Soviet resentment was muted; or perhaps we who were so close to Tito did not sense it, because for us Stalin was in a class with Lenin alone.

The attack on Tito was triggered by a speech he gave in Ljubljana on May 27, 1945. Intoxicated with victory, but feeling bitter toward the Western allies for having forced our troops out of Trieste and toward the Soviets for going along with it, Tito expressed aloud what top party leaders commented on with amazement, and bourgeois leaders considered natural and unavoidable in Great Power politics:

It has been said that this was a just war, and we have regarded it as such. But we also seek a just conclusion. Our goal is that everyone be the master in his own house. We are not going to pay the balance on others' accounts, we are not going to serve as the small change in anyone's currency exchange, we are not going to allow ourselves to become entangled in political spheres of interest. Why should it be held against our peoples that they want to be independent in every respect? And why should that autonomy be the subject of restrictions and dispute? We will not be dependent on anyone ever again, regardless of what has been written and talked about—and a lot is being written, and what is written is ugly and unjust, insulting, and unworthy of our allies.* Today's Yugoslavia is no object for bartering and bargaining.†

This speech led Moscow to lodge a protest with our government. Actually, our government was by-passed; the diplomatic note was made known to the smallest circle of Central Committee members. Stalin, we know, did not act in haste, but neither did he dawdle. The letter arrived at the beginning of June, in the form of official instructions to Ambassador Sadchikov to be relayed to Kardelj. I don't know where that note is today—most likely in Tito's personal archive along with other important documents. Although

---

* Tito was thinking of the Western press: Yugoslavia had fallen into the Soviet sphere of influence, and was viewed as a satellite of the U.S.S.R.

† *Borba,* May 28, 1945.

rumors about Soviet collusion with the "imperialists" at our expense had not yet taken shape, I remember that Moscow took offense at being lumped together with the Western imperialist powers. The Soviets justified their refusal to support Yugoslavia by the senselessness of going to war over Trieste so soon after the recent terrible war. Their instructions to Sadchikov included the threat of public disavowal:

We regard Comrade Tito's speech as unfriendly to the Soviet Union, and Comrade Kardelj's attempts to explain it away as unsatisfactory. This is how our readers understand Comrade Tito's speech; it cannot be taken otherwise. Tell Comrade Tito that if he should once again mount such an attack on the Soviet Union, we would be compelled to respond openly in the press and disavow him.*

It is possible that the Soviet government's pressure was co-ordinated with the concealed pro-Soviet opposition inside our Central Committee from Andrija Hebrang and Sreten Žujović, and that it took into account our excessive loyalty to the Soviet Central Committee and Leninism. But at the time it passed un-noticed. We were aware that while Hebrang was in Moscow at the beginning of 1945 he had written a report to the Soviet leaders on the situation within the Communist party of Yugoslavia, but that was considered as merely bad or unfriendly behavior, not as fac-tionalism or betrayal. Those who had gone to party school in Moscow were no strangers to such modes of operation, which they in turn passed on to functionaries who had matured politically within Yugoslavia. The Soviet party was the acknowledged leader and model. More than that, the Soviets were our friends. Differ-ences arose on the level of international relations but our ideology and way of thinking were similar.

Even so, we at the top—the only ones familiar with the Soviet instructions to Sadchikov—felt uneasy: we could hardly imagine diverging from the Russians, but we were unwilling to abandon

---

* Quoted from S. Kržavac and D. Marković, *Informbiro—šta je to* (The Cominform: What It Is), Belgrade, 1976, p. 95.

Tito. We were torn between theory and life, between an idea and our own achievements.

It may have been Kardelj's idea that we bring our influence to bear upon Tito, because Kardelj came over to see us at the Central Committee—a rare occurrence, since the burden of government rested on his shoulders. Ranković and I eagerly received him. Kardelj often consulted with Sadchikov in those days, but nothing led us to suspect that this had any bearing on his present initiative, even though Kardelj was then in the habit of making passing criticisms of Tito as arbitrary and lacking a broad perspective. We gathered in Ranković's office around ten in the morning and without much discussion agreed to speak with Tito about the senselessness of conflict with the U.S.S.R. and the need to smooth ruffled feathers. We telephoned to request a meeting and were told to come right away.

Tito's expression was usually self-confident and energetic, but on this occasion he was subdued and uncomfortable. We entered his study, and Kardelj began emphasizing that a quarrel with the Soviet Union—one that might well become public—made no sense. "Nonsense!" snapped Tito. "That won't happen. Of course we'll settle it."

Tito quickly recovered his composure. Ranković and I were delighted—like two schoolboys. After talking a little more on the subject, we passed on to other matters. We spent about an hour with him. Tito had obligations and did not ask us to stay for lunch. Returning in the same car, Ranković and I glowed in our separate ways over Tito's nerve when the chips were down; Kardelj admired his ready understanding. The idea must already have dawned on Tito that we and the U.S.S.R. might travel different paths, perhaps be at odds on some issue, but none of us dreamed that real divergence or conflict was inevitable.

Even within our small group there was no talk about any of this, as if it had no importance for our country and party. But it was a turning point, I think. The four of us drew closer and talked freely about Soviet actions, while at the same time Tito became much more cautious about making statements that might be construed "erroneously" by Moscow. This was no plot: we simply looked upon our power as our own—Yugoslavia's—business. None of us saw through Soviet intentions, let alone the nature of the Soviet system under Stalin. Yet there spread a critical attitude toward the U.S.S.R., and with it a certain intellectual and emotional independence.

The incident with the Soviet leadership over the Ljubljana speech was smoothed over. Tito made his "explanations" to Ambassador Sadchikov; the Soviets made a tactical withdrawal; more important common problems emerged. Yugoslavia's internal situation at that juncture—the bourgeois democratic leaders Grol and Šubašić had passed over to the opposition—did not play into the Soviets' hands for purposes of dividing us Communists and openly imposing their own hegemony through public attacks on Tito. But the incident did prompt us at the top to accelerate the popularizing of Tito as our leader.

Tensions and frictions with the Soviets carried over to other areas, especially economic. The sharpest differences had to do with the jointly owned companies they were establishing all over Eastern Europe. These companies were regarded with mixed feelings by our leadership. It did not escape our notice that Moscow, like all victors, meant to perpetuate its political dominance. On the other hand, we felt that Moscow was justified because of the weakness of socialism and the danger that prewar economic relations might be restored in those countries. At home, however, we saw no such weaknesses and dangers, and our negotiations with the Soviets in no time at all got down to hard bargaining, which led to strain and disagreement. This in turn prompted us to compare Soviet intentions with exploitation by Western companies before the war—exploitation that had been milder by comparison, for all its shameless injustice. Appeals to socialism's so-called weakness now began to lack credibility as a justification for the subjection of the East European countries, some of whom were our allies, and every one of whom was intensely aware of itself as a people and a nation. As we played host to the representatives of these countries and visited them in turn, we could see that their leaders were unhappy with the joint companies. Our independent and sometimes overconfident bearing must have been painfully conspicuous.

If we refrained from openly criticizing this exploitation of East European countries, we could not and did not conceal the tensions provoked by such companies in our own country. Differences grew and spread, transforming themselves into the doubts and casuistries of doctrinaire minds: indoctrinated spirits remain creative and potent only through preserving and developing their doctrine.

The ambiguity of our position was manifest: no one was against joint companies, but at the same time no leader was willing to surrender our sovereign rights and forgo a mutual, fair profit. No one, that is, but Hebrang and Žujović, for whom sovereignty and independence in relations between socialist states were "purely bourgeois prejudices." Our ambivalence toward these companies was reinforced by ostracism, boycotts, and denigration from the West, especially the United States. It is true that our unreasonable ideological hatred shut us off from the West. But the West for its part did not open up to us economically, and did not return to us property the war had tossed in its lap.

Once, I happened to be at Tito's on business when Vladimir Velebit, then assistant minister of foreign affairs, warned him that the agreement with the Soviet government for a joint air transport company violated state sovereignty, since it provided for Soviet staff at our airports. Tito exploded: "That can't be! Sovereignty has to be preserved!" His reaction was clear enough, but his proposed solution was not: our position had to be explained to the Russians; the agreement must be accepted, but our sovereignty must be retained.

We, more than the Soviet representatives, were the victims of propaganda, having created our own private idyll about their system and their economic might. For us, industrialization was not only a vital necessity and a vindication of our sacrifices and wartime destruction, but also the *sine qua non* of a future classless society. For us, socialism meant not just a better life, but the brotherhood of peoples and nations.

So it seemed natural and logical that the Soviet Union would help us to industrialize. It was a country with the same ideals; it had, we thought, a highly developed industrial base. Our excessive demands on the U.S.S.R. were often born of these delusions and self-deceptions. Not only were the Soviet representatives in no position to satisfy our often unrealistic and sometimes megalomaniacal needs, but they did not even deliver the equipment for the joint companies. In 1947, in the corridor outside his office at the Planning Commission, Boris Kidrič showed me a meticulously detailed model of an electric power station, the gift of some Soviet colleague. "I wish he'd given me the real thing!" said Kidrič with whimsical cynicism. Another time he told me that our enterprises were behind in commodity deliveries to both the Soviet Union and the other East European countries. "But among socialist countries these matters get straightened out in comradely fashion," he added.

Yet, though we might be impatient and unrealistic, in Soviet attitudes there was something grotesque and insulting. In negotiating joint companies for copper production—or, rather, the existing copper plants at Bor—they tried to prove that there cannot be any value in ore alone, because, according to Marx, value is not established until labor has been invested in something: labor alone creates value. These arguments confused some top leaders. No one could contradict Marx, but we knew that at the Bor facility—under French ownership before the war—capitalists had paid separately for the ore and for labor. Incidentally, even going by Marx, the Soviet argument was incorrect, as "anti-Soviet" theoreticians like Kidrič quickly figured out. It was contrary both to his theory of differential rent and to the theory of value itself, according to which the price of a uniform product can be set lowest by the producer who invests the least labor in it. To apply Marx to this case, the refining of poor-quality ore would not yield the same income as refining concentrated ore.

We were then buying weapons, too, from the Soviets. Only in 1948, after the conflict had broken out, was it discovered that they had sold us used, repainted fieldpieces that we paid for in dollars. Our commissions noticed this upon receipt but did not sound the alarm. All was as it should be, they thought, because it came from the Soviets; few cared about the cost. It was the same in sending students to the U.S.S.R.: sending them was easy; the pinch came when we began paying for it at the official ruble-to-dollar exchange rate, which was highly unfavorable to us.

Negotiations over joint companies progressed slowly and came in secondary branches of the economy. Tensions were for that reason less noticeable and were obscured by other distractions. We had domestic problems with the bourgeois opposition and the Catholic church, and international problems with the West, especially the United States. Moreover, the Soviets, in a hurry to consolidate in Eastern Europe, were being cautious in dealing with the United States. Furthermore, when Kardelj visited Stalin in March 1947, in connection with a Big Four foreign ministers meeting in Moscow to negotiate a treaty for Austria, Stalin reasoned as follows:

How would it be if we didn't set up any joint companies? Clearly, this isn't a good form of collaboration with a friendly ally like Yugoslavia. It will always end up in discord and disagreement, the country's independence will suffer, and friendly relations will be undermined. Such companies are appropriate for satellites.*

Stalin's reasoning—classifying the socialist countries as either satellites or independents—seemed curious to us at first. He often surprised non-Soviet Communists by reacting and thinking "unidealistically," a style more associated with the power politics of autocrats. But we adjusted to it, and even found it acceptable, as if it had nothing to do with us. Having had a taste of power, we were reasoning like those used to power politics. We could not yet grasp that Stalin was seducing us precisely by such "reasoning."

There were no attacks on Tito, at least no visible ones. The Soviet leadership did not retreat; it simply lay low while Tito, preoccupied elsewhere, calmed down. During Kardelj's visit, Stalin, in fact, took a keen interest in Tito's health. Tito had recently undergone a hernia operation. His surgeons were Soviet, which

---

* Vladimir Dedijer, *J. B. Tito, prilozi za biografiju* (J. B. Tito: Contributions toward a Biography), Belgrade: Kultura, 1953, p. 465.

again shows that relations at the time were close. Tito told his story about a drunken Soviet doctor trying to thrust his hands into his dressed wound only after 1948, when evil Russian designs were seen even where they didn't exist.

Not even our conflict with Hebrang, which surfaced in April 1946, had any impact on our relations with the Soviets, whose affection for Tito seemed to blossom with renewed vigor. This conflict had been smoldering ever since Hebrang was dismissed as secretary of the Communist party of Croatia in the autumn of 1944. The Politburo's careful, emphatically friendly treatment of him, and his conscientiousness and diligence on the job, aggravated rather than allayed the antagonism—an antagonism perhaps grounded in ambition as much as in differences of opinion. Tough and obstinate, Hebrang had retreated into his shell from the beginning. But the Politburo—those of its members who had risen to the top with Tito on the eve of the war—had also shut the door on him. When a Politburo member took some initiative in which Hebrang had no part, he would see this as undermining his status. It was as if he thought we viewed his every difference of opinion as oppositional, factional activity. My own duties rarely brought me into contact with Hebrang, but whenever I did turn to him for anything, I encountered an attentiveness so pronounced as to seem unnatural and insincere.

The Politburo, into which Hebrang and others had been co-opted, convened less and less often. Tito decided everything by himself, or in consultation with the comrades most directly involved. In the end this meant his own men, the prewar Politburo members—Kardelj, Ranković, and me—thus quietly restoring the impenetrable inner circle. This could only provoke resentment and suspicion in Hebrang.

Once such an antagonism gets a foothold in the body politic, it takes on a life of its own. Not only do actions and views acquire importance, but also intonations and facial expressions, and even the way one dresses or spends one's leisure time. A relationship like this cannot last; inevitably, it evolves into either an open clash or the capitulation of one side. Hebrang withdrew into his work as into a cocoon. Often—in fact, daily—he saw Mikhail Sergeichuk, the Soviet official in charge of UNRRA for Yugoslavia, and Sreten Žujović. This would not have aroused any suspicions had we been on "comradely" terms, since other leaders also met with Soviet representatives and, particularly with Žujović.

Occasionally, Hebrang voiced open disagreement and criticism. Even if he had not already painted himself into a corner, this would have aroused suspicion. The war had hardly ended when he began to speak out in his circle, narrow as it was, arguing for the Croatian borders with Serbia as they had existed in Austria-Hungary before 1918. He managed to moderate his tone to the extent of not seeking "borders on the Drina," since Bosnia and Hercegovina together had already been proclaimed a federal republic on a par with Serbia and Croatia. But in the north, in Vojvodina, a border between Serbs and Croats did not become an acute issue until the end of the war, and the issue was argued with emotions still steeped in blood and hatred. "The border of Croatia is known," thundered Hebrang, unappeased and belligerent. "It extends to the town of Zemun, right across the Sava from Belgrade!" That made the Serbs of Vojvodina and Srem uneasy. These Serbs were all the more resentful because throughout the war, by rebellion and sacrifice, they had linked their destiny with that of the Communists, with the destruction of fascism and the fascist Croatian "state."

There were complaints, too, from the Serbian leadership. At Tito's suggestion, in a meeting which I am sure Hebrang did not attend (though I cannot recall who did), the Politburo appointed a border commission, which was formally confirmed by the National Assembly. I chaired the commission, probably because I was thought to have a feel for nationality problems. On the commission were Serbs, Croats, and others. We held to the principle of ethnicity: that there be as little "foreign" population as possible in either Serbia or Croatia, that we disturb the national fabric as little as possible. Only the towns of Ilok and Bunjevci remained in dispute. At my suggestion, Ilok, with its Croatian majority, went to Croatia, even though it protruded like a useless appendix into the Serbian expanse of Vojvodina. Bunjevci, with its substantial Croat population, remained part of Vojvodina by decision of the Politburo, as the commission had proposed, because its inclusion in Croatia would have affected a still more substantial group of Serbs and disturbed the ethnic composition of Vojvodina to the advantage of the Hungarian minority. Our realignment of the borders was approved: in those days Serb and Croat nationalism was muted.

Hebrang also opposed the construction of the modern highway from Belgrade to Zagreb. We leaders envisioned such a highway as bridging over the lingering feelings of hatred and resentment at mutual butchery that divided Serbs and Croats. It justified our confidence and our determination to build even the most incredible project, if it served "the peoples interest." We believed that we knew what that interest was, having fought and won the right to be the people's sole representatives. No one was against the highway; no one dared to be. As for Tito, he campaigned for it more passionately and stubbornly than anyone because his aspirations and prestige were at stake. In opposing the highway, therefore, Hebrang took cover behind an economic argument: it would be an unprofitable venture because of the negligible number of motor vehicles. Hebrang's argument inflamed our suspicions, although it was not entirely groundless. For several years after its construction, the highway was deserted. However, for the past fifteen years it has been an essential link between the two centers.

Tito and Hebrang were both so independent, ambitious, and power-loving that their ideological differences—Tito's Yugoslavism, Hebrang's Croatianism—surfaced only sporadically, though not insignificantly. Hebrang insisted on the special autonomous position of Croatia, an aspect of his personal affirmation and power. But this would have brought about similar demands from the other Yugoslav republics, thereby weakening both the federation forged by the revolution and Tito's dominating role. Tito had won the right to play that role throughout Yugoslavia; to permit Hebrang a similar right over Croatia would only have undermined Tito's idea of "brotherhood and unity" and his prestige. Everyone at the top knew from party experience that political disagreements between such personalities end up in an ideological and personal reckoning. Those who wanted it to happen—including Kardelj and Ranković, and me as well, though with a sense of guilt—did not have to do a thing. By our silence alone we deepened the estrangement and hastened the clash. It was harder for Hebrang's onetime fellow fighters and ideological sympathizers, such as Moša Pijade. If his friend's conduct was mentioned, Moša would remain silent, or, if cornered, he would remark: "I don't know what's wrong with Andrija. What does he want?"

The occasion was anticipated, awaited. In the spring of 1946 it presented itself. A government delegation was to go to Moscow for important, even crucial, economic negotiations. The issue was Yugoslavia's industrialization, which was built into the five-year plan and which for its fulfillment depended largely on the Soviet Union. Since Hebrang was instrumental in devising the plan and in selecting the delegates, it was logical that he should lead the delegation. In politics, though, logic is transient, illusory. Instead of Hebrang, a less authoritative but more reliable minister was named head of the delegation. That elicited a letter from Hebrang to Kardelj, complaining of being passed over and of intolerance on the part of Tito.

The means of protest chosen—a letter, even though both men were in Belgrade—was itself indicative of a challenge to the Politburo. Two days later, on April 19, 1946, the Politburo met, augmented by important officials whose conduct was above suspicion. We avoided any broad discussion, handing Hebrang's "grievance" over to a commission headed by Ranković, which was no accident, since he was closest to Tito and not so kindly disposed toward Hebrang. Defending himself before the commission, Hebrang was obdurate, or "unhealthy," as we used to describe such behavior. Žujović's testimony at a meeting of the Central Committee was hesitant, but he clearly favored Hebrang; it was not then obvious that he was actually expressing his feelings for the Soviets. The commission criticized Žujović for being too conciliatory and supportive of Hebrang and proposed reprimanding Hebrang and excluding him from the Politburo. The proposal was adopted.

Soon after, in mid-May, Kardelj and I were in Paris for the Italian peace treaty negotiations, in which the Big Four were ironing out disagreements. We knew in advance that Molotov would represent the Soviet Union, and had agreed with Tito to inform Molotov that Hebrang had been ousted from the Politburo because of "factional activity." We also knew that the Soviet leadership would hear the news one way or another, most likely from Hebrang himself, and we felt it wiser to take the initiative ourselves.

Kardelj and I went to see Molotov about the treaty and other questions of mutual interest. Conversation flowed briskly and smoothly, as always with Molotov. When Kardelj gave him the news, adding that there were also doubts about Hebrang's conduct with regard to the Ustashi policy, Molotov was icy and silent. But his silence and coldness spoke for itself. Though restrained when necessary, Molotov would lose his temper whenever the words "lie" and "falsehood" crossed his path, and "factionalism," for him, was a loaded term implying still worse evils. But since on this occasion he let nothing betray his thoughts, he had probably already been told about Hebrang.

That was when Kardelj told Molotov that Velebit was suspected of spying for the British. Kardelj's motive was probably to build up a deeper trust. "Aha, Velebit a British spy . . . ," Molotov commented casually, indifferently. Doubts about Velebit stemmed from Ranković and his police, and were taken as a warning by the inner circle.

Ranković was suspicious by nature and given to investigating private lives; desirable traits, as it were, in a chief of secret police and organization secretary for party affairs. At the end of the war a certain Englishwoman came to Belgrade, and OZNA photographed a letter she wrote to Velebit. I saw the copy: a sentence or two, revealing nothing but sentimental affection. Yet that was enough for our intelligence—overzealous, like all secret services, even without the Soviet model.

The "Velebit case," that is, Kardelj's confidential remark to

Molotov, was later exploited by the Soviet leadership in their letter to the Yugoslav Central Committee of March 27, 1948, and in all the ensuing propaganda. Tito did not suspect Velebit, and said as much in a rebuff to Ranković: "Nonsense—I've never doubted him." I always felt uneasy with Velebit because of my passivity when Kardelj was denouncing him to Molotov—or, more precisely, because of my passivity with regard to the secret service's suspicions. After the conflict with the U.S.S.R. broke into the open, this uneasiness prompted me to tell him that the Englishwoman's letter had aroused suspicions. Velebit was jarred; yet at the same time he understood the society of which he was a part.

Molotov probably remained silent when informed about Hebrang because relations with Yugoslavia were "friendlier" at that point, and Tito was well liked and highly respected. Soon after I returned from Paris, on May 27, 1946, Tito departed for Moscow at the head of a delegation that included nearly all our most trustworthy comrades. At stake was nothing less than our industrialization and rearmament with the help of the Soviet Union.

Tito's visit to Moscow lasted longer than usual for a national delegation. A contributing factor, perhaps, was the death of Mikhail Kalinin, which coincided with the visit. Kalinin, president of the Supreme Soviet, was not an influential person, but protocol required that he be duly mourned by the top Soviet leadership. In general, the Soviets did not observe strict protocol with delegations from the socialist countries—in other words, the schedule would shift to accommodate the Russian leaders. At a meeting of the Cominform once, Rumanian Communist leader Ana Pauker told me of a saying among the top Communists, dating from prewar times: "To Moscow whenever you please, from Moscow when they let go of you." She spoke with blissful tranquillity, probably unaware that she was uttering a medieval adage adapted to present-day Moscow. There was much carry-over of the Kremlin's prewar style in dealing with foreign Communist parties to the heads of the new Communist states. The "world revolutionary center" simply adopted the role of "chief autocratic state," and yesterday's leaders and heroes were more or less obedient vassals.

"Stalin gave a dinner for Tito and our delegation on June 9," said the press releases in our country; there was nothing about the working sessions. As far as I can recall, there was no return dinner. Stalin's invitation was not entirely according to protocol because of the presence of Radovan Zogović, who was in Moscow as a writer, and Tito's son Žarko, who was there simply out of curiosity. The delegates were carried away by the host's wit and personality.

Stalin was reserved on the issue of joint companies, but after Tito endorsed them as beneficial in the development of the Yugoslav economy, Stalin and Molotov went along. These companies, as I have mentioned, led to nothing but bickering and misgivings. Other economic agreements with the Soviets came to the same dead end, though, in all fairness, it must be noted that we, too, failed to carry out our obligations.

Even at that time, Stalin took a lively interest in Albania. He was perhaps better informed than our own leaders, despite our proximity to the country and our many ties. He wanted detailed information about personalities and trends in the Albanian leadership. Speaking of the Albanians' desire to visit Moscow, he remarked: "The Albanian Central Committee won't let Enver Hoxha travel alone, but insists that Kochi Xoxe come with him, as a kind of security." After a brief pause, he turned to Tito: "What do you think about that?" Tito replied that he had no knowledge of any major disagreements in the Albanian Central Committee. "Should we receive them here in Moscow?" Stalin asked. "We see no need for it. We'll assist them through Yugoslavia." Then he pressed on: "You know, there's some problem with the Albanian Politburo. . . ." Here, party-minded, strait-laced Ranković put in: "There are no major differences. The point is that the Politburo comrades don't regard Hoxha as enough of a party-liner, so they want Xoxe, the Politburo's senior party member, to come with him." Ranković went on to observe that at the last Albanian Central Committee session certain errors had been discovered, and that the man responsible for them, Sejfulla Malleshova, had been dropped from the Politburo. Tito added, "We can resolve these problems with our Albanian comrades." Stalin simply said: "Good."

This conversation about Albania was not accidental. I strongly believe that Stalin already had in mind the subjugation of Yugoslavia. In early 1948, our friction with Moscow over Albania would serve Stalin as the most convenient and convincing cause for an attack on Yugoslavia. His offering Albania to Yugoslavia was a snare, but one he wove out of actual relationships, out of unequivocal designs our top leadership entertained toward Albania, out of our ever less idealistic, ever more power-seeking ambitions. It was not just in Stalin's rise that the ability to exploit revolutionary idealism and create a privileged class proved decisive.

We were still in thrall to ideological concepts and revolutionary idealism, however unbridled our craving for power and our pretensions of being a great state. Stalin knew this better than anyone, both from the experience of the Russian Revolution and instinctively. The Albanian issue was only one move, albeit the most sensitive, in his scheme to inflame our egos and lead us down the path of his choice.

During the dinner at Stalin's villa he dispensed opinions, mainly negative, about the leaders of the European parties. Thorez didn't know how to bite; La Pasionaria couldn't collect her thoughts and had no capacity for leadership; Togliatti was a professor who could write a good theoretical article but couldn't lead people toward a well-defined goal; Pieck was a senile old man, only up to tapping you on the shoulder.

On the other hand, he announced: "Tito must look out for himself. I won't live long, and Europe needs him. Yes, Europe needs Tito!" This European mission that Stalin had in mind for Tito never made sense to me. I tried to explain it to myself in terms of the intoxicated state of the Soviet leaders that evening. In that curious context, Tito had been assigned the role of Soviet, or Communist, deputy in Europe. I have never been convinced that Yugoslavia, the Yugoslav revolution, had any part to play outside Yugoslav and Balkan relationships, in spite of our popularity in the "people's democracies," which caught the eye of the Soviets before we had even begun to make use of it. Yet when our leading comrades told and retold these scenes from Stalin's dinner party, they were in ecstasy, with reason suspended, eyes shining, smiles gleaming. Even Tito would glow with pride in "humble" silence and self-restraint. That transport was perhaps best demonstrated by Ranković, who, urged by Stalin, drained one glass of vodka after another, though he never cared for hard liquor. "I would have taken poison if Stalin had offered it," he later said.

Another dinner, this one including the Bulgarian leaders Dimitrov, Kolarov, and Kostov, let Stalin and his entourage reopen unhealed wounds and stir up fresh competition between Bulgaria and Yugoslavia. Stalin demonstrably valued Tito more than Dimitrov. Beria said loudly enough for all to hear that Kolarov had lost his intellectual grasp forty years before. And when a bottle of Bulgarian wine was opened, Stalin quipped, "This is Yugoslav wine—the Bulgarians plundered it from them during the war."

Our delegation was granted exceptional consideration; for example, we were allowed to stand honor guard over Kalinin's bier. Tito himself was singled out for honor during the burial ceremony by Stalin, who called upon him to take a place among the members of the Soviet Politburo.

What did Stalin want? Why did he do all this? There is no one clear answer, I think, nor can there be. Certainly he was enthusiastic about Tito and the Yugoslavs, but at the same time he was misleading them. Stalin's mind worked in many directions, up to the point where, realities having come into focus, he found the right way to strengthen his power. In Tito he saw not only the master of a new Yugoslavia, but also an independent, gifted politician, an exceptional collaborator—or an unparalleled antagonist. Or perhaps all these at once, good for various periods and various forms.

Stalin's opinion of Tito can perhaps be explained by Tito's past, the time he spent in the Soviet Union, his training there, his special links with Soviet intelligence. The scope and nature of these links were never clearly disclosed, to me or to other members of the Politburo. Perhaps the following details will help confirm my conjectures. Besides the wartime radio link to the Comintern, with Tito's co-operation a radio link out of Zagreb was maintained with Soviet intelligence. The secret agent "Vazduh" ("Air"), Josip Kopinić, who was foisted on the Croatian Central Committee at the beginning of the war, when Tito replaced their Politburo, operated that link. Tito forbade Pavel Savić, a physicist and wartime code clerk at the High Command, to show communiqués from Moscow to the Politburo members without his approval. Why? Because of his special relations with Moscow, or because he wished to conceal any criticism Moscow may have directed at his work? Such criticism existed—Tito did not hide it from his Politburo comrades—and I never noticed him concealing anything else of greater significance. Still, he would not allow communiqués to be handed over before he had read them. And Soviet intelligence paid special attention to Tito at the end of the war. Lest the reader be misled about my motives in presenting these details, I should mention that a link with Soviet intelligence was necessary to the party—especially given its illegal status—for organizational reasons, and a link between an individual party member and Soviet intelligence was regarded as a recognition, even an honor, and fortified one's prestige. But Tito never became a slave to this connection or to the honors the Soviet leadership showered upon him, however much he enjoyed them.

# 10

Our confrontation with the U.S.S.R. was conceived in anger over questions of influence and prestige in the so-called people's democracies of Eastern Europe, and was inseparably linked to Soviet pressure and provocation. A small, undeveloped country whose revolution was young and unbureaucratized, eager to assert its claims, clashed with a stable Great Power conscious of its "historic" imperial role. Our highly idealistic initial aspirations in relation to these countries may have carried the seeds of hegemony, if only ideologically. Does not politics by definition contain such seeds, though unaware of their presence? Soviet aspirations, on the other hand, were consciously hegemonic and only superficially cloaked in a codified, ossified ideology.

The tight little group around Tito were not in disagreement on the people's democracies or the U.S.S.R. Insofar as there were minor differences, they arose either from personal style or from more or less idealized views. Not that our relations with each people's democracy had to conform to a single pattern. We were all in agreement that these relations should be cordial and open, because those countries had their own structural differences and suppressed aspirations which dictated a variety of approaches. This was especially true of Albania and Bulgaria, which were associated by us with so much past strife, not to mention the tangled legacy of ethnic disputes and national jealousies.

Nuances of difference in our top leadership over the way we should treat Albania were already evident when I visited that country in May 1945, following a tour of Montenegro. My visit was semiofficial, for in those days nothing went strictly by protocol among the new regimes. Nevertheless, the Albanians received me with warm solicitude, knowing that I was there at the Politburo's behest and that I had been a close colleague of Tito's since before the war.

Full of excitement and curiosity, I drove out of Ulcinj, over a bad military road. A foreign country, yes, but part of our own history. Even after my Albanian hosts had taken me in hand, I could not resist stopping on the improvised bridge over the Bojana, because our folk poetry echoes with the silvery resonance of that river. Nor could I resist gazing at the bare, mountainous terrain around Lake Scutari and asking about the villages where several thousand Montenegrins perished in those last futile battles against the Turkish Empire in 1912 and 1913. The town of Scutari itself, though picturesque in its Balkan way, and with all its seemingly chaotic splendor intact, was a disappointment simply because it was not the incredibly marvelous, enchanted city of our folk poetry.

After a formal meal in a rambling restaurant, so low-ceilinged that I felt uncomfortable standing up, we continued on to Tirana that same day. The short-lived Italian occupation of 1939 had been one of those foolish adventures that cost the occupier dearly, as I could observe on this brief ride: the highway from Scutari to Tirana was paved with asphalt. Reluctantly, my Albanian escorts confirmed that Il Duce, seeking to outshine Roman culture and to uproot the "primitive" patriarchal mentality of the natives and facilitate Albania's exploitation and colonization, had had to build and thus invest capital. The future deceived him all the more unexpectedly in that he regarded himself as its creator. That there had been certain "benefits" from the Italian occupation was borne out by the sight of the capital, whose downtown area had been rebuilt with the skill and delicacy of Italian architecture. Several thousand Italian laborers still remained in Albania, and the government, for all its ideology and nationalism, could not expel them because they were so productive. I imagine that the Albanians rose in arms under Communist leadership more from national pride, or for want of patriotism among the beys and the merchants who formed the upper classes, than because of foreign plunder and oppression.

It is hard for me to adjust to new people and places. A string of formal meetings and informal visits should bring soothing fatigue, but instead they increase my tensions and insomnia. So it was in Tirana, where I had too much to do, meeting leaders, attending dinners, participating in conferences. The Albanians were then largely oriented toward Yugoslavia—indeed, there was unofficial talk of their joining Yugoslavia as one unit in a future Balkan federation.

Revolutions awaken endless aspirations, so the Albanians wanted to reach a high cultural level overnight. Both a theater and a stadium in Tirana had been nearly completed by the Italians and awaited only the finishing touches and the development of a theatrical life. We agreed to provide them with a theater expert from Belgrade. Similar assistance was agreed upon for other cultural areas.

These were complex, though not really sensitive, issues. Language was a barrier, but one that could be surmounted. To a man, Albanian intellectuals spoke French, and since there was a tradition of French cultural influence in Serbia, it was not hard to find French-speaking professionals for work in Albania. My own French was serviceable—I understood it and, when I had to, could speak it—but I had brought with me, as a kind of secretary, a young man by the name of Nijaz Dizdarević, who knew French quite well.

Enver Hoxha was by then the acknowledged leader in Albania. He was thirty-five years old, on the heavy side, of modest bearing, eager to learn. But behind the unpretentious, Europeanized exterior loomed a personality bent on its own course, turned in on itself, and inaccessible. He was absorbed in domestic problems that, if they did not entirely coincide with, at least overlapped his personal role as he saw it. At times his face would break into a sudden and strangely cruel smile. His wife was young and beautiful, with dark skin, large eyes, and long lashes. They lived in a villa, but the royal palace on a hill in Durres was being prepared for them. I hear that Hoxha later turned modest, except in matters involving power and ideology. But those were different times. We imitated the Russians in management; the Albanians imitated us in management and autocratic luxury. The president of the presidium, Omer Nishani, was known for his education and culture. A patriot free of national prejudices, he had placed his hopes in a new Albania and in Balkan reconciliation. Though respected by all, and most pleasant to deal with, he had no power or political influence.

Nako Spiru was in the top circle, though not one of the most prominent leaders. He was distinguished by a fine intelligence and by forthrightness. Slender in build, almost tiny, he was a bundle of nerves. One sensed in him an unhappy childhood, or some enduring, inconsolable sorrow. On that idyllic threshold of Yugoslav-Albanian relations, Spiru teemed with ideas for economic collaboration. Even though I was uninformed about economics, and still less interested, we "planned" brotherhood and progress together. When, isolated in his resistance to Yugoslavia, he committed suicide in 1947, I felt sadness at something inexplicable that was involved there, in spite of the generally accepted belief that Spiru was carried away by nationalistic ardor.

Kochi Xoxe was the number-two man in the Albanian leadership. Like Ranković, he was chief of internal affairs and secretary of the Central Committee. Coarse-featured and fleshy, he was of short stature and solid build. His education had been skimpy, but he was brave and methodical, modest in his tastes. Slow to come to a decision, he was steadfast once he had made it. He had spent some time in Macedonia, and through Macedonian had come to understand Serbo-Croatian rather well, though he avoided speaking it. Ranković and Tito judged Xoxe to be the most stalwart and proletarian figure on the Albanian Central Committee, unlike Enver, who was considered intelligent and deserving of esteem, but encumbered with petit-bourgeois values and intellectualism. My encounter with Xoxe in Tirana was mainly a matter of protocol, since we worked in different fields. Later I got to know him better because he often came to Belgrade on government and party business and invariably saw Ranković in the Central Committee building, where I too worked.

Our evaluation of the Albanian leaders was based mainly on reports from our Yugoslav representatives, Miladin Popović and Dušan Mugoša—Communists who during the war had wound up in Albania after escaping from an internment camp. Their role, as I see it, was more that of experienced revolutionaries adapting to a young, undeveloped movement of a neighboring people than of official representatives of the Yugoslav party. The help they rendered their Albanian comrades was substantial. But in Yugoslav historiography after 1948—when Albania joined the Soviet campaign against us—their role was overestimated to the point where without Popović and Mugoša, Albania would have had no revolution and no party at all.

Transferring one's own experience to a foreign country first causes dissidence and opposition, then domination and subjugation. Though aware of this, I had no idea that it might hold true for relations between Communist parties and socialist states. It was on my trip to Albania that I first noticed something incongruous and unnatural about the transfer—the imposition—of our experience. I believe I brought the matter up in my talks with the Albanians, but I distinctly remember my frequent arguments on the subject with our party delegate in Albania, Velimir Stojnić.

Stojnić was a prominent insurgent from the Drvar area, a teacher by training and devoted to his job. But persistence and initiative become failings if they go against the currents of life and creativity.

112

That is what happened to Stojnić in Albania: he adamantly insisted on Yugoslav forms and views. Naturally, my warnings did not sit at all well with him. Upon returning to Belgrade, I alerted the leadership to the problem. Tito's response was that one had to act with caution and tact in these relationships. Ranković listened carefully, a sign that he realized we had to change our ways, though not our orientation. Stojnić was subsequently recalled and placed in a high and sensitive position on the Central Committee. When Ranković fell in 1966, Stojnić criticized his personnel policy, although he himself had been its direct administrator. People jump off a sinking ship in hopes of boarding a bigger, better one.

Before leaving Albania I gave an informal, friendly interview to the newspaper *Bashkimi*. Flying home over the Prokletija, I felt that I was crossing my own awesome mountains, that I was merging at last with this people with whom we have ties of bloody struggles and hopes, but from whom we were separated by inexorable national differences.

The following year, on June 23, Enver Hoxha paid us an official visit. He was clearly flattered when Tito personally met him at the airport. Tito for his part made a concentrated, almost ostentatious, effort to show that this was a partnership of equals. All in all, it was a warm and friendly visit. Hoxha was accompanied by several members of his government and other high officials. They were assigned to Yugoslavs equivalent in rank and responsibility, to establish working relationships and to be entertained. Three or four fell to me. My sister Milka, because of her wartime association with Albanians in Kosovo, served as interpreter. Our guests took this as a mark of special attention.

Relations between the two leaderships in those first postwar months were such that we all assumed we were heading toward economic and political unity, with due regard for national and ethnic identities. Such fantasies could not be entertained in relation to the other people's democracies, except possibly Bulgaria, and that only temporarily. Those states had not sought revolutions; they had coalition governments, which were more concerned with formal independence than with "internationalism." And because they were less handicapped by the emotional and ideological factors encumbering our relations with Albania and Bulgaria, they were on more open and stable terms with us.

Since all these socialist regimes, including our own, were new, they relished official parades and the external symbols of nationhood. So began an exchange of state visits full of pomp and ceremony. It was as if the new power brokers and the people, too, craved these demonstrations.

Tito's first state visit was to Poland, on March 14, 1946. We traveled by train. The Soviet government took a special interest in this visit. We learned from our escort that no sooner had we set foot on Polish soil than security was provided by Soviet police units—a whole NKVD division in Polish army uniforms. Only the leading Communist faction of the Polish government received us with open arms. They did so because of Yugoslavia's and Tito's popularity with the Polish resistance movement. The conduct of Stanislaw Mikolajczyk, head of the Agrarian party, was correct but restrained, while the Socialist Edward Osobka-Morawski made no effort to hide his differences with us regarding the future of society.

At that time all the people's democracies were not just pro-Soviet but, each in its own way, loyal and obedient to Moscow. Traditionally independent, Yugoslavia was at pains to prove its Leninist-Stalinist orthodoxy. The Czech coalition government emphasized its Slavic and national solidarity with "the great Russian people," Rumania and Hungary avoided the least move that might seem anti-Soviet, and Bulgaria boasted of having been liberated twice by Russia. Poland, though, was a world unto itself.

The Poles are, perhaps, the strongest, most independent Slavic people. Slavism and Pan-Slavism, which Moscow was still forcing down our throats, found an echo only in the top echelons. Even in Belgrade, carried away by its own revolutionary exploits, the "Slavic idea" met no deep response. But top Yugoslavs—perhaps I most of all—tried to motivate the new Stalinist Slavism by appealing to the need to defend ourselves against foreign invaders, bearing in mind the recent Nazi attempt to exterminate the "inferior" Slavic race. In Poland, however, Slavism amounted to the forced obligation to drink banquet toasts to Moscow. Fervor and conviction, especially among the broader strata of society, were conspicuously absent.

Externally, everything in Warsaw had a Polish look: banners, four-cornered officers' caps, cruciform decorations, even the president, Boleslaw Bierut, the somewhat dejected emblem of Polish statehood. He was still hiding his party membership while "consulting" with the Soviet ambassador about the pettiest details. He lived in a beautiful palace, rather small, the sole surviving public building, spared because a unit of the Gestapo charged with the city's destruction had been quartered there. He was accompanied by an unattractive older woman, whose official status was unclear; yet Tito had to show her due respect.

The Polish marshal Michal Rola-Zymierski, a malcontent from the prewar officers' cliques, also concealed his party membership. He made every effort to befriend Tito, who seemed to reciprocate. At a private meeting with Tito, he confided that he was indeed a party member, though nothing in this man's views or manners was Communist. But even he resented the way Soviet publications belittled Polish troops and their losses in the final military operations against Germany. His wife, plump and white-skinned, always gracious and smiling, reflected the personality and beliefs of this smug, superficial officer.

Wladyslaw Gomulka stood off to the side, though as party leader he was said to be important. He appeared on only one or two occasions, dressed with striking modesty and conspicuously reserved. His modesty was a pose—of that I was convinced after meeting him when the Cominform was founded in 1947. It was a pose he had selected as the most suitable for his assigned role. No doubt his conduct had more to recommend it than the overbearing manner of the Polish and Yugoslav marshals, but beneath it lay a somewhat crude, petty love of power. His "modesty" was too modest, too contrived not to be suspect.

At a dinner given by Marshal Rola-Zymierski outside Warsaw, a Soviet army officer sat next to me in the uniform of a Polish colonel. At first he spoke Polish, but so badly that I noticed it, though I don't really know the language. However, his true allegiance was revealed when he remarked that he was "by origin" a Pole. Soviet "instructors" of that kind were there in abundance, besides the official representatives of the Soviet army. Yet something else was strongly in evidence—an undercurrent of Polish nationalism. Whenever Poland and her people's struggles came up in the toasts, the hall would shake with applause. Allusions to the Soviet Union and the Red Army, on the other hand, met only a guraded reception, much more guarded than that provoked by mention of Tito and the Yugoslav Partisans.

Our encounter with the citizens of Warsaw was painfully different. Their government had decided—with Communists taking the lead, of course—to organize a parade of soldiers and civilians. The troops did not turn out in force, however, and those that did were listless and passive. It was the civilians—five or six thousand in all, mostly petits bourgeois and clerks—who revealed a bit of the true mood of Poland, crushed, tortured, and bleeding. The Polish leaders apparently believed that the popularity of Tito and the Yugoslav Partisans would attract even those citizens who disliked the Russians. But they were wrong. Any possible sympathy was overwhelmed by the fact that we were visiting a Warsaw dominated by Moscow, that Moscow was blamed for Warsaw's tragedy, that the stage setting itself was Soviet, and that we had pro-Soviet slogans on our lips. The morning was cold, overcast, and gloomy as the people of the city, undernourished and shabby, marched past in silence. If someone shouted a shopworn slogan, it would be caught up by so few marchers that it conveyed only discontent. On the reviewing stand the mood was one of repressed dissatisfaction. We could hardly wait for this funeral-like procession to be over, to get on to the next planned event.

The city itself made an impression we could not foresee or imagine: it was appalling. We knew, of course, that on Hitler's orders, the Polish capital had been totally destroyed during the 1944 summer uprising, and had read descriptions in the press. But no description could possibly match this devastating, horrifying reality. We toured the city and saw through the charred cavities of doors and windows the gutted recesses of homes stretching endlessly, row upon row, down to the huts scattered in outlying fields. Warsaw had kept its face but it was a dead city, a skeleton without body, without soul. By some miracle or through oversight, or perhaps owing to the cultural preference of the German commandant, the monument to Copernicus had been saved. It stood in an empty square, surrounded by burned-out wrecks of buildings.

The Germans had no time or lacked the means to mine the city thoroughly or bomb it into dust—though they had certainly done plenty of both. They had put Warsaw to the torch quarter by quarter, street by street, house by house. During two months of combat by General Bor's nationalist insurgents, Warsaw went up in flames. And, from the right bank of the Vistula, Polish units formed in the U.S.S.R. or on Polish free territory looked on in despair as their capital was wiped out, along with its inhabitants, as the elderly and the youth of their nation were being destroyed. They, too, were destroyed—by anguish and impotence. I was told the story by the then Polish ambassador to Yugoslavia, who had been an officer in the Polish army under Soviet command. Yet, according to the ambassador's sober, cautious account, the Soviets did permit one Polish division to try to force the river; decimated, the remnants had to pull back.

The suburb of Praga, where the Nazis had concentrated Jews, looked like a classical ruin. Several hundred thousand Jews had been packed into a lower-middle-class and working-class quarter. But the Jews had resisted and the Nazis had to fight house by house for every Jewish death. And although architects of the Warsaw to come pointed out to us the bright, harmonious expanses of future boulevards—as if only such vast destruction had set their minds free to dream and their skills to be used—still it was decided later that Praga should not be restored but kept exactly as the desperation of the Jews and the Nazi madness had left it.

There was no problem in concluding a treaty of alliance between Poland and Yugoslavia, especially since the treaty was directed against German imperialism, now crushed beyond hope.

But the Poles did not want to sign it without Soviet consent. Moscow had already been provided a text; it awaited Stalin's approval.

Between Warsaw and Moscow—or, rather, between President Bierut and Stalin—there was a special telephone line. It was like the one installed between Moscow and Belgrade in late 1947 or early 1948, when the editorial offices of the Cominform organ *For a Lasting Peace, for a People's Democracy* were set up in our capital. Stalin could call Bierut directly at his palace, whereas Bierut had to arrange for his call in advance and get confirmation of the hour. At this point, however, the Bierut-Stalin line was out of order, so we were transferred to the Soviet ambassador's residence, where there was also a special line to the Kremlin. Stalin had no major criticism of the treaty.

After speaking with Bierut and Tito, Stalin called me to the phone. He began with banalities; I was embarrassed, wondering what to ask him. "How is your health?" I finally ventured. He replied that he felt fine, but I sensed astonishment at such a question. I explained that the Western press had lately given a lot of coverage to his poor health. "They're lying," said Stalin. "They're simply lying. It works to their advantage to lie."

The Soviet ambassador asked us to stay on after we had talked to Stalin and the Poles had left. This ambassador was just what ordinary, inexperienced people picture a diplomat to be: adroit, adaptable, educated, unprincipled. No sooner had the Poles left than he began to complain about them: they weren't resolute enough; their units wouldn't fight rebels, of whom there were plenty left; even with mortars and artillery they wouldn't fight. So three Soviet divisions in Polish uniforms had to bloody their hands.

Our impressions of Czechoslovakia and Prague, which Tito visited on his way back from Poland, were very different. The Czechs were just as we had imagined them to be: happy, kindly, well dressed, in ecstasy over their democracy and their Slavism and fond of the South Slavs. Their squares had been transformed into flower gardens, their streets into fields of human grain and blossoming meadows. There were people of all ages festively dressed, and swelling tides of young girls and boys in folk costumes. Sitting there next to Tito—and concerned for his security, because in this country there were fugitive Ustashi—I was nevertheless carried away by the enthusiasm, fervor, and colorful crowds. And Tito even more: he smiled, waved his hand, jumped up from his seat, and all but lost his dignity. We did have an escort as we moved about—both our own people and Czechs—but the human wave of young people would occasionally close around us, forcing Tito to squeeze through, arms spread, while the police entreated and admonished the crowd to free a passage.

If in Warsaw all had been empty and desolate, in Prague nothing, or almost nothing, had been touched. There were only slight traces of destruction, going back to the fighting in the last days of the war, which the Czechs proudly pointed out. Not only had this supremely beautiful city been preserved, but the markets were packed with goods and the coffeehouses and restaurants gleamed and smelled of fine food. In Hradčany Castle nothing had changed; President Beneš and his government, unlike the Poles, maintained strict diplomatic protocol, right down to the proper dress. I was well but not "properly" dressed; on one occasion Tito had to lend me a pair of striped pants—too short and much too wide. Somehow we managed to please even in this regard, and high orders were bestowed on us, just like the ones the republic used to hand out before the war to Yugoslav statesmen. We were housed in a palace above the Vltava, overlooking tidy villages and low hills with symmetrical patches of woods, reminiscent of landscapes by primitive artists.

Communists formed the strongest party, more because of their organization and key positions (Vaclav Nosek, the minister of internal affairs, was a Communist) than because of voter support. The vice-president of the governing body was the Communist party leader, Klement Gottwald; and the president, the Socialist Zdenek Fierlinger, favored unity with the Communists. But it was Moscow's influence that made the greatest and most decisive difference. The power balance had shifted during the war because the U.S.S.R. contributed the most to winning it and thereby won predominance in Eastern Europe.

Eduard Beneš, as president of the republic, enjoyed a reputation greater than what we in Yugoslavia had supposed. We had believed he was more the formal than the real head of state, and only to please the West. But for Czechs, the formal was inseparable from the real. We had also thought that Beneš, though perhaps not quite like our "patriots"—adherents of the democratic parties who had joined the Communists—had little more importance. Besides, we were convinced that his reputation had been undermined by his pusillanimous "appeasement" in 1938. But Beneš was now indeed the head of state, albeit with limited powers. As for 1938, almost no one in Czechoslovakia criticized him for it, not even the Communists. What else could Beneš have done, other than hurl his own people into a bloodbath, after France and Britain left him in the lurch? We Yugoslav Communists thought otherwise: one had to fight. Not everything was hopeless, and even if it were, one had to defend one's nation and way of life. Maybe both we and the Czechs were right, each of us in the light of our own perspectives and traditions.

No matter what our views, we could not escape the Beneš personality. He behaved gently, wisely, with moderation and thoughtfulness in all things. His least little gesture or passing remark breathed a cultivated feeling for democracy, precisely that democracy whose prime mover he had been. He spoke the major languages fluently—his Russian was superb, incomparably better than Tito's or mine. He had had an excellent musical education. At a performance of Smetana's *Bartered Bride*, he joked about being fed up with it because it was always given on official occasions; listening now for the hundredth time, he would be aware at once if a note was left out or off-key.

Yet there was resignation in the man. It showed in his gentle cynicism, especially when politics as an activity—not concrete political issues—was touched upon. When someone offered him a cigarette, he said, "One poison is enough—politics." He didn't drink or smoke. In giving a toast to Tito, he merely moistened his lips with champagne. Withdrawn and meditative, he would reflect not on his place in history, but on the physical and spiritual survival of his people. I exchanged only a few words with Beneš, at receptions and the theater. Yet I was told that long before I was denounced by the Central Committee as a "revisionist," Beneš had said of me: "That Djilas will wind up a Communist heretic."

The liveliest and most attractive person among the top leaders of Czechoslovakia in those years was Jan Masaryk, minister of foreign affairs and son of the republic's founder, Tomaš Masaryk. He was the subject of anecdotes and was everyone's favorite, even the Communists'. He owed this more to his personal charm than to his famous father. Tallish, bald, pale, and gaunt, Jan looked like someone who was in the habit of staying up late and having a good time. He was, however, moderate in all things except—so it was rumored—love: unmarried at fifty, he made no effort to conceal his passion for women. He had a fine, quick intelligence, was broadly educated, and, above all, was a magnificent raconteur. I never heard anyone tell off-color stories with such easy, quiet, inoffensive salacity, and that in the most unlikely circumstances— at banquets, before the highest and most dignified guests. In fact, the King of England had once been late for a reception—I think it was when the United Nations met in London—because Masaryk was telling jokes. That actually happened!

On that particular visit to Prague, I heard about Jan Masaryk's "eccentricities" from Communists, both our own and Czech. But later, when the Czechs reciprocated our visit, I talked with him in Belgrade and got to know him better. Our talks were, unfortunately, brief. Naturally, what I saw in him was a bourgeois democrat in the tradition of his father, although he was not active in Masaryk's National Socialist party and never invoked his father's name. He wanted to be his own man and he succeeded. One of us once asked him why he had left Czechoslovakia during his father's presidency. He answered: "My father was a philosopher, a president, a living monument, and he would see me only when he had to give me money or when I was mad at him. I wanted to get out from under the aura of his majesty."

My narrow Communist view did not prevent my appreciating

that Jan Masaryk was not one of those manipulators from a social democratic party who adhere to their principles in order to hold on to their followers, to realize their ambitions, and to maintain an easy life, while siding with the Communists. He favored collaborating with the domestic Communists and especially with foreign Communist governments, but not at the expense of his own or Czechoslovakia's integrity. In one banquet toast he remarked: "In the West, Czechoslovakia is described as a bridge between East and West. We have no wish to be a bridge. Bridges are where horses commit indecencies." And in Belgrade, likewise in a toast: "United States senators are rarely informed when it comes to foreign affairs, nor are they sharp when it comes to geography: they've been getting Czechoslovakia mixed up with Yugoslovakia; Czechoslavia with Yugoslavia. That doesn't look good for the senators or for the U.S.A. But we ought to be friends, so that when they get us mixed up, *we* are not confused."

Masaryk was an exponent of collaboration and rapprochement with the Soviet Union and especially with Yugoslavia. Underlying the affection between Czechs and Yugoslavs is there not a spontaneous yearning that their patience and our readiness for violence should complement each other?

Still another mutual assistance treaty was signed in Prague, directed against a Germany that was by now defeated and occupied. The only significance of this one was, essentially, our taking a stand against American hegemony. We felt certain that the Americans would not go to war until they had put Germany on its feet. Though we were aware that this treaty and the others were binding the East European countries together around the Soviet Union, we did not recognize that by the same token we were being included in the Soviet empire.

Perhaps that was Masaryk's suspicion. He behaved with real warmth toward Yugoslavia, but attributed only formal significance to the alliance. Beneš, too, had reservations about such a treaty with Yugoslavia. He put them mildly to Gottwald, who quoted Beneš to us with a laugh: "I'm not against the treaty, but you know what they're like as a people, quick to stir up war—just think of 1914!"

Jan Masaryk died under mysterious circumstances, just after the Communist takeover, in March 1948. Whether he was killed or committed suicide is a question I cannot and do not wish to speculate on. I am sure of this: he could not accept dictatorship and Soviet domination, nor could he survive them politically and remain true to himself and his father.

I stayed on in Prague after Tito's visit ended, representing our party at the Czechoslovak party congress. I was staying at the apartment of our ambassador, Darko Černej, which was not far from where the Gottwalds lived. One morning on my way to the congress I dropped in to see him. He was a fair-haired, heavy man with the ruddy nose of a drinker and slow movements, rather like a Slovenian innkeeper.

The furnishings in the Gottwalds' apartment were of good quality but ordinary. On the shelves of the glass-enclosed cabinets crystal gleamed. On the walls hung pictures of the socialist realist school. My awareness back then had not gone beyond socialist realism in theory, but I resisted the stereotypes of Soviet painting and its imitators. In our country, happily, they were few. I asked Gottwald why he didn't have paintings that were more contemporary and of higher quality. He replied that he liked such pleasant, simple, obvious pictures, adding, "This crazy modernistic stuff isn't for me, though I'm against party interference in the matter. I'm against any sort of censorship."

The conversation turned to our use of Soviet experience. Like all of us in the narrow circle around Tito, perhaps more instinctively than consciously, I already resented Soviet high-handedness and spying. But I still thought of Soviet models and experience in "building socialism" as invaluable. Gottwald was of another opinion: "The Soviet Union is still undeveloped. We are developed, we have strong democratic traditions, and socialism here is going to be different."

Gottwald, like most of the Czech party leadership, was obviously not inclined to copy Soviet forms or to be unconditionally obedient to Moscow. But Czechoslovakia, unlike Yugoslavia, had not passed through a revolution, and it had no independent power to fall back on.

As at congresses and public assemblies throughout Eastern Europe, pictures of Marx, Engels, Lenin, and Stalin were prominently displayed. But this was Czechoslovakia, and a picture of Tomaš Masaryk was also there. Communist officials were perfectly aware that Masaryk, working with the Entente powers to create an independent Czechoslovak state, had supported the anti-Bolshevik intervention through a Czechoslovak legion organized in Russia among exiles and prisoners of war. The Soviets and their representatives, however, did not openly object to the picture. It was prominently displayed at all demonstrations and, beside that of Beneš, on public buildings. But for me, this emphasis on Masaryk's picture at a party congress was not just an instance of bourgeois-democratic behavior, but a step backward from ideological purity. When I asked Gottwald for an explanation, he offered the following, almost as an excuse: "Masaryk's picture is there because, in the minds of the masses, he symbolizes the creation of the republic."

As in the rest of the East European countries liberated by the Red Army, the Czech Ministry of Internal Affairs was in the hands of a Communist, Vaclav Nosek, a Politburo member. But Nosek had not yet built his own Communist police apparatus, and he was not of the same mettle as his Balkan counterparts, tempered by prison and underground struggle, and dedicated to consolidating a new, dictatorial power. The Czech authorities, still relying on the old police organization, provided for Tito's security by a proven technique: they arrested all citizens of Yugoslav origin. To be sure, many wartime deserters, especially Ustashi, had found refuge in Slovakia and were not ordinarily under strict control.

On the very first day of our stay in Prague, Tito started receiving letters entreating him to intervene on behalf of arrested husbands and fathers—old men who had settled in Czechoslovakia back in the days of the Austro-Hungarian Empire. Tito did intervene with the top Czech leaders, who explained that it was a matter of preventive arrests that would continue for the duration of his visit. When I mentioned this to the Gottwalds in jest, Mrs. Gottwald told me that the police came to their door to inquire about a Yugoslav woman registered as living there. She was baffled until she realized that her two-year-old granddaughter was that "woman." When the Gottwalds lived in exile in Moscow, their daughter had married a Yugoslav immigrant. She had since obtained a divorce but their little girl, registered as a Yugoslav, was being brought up by the Gottwalds.

The congress itself placed more emphasis on the national than the international, favoring democracy over the dictatorship of the proletariat. I realized that their approach was dictated by domestic and foreign relations, so I did not object. On the other hand, I was not enthusiastic about such concepts and positions. In my country, reality was different: a "dictatorship of the proletariat" already existed, and I myself was obsessed with the "perfection" of dogma.

I also represented the Yugoslav party at the congress of the French Communist party in Strasbourg in June 1947. On the train to Strasbourg an elderly Frenchman, on discovering that my group were Yugoslavs, vented his fury on us for nationalizing the Bor copper mine, which had been owned by French capitalists and in which he had obviously been a stockholder. I explained to him with quiet irony that we had not nationalized French, but German, capital. The French had sold Bor to the Germans during the war, and we were thus "discharged" of any obligation toward France as our ally. Blaming the Germans for all the evils of this world was fashionable in Germany itself, to say nothing of France. "That idiot Pétain!" exclaimed this French bourgeois bitterly.

At the congress, I was in close contact with Etienne Fajon, a Politburo member and a functionary of narrow but firm views. Maurice Thorez dominated the congress through his impressive bearing and great powers of expression. He did not grasp, however, the change initiated by the strain in Soviet-American relations. The previous French government had just fallen, and the Communists were left out of the new one. During a break in the proceedings I approached Thorez and conveyed Tito's greetings, with an invitation to visit Yugoslavia. "Yes, yes, this autumn," he replied, "if we're not in the government—but we will be, I'm sure." I did not like this graceless, manipulative reply, particularly with regard to a country that had battled fascism so heroically; nor did I believe he would enter the government again. On another occasion I visited Thorez in his Paris apartment and once again felt looked down upon as a Yugoslav. French Communists, in their condescension toward us, adopted something of French officialdom's haughtiness.

At the Strasbourg congress it was brought out strongly—too strongly, to my way of thinking then—that the French Communist party was implementing a national policy. The West European parties, like their counterparts in Eastern Europe, were eager to differentiate themselves from the Soviet Union, without actually opposing Moscow. If the French Communists were not the steadiest in pursuit of this goal, they were, I would say, the noisiest.

Like the rest of our leaders, I had been critical of the French party, partly out of ignorance, partly from "revolutionary" vanity. But I changed my mind at that congress, at least so far as the middle ranks—the functionary level—went. Tempered in war, confident of their ideology, and prepared for sacrifice, they did not differ essentially from the Yugoslav Communists who had led a revolution. They also expressed enthusiasm for Stalin and the Soviet Union.

Soon thereafter, Molotov came to Paris to consult with the Western ministers about the Marshall Plan. I was still in the city, and Molotov invited me to lunch. We talked in the embassy drawing room before lunch, and then, after lunch, while strolling in the embassy garden. In the drawing room the Soviets turned on the radio to prevent electronic eavesdropping, commenting that jazz was most effective for this purpose, though they preferred classical music.

Molotov wanted my impressions of the congress. I was critical of our French comrades, who operated under the illusion that American imperialism was not skillful enough to prevent their return to the government, and of their preoccupation with a "national policy." Molotov corrected me: "It's fine for them to have a national policy, but that policy isn't co-ordinated with the people's democracies and the Soviet Union." This was what I'd meant, I said. As we talked further about the lack of co-ordination between the Communist parties of Eastern and Western Europe, Molotov remarked that there ought to be a joint ideological periodical. I reminded him that in Paris a journal called *La Démocratie Nouvelle* was already appearing, edited by our French comrades. (Formally, I was a member of the editorial board.) "That's not the point!" said Molotov. "There's no common line. Everyone advances his own ideas. What's needed is an ideological review with a single editorial office and unified positions." I agreed.

Molotov was not much interested in conditions within Yugoslavia, though he did not seem uninformed. He wanted to hear my opinion of the East European countries' participation in the Marshall Plan. Belgrade did not have a fixed position, but from the general mood and various conversations, I judged that our leadership was opposed and told Molotov so. Moreover, I was against our attending any meeting concerning it. Molotov then said that he had at first leaned toward participation, but that the Politburo had disavowed the Marshall Plan and directed him to oppose it. Upon my return to Belgrade, incidentally, I was supposed to go to Moscow to do some persuading among the Czechs, who had agreed to participate in the plan. A Soviet plane was waiting for me, but at the last minute my departure was canceled, because the Czechs had backed down.

Molotov and Vyshinsky were on their way to a cocktail party or to supper and offered me a ride back to my embassy. Driving along the luxurious boulevards of Paris, Molotov remarked, apropos of a loan the French had just negotiated with the United States: "They'll spend it on brothels and luxuries and be right back where they started."

Those were the years—especially 1947—of a series of mutual visits among the people's democracies, with our country taking much of the initiative. However, members of the Hungarian Central Committee were, I would say, the most active in seeking ties with our Central Committee. Many times they came to Belgrade unofficially to consult about their own domestic affairs. The meetings were usually held in the White Palace, and they were attended by Tito, Politburo members, and, from time to time, by others from relevant sectors, such as Boris Kidrič.

Those unofficial Hungarian delegations were led by the party chief, Mátyás Rákosi, a well-known figure in the Communist movement. He was most often accompanied by Erno Gero and three or four Central Committee members, and our relations were, on the whole, cordial. The Hungarians looked to Belgrade for support, and until 1948, Belgrade, one might say, was a second Moscow for their party leadership.

Along with Tito, Ranković, and Kidrič, I was in the state delegation which in turn visited Budapest on December 8, 1947. The rather cold reception given Rákosi's speech at a well-attended mass meeting did not escape me.

There were still Socialists in the government at that time. Though the Hungarians observed protocol, it was impossible to conceal a special closeness between the Hungarian leaders and us. There was an unofficial meeting of our respective top leaders, with Laszlo Rajk and János Kádár in attendance. We Yugoslavs singled out the two of them as "domestic" cadres—those who had not had their training in Moscow. Kádár was reserved and taciturn. His working-class origin was played up as a special distinction. He was modest and steady, but still not sufficiently mature "ideologically," which was all the more apparent because the other leaders were so quick in responding with theory to every question that arose in conversation.

Rajk was an intelligent, sensitive, and conscientious official. He, too, was taciturn. It was as if in those days taciturnity were a characteristic—more congenial than acquired—of all the ministers of internal affairs in Eastern Europe. Ranković and Rajk held special meetings as ministers of internal affairs. Their bond grew especially strong, and Rajk came to Belgrade on an official visit. What was the nature of this bond? Undoubtedly, it was more than just an exchange of experiences, but in no way was it a conspiracy to detach Hungary from the Soviet Union: the later trial of Rajk was based on fabrications. Nevertheless, it did have some basis in reality, in that Rajk subconsciously objected to Soviet dictation; we knew it. Perhaps Ranković would have something more precise to say on the subject, but I believe the essence of the matter was the mounting protest in Hungary, as in the other Eastern European countries, against Soviet positions and actions. This protest grew little by little and was associated with us. As a repressed malcontent, Rajk sensed our backing. I think that Tito, acting primarily through Ranković, was trying to channel that protest in our direction as a way of strengthening his own role and that of Yugoslavia. The 1948 confrontation was conceived in various countries—all the centers of Eastern Europe. The Soviet leaders were not about to renounce hegemony, and so their only choice was confrontation.

Our relations with Bulgaria have never been good. Cold suspicion has alternated with romantic, childish ecstasies. The burden has been borne by Serbs and Macedonians; Croats and Slovenes, less sensitive to the problem, have been less involved. Tito was the exception: he recognized the significance of the Bulgarian connection for Yugoslavia and for the Balkans generally. Besides, he had an emotional bond with Georgi Dimitrov, who, by helping to place him at the head of the Yugoslav party in the 1930s, had set the course for Tito's rise. The Macedonian Communists were less enthusiastic about the Bulgarians and more suspicious than the Serbs. This resulted from their painful, humiliating experience at the time of our revolution with the Bulgarian party, which took over the Macedonian organization and stopped the Macedonian uprising dead in its tracks.

Our relations have also been burdened with four wars in half a century: in 1885, 1913, 1915, and 1941. The attitude of Serbian Communists—or, more broadly, the Serbian people—has been ambivalent. Recognition of their own mistakes was mixed with bitterness over Bulgarian treachery and brutality during periods of occupation. The Serbs felt—and probably still do—that they themselves were to blame for the war of 1885; that both sides were equally at fault in 1913; but that they were attacked by the

Bulgarians despite treaty obligations and vows of "eternal friendship," in the tragic events of 1915 and 1941. But the Bulgarians were rarely capable of such insight and openness in assessing the history linking our two nations, and the Communists, curiously enough, less so than Bulgaria's Agrarian party leaders.

However, with Dimitrov's return from Moscow, relations took a turn for the better, and the flood of fraternal feelings promised to wash away hatreds and misunderstandings forever. Receptions given by the Bulgarian ambassador, who was not a Communist, were more like family gatherings than diplomatic receptions.

A Bulgarian state delegation reached Belgrade on July 26, 1947. It was led by Dimitrov, who was popular in Yugoslavia and well liked by our party's top leadership. I did not attend the welcoming reception, because I was on vacation in Slovenia, writing a novel. But when the delegation went to Lake Bled, where several mutual assistance treaties were signed, I joined our leaders. Dimitrov told us then with genuine feeling that he had been especially moved by the welcome Serbian peasants gave him at train stations on the way to Belgrade. They were rejoicing that an end had come at last to the hatred and bloodshed between two neighboring peoples.

In the Lake Bled talks, official and otherwise, one sensed hope for rapprochement, for unification. No one ever thought, let alone spoke, of breaking away from the Soviet Union. But our absorption in solving mutual problems channeled both sides in the direction of independence. And since a peace treaty with Bulgaria had not yet been concluded, the understandings and demonstrations in Yugoslavia meant for the Bulgarian government a step toward full national rights and diplomatic parity. These understandings, along with the alliance concluded later in Evsinograd, were to be the core of Stalin's savage criticism when Yugoslav and Bulgarian representatives met with him in February 1948.

The Bulgarians were surprised and impressed by what they saw in Yugoslavia—even by our factories. Tito was pleased. "It's good for them to see all this, or they might think we don't have anything."

In one unofficial conversation, an altercation broke out between Dimitrov and Lazar Koliševski, prime minister of our republic of Macedonia. I supported Koliševski. There had been talk about future unification, a Bulgarian-Yugoslav federation. It went without saying that in such a federation Macedonia would annex the Pirin region, the part of Macedonia that had remained in Bulgaria. In a devilish moment I goaded Koliševski to ask Dimitrov why annexation should wait until the unification of Yugoslavia and Bulgaria, now that the Macedonian character of the Pirin region was established and recognized by all. Such an annexation, I added, would reflect Marxist views on the nationality question and be an inspired beginning to the unification of our two countries.

His back to the wall, overwhelmed by our arguments, Dimitrov reacted with nervous confusion: "We can't do that now—the bourgeoisie would exploit the issue!" For Koliševski and me, this answer was like waving a red flag. Bulgarian Communists, we believed, were duty-bound to fight the bourgeoisie. But just as the argument was gaining momentum, Tito cut it short: "This is no time to discuss the matter."

On the whole, Dimitrov went further than any other Bulgarian in acknowledging the special character of the Macedonians, though it was never clear how much sprang from his own conviction and how much from the desire for a rapprochement with Serbia and Yugoslavia. That his mother was Macedonian and his first wife a Serb may have been significant, but what was crucial was the legacy of Balkan socialist movements that had championed a Balkan federation before World War I. Dimitrov was dreaming of fulfilling the ideals of his youth. The year 1948 would dispel those ideals. The fact that at the Bulgarian party congress in the autumn of that year Dimitrov directed his criticism at Koliševski and me, not Tito, may have stemmed more from his hesitation and hope for a compromise solution through the sacrifice of expendable Yugoslav officials than from our quarrel at Bled over Macedonia.

This interpretation is supported by the circumstances of our return visit to Sofia on November 26, which was less the encounter of two chiefs of state than the long-desired merger of kindred victorious movements. To show off a little, the Bulgarians

131

drove us to Varna and the royal palace in Evsinograd, on the Black Sea, where the mutual assistance treaty was signed. Along the way, Bulgarian peasants greeted Tito with genuine warmth, just as the Serbs had welcomed Dimitrov. It was this treaty of alliance, if I recall correctly, that, at the Bulgarians' suggestion, was to include a provision for "eternal friendship." Although we Yugoslavs recalled the "eternal friendship" pledged by the kingdoms of Yugoslavia and Bulgaria—a friendship whose "eternity" hardly lasted until the signatories' ink was dry—the provision would have passed muster had not the Soviet government advised us to replace it with "twenty years." This was done without any objection from the Bulgarians. Soon after our confrontation with Moscow, the Bulgarians abrogated this and all other treaties. Communist "eternity" proved no more eternal than the royal kind.

During the meetings, Anton Yugov and Ranković, the ministers of internal affairs, "exchanged experiences" of the struggle against the class enemy and other common foes.

At the farewell banquet Tito had more to drink than usual, and the hugging at the railroad station knew no limits.

I was not in the delegation that visited Bucharest on December 18, 1947, but Ranković told me that the Soviet representatives could not conceal their envy when hundreds of thousands, standing in slush, cheered Tito. We also felt Soviet disapproval during our visit to Hungary. East European protests against Soviet domination had found an outlet in Yugoslavia.

# 11

The idea of sharing experience and co-ordinating actions of the Communist parties came up often, especially in meetings among the East European leaders. It was not so much ideological unanimity that brought the issue up, as it was the rivalry between capitalism and socialism—between the United States and the Soviet Union. But no one favored reviving the Comintern, which Stalin had dissolved in 1943 to strengthen his country's position. Stalin discussed the matter in general terms with Dimitrov and Tito during a Yugoslav delegation's stay in Moscow in June 1946. They agreed that any future organization should be informational in character. The launching of *La Démocratie Nouvelle* in Paris was one step in this direction, and Molotov's later conversation with me another.

The final decision to hold a meeting to found a Communist Information Bureau (Cominform) was made by the Soviet top echelon without any direct consultation, but with the agreement of all concerned. Kardelj and I, representing the Communist party of Yugoslavia, took off by special plane for the Polish city of Wroclaw (the former Breslau) in late September 1947. When we landed, the day was overcast, but without rain. We were met by Jakub Berman, the stocky, coarse-featured, uncommunicative chairman of the Polish Central Committee, then had to wait two hours on the barren airstrip because security measures did not permit us to move into the waiting room, and no automobile came for us. We joked about this a little, and Berman observed apologetically that organization was in the hands of our Soviet comrades.

The meeting was held at the resort of Szklarska Poreba. I didn't learn the name of the place until later, because they didn't tell us, nor did we ask, so scrupulously did we observe the security arrangements. It took about three hours to drive there, between tidy lines of fir trees and through villages laid out all straight and even. The delegates were put up in the small lodging house of a rest home belonging to State Security; the meetings were held in its dining hall. Other small buildings were scattered about, but I do not know who was housed in them. Around the lodging house stretched meadows, where the delegates strolled in casual conversation during the breaks.

The following represented their parties at this meeting: Zhdanov and Malenkov (U.S.S.R.), Chervenkov and Poptomov (Bulgaria), Pauker and Dej (Rumania), Farkas and Revai (Hungary), Gomulka and Minc (Poland), Slansky and Bashtovansky (Czechoslovakia), Longo and Reale (Italy), Duclos and Fajon (France), and Kardelj and I (Yugoslavia).

The meeting lasted seven days, with morning and afternoon sessions. The opening report, on the international situation, was given by Zhdanov. Thereafter one representative reported on each party's work and situation, Kardelj speaking for Yugoslavia. Malenkov stressed that the Soviet party was making the transition from socialism to Communism, and that studying the utopian socialists had therefore taken on new interest and importance. All the delegates except the French spoke Russian; and since there was no simultaneous translation, everything had to be put into French. As a result, the conference dragged on, even longer because the Soviet translator was not familiar with political problems and terminology. Zhdanov and I kept having to break in, until finally Minc, of Poland, undertook to do the translating.

No agenda had been fixed in advance. Reports had to be prepared overnight and in the morning, so the delegations—especially ours, which was preparing a critique of the French and Italian parties—worked very hard. Even before the discussions took place, disagreements surfaced, particularly with the French and the Italians. Actually, we were out gunning for them because of their "parliamentary illusions," their tendency to underrate American "aggressiveness," and their feeble support of the Soviet Union and the people's democracies. Criticism of the French and the Italians was implicit in Zhdanov's report, because he drew a sharp distinction between capitalism and socialism, accusing the United States of blackmail and pressure, and preparations for a war of aggression. More specific criticism of the two parties fell to us, first me and then Kardelj. Even before Duclos and Longo gave their reports, Kardelj and I discussed our critiques of their parties with Zhdanov and Malenkov. Zhdanov could hardly wait: "They must be criticized!"

We worked very closely with the Soviets. We sat next to them and consulted in whispers or passed notes back and forth. Ana Pauker interpreted it her own way when we were outside in the meadow, relaxing with small talk: "Unlike the Soviet and Yugoslav parties, the rest of us haven't much to boast about."

Kardelj's criticism of the Italians went deeper and was more concrete than mine of the French. My knowledge of conditions in the French party was superficial, just enough to be included in the scheme set up by Zhdanov. But my superficiality had no more to do with Duclos's angry rejection of my criticism than Kardelj's depth with Longo's acceptance of Kardelj's critique. Unlike the Italians, the French Communists were supercilious and self-confident. Jacques Duclos had not even gone through the Soviet "school" of criticism and self-criticism, and had lived in the U.S.S.R. for only short periods. He vented on me all his resentment of the gathering itself, including the Soviet delegates. Just before the end of the session Zhdanov and Malenkov toned down their positions, lest the French feel rejected personally.

Luigi Longo, on the other hand, accepted the criticism with equanimity. Furthermore, with Eugenio Reale he visited Kardelj and me in our room. He even swallowed Kardelj's charge that their party press printed almost nothing about Yugoslavia. We parted with mutual understanding, but without any of the warmth characteristic of relationships during our illegal period and in wartime. Still, we continued to have spirited contact with the Italian party. Palmiro Togliatti, its leader, came to Belgrade two or three times after the war. A mutually accceptable, sensible agreement could always be worked out with him, thanks to his flexibility and Tito's practicality.

At the beginning of 1948, on the eve of elections in Italy, two members of the Italian Central Committee came to Belgrade, and agreement was reached on everything touching our relations. But on the train to Zagreb a sharp difference of opinion arose between Kardelj and me and these two Italians over their notion of where Italy was headed. They were convinced that they would win a majority in the forthcoming elections, thereby creating conditions for a system like Yugoslavia's. We were dubious of any such victory and kept trying to convince them that such a system depended on destroying the status quo through armed struggle. The term "revolution" was not yet official in Yugoslavia, though Kardelj and I felt that that was what our struggle against the occupation had been. If we were trying to apply Yugoslav experience to Italy somewhat schematically, it was obvious that our Italian comrades had delusions about winning power by peaceful parliamentary means. The story related here and my accompanying judgment cannot be applied to the Italian party's current "Eurocommunism," because circumstances have changed in Europe and the world since then, as has the Italian party itself.

The French and the Italians were similarly attacked at this first Cominform conference, mostly by Zhdanov, for their illusions about their chances of staying in power and about parliamentarism in general.

A quarrel erupted between the Hungarian and Czech delegations, the former accusing the Czechs of persecuting and expelling their Hungarian minority. As evidence, drastic cases were cited, such as the expulsion of veterans of the Spanish Civil War, as well as party members and persons in the Communist youth movement. Their delegation had the support of the rest of us. Broader discussion was avoided at the working session, but in the corridors no holds were barred: we Yugoslavs lectured the Czechs on internationalism.

The only real ideological divergence emerged when Gomulka outlined, in no uncertain terms, a "Polish road to socialism." A notion like that never occurred to us Yugoslavs; even when our confrontation with the Soviets began, we disputed false Soviet accusations, not their form of socialism. Gomulka also expressed reservations about collectivizing the Polish villages. When he did this, Kardelj muttered loudly enough for Zhdanov, sitting next to him, to hear: "A 'Polish' road to socialism—why, it was the Red Army that liberated them!" Yet Gomulka's idea was not met head on and refuted; this was done in the corridors, where we, needless to say, excelled in our zeal.

Zhdanov and Malenkov had reason to be satisfied with the delegates from Yugoslavia. They enjoyed our unqualified support, even though differences were already smoldering between the two countries. The decisions taken by that founding session of the Cominform would not, I believe, have turned out otherwise had the Yugoslavs behaved more independently, but the atmosphere and relationships would certainly have been different. The Soviet delegates would have been less self-confident, and the other delegations—especially the Poles, the French, and the Italians—would have been supported by a party that had brought off a revolution of its own.

The reports may not have extolled us to the degree our party deserved, but the Soviets did pay us special attention. Our position there was that of their most deserving junior partner, which at the time was enough to avoid ruffling Yugoslav vanity and aspirations. Later, when conflict broke out, our top people viewed the Cominform, and its location in Belgrade, as a diabolical scheme of Stalin's to subjugate Eastern Europe, with Yugoslavia as target number one.

Today, on reflection, I believe that this thinking was not

quite right. By organizing the Cominform, Stalin certainly intended to impose obedience on Eastern Europe and on those Communist parties, the French and Italian, whose influence was important in the West. There was corridor talk to the effect that some other parties ought to have been invited—for instance, the British, the Albanian, and even the Greek, which was then embroiled in a civil war. But the Soviets quashed the idea without much explanation. To this day I don't understand why the Albanians were not asked; we Yugoslavs certainly had no objections. Perhaps Moscow did not regard Albania as of much consequence, or perhaps it thought Albania not wholly weaned from capitalism. Greek attendance was rejected because it could be interpreted in the West as open involvement in the civil war. Yet no greater importance was ascribed to the Greek party than to any of the other parties left out. The British party was judged too weak, especially when compared with the French and Italian; had it been present, the absence of other parties could not have been justified. Anyhow, the delegates felt that these nonparticipating parties would support the decisions of an information bureau and observe any positions it might adopt—a judgment that proved correct.

All in all, the organization and composition of the Cominform answered to the interests of Moscow. But I don't think that the choice of Belgrade as its site was at that moment motivated by plans to subjugate Yugoslavia. In fact, Zhdanov had suggested Prague, as the least exposed capital in the worsening relations with the West and the "weakest link" in the East. But Slansky could not accept the obligation without consulting Gottwald, and since there was no direct telephone line between Szklarska Poreba and Prague (there was such a line only to Moscow), he went back to Prague. After driving all afternoon and all night, he returned to the meeting about noon the next day, with Gottwald's reluctant assent. Meanwhile, Zhdanov had talked with Stalin overnight on the special phone and of course conveyed Slansky's hesitation. Stalin then decided to make Belgrade the site, and Kardelj and I accepted with enthusiasm, even though this would subject Yugoslavia to additional pressures from the West and to new international commitments. But Belgrade would now be recognized as the new revolutionary center, second only to Moscow.

It was agreed at the conference that the Cominform would publish a fortnightly organ, but its title, *For a Lasting Peace, for a People's Democracy*, was settled on later. The editor-in-chief, Pavel Judin, used to say that the title was concocted by Stalin on the premise that, when Westerners referred to it, they would have to utter a Communist slogan. But this expectation was disappointed, as were hopes for the Cominform itself. The Western press services, if only because the title was too long, referred simply to the "organ of the Cominform."

Kardelj and I saw Tito immediately upon our return—that same afternoon, in fact. In the evening, ten of our leading comrades, including Koča Popović, Ivan Gošnjak, and Blagoje Nešković, gathered for an informal meeting around the billiard table at our bowling alley, there to hear the good news. They were bursting with childlike pride and joy, as if we had come full circle to the "romantic" period of interparty relations, as if the blood and suffering of us Communists and Yugoslavs had at last won recognition. Yet for all our romantic glow, we felt pretty smug in reviewing all the criticism and self-criticism of everyone except the Yugoslavs and the Russians. Shortly thereafter, by agreement with the other parties, we published the conference's declaration, on which occasion I wrote an editorial for *Borba*'s October 8 edition. It illustrates our unbridled conceit.

The peoples of Yugoslavia can be proud that their capital has become the place where Communist parties will carry out future consultation and reach agreements on the struggle against the instigators of new wars and their henchmen. We can only take pride that our country will thus help promote the activity of the most progressive forces in contemporary society, for the welfare of peace-loving, toiling humanity and all peoples fighting for emancipation from the imperialist yoke.

The Soviet representative, Pavel Judin, soon arrived in Yugoslavia. Measures were promptly taken to house the Cominform and print its publications. This was mainly the job of Ranković and his staff. One of the most imposing mansions, a former bank, was emptied and refurbished. We took the duty entrusted to us as a "historic responsibility" and carried it out conscientiously. Even the Soviets found nothing to criticize.

A special telephone line was installed to connect Judin with Moscow. According to a decision made at a Cominform meeting in mid-January 1948, at which Gošnjak represented the Yugoslav party (I was in Moscow at the time), the editorial board was to include one representative from each Cominform country. In actual fact, editing was in the hands of Judin—"the best philosopher among the secret agents and the best agent among the philosophers," as they said in Moscow. Yet even he had no more authority than an intelligent copy editor. A proof of the newspaper was flown to Moscow for the approval of Stalin and Molotov, and no less a figure than Judin's deputy, Olenin, stood guard over the *Borba* printing press lest a copy be filched before the imprimatur arrived.

Boris Ziherl was our member on the editorial board, and I was the party representative to the Cominform itself. Ziherl was satisfactory from a journalistic, and especially a theoretical, point of view, though he was not firm and courageous enough with the Soviet representatives. To be sure, there was then no reason to be, and at first glance it seemed there never would be. The very founding of the Cominform—still more, its establishment in Belgrade—implied harmony with the Soviet Union.

But all this was mere outward show dictated by our need for ideological unity with the Soviet Union. Differences and disagreements "in the government line," which meant real and vital issues, continued to exist, and even to intensify. In the press, an observer of the time would have noticed an even stronger, almost feverish, support by Yugoslavia of Soviet foreign policy, and for Vyshinsky's long and bathetic speeches. The thirtieth anniversary of the October Revolution dominated entire newspaper editions and was celebrated more noisily than in Moscow. In 1947, Yugoslav Army Day was still being celebrated on Stalin's birthday, December 21. Yet such ostentation only served to conceal the underlying reality.

This was the period of Tito's visits to Budapest, Bucharest, and Sofia, when the spontaneous sympathies of those three peoples for Yugoslavia were so strikingly apparent. It was the period when some of their leaders showed an inclination toward our country because of her independent, "Yugoslav" position. Behind the scenes, as if inadvertently, conflict was growing through gossip about the stupidities, arrogance, and crudeness of the Soviet representatives. Soviet Ambassador Lavrentiev was a frequent topic of this backstage mud-slinging, often with good reason.

Our first Soviet ambassador had been Sadchikov. Appointed immediately upon recognition of the Tito-Šubašić government, he remained a little more than a year. When the question of an ambassadorial appointment originally came up, Kardelj had emphasized that we ought to insist that the Soviet government send us, not a professional diplomat, but a party man, someone who could help us with internal development and party matters. I don't recall who did the insisting—maybe Tito, maybe Kardelj himself in Moscow at the end of 1944. So Sadchikov was pulled from the Central Committee apparatus of the Soviet party and sent to Yugoslavia. He wore the recently introduced uniform of an ambassador and behaved as a diplomat should, especially in the presence of the Western Allies. In addition, he followed our internal affairs and gave us counsel through our leaders, most often Tito or Kardelj. He was reserved, patient, and unobtrusive. I remember the result of one significant piece of advice he offered: the draft constitution of 1946 provided medical, disability, and pension insurance for the peasants, but this was eliminated from the final text on grounds that even the Soviet Union lacked the material means for such guarantees.

It was never clear to us why Sadchikov was replaced; we had no reason to be suspicious. The new ambassador, Lavrentiev, was even more energetic about establishing contacts; he gave generous dinner parties and receptions. Yet, he was too much the official representative, even when there was no formal reason for such conduct. He made no effort to explore circumstances and relationships, and in conversation was noticeably stiffer than his predecessor. He was incapable of accepting even the mildest criticism of the Soviet Union or its representatives. Differentiating among us Yugoslav leaders, he cultivated, one after another, those a rung higher on the ladder. A change could be felt also in the embassy officers, who grew more official and reserved. At one dinner party, when I was explaining to Lavrentiev the trouble we had translating a certain Russian term, he at once suggested, "Why don't you adopt the Russian term?" He would needle Serbian officials as if in fun, implying that they were neglecting the Serbian people's "leading role," while others of his country's representatives were at the same time maintaining strong ties with Hebrang and other Croatian officials, and alluding freely to the subordinate position of Croatians and Croatia. Pointing out that we were underrating the Orthodox church, Lavrentiev attempted to resuscitate the ties between the Soviet and Serbian churches.

He was a typical representative of Stalinist diplomacy: rigid, unassailable, manipulative. His task was not to understand but to bring to heel, which made him seem more narrow-minded and tactless than he really was. Judin had close ties to Lavrentiev, as was evident from their daily meetings and from conversations at dinners and receptions. When the confrontation started, however, Judin avoided letting himself or his publication get caught in too exposed a position.


Toward the end of 1947, vast and insuperable differences developed with the Soviet government over our economy. In its helter-skelter rush to realize our first five-year plan, the leadership had pulled our whole people along, willing or not, and the country was being wrenched apart by the effort. That plan, framed by Hebrang and implemented by Kidrič, was overreaching and unrealistic in all its premises. When Hebrang had argued for it at a Politburo session, everyone was enthusiastic. There was hardly any discussion. I was the only one to make even the smallest comment: it was impossible to have so many cows and so much dairy production, I said, because cattle breeding had suffered greatly during the war and cows calve only once a year. My observation was taken as made in jest, and it *was* made half in jest, but Hebrang replied that cows would be imported from Holland, and so I, too, was enthusiastic. Planning was done on the basis of wishes and ambitions, not possibilities and needs. As anyone else would have done in his place, Hebrang had surrendered to the general mood, which was prevalent even among our specialists, most of whom were party people rather than professionals.

Later, when the conflict with the U.S.S.R. was at its height and the East European governments broke off economic relations with our country, Yugoslav leaders claimed that this blockade had scuttled our plan. There is some truth in that, but only after first conceding that the plan was unrealistic from the start. Further, it was carried out like a military campaign, half coercively, as if the nation's destiny hung in the balance. The critical, irreducible fact was our lack of an adequate labor force. A significant role in the conquest of "key objectives" was carried out by our more than 50,000 political and other prisoners and over 100,000 German prisoners of war. But in January 1946, forced labor had been abolished as a form of punishment, having proven costly and inefficient. As for "voluntary" labor, that test of one's patriotism yielded no better results.

Passing through Bosnia in the spring of 1946 or 1947, I reached the Romanija Mountains, to the east of Sarajevo, where I saw hundreds of people, half-starved and freezing, sitting idle in logging camps. Talking with them, I found that they were mostly from Serbia and that they had neither been sentenced to work nor had they truly volunteered. Although they were supposed to work for as long as two months, they got no pay, and their food consisted of soup without meat or fat, plus half a kilo of corn. Such a listless, underfed force, unpaid into the bargain, could not possibly have been induced to work hard, even if the proper specialists had been on hand. I encountered similar "volunteers" elsewhere—in Yugoslavia they could be found all over. Upon returning to Belgrade, I conveyed my impressions to leading comrades, most of all to Kidrič. Everyone saw the disadvantage and unreasonableness of so-called voluntary labor, but no one knew how else our projected tasks could be carried out. Soon thereafter, Kidrič and his staff figured out that the cost of it all, including transport, food, medical care, and so forth, exceeded the return. "Voluntary" labor was abolished. What remained was voluntary work for the young, as part of their ideological upbringing, and, on the local level, labor that was truly voluntary.

This irrational, ideological strain on the economy was somewhat alleviated by UNRRA aid. With the help of UNRRA's experts, our government saw to its rational and competent distribution. The speedy repair of our badly damaged rail system offered the most striking example of such aid being put to effective use. But it could not be of any fundamental use in carrying out plans that were overambitious and unrealistic to begin with.

Our insistence on rapid industrialization and modernization was fed with false promises by Moscow. From all the high-level talks, especially those between Tito and Stalin in June 1946, one might have concluded that Soviet assistance would be plentiful and comprehensive. In practice, very little if any was rendered. The Soviets made every effort to take over the Yugoslav economy and keep it agrarian, a source of raw materials. But we had a long, painful road to travel, through disbelief and indecision, before we could recognize their selfishness for what it was, grasp the degeneration of the Russian Revolution, and realize that they were asserting their hegemony; a long road to travel before we could see ourselves as a separate entity whose ills were curable only by our own efforts.

Kidrič, whose duty was to execute the plan and to develop and sustain relations with the East, wore himself to a frazzle, although he was fully aware of the futility of it. Both our day-to-day commercial contacts and our contract negotiations proved that economic relationships with the Soviet Union and other East European countries were no different from those with the West— worse, in fact, burdened as they were with ideological obligations and associated pitfalls. The leadership was in a painful dilemma, and so was Kidrič. (I am singling him out here because he personally administered an economy whose development was supposed to justify our immeasurable war sacrifices and secure the necessities of life.)

Our dilemma would perhaps have continued far longer had our problems with the Soviet government not become interwoven with ideological disagreements. In these matters our leadership could not and would not submit in silence, conscious as it was of having carried out a revolution on its own. Starting from the innermost circle and spreading outward in widening ripples, resentment and dissent were gradually transformed into conscious criticism.

This criticism could not have been concealed, even if we had attempted it. Within and around the leadership were comrades who took any act of criticism—particularly any step toward independence from the Soviet Union—not just as a retreat from ideology but also as a betrayal of the revolution and their own essential, revolutionary selves.

So a confrontation became inevitable. No one knew what form it might take or the proportions it would assume. No one sought a pretext or meant to strike a match. The conflict was touched off by the disagreement between Yugoslavia and the U.S.S.R. over policy toward Albania. Even today in Belgrade and Tirana, those postwar relations are subject to different and opposed interpretations, in accordance with conflicting ideological and state interests. It is often said that Belgrade treated Albania the way Moscow treated Belgrade. That is an oversimplified, superficial comparison. The problem lies much deeper.

From what I know and what I have been able to gather from published Yugoslav materials, economic relations between the two countries bore only a superficial resemblance to those between the Soviet Union and the countries of Eastern Europe: joint ownership companies, for instance, were established in both. But all told, Yugoslavia gave more than it received from Albania. Through joint companies, Yugoslavia constructed the first railroad in Albania (between Durres and Peqin), as well as several small factories, and extended credit in the amount of two billion leks, or forty million dollars. A considerable quantity of grain was given outright when Albania was hit by a drought in 1946, although our own country was also war-torn, hungry, and beset with shortages.

Such an economic relationship, costly and inequitable for Yugoslavia, was possible only because, since the end of the war, the leaders of both countries had taken the view that the two should become one nation. Albania was to be the seventh Yugoslav republic, a republic that would include the Kosovo-Metohija Region, which had an Albanian majority. It was hoped that territorial quarrels and national prejudices would thus be disposed of for good. Although joint companies and trade were governed by contractual agreements, the larger context involved this expectation of political unity. Accordingly, our relationship with Albania was one of selflessness and largesse, as if Albania were an undeveloped republic of our own.

But that would have been unacceptable to the people of Albania, even though autonomy and a sense of national identity were not essential to them. And a rapprochement looking to unification was still less likely to suit the Soviet government, which favored a controlled and dependent Yugoslavia, not a Yugoslavia that was an independent, powerful Balkan state.

As Albania established ties with the other Eastern European countries, particularly the U.S.S.R., it saw possibilities—both economic and, especially, political—other than reliance on Yugoslavia. The mere suggestion of such possibilities, however unrealistic, was sufficient for the Albanian leadership to question the correctness of fixed, exclusive relations with Yugoslavia. Yet our country may have shown more equity in dealing with Albania than the U.S.S.R. ever showed toward any Eastern European country, including Yugoslavia. But by its very nature, an exclusive relationship had to incur Albanian opposition sooner or later. Joint enterprises, the role of our consultants and specialists, our attempts to synchronize Albanian development with our own in anticipation of unification—all these, and much more, combined with insuperable national and other differences, were bound to provoke disagreement.

Yugoslav-Albanian relations were not then burdened with the issues of Kosovo and Metohija. Both leaderships had taken a stand in favor of unification, so that the problem of this border-land would be resolved most naturally by its inclusion in an Albanian federal unit. Here the Yugoslavs masked an inconsistency, not unlike the Bulgarians when they linked our annexation of the Pirin region of Macedonia to unification with Yugoslavia. The Albanian leadership did not make an issue of it, but the question must have been on their minds or lurking in their unconscious, especially after relations with us began to grow complicated.

In 1947, and particularly toward the end of that year, our leadership stepped up its activity with regard to Albania in the political, economic, and military spheres. This happened at Tito's initiative and under his direct supervision. Yugoslav instructors strove to transmit our experience to the Albanian party and army, and to bind the two economies together. For their part, the Albanians seemed to adjust to these developments. Federation with Yugoslavia represented the still-living legacy of Balkan socialism, reinforced by recent wartime experience, as well as resistance to pressures from the West.

The Soviet government showed no enthusiasm for the unification of the two countries. At the end of 1946, Ambassador Sadchikov had expressed reservations about the Yugoslav-Albanian assistance treaties and had warned Albania to think twice about what it was doing.

The beginning of 1947 saw open friction on economic issues. Nako Spiru, the man responsible for Albania's economy, voiced opposition to the mutual assistance pacts signed in 1946. An Albanian delegation headed by Spiru came to Belgrade to talk about the matter. Our differences were smoothed over. But when I saw Spiru at the time, he asserted, without hatred or bitterness, but citing figures, that our economic relations, as projected, were neither good nor equitable for Albania. The smoothing over was illusory and did not last long: Spiru continued to oppose us, along with Soviet representatives in Tirana—especially the Soviet ambassador—and to criticize any strengthening of Yugoslav-Albanian relations.

To what degree Spiru's disagreements were connected with the ambassador's intrigues, I don't know, but they happened simultaneously. However, a majority on the Albanian Central Committee still supported rapprochement with Yugoslavia and took concrete steps in that direction. So, too, did Enver Hoxha, though he did so without enthusiasm or initiative—one of the reasons Belgrade looked on him as a Communist of the petit-bourgeois kind.

Spiru's nervous, contradictory, but persistent attempts to block the fulfillment of contract obligations with Yugoslavia created a crisis in the Albanian Central Committee. No doubt our representatives in Tirana played a part. Spiru was expelled from the party and a replacement was found—a decision not opposed by Hoxha, at least not in public. Finding himself isolated and accused of "nationalist deviations" because of his opposition to the rapprochement of two socialist countries, Spiru committed suicide in the autumn of 1947. To the top leadership in Belgrade, and even more in Tirana, his gesture brought confusion, uneasiness, and a sense of something ominous—this in spite of superficial ideological explanations and soothing comments about his having been a weakling, an intellectual, and a nationalist.

The founding of the Cominform and the establishment of its headquarters in Belgrade mitigated for a time our disagreements with the U.S.S.R. over Albania. But no sooner did the honeymoon of ideological internationalism come to an end than the conflict broke out again, with unpredictable violence.

Increasingly nervous, Tito pressed for unification with Albania. Within his narrow circle he did not and could not hide his fears that the Russians would get the jump on us and "grab" Albania. So unification, instead of being founded on mutual good will, looked more and more like an invasion by Yugoslavia. For no good reason, but under the pretext of danger to Albania from "Greek reaction" and "imperialists" hiding in Greece, Tito prepared to send two divisions to Albania. Like all our military affairs in that country, this was in the hands of Milan Kuprešanin, one of the more capable, moderate, and disciplined of our generals. I happened to be present when Tito gave him his initial instructions.

Neither the preparations nor the decision to send two divisions was discussed in the Politburo or in Tito's inner circle—Kardelj, Ranković, and myself. Of that circle, only Ranković was privy to all the details, since a substantial part of the affair fell on his shoulders: intelligence, interparty relations, selection of personnel. Leading comrades from the army were also informed: Gošnjak, Popović, and Vukmanović-Tempo. The line about "saving" and "defending" Albania was the official one, even for the upper echelons. But my conscience was not easy; bringing Albania to heel was inconsistent with our teaching about voluntary merger and the self-determination of peoples.

True, this would not be the first time that reality "corrected" theory, but it was a new, very drastic case—our own case—of such correction. On the other hand, it was an unpleasant thought that Moscow might gain the upper hand in Albania, and thereby "encircle" Yugoslavia and prevent unification of the two countries. I could find no support for these reflections; I was alone with my doubts. Above all, I felt that the maneuver would not succeed. Tito was tense, our actions seemed hasty and impulsive, and the times were not propitious. Civil war was raging in Greece, and our country was being accused in the United Nations of intervening in it; and it was a time of feverish endeavors by Tito and the government to draw close to the people's democracies and consolidate our special influence on them, independent of the Soviet Union.

Is deceit possible in politics? Yes, in small ways, in everyday behavior. But when large-scale changes or turning points are involved, then it is possible only to the extent that reality itself—the totality of relationships—is "deceitful" and suits the purpose of those who deceive. Such was not the case with the Albanian issue. The Russians and part of the Albanian leadership, headed by Hoxha, did not seem to realize fully what was going on. In the first issue (January 20, 1948) of the journal *Albania-Yugoslavia*, the organ of the Society for Cultural Co-operation between Albania and Yugoslavia, Hoxha congratulated Tito and Yugoslavia, but emphasized that his country had been liberated by its own efforts. No doubt he had his suspicions and was playing dumb, as yet lacking guaranteed Soviet support.

# 12

At the end of December 1947, we received a cable from Stalin requesting that I or some other Central Committee member come to Moscow to reconcile the policies of our two governments toward Albania. Differences had multiplied following Nako Spiru's suicide and the flagrant intriguing of Hoxha and other top Albanian leaders with Soviet representatives. The Soviets in Tirana were more or less openly critical of Yugoslav policies in Albania. Their objections enjoyed the logic and plausibility that politics so easily hits upon, especially when it feels the common pulse. Why, they asked, did Yugoslavia insist on joint companies with Albania while rejecting such arrangements with the U.S.S.R.? Why was Yugoslavia increasing the number of its instructors in the Albanian army while seeking Soviet instructors for its own? Why were Yugoslav civilian advisers working in the Albanian economy while Yugoslavia was hiring foreigners for its own? Why was Yugoslavia, poor and undeveloped, now developing Albania? And so on.

It was not entirely clear why Stalin asked for me personally. In my book *Conversations with Stalin,* I advanced two possibilities.

First, Stalin knew me as a frank and open man; second, he may have wanted to win me over to his side. After all, unlike Hebrang and Žujović, on whom he could count already, I had belonged to Tito's closest circle since 1937, the year Tito took over the party leadership.

Since I was generally abreast of Yugoslav-Albanian relations, including what we called the "tactless" and "irresponsible" scheming by the Soviets in Tirana, I received no special instructions. A small delegation from the Yugoslav army joined me: the current chief of the General Staff, Koča Popović, and the head of our military industry, Mijalko Todorović, who wanted to discuss armaments and the development of our arms industry. Svetozar Vukmanović-Tempo, head of the army's political administration, also came along to familiarize himself with the Red Army's experience in political work. We set off by train on January 8, buoyant and full of hope, but convinced that Yugoslavia must solve its problems in its own way and rely on its own resources.

It was in Bucharest that we realized we were not alone in our opinion that the Soviet Union need not be an inviolable pattern in "building socialism." At a dinner given by our ambassador, Golubović, one Rumanian leader agreed with us, a second was unconvincingly opposed, while Golubović himself and Ana Pauker, then minister of foreign affairs, listened carefully. I felt such conversations to be inappropriate, since in Bucharest, and later in Moscow, I was sure that Soviet intelligence would record, and possibly distort, every word uttered. But this time it could not be avoided: the Rumanians had grievances and were much concerned, and our delegation was irrespressible, especially Vukmanović.

As fate would have it, the trip abounded in episodes that only added fuel to the fire of our discontent. In the Rumanian border town of Jassy, the Soviet commander expressed shock at the muddy squalor of the place, as if Soviet towns were not worse; our Soviet escort was unexpectedly official, even cold; the huge brass handles of our compartments seemed ridiculously pompous; we were appalled at the poverty of our porter, who kept hens in his tiny compartment. At the sight of the Ukraine, war-torn and desolate, the sadness that swept over us was highlighted by the ironic contrast of ourselves riding along comfortably in the Soviet government's magnificent parlor car, furnished with every amenity.

In Moscow, only hours after our arrival, we were recounting the news from home to our ambassador, Vladimir Popović, and wondering what our prospects with the Soviets might be, when all of a sudden the phone rang. It was the Ministry of Foreign Affairs calling to say that, if I was not too tired, Stalin wanted to see me. *Tired?* What could have tired me on a trip of several days in a comfortable parlor car, spent in reading and idle chatter? Even if I had been completely exhausted, I would have rushed at Stalin's beck and call. I was the object of envious looks from all, and Popović and Todorović begged me not to forget their own reasons for coming. Yet in all my joy at the imminent encounter with Stalin, there was sobriety and wariness. The duplicity of Yugoslav-Soviet relations haunted me through the night I spent with Stalin and his aides.

At nine o'clock I was driven to Stalin's office in the Kremlin. Stalin, Molotov, and Zhdanov were there, the latter because he was responsible for relations with foreign parties. Once the greetings and the usual inquiries about health were over, Stalin sat down at the table and turned to the matter at hand, Albania: "Members of the Albanian Central Committee are killing themselves on your account! That's most unpleasant, most unpleasant. . . ."

I agreed it was unpleasant and started to explain—that by opposing rapprochement between Albania and Yugoslavia, Nako Spiru had isolated himself in his own Central Committee. But before I could finish, Stalin unexpectedly broke in: "We have no special interest in Albania. We agree that Yugoslavia swallow Albania." Here he put the fingertips of his right hand to his lips and pretended to swallow something.

I must have looked surprised, but I made an effort to interpret it in the spirit of Stalin's drastic and picturesque humor. I tried again: "It is not a matter of swallowing, but of unification."

At this Molotov interjected: "But that is swallowing."

Stalin caught up the phrase, gesturing again with his fingertips. "Yes, yes, swallowing. But we agree you ought to swallow Albania —the sooner the better!"

Otherwise the atmosphere was very cordial; even Molotov delivered that line about swallowing with great good humor.

Yet Stalin's gestures and approval of swallowing roused my suspicion that something was amiss in our Albanian policy. Unification was not proceeding voluntarily—no more than in the Soviet Union's annexation of the Baltic countries.

But Stalin brought me back to business: "What about Hoxha, what is he like in your opinion?" I avoided a clear, direct answer. Stalin then expressed precisely the opinion about Hoxha current among Yugoslav leaders: "He is a petit bourgeois, isn't he, inclined to nationalism?"

"Yes, we think so, too," I concurred.

Bringing the conversation about Albania to a close, Stalin declared: "There are no differences between us. You personally write Tito a dispatch about this in the name of the Soviet government and submit it to me by tomorrow."

Not sure that I had understood Stalin's unusual instructions— to write a telegram in the name of the Soviet government—I asked him what he meant, and he said it again, distinctly. At that moment I was flattered by Stalin's confidence in me, but when I framed my words the next day, I avoided saying anything that could be used against Tito and our government. The dispatch was never delivered, probably because it contained nothing that Stalin's evil cunning could turn to advantage. I stated simply that Stalin had received me and that the Soviet government agreed with our policy toward Albania.

With the main topic out of the way, the conversation turned to nonessential matters such as the location of Cominform headquarters, Tito's health, and the like. Choosing the right moment, I brought up the question of equipment for our troops and our arms industry, noting that we were running into problems with the Soviet representatives because of "military secrets." At this, Stalin rose from his chair. "We have no military secrets from you. You're a friendly socialist country—we have no military secrets from you."

He then went back to his desk, got Bulganin on the phone, and gave him a brief order: "The Yugoslavs are here, the Yugoslav delegation—they should be heard immediately."

Our talk in the Kremlin lasted about half an hour, and then the four of us—Stalin, Molotov, Zhdanov, and I—were driven to Stalin's dacha for dinner. Malenkov, Beria, and Voznesensky were also invited to attend.

While waiting for the guests to arrive, Zhdanov and I lingered in the hall before a map of the world. Stalin joined us. He was clearly pleased when I noticed his blue pencil mark encircling Stalingrad. He began looking for Königsberg, which was to be renamed Kaliningrad, and came upon some German place names around Leningrad that dated back to the time of Catherine the Great. "Change these names," he ordered Zhdanov. "It's senseless for those places to bear German names today!" Zhdanov pulled out a little memo pad and made a note of it.

The dinner began with someone—Stalin himself, I think— proposing that each guest tell how many degrees below zero it was outside, and be penalized by being made to drink as many glasses of vodka as the number of degrees he guessed wrong. No drinker, I was happy to miss by one degree. Beria was off by three, remarking that he had done it on purpose. That little game of degrees of coldness matched by glasses of vodka inspired a heretical thought in me: "Just look at these people on whom the fate of the world hangs, look at their senseless, worthless way of life!" That heretical thought was enhanced by Stalin's poor physical condition. In the three years since I had last seen him, in March 1945, Stalin had grown flabby and old. He had always eaten a lot, but now he was positively gluttonous, as if afraid someone might snatch the food from under his nose. He drank less, though, and with more caution. It was as if his energy and power were of use to no one now that the war had ended. In one thing, though, he was still the Stalin of old: he was crude and suspicious whenever anyone disagreed with him.

Stalin led the conversation, but now and then others could

initiate a subject, as a rule only after Stalin had finished. Usually, though, it was Stalin who introduced topics, according to some bizarre order that alternated current events and complex problems with anecdotes.

He made no attempt to hide his admiration for the atomic bomb. "A powerful thing!" he exclaimed, two or three times. His often cited remark that the bomb impressed only people with feeble nerves is interpreted to mean that he underestimated its importance. However, one must not lose sight of the fact that the U.S.S.R. did not possess that weapon when Stalin made the remark. Whether Stalin possessed it on the evening he glorified it in front of us, I don't know. I believe that he then knew its secret as well as its power. When, a month later, Kardelj, Bakarić, and I met in Moscow with Dimitrov, he told us that the Soviets already had an atomic bomb, and that it was better than the Americans'. Did they really have it, I wonder, or were they simply trying to frighten us?

When Germany was discussed, Stalin concluded: "The West will make West Germany their own, and we shall turn East Germany into our own state." This seemed to me logical and comprehensible. But I could never understand the statements by Stalin and the Soviet leaders, made before the Yugoslavs and Bulgarians in June 1946, that "all Germany must be ours . . . !" It was simply unrealistic.

We sat at one end of a long table; at the other end, there was food in heated silver serving dishes. Stalin did not sit at the head of the table. Beria sat there, on Stalin's right, and the rest of us sat on the other side facing Stalin. On my left, next to Beria, sat the uncommunicative Molotov; on my right was Zhdanov, followed by Bulganin and Voznesensky. Zhdanov started talking about Finland, about its punctual deliveries of war reparations and their high quality. "We made a mistake in not occupying her," he concluded. "Everything would have been all set up if we had." To which Stalin added, "Yes, that was a mistake. We were too concerned about the Americans, and they wouldn't have lifted a finger." "Ah, Finland!" observed Molotov. "That is a peanut."

Zhdanov then turned to me. "Do you have an opera house in Yugoslavia?" Astonished at this question, I answered, "In Yugoslavia, operas are presented in nine theaters," but I was thinking how little they knew about us, how little interest they took in our life. Zhdanov was the only one who did not drink alcohol; he drank orangeade instead. He explained to me that he had a heart condition, adding, in derision, "I might die at any moment, and I might live a very long time."

Bulganin and Voznesensky were for the most part silent. At one point Stalin spoke of the necessity of increasing pay for teachers, and Voznesensky agreed. Then Stalin asked whether more resources could not be made available for the Volga-Don canal, in the just adopted five-year plan, and Voznesensky agreed again.

I raised two theoretical questions that I was anxious to know what Stalin thought about. The first concerned the distinction between "people" and "nation." In Marxist literature, no formulation clearly defined the difference, and Stalin—the author of a book entitled *Marxism and the Nationality Question*, written prior to World War I—was considered the greatest expert on the nationality issue.

As I put my question, Molotov interrupted. "People and nation are the same thing." But Stalin did not agree. "No, nonsense! They are different. You already know what a nation is: the product of capitalism with given characteristics. All classes belong to it. And 'people,' these are the working men of a given nation—that is, working men of the same language, culture, customs."

When I praised his *Marxism and the Nationality Question* as an exceptional book, still of current interest, Stalin retorted, "That was Ilyich's [Lenin's] view. Ilyich also edited the book."

My second question was about Dostoevsky. From early youth I had looked on him as the greatest writer of modern times and had never succeeded in coming to terms with his neglect in the Soviet Union, even though I was opposed to his political ideas. Stalin had a simple explanation for this, too: "A great writer and a great reactionary. We are not publishing him because he is a bad influence on youth. But, a great writer."

As regards Gorky, Stalin did not agree with me that *The Life of Klim Samgin* was Gorky's most important work, both in its method and in the depth of its portrayal of the Russian Revolution. "No, his best things are those he wrote earlier," he said. *"The Town of Okurov,* his stories, and *Foma Gordeev.* And as far as the depiction of the Russian Revolution in *Klim Samgin* is concerned, there's very little revolution there. . . ."

Stalin also singled out two contemporary Soviet writers, one a woman. When the discussion turned to Sholokhov, Zhdanov recounted Stalin's remark apropos Konstantin Simonov's book of love poems: "They should have published only two copies—one for her, and one for him," at which Stalin smiled demurely while the others roared. Then Zhdanov told us with a sneer that the Leningrad officials interpreted his criticism of Zoshchenko to mean that the writer's ration card should be withheld and Moscow had to tell them not to do that.

Someone—I think it was I—mentioned the vitality of Marx's and Engels's view of the world. Stalin, speaking as one who had thought long on the matter and had come to irrefutable conclusions, perhaps against his will, made the following observation: "Yes, unquestionably they were founding fathers. But they have their shortcomings, too. It should not be forgotten that Marx and Engels were under the excessive influence of German classical philosophy, especially Kant and Hegel. Lenin, however, was free of such influence. . . ."

This position of Stalin's—clearly very important—was left out of my book *Conversations with Stalin* due to a slip of the memory. No one in the Communist movement until then had had the courage to speak so critically of the *Weltanschauung* of Marx and Engels; at the time, I was full of admiration for the daring and farsightedness of Stalin's judgment. Reflecting on it today, I feel that in arriving at such a critical, "revisionist" position on the two founding fathers, Stalin was swayed more by the practical experience of running a state than by theoretical considerations. If the Soviet Union was to be the leading power of socialism—which, according to Stalin, it was—then to the Soviet Union belonged priority in matters of theory, meaning the revision of theory. In practice, this meant adopting Lenin as more correct, more trustworthy than Marx.

Shortly before the gathering broke up, Stalin suddenly asked me why there were no Jews on our Central Committee. I explained to him that there were not many Jews in Yugoslavia in the first place and most belonged to the middle class. I added, "Pijade is the only prominent Communist Jew on the Central Committee." Stalin thought back: "Pijade, short, with glasses? Yes, I remember, he visited me. And what is his position?" "He is a member of the Central Committee, a veteran Communist, the translator of *Das Kapital*," I explained.

"On our Central Committee there are no Jews!" Stalin broke in, with a provocative laugh. "You are an anti-Semite; you, too, Djilas, you, too, are an anti-Semite!"

I realized that Stalin was trying to goad me into declaring my stand concerning Jews. I smiled and said nothing; I have never been anti-Semitic. And Stalin quickly abandoned the subject.

The evening did not pass without vulgarity. After forcing me to taste the *pertsovka*—strong vodka with pepper—Beria explained with the crudest of expressions and a leer that it had a bad effect on the sex glands. As he rattled on, Stalin looked at me intently, with suppressed amusement, but kept himself from laughing outright because I wore such a sour expression.

Quite apart from this incident, above and beyond words, there was some ill-defined tension during the entire six-hour-long dinner. I had forebodings that they would begin criticizing Tito and the Yugoslav Central Committee. I felt gathering within me a vague resistance and began carefully measuring my every word. To consolidate my position beforehand, once or twice I mentioned Tito and our Central Committee.

So, not even Stalin's injection of a personal element—why had I not responded to his invitation in 1946 to visit on the Black Sea?—changed anything, either in my conduct or in that something in the air that went beyond words. Stalin ended the dinner by raising a toast to Lenin: "Let us drink to the memory of

Vladimir Ilyich, our leader, our teacher—our all!" We stood and drank to this deity in utter humility. The expression on Stalin's face was earnest, grave, even somber. But before we dispersed, Stalin turned on a phonograph and tried to dance, flailing his arms to the rhythm of the music. However, he soon gave up, with a resigned "Age has crept up on me and I am already an old man."

Stalin's entourage reassured him with words full of flattery. Then he put on a record on which the intricate flights of a coloratura were accompanied by the yowling and barking of dogs. Stalin laughed hard, too hard, as did the others, but not I. Noticing my discomfort and incomprehension of their way of having fun, he stopped the record. "Well, still, it's clever, devilishly clever," he said, as if apologizing.

On that note, the evening at Stalin's came to an end.

We waited no more than a day or two to be called to the General Staff headquarters to present our requests. The meeting was chaired by Bulganin, who sat surrounded by high-ranking specialists, including the chief of the General Staff, Marshal Vasilyevsky. First I set forth our needs in broad terms, leaving the details to be filled in by Popović and Todorović. Our requirements seemed excessive to me, especially in relation to building up our military industry and our navy. We had talked about it in the train on our way to Moscow, but since it had all been closely worked out with Tito in Belgrade we did not deviate. The Soviet officers asked questions and made notes, but remained noncommittal. Still, things appeared to be moving off dead center, and even more so when Popović and Todorović held meetings over the next few days with military specialists.

But some ten days later it all ground to a halt, with Soviet officials hinting that "complications had arisen" and that we had to wait. We suspected, of course, that the complications were between Belgrade and Moscow.

We started killing time by visiting museums and theaters, taking long walks and chatting. This only served to deepen our criticism of Soviet patterns, Soviet reality—which some of us were unable to hide. This criticism had not yet assumed the proportions of outright rejection and would have been understandable, though not acceptable, if directed at any normal law-abiding nation. No doubt a meeting that we had with high-ranking Yugoslav officers, mostly generals who were going to school in the Soviet Union, contributed to poisoning our relations with the Soviet government. We informed the officers about conditions back home but also warned them that Soviet army experience was not to be blindly taken as a model.

There were also some careless overstatements about the stodgy conventionalism and rigidity of the Soviet army, of the sort that are hard to avoid when the ways of partners begin to diverge. A certain resistance to our suggestions could be detected in individual officers. Vladimir Popović had acquainted us with the deteriorating relations among some of our most prominent officers, especially between Peko Dapčević and Arso Jovanović, and these surfaced at the meeting. I left with a painful impression, not only of the influence of Soviet doctrines and resistance to the intentions of our Central Committee, but also of the active presence of Soviet intelligence among the ranks of our people who were being schooled in the U.S.S.R.

Just then Bogdan Crnobrnja arrived in Moscow. He was a Yugoslav foreign trade representative and an energetic and skillful negotiator. He insisted that I seek an audience with Mikoyan, in order to give more weight to our requests and greater authority to our discussions. Several matters had to be thrashed out, specifically, the delivery to us by the Soviets of rolling stock the German troops had taken with them when they retreated.

Mikoyan received us coldly, never bothering to conceal his impatience. When the discussion turned to our rolling stock, he was tough: "What do you mean, they should be given to you? Under what conditions, at what price?"

Crnobrnja and I had anticipated this, and accordingly I retorted, "Make us a gift of them." Mikoyan curtly replied: "My business is trade, not gifts." We also wanted to amend the agreement to purchase Soviet films, which was damaging to Yugoslavia

160

and discriminatory. Mikoyan rejected this as well, under the pretext that it would constitute a precedent—and why not?—for other East European countries. He was cordial only when Yugoslav copper was up for negotiation: he offered to pay in whatever foreign currency we liked, and in advance.

We wanted to visit Leningrad, city of revolution, suffering, and beauty. I called on Zhdanov; oddly enough, arrangements for such a trip could not be handled on a lower level. He already knew the purpose of my visit and kindly agreed to our request, but he was strikingly reserved. He did ask my opinion of an article by Dimitrov on his visit to Rumania that had been published in *Pravda*. *Pravda* later disowned the positions he had taken. I expressed reservations: Dimitrov was treating Rumanian-Bulgarian relations in isolation; and as for co-ordinating their economic plans—his point, in the article—it seemed to me premature. Zhdanov was unhappy with Dimitrov's statement, but did not give his reasons. They would be presented by Stalin in the meeting with the Yugoslav and Bulgarian delegations that was soon to take place.

Leningrad. Fascination with the city, sadness over its suffering. And an inexplicable, deep closeness to its officials. Neither they nor we spoke a word in criticism of the Soviet system, its leaders, or the status quo. And yet among us there arose a certain implicit understanding, as between exiles or survivors of a shipwreck.

After days of idleness, Popović decided to return to Yugoslavia. I would have gone back with him had a wire not come notifying us of Kardelj's and Bakarić's imminent arrival and directing me to join them to help straighten out the "complications" that had arisen with the Soviet Union. Tito had been included in the Soviet invitation, but mistrust had taken such firm root by now that the Yugoslav leadership declined to let him go—on grounds that he was not feeling well. Representatives of Bulgaria were invited simultaneously, and the Soviets made sure to let us know that Bulgaria was sending its "top people."

Kardelj and Bakarić arrived on February 8 to a cold and perfunctory welcome. They were put up in a dacha near Moscow, and I moved in with them.

That same night, while Kardelj's wife was sleeping, and Kardelj was lying next to her, I sat down on the bed by him and, as softly as I could, informed him of my impressions from my stay in Moscow and of my contacts with the Soviet leaders. They came down to the conclusion that we could not count on any serious help but had to rely on our resources, for the Soviet government was carrying on its own policy of subordination, trying to force Yugoslav down to the level of the occupied East European countries.

Kardelj told me that the direct cause of dispute with Moscow was the agreement between the Yugoslav and Albanian governments to send two Yugoslav divisions into Albania. Moscow did not accept our reasons—that the two divisions were to protect Albania from Greek "monarcho-fascists"—and in his wire Molotov threatened a public breach.

"Whatever possessed you to send two divisions now?" I asked Kardelj. "And why all this feverish involvement in Albania?" With resignation in his voice, Kardelj replied, "Well, the Old Man is doing the pushing. You know, yourself . . ."

Indeed I did! The top echelon, insofar as it participated in the most important decisions, had no greater actual role than did advisers to an absolute monarch. Such a relationship was conceived during our illegal period—when Tito had been appointed by the Comintern to lead the party and was given the right of veto. He then proceeded to consolidate his position systematically, imperceptibly, irreversibly. I have written about these matters in previously published works and am resurrecting them here only to round out the picture. Also, I left the description of my intimate talks with Kardelj in Moscow out of *Conversations with Stalin*, to avoid feeding Albanian-Soviet propaganda with ammunition at a time when this was still a living issue.

The next day Kardelj, Bakarić, and I took a walk in a park, whose paths had been swept clean. There I reported more fully to them, and the three of us gave our relations with the Soviet Union a thorough airing. Our long walk that frosty day caused astonishment, as well as resentment, in our Soviet escorts, because we had done our talking outside and not in the dacha. One of them asked us later why music was always being played in the living room. My answer was that we loved music, especially Kardelj—which was not entirely inaccurate.

We did not hear from the Soviet government until the evening of February 10, when we were picked up and driven to Stalin's office in the Kremlin. In the little anteroom occupied by Stalin's secretary, Poskrebishchev, we waited fifteen minutes for the Bulgarians to appear—Dimitrov, Kolarov, and Kostov—and then were ushered into Stalin's office. The exchange of greetings was cold and brief. Stalin sat down at the head of the table. To his right were Molotov, Zhdanov, Malenkov, Suslov, and Zorin; to his left, Kolarov, Dimitrov, and Kostov, followed by Kardelj, myself, and Bakarić.

Upon returning to Belgrade I wrote a report about that meeting for a session of the Politburo of the Central Committee, which took place on March 1, 1948. I wrote the report by hand and did not have it typed for fear it might fall into unwanted hands. As soon as I finished reading it, Tito took it for his personal archive. The report more or less covered the facts presented here, but it ended with my expressing faith in Stalin and confidence in his great love for our party and particularly for Tito. This conclusion was at variance with the spirit of the text and particularly with the facts laid out in it. Idolatry dies hard. Besides, I surmised, and it was later confirmed, that Žujović was reporting to Ambassador Lavrentiev on the state of affairs in the Central Committee and on the views of its members. Stalin would continue being glorified when we had our Fifth Party Congress, but with less illusion and more guile.

Molotov had begun the meeting with a brief presentation of the disagreements between the Yugoslav and Bulgarian governments and the Soviets. He cited examples: Bulgaria and Yugoslavia had signed a treaty of unification without the knowledge of the Soviet government; in Bucharest, Dimitrov had made a statement about the establishment of East European federations, to include Greece. Such acts were not allowable, Molotov emphasized, from the point of view of either party or state.

Stalin interrupted and turned to Dimitrov. "Comrade Dimitrov gets too carried away at press conferences. For example, the Poles have been visiting here. I ask them: 'What do you think of Dimitrov's statement?' They say: 'A good thing.' And I tell them that it isn't a good thing. Then they reply that they, too, think it isn't a good thing—if that is the opinion of the Soviet government. For they thought that Dimitrov had issued that statement with the knowledge and concurrence of the Soviet government, and so they approved of it. Dimitrov later tried to amend that statement through the Bulgarian telegraph agency, but he didn't help matters at all. Moreover, he cited how Austria-Hungary had in its day obstructed a customs union between Bulgaria and Serbia, which naturally prompts the conclusion: the Germans were in the way earlier, now it is the Russians. There, that's what is going on."

Molotov went on, accusing the Bulgarian government of moving toward federation with Rumania without consulting the Soviet government.

Dimitrov tried to smooth things over, claiming that he had spoken only in general terms about federation.

But Stalin interrupted him: "No. You agreed on a customs union, on the co-ordination of economic plans."

Molotov followed up: ". . . and what is a customs union and a co-ordination of economic plans but the creation of a single state?"

The purpose of this meeting convened by the Soviet leadership was painfully obvious now: the "people's democracies" could not develop their own relationships without Moscow's approval. Dimitrov's initiative and Yugoslavia's obstinacy were not merely "heresy" but also a direct challenge to the "sacred rights" of the U.S.S.R. Dimitrov tried to justify and explain, and Stalin kept interrupting him. Stalin's colorful wit turned into malicious vulgarity, and his exclusiveness into intolerance. But he never lost a sense of actual relationships; while upbraiding and reproaching the Bulgarians, because he knew they were "softies" and more manageable, he was taking open aim at us Yugoslavs.

"We learn about your doings from the newspapers!" Stalin shouted in answer to Dimitrov's excuses. "You chatter like women . . . whatever comes to your mind, and then the newspapermen grab hold of it."

Dimitrov continued obliquely justifying his position on the customs union with Rumania: "Bulgaria is in such economic difficulties that without closer collaboration with other countries it cannot develop. As far as my statement at the press conference is concerned, it is true that I was carried away."

Stalin interrupted him once again: "You wanted to shine with originality. It was completely wrong, for such a federation is inconceivable. What historic ties are there between Bulgaria and Rumania? None! And we need not speak of Bulgaria and, let us say, Hungary or Poland."

When Dimitrov protested that there were no differences between Bulgaria's foreign policy and that of the Soviet Union, Stalin roughly retorted: "There are serious differences. Why hide it? It was Lenin's practice to recognize errors and remove them as soon as possible."

"True, we have made errors," Dimitrov obediently took him up. "But through errors we are learning our way in foreign politics."

"Learning!" scoffed Stalin. "You have been in politics for fifty years, and you talk about learning! About correcting your errors! Your trouble is not errors, but a stand different from ours."

Dimitrov's ears were burning, red blotches had appeared on his face, and he looked so dejected and hangdog that one couldn't help wondering: Is this the same man who defied Göring and fascism at the Leipzig trial?

Stalin went on: "A customs union, a federation between Rumania and Bulgaria—this is nonsense. A federation of Yugoslavia, Bulgaria, and Albania is another matter. Here there are historic and other ties. That is the federation that should be

created, and the sooner the better. Yes, the sooner, the better—
right away, tomorrow, if possible. Yes, tomorrow, if possible!
Agree on it immediately."

Someone mentioned—I think it was Kardelj, because Bakarić
and I sat silent throughout the proceedings—that a Yugoslav-
Albanian federation was already in progress.

Stalin broke in with an emphatic "No. First a federation
between Bulgaria and Yugoslavia, and then both with Albania.
We think that a federation ought to be formed between Rumania
and Hungary, and also Poland and Czechoslovakia."

Stalin did not develop the question of federation further. Judging by indications from top Soviet circles, the Soviet leaders were
toying with the idea of reorganizing the U.S.S.R. by joining Poland
and Czechoslovakia to Byelorussia; Rumania and Bulgaria to the
Ukraine; and the Balkan states to Russia. A grandiose, insane
federal-imperial conception.

Just as it seemed that the dispute over a Bulgarian-Rumanian
treaty had been settled, old Kolarov revived it: "I cannot see
where Comrade Dimitrov erred. We sent a draft treaty with
Rumania to the Soviet government in advance and the Soviet
government made no comment regarding the customs union, only
regarding the definition of an aggressor."

Stalin turned to Molotov, asking if this was the case. "Well,
yes" was the ill-tempered reply.

With angry resignation, Stalin said, "We, too, make stupid
mistakes."

Dimitrov latched on to this detail: "This was precisely the
reason for my statement. The draft had been sent to Moscow. I
didn't think you could have anything against it."

But Stalin was not easily moved by facts. "Nonsense. You rushed
headlong like a Komsomol youth. You wanted to astound the
world, as if you were still secretary of the Comintern. You and
the Yugoslavs don't let anyone know what you are doing, and
we have to find out about it on the street. You present us a fait
accompli!"

Kostov, who administered Bulgaria's economy and had come
prepared to raise economic problems, broke in: "It's hard to be a

small and undeveloped country. I would like to raise some economic questions."

But Stalin cut him short and directed him to the proper ministries. "Here we're discussing foreign policy disagreements among the three governments and parties."

Finally Kardelj was recognized. He turned red, pulled his head down between his shoulders, and paused where there was no reason to, a sign that he was upset. His point was that the Soviet government had been provided with advance copies of the agreements between Bulgaria and Yugoslavia, and that the Soviets had made only one minor criticism: replace "for all time" with "twenty years." "Except for that objection, which we took care of," said Kardelj, "there was no disagreement."

Stalin kept glancing at Molotov, who lowered his head in confirmation of Kardelj's statement.

Stalin interrupted Kardelj, as angrily as he had interrupted Dimitrov, but not as offensively: "Nonsense. There are differences, and serious differences at that. What about Albania? You didn't consult us at all about sending troops into Albania."

Kardelj: "That was done with the assent of the Albanian government."

Stalin: "It could lead to serious international complications. Albania is an independent state. What are you thinking of? Excuse or no excuse, the fact is that you did not consult us about sending troops into Albania."

But Kardelj went on making excuses that none of this was final, that he did not recall a single foreign issue on which the Yugoslav government had not consulted with the Soviets.

"Not so!" shouted Stalin. "In general, you don't consult. With you, it's no mistake; it's your standing procedure."

And so Kardelj never managed to present his case.

Molotov picked up a piece of paper and read a passage from the Yugoslav-Bulgarian agreement: that the two countries would "work in the spirit of the United Nations and support any action to maintain peace against all hotbeds of aggression." "What does that mean?" asked Molotov, pointedly.

Dimitrov explained that these words meant solidarity with

the United Nations in the struggle against all hotbeds of aggression.

"No, that's preventive war," Stalin interrupted him. "The commonest Komsomol stunt. A tawdry phrase, which only brings grist to the enemy mill."

Molotov returned to the Bulgarian-Rumanian customs union, underscoring that this was the beginning of a merger between the two states.

Stalin interrupted with the remark that customs unions are generally unrealistic. This, for some reason, eased the atmosphere a little, and Kardelj observed that some customs unions have in fact worked out.

"For example?" asked Stalin, disinclined to make any concessions.

"Well, take Benelux," Kardelj replied, cautiously. "Belgium, Holland, and Luxembourg . . ."

"No, not Holland," Stalin barked. "Only Belgium and Luxembourg. That's nothing; it's trivial."

"No, Holland is part of it," Kardelj explained.

"No, not Holland," Stalin said finally. He looked inquiringly at Molotov, Zorin, and the rest. It occurred to me to explain that the "ne" in the acronym Benelux refers to the initial syllable for Holland (the Netherlands), but since no one else responded, I didn't either, and so we left it: there is no Holland in Benelux.

Stalin returned to the co-ordination of economic plans between Bulgaria and Rumania. "That's ridiculous! Instead of collaborating you'd soon be quarreling. Unification of Bulgaria and Yugoslavia is another matter entirely—there we have affinities, aspirations of long standing."

Kardelj immediately noted that at the Lake Bled meeting it was decided to work gradually toward a federation of Bulgaria and Yugoslavia, but Stalin broke in with a categorical "No! Right away. Tomorrow, if possible! First, Bulgaria and Yugoslavia should be united, and later Albania should join them."

Next Stalin passed to the uprising in Greece: "It has to wind up!" Then he turned to Kardelj. "Do you believe," he asked, "in the success of their rebellion?"

"If foreign intervention doesn't escalate," said Kardelj, "and if the Greek comrades don't commit big military and political blunders..."

"If, if!" Stalin retorted sarcastically. "No. They have no prospects of success at all. Do you think that Britain and the United States—the United States, the strongest country in the world—will permit their arteries of communication in the Mediterranean to be severed? Nonsense! And we don't have a navy. The uprising in Greece must be wound up as soon as possible."

Someone mentioned the recent successes of the Chinese Communists. But Stalin remained adamant. "Yes, our Chinese comrades have succeeded, but the situation in Greece is entirely different. Greece is on a vital line of communications for the Western powers. The United States is directly involved there—the strongest country in the world. China is a different case, relations in the Far East are different. True, we too can make mistakes. For instance, when the war with Japan was over, we invited our Chinese comrades here to discuss how they might reach a modus vivendi with Chiang Kai-shek. They agreed with us in word, but when they got home they did things their own way: gathered their forces and struck. It turned out that they were right and we were not. But the rebellion in Greece is a different matter. No hesitation here—it must be laid to rest."

What prompted Stalin to oppose the uprising in Greece? Probably he was reluctant to see still another Communist state created in the Balkans before those that had been established were brought into line. Even more did he shy away from international complications before the Soviet Union had recovered from war losses and destruction. Stalin was just as anxious to avoid conflict with the West, particularly the United States, over China, and probably wary of creating a revolutionary power that, with its innovations, its sheer size and autonomy, could become a successful, invincible competitor.

The discussion slacked off, and Dimitrov raised the issue of economic relations with the U.S.S.R. But Stalin did not give an inch: "We'll talk about that with a unified Bulgarian-Yugoslav government." And to Kostov's remark that the treaty on technical assistance was unsuitable for Bulgaria, Stalin curtly replied: "Send Molotov a note."

Kardelj asked what position should be taken concerning Italy's demand that Somalia be placed under its trusteeship. Yugoslavia was not in favor of it, but Stalin held the opposite point of view, and he asked Molotov if a reply to that effect had been sent. Stalin explained his motivation: "Once, kings, unable to reach an agreement on division of spoils, would give disputed territory to the weakest feudal vassal, so they could snatch it back at the right moment."

At the end of the meeting, Stalin conveniently evoked Lenin and Leninism: "We, too, Lenin's disciples, often had differences with Lenin, and even quarreled over some matters. But then we would have a sound discussion, fix positions, and go on."

The meeting had lasted about two hours, but this time Stalin did not invite us home for dinner. I felt a sadness and emptiness, both because of my sentimental, worshipful attitude toward Stalin and because of my disappointed hope that over a feast tensions might dissipate and disagreements become clarified, if not smoothed over. Once outside, in the car, I began to express my bitterness over the meeting to Kardelj and Bakarić, but Kardelj, depressed, motioned me to stop. For me, that was a sign that we saw eye to eye—as indeed we did in all things at the time of those Moscow tribulations. Each man reacted emotionally in his own way.

Although Kardelj did later confirm that we were in agreement, a year or two before he died he alleged that, as we emerged from the Kremlin, I had said: "Now we really must unite with Bulgaria!" That is quite possible. But that he replied "We should not do so at this point" is not true; rather, he construed his reply in retrospect to fit the context of the situation as it evolved. At the time, there in the Kremlin, in Stalin's anteroom, we and the Bulgarians agreed to meet the next day for preliminary discussions on future unification.

And, indeed, the two delegations gathered for lunch in the dacha outside Moscow which had been at the disposal of Dimitrov since he was secretary of the Comintern. We did not go into the details of federation but agreed to revive contacts between Belgrade and Sofia on this question. Nor, after we returned to Belgrade, did anyone, including Tito, raise any objections to our federating with Bulgaria and Albania. But our enthusiasm was kept under control as Stalin's orders replaced the romantic good will of earlier times.

From that lunch emanated a closeness we had never before experienced with the Bulgarians—the closeness of the oppressed and tyrannized. It was then that Dimitrov told us in confidence that the Soviet Union had the atomic bomb. Kostov made an effort to be friendly toward us, but neither then nor later did we show any understanding of him—not even when he was tried and shot. Our top people were firmly convinced that Kostov was Yugoslavia's opponent and that he leaned toward a greater Bulgaria. During his trial our intelligence service provided us with erroneous and confused facts and evaluations, so that even our propaganda failed to take him under its wing. He deserved protection, if for no other reason than his exceptional, heroic conduct, both in the prisons of the Bulgarian king and in Stalin's gulags. As for Dimitrov, without a doubt he felt as we did. Talking to us in front of the dacha, he said, as if in passing: "Criticism of my statements is not at issue here; something else is."

That evening, Kardelj was pulled from the theater to sign an agreement with Molotov—in accordance with Stalin's directive from the Kremlin meeting—an agreement to consult in matters of foreign policy. And since the agreement was presented without explanation, the signing was done without ceremony. But Kardelj signed in the wrong spot. The error was discovered, and the next day Kardelj had to go sign again.

Three days later, at dawn, we were taken to Vnukovo airport and put on a plane for Belgrade, without ceremony or protocol. We were weary. And homesick.

# 13

Back in Belgrade the leadership accepted Stalin's order with little argument, yet relations with Moscow became more strained than ever. New Soviet measures, new pressures, followed and with such speed and highhandedness that they generated sober-minded resistance instead of confusion and panic. We continued to maintain a pro-Soviet line with feverish determination, especially in propaganda: we expressed enthusiasm over the February coup d'état in Czechoslovakia, we "unmasked" Greece's "provocations" of Albania, and backed the Soviet government in protesting the Western powers' "illegal" decisions concerning Germany. But on February 12 the French newspaper *Le Figaro* noted that in Rumania Tito's pictures were being taken down. Barely two weeks later, on February 28, while Vukmanović-Tempo was hailing the Red Army with the usual stereotyped hymns of praise, in Tirana the Soviet chargé d'affaires accepted a toast to Tito's health only insofar as Tito's work strengthened the democratic front around the world. And in the most drastic step of all, the Soviet government refused to broaden and extend our trade agreement

—although Mikoyan had promised to do so when Crnobrnja and I met with him in Moscow, and 50 percent of our foreign trade was conducted with Eastern Europe, predominantly the U.S.S.R.

In addition to the official disagreements and pressures, there were—as always in such cases—all kinds of seemingly inconsequential indications, reflected in the behavior of the Soviet representatives, in nuances of protocol, and especially in our own critical recollections and insights. Scarcely ten days after our return from Moscow, we were more guarded about uniting with Bulgaria and Albania. We had not yet shaken off that time-hallowed ideal of Balkan socialists and democrats, but it was now subordinate to political considerations.

Our strained relations with Moscow prompted Tito to call a session of the expanded Politburo. There were only four regular members of that body—Tito, Kardelj, Ranković, and I. An "expanded" meeting would include other influential comrades: Moša Pijade, Ivan Gošnjak, Sreten Žujović, Blagoje Nešković, Svetozar Vukmanović-Tempo, Vladimir Popović, Boris Kidrič, and Krsto Popivoda. These men had not yet been voted in, hence were not yet members in a formal sense.

The following items constituted the agenda of that session: reports by Kardelj and me on the Moscow discussions, the five-year plan, the army and the armaments industry, and federation with Bulgaria. First, Tito presented our disagreements with the Soviet Union, dwelling particularly on the Soviet refusal to sign a trade agreement, which he termed economic pressure on Yugoslavia. He mentioned Moscow's stirring up of Albania against us and its refusal to let our army equip itself, allegedly because we had no need of a strong army while the Soviet army served as our protector. His conclusion was that relations with the Soviet Union had reached an impasse. To which he touchingly and unexpectedly added: "If they continue such a policy toward us, I will resign."

Probably no one there was so naïve as to take this threat seriously; certainly not I. He threw it out to test us, to see if anyone would approve of his resignation as the most sensible way out. But everyone—except for Žujović, who was noticeably silent—cried out against any such action. Tito did not mention it again.

Next, Kardelj presented the substance of our conversations with Stalin, emphasizing Stalin's coarse and degrading manner. He stressed also that under such dubious and coercive circumstances unification with Bulgaria would be a dangerous mistake. I then read the report of our trip to Moscow. It carried conviction, and Mikoyan's statement—"My business is trade, not gifts"—provoked bitter laughter and became almost a proverb.

Vukmanović stated that the Soviets had no grasp of our army's problems and were essentially trying to subordinate the armies of the East European countries. Kidrič presented the difficulties dogging our economic relations, dwelling particularly on the Soviet refusal to sign the trade agreement. He emphasized that we must pursue our own independent path economically, since disagreements with the Soviets were multiplying and becoming ever riskier for us.

The discussion then turned to our differences with the Soviets regarding socialism in our country and the world. Kardelj stressed that our policy toward the Soviet Union had remained unchanged, but that two distinct points of view had emerged: we were for co-operation among socialist states on the basis of equality, whereas their top ranks were for broadening the role and influence of the Soviet state. At one point he exclaimed, as if to himself, "Damn it, they have *their* country and we have ours!"

In the discussion of economic issues, Kidrič stressed the importance of thrift and proposed specific measures. Although this question was of primary importance to us, in the context of resistance to the Soviet Union it was secondary. The economy had to concede to "pure politics," because political success was prerequisite to economic success.

When federation with Bulgaria was under discussion, Tito, though not opposed in principle, obviously had doubts: "For our party and our country, it would be a Trojan Horse." Ranković expressed reservations, pointing to the disunity of the Bulgarian party. My contention was that the Soviet government would continue to tighten the screws on us economically because the actual issue was something much deeper—the free development of social-

174

ism as opposed to its development through expansion of the Soviet state.

After a discussion of military problems, the session was concluded. It was held in Tito's villa at 15 Rumunska Street in the afternoon, if I remember correctly, and lasted some four hours. All those present participated in the discussion in some way. And all agreed that we were not to give in—all, that is, except for Žujović, who never took the floor but nevertheless made copious notes, as was his habit. He had begun keeping notes during the war and by now had several volumes, not only of presentations at Central Committee meetings, but of private conversations as well. He once read back to me some incredible remark I had made, to which I retorted: "People say all kinds of idiotic things because they react on impulse, before forming a position. No one should be held responsible for such remarks—only public speeches and deliberate decisions entail responsibility!" Later, when Stalin and Molotov attacked our Central Committee through a series of letters, Žujović handed over his volumes of notes to Soviet Ambassador Lavrentiev "for safekeeping."

Žujović's estrangement from our leadership had been obvious for some time. His restrained, taciturn behavior at the meeting was all the more unpleasant and provocative because of his hurried and detailed note-taking while his comrades were speaking. This behavior drew comment in our narrow circle as a definite sign our minister of finance was siding with the Soviets.

At the session we had decided to keep what was said in strictest secrecy, in order to preclude twisted interpretations and further exacerbations of our relations with the Soviets. But Žujović surely disclosed our speeches and resolutions to Lavrentiev. The hasty surprise measures undertaken by the Soviet government in March cannot otherwise be explained: the recall of its military instructors on March 18, its economic experts on March 19, and the detailed letter of criticism from Molotov and Stalin on March 27.

Meanwhile, between the expanded Politburo session of March 1 and the recall of the military instructors, resistance was hardening in our top echelon and ideological discussions were taking place.

What was the nature of the Soviet system? What was going on in the Communist movement? Could it be true that the socialist U.S.S.R. was an imperialist power? As examples of such questioning, I recall my prolonged, usually nocturnal arguments with Kardelj, Kidrič, and a few others; the instructions Tito gave me before I went off to the celebration of the centenary of the Hungarian revolution of 1848; and the tough stance I assumed on that occasion.

I headed a delegation that departed for Budapest on March 13 by car. A day or two before, I had had a talk with Tito. From agency news reports we knew that the Soviet delegation would be led by Marshal Voroshilov. So Tito said, "You know, if Voroshilov wants to talk with you, go ahead and talk. It could be useful. But don't humiliate yourself." In addition, Ranković told me that in Budapest I could count on Lazar Brankov, the ranking officer in our embassy, in charge of intelligence. Brankov was from Vojvodina and spoke fluent Hungarian.

At the official session of the Hungarian parliament I gave a speech. Marx and Engels had harshly criticized the Croatian and Serbian intervention against the Hungarian revolution in 1848. With that in mind, and trying to ingratiate myself with contemporary Hungary, I mounted an extremely sharp attack, one-sided and unhistoric, on the interventionists. At the same time, and contrary to the predictions of Marx and Engels about the inevitable disappearance of the slavery of our peoples, I emphasized that "the business of freedom and progress is not only linked with them [the peoples of Yugoslavia] but, if I may say so, is identical with their survival." Even Jozsef Revai, a member of the Hungarian Politburo, said that I had exaggerated, that the Hungarian side of the picture should also be looked at—their nationalism and intolerance, which had provoked the intervention. Doubtless he had a better grasp of the Hungarian revolution, but I replied that this criticism was for them, the Hungarians, to make, and that I would carry out my own duty.

But more important, and probably most conspicuous, was the

fact that I was the only one not to mention the Soviet Union as Hungary's liberator, not even in my concluding slogans: "Long live the democratic and independent republic of Hungary! Long live friendship and collaboration between the new Yugoslavia and the new Hungary!"

The Hungarian Communist leaders treated me with a vague coldness, all the more striking because they had, as a rule, been obtrusively cordial toward our leadership. Obviously they had been apprised of the deterioration in our relations with the Soviets, and just as obviously had come to a decision. I therefore assumed a pose of official reserve toward them—toward everyone, in fact, but my escort, a simple, warm-hearted veteran of the Spanish Civil War whose name I have unfortunately forgotten.

But I talked frankly with Brankov, asking more about the attitude of individual Hungarian leaders toward us and the Soviets than about conditions in Hungary. I sensed in him a certain reticence and embarrassment. This may have had no connection with his subsequent conduct in the trial of Laszlo Rajk, where he was the main "crown witness" against the accused and Yugoslavia, but it cannot be ruled out that even then he was on the fence, if not already recruited. Our conversations were conducted while sightseeing, because I was wary of listening devices in my rooms at the Hotel Gellert. The conversations revealed nothing that I did not know already.

The Hungarian party and government attached great significance to commemorating 1848, no doubt in an effort to present themselves as heirs to the patriots and democrats of those glorious, unforgettable days. But their observance was limited—more so, I thought then, than necessary. The crushing of the Hungarian revolution by Czarist Russia was passed over in silence, while the Soviet Union's liberating, fraternal role was brought out strongly. Moreover, the citadel of Buda, the city's most conspicuous and beautiful spot, witnessed the unveiling of a monument, not to the year 1848, or to the Hungarian Commune of 1919, or to the slain Hungarian revolutionaries, but to the Red Army. The celebration, therefore, glittered more than it convinced.

All this I noticed, and much else besides. Of course my field of vision was now both sharpened and expanded by the ominous relations between Yugoslavia and the U.S.S.R. At the unveiling of the monument, I found myself standing next to Rákosi. He asked how I liked the sculpture, and I could not resist replying: "It's good. But why didn't you erect a monument to Hungarian revolutionaries? Your history is so full of revolutions and revolutionaries!" Obviously uncomfortable, Rákosi answered: "Yes, yes, we'll raise one to them, too."

Far fewer people attended the mass celebration than the crowds our Belgrade, a city half the size of Budapest, would have turned out, and the lack of interest was striking. Speeches delivered by non-Communists in the government got a lukewarm reception, and Rákosi's speech met with downright restlessness and boredom. Loud enthusiasm came only from organized groups.

Banquets and receptions dispensed food lavishly to throngs of invited guests. But the atmosphere was more gluttonous than festive. Marshal Voroshilov, who until recently had presided over the Allied Control Commission in Hungary, was in his eighties, still hale but completely senile. At a crowded banquet, in a toast delivered off the cuff, he declared that a certain people who had settled in the Danube River basin were destined to live a happy, carefree life now that they had been liberated by the Red Army.

At that reception I exchanged a couple of words with Voroshilov. If he noticed me at all, he did not remember me, let alone ask me to call on him. He was the center of attention, self-satisfied, pompous, aglitter with medals, and dispensing forced, condescending amiability. As the celebration was winding down, I gave up the hope that Voroshilov would call me over. My feelings were hurt; I felt the bitterness, but also the pride, of the small, who long to be understood by the great. Then a Soviet colonel approached. I had seen him somewhere earlier but knew nothing about him. He struck up a conversation, in which Voroshilov was mentioned. I pronounced a few conventional phrases about the marshal's brilliant appearance and dignified bearing. He said: "I know the marshal would like to talk with you. He's simple and warm—surely he'll receive you."

"All the marshal has to do," I replied, "is say so."

"He's so busy," said the colonel. "All these receptions and duties. But he'll find time for you, I'm sure. Just ask to see him."

"I'd be happy to call on him if he requests it."

On this note our conversation ended. Voroshilov did not express the desire, and I did not beg.

Two days after my return to Belgrade, on March 20, Tito called a meeting with Kardelj, Ranković, and me to inform us that the Soviet government was recalling its military instructors. The news that they were pulling out their economic experts as well reached us while the meeting was in progress. Tito had prepared an answer in the government's name. That was when he observed, as if noting something very important: "It's better to shift the whole matter over to the sphere of international relations. Relations between parties aren't all that's at issue here."

Tito's reply to the Soviet government was mild and unprovocative, but at the same time firm and searching. He insisted on the truth by rejecting Moscow's contention that we were unfriendly toward Soviet specialists, that we "distrusted" them and kept them under "surveillance." We accepted his reply without criticism.

We decided at the meeting to inform the leadership groups in each republic and leading comrades throughout the federal and party organizations about our deteriorating relations with Moscow. I was assigned Montenegro and Bosnia, and left immediately. In Cetinje, vacillation in the leadership was plain. With Božo Ljumović this meant gnawing on the old bone of "internationalism": revolution and the Soviet Union were inseparable. V. Tamšić maintained a confused, "irresolute" silence. Blažo Jovanović, secretary and head of the Montenegrin government, was puzzled by this new turn of events, and kept asking too many questions and wondering out loud what it all meant. At that time, the conflict, as yet ill-defined, had not taken on a sharp edge; it was the stage of information and discussion. Everyone did agree to support the Central Committee. In Sarajevo there was no hesitation. The head of the government, Rodoljub Čolaković, was absent from the meeting; later, he wavered. Djuro Pucar, the

179

committee secretary, rationalized a bit, but this was not hesitation, only slowness in adapting to new and uncomfortable circumstances. Indeed, he proved to be one of our staunchest officials in resisting Soviet pressures.

It was around this time that Judin, the Soviet representative on the Cominform and editor in chief of its publication, asked Tito for an article, as if nothing were amiss between the two leaderships. Tito agreed, but no one believed Judin's visit to be prompted only by hopes for an article. Nothing was accidental any more. Judin's visit was part of a scheme to drive a wedge between Tito and the rest of the leadership, while offering him a chance to save himself. Stalin and Molotov attacked neither Tito nor Kardelj until the Cominform convened in Bucharest on June 26, 1948, at which time the Yugoslav leadership and its policies were anathematized.

While waiting for the Soviet response to Tito's letter, we polemicized with the "imperialists" over Trieste and issues of peace, and were savagely attacked by the Western press for allegedly massing our troops against Italy and interfering in the civil war in Greece. The Soviet answer came quickly—obviously prepared in advance. It bore the date March 27, the anniversary of the royal Yugoslav government's overthrow for acceding to the Tripartite Pact in 1941. I believe this to have been purely accidental, but it served as a further, symbolic stimulus to resistance. The letter bore Molotov's and Stalin's signatures, in that order. Why Molotov first and not second, according to the hierarchy and his intrinsic importance, was never explained. We interpreted it to mean not that Stalin was "hesitating" or "leaning our way," but, rather, that he wished to remain somewhat in the background. But to what purpose? To blame Molotov if the undertaking failed? Or to ascribe a secondary importance to it in the Communist movement? Or—most likely—to nourish among us the illusion that he was not so deeply committed that he could not "pardon" us someday? Be that as it may, neither then nor later did Stalin mount a public attack on Tito or Yugoslavia. The man died without publicly uttering a word against his most successful adversaries.

In certain Yugoslav historical papers* this letter's date, March 27, is said to be the same as the date it was handed to Tito in the Croatian government's Villa Weiss in Zagreb. But Tito could not have received the letter that day, nor could he have been in Zagreb. On that day the remains of Ivan Milutinović and Ivo-Lola Ribar, two Central Committee members killed in the war, were being reinterred in Belgrade. Tito attended the ceremony, waiting for the official part of the procession to reach him on Kalemegdan. We by this time feared attempts on Tito's life, less from reactionaries than from Soviet agents. We knew that they existed within the party, and in important positions to boot. My speech at the grave stressed Yugoslavia's independence as well as our love for the U.S.S.R. The idea of interring Central Committee members on Kalemegdan was mine, in obvious mimicry of burial in the Kremlin walls. And yet, did we not thus put ourselves on an equal footing with the Russians, revealing a latent wish to be our own masters?

A curious incident took place at the funeral. Djuro Salaj, president of the trade unions, was scheduled to speak when the procession reached Terazije, the main downtown square, but he couldn't find his text. Having rummaged through his pockets in plain sight of the public and the procession, he signaled to me, as the man responsible for propaganda—and apparently for forgotten speeches as well. I joined him on the sidewalk and told him to give his speech from memory: "You've been a people's representative, you're the union leader—it won't be the first time you've spoken from memory." So he spoke, maybe not as fluently as he would have, but surely more naturally. (As if speeches had any significance!)

Tito most likely received the Soviet leaders' letter at the beginning of April. No sooner did Lavrentiev present it than Tito phoned Kardelj, Ranković, Kidrič, and me. We caught a train to Zagreb that very evening. He gave us the letter to study, along

---

* See, for example, S. Kržavac and D. Marković, *Informbiro—šta je to* (The Cominform: What It Is).

with a draft of his reply. The four of us read it and then conferred for two or three hours.

The letter blamed the Yugoslav leadership for the deteriorating relations and pointed to the absence of inner-party democracy and to the irregular work and composition of the Central Committee. "It is understandable," the text read, "that we cannot regard such an organization as Marxist-Leninist, as Bolshevik." It was addressed to "Comrade Tito and the other members of the Central Committee." Although Tito and Kardelj were not criticized by name, the Soviet leaders warned that "the political career of Trotsky is quite instructive." Mentioned by name were only "such questionable Marxists as Djilas, Kidrič, Ranković, Vukmanović, and others." But it was clear to everyone, and most decidedly to Tito, that the criticism was directed at him and Kardelj. When I said that the four of us cited in the letter could resign, Tito retorted bitterly: "Oh, no! I know what they want— to smash our Central Committee. First you, then me."

We took no exception to Tito's reply except for its conclusion. During our private deliberations I pointed out that it would annoy the Soviet leaders because its emphasis on independence and equality between the people's democracies and the U.S.S.R. challenged the dominance of the Soviet Union. Kardelj, Ranković, and Kidrič agreed. But who would say this to Tito, now more nervous and intolerant than he had ever been? Someone—I think it was Kardelj—suggested that I do it. I did, and Tito agreed. Obviously, he realized that he could not carry on the battle with Stalin and the Soviet system alone; overnight, as it were, he had become more disposed to collective action and more open to criticism.

In hindsight, it is clear that Tito's letter, approved with minor changes at the plenary meeting of the Central Committee on April 13, was just as aggravating to Stalin and Molotov as it would have been had the first version of the conclusion been retained. They had already decided to settle accounts with the Yugoslav leadership. My criticism was in part an outgrowth of my dogmatic, ideological approach, as opposed to Tito's. From the beginning of the confrontation, he tried to place relations with the Soviets predominantly on a governmental, not a party, basis. For Tito, what counted was to preserve the state, to maintain power, whereas for me it was the purity of the idea.

It was decided at that first meeting to call a plenary session of the Central Committee for April 12—the first such meeting since the committee had been selected in October 1940. If I recall correctly, at this meeting Tito proposed convening a Fifth Party Congress in order to strengthen our national legitimacy, as opposed to that of the Soviet leadership, which represented "international" legality. On the train returning to Belgrade, Kardelj commented, "They'll call us fascists. I know the Russians. This is just the beginning." That sort of thing seemed incredible to me, and I said as much to my colleague. Yet its very improbability— its absurdity—did not depress me; it drove me to reflect more deeply, strengthening my inner resistance and arousing my fighting instincts.

The plenum of the Central Committee convened on the appointed day, before noon, in the library of the Old Palace at Dedinje.* After a brief introduction by Tito, the letter from the Soviet leaders was read aloud, followed by the reply he had drafted. Tito then spoke for nearly an hour, stating that the Soviet leaders were taking advantage of so-called ideological differences to put pressure on our country. He called on us to keep our heads in the discussion and insisted that each member make a statement individually. He also said that a transcript of the meeting would be sent to the Soviet Central Committee, if they asked for it. They never did, nor did it occur to anyone to send it.

Next, Kardelj summarized the experience and achievements of our party. With a burst of feeling, he concluded, "It would be contemptible of us to concede that these were wrong." Other

---

* Remarks by the various speakers are quoted for the most part as they appear in Vladimir Dedijer, *J. B. Tito, prilozi za biografiju.* I made my own notes at this meeting, but they are not in my possession; they may be in the Central Committee archives.

speakers rose in turn. To a man, they were angry and ready to fight—and I among them, outraged by the lies and unfairness of it all. Most of the Central Committee members fell into line, including the comrades from Montenegro: Blažo Jovanović supported the Politburo with watered-down phrases; Božo Ljumović concealed his support of the Soviet leadership in confused, old-fashioned "internationalist" phrases.

At this point Sreten Žujović, pale and nervous, rose to speak. His declaration against the Politburo and in favor of the Soviets had been anticipated. We had been struck by his frequent tête-à-têtes with Hebrang, who was openly dissatisfied with his own position and with the Politburo's orientation toward independent development. We had been struck by Žujović's extraordinary closeness to the Soviet ambassador, and Hebrang's all-too-frequent get-togethers with the UNRRA chief for Yugoslavia, another Soviet official. All this had seemed innocent enough until our differences with the Soviet government erupted into open conflict. Thus one episode—Žujović's visit to the Soviet ambassador several days after the expanded Politburo session of March 1—had taken on a sinister meaning.

That day I had left my office early, around noon, and while driving past the Soviet embassy I had noticed Žujović's ZIS limousine and his mustachioed bodyguard in front of the gate. I was not surprised, but, to make sure, I ordered my chauffeur to turn back and drive up close to the car and bodyguard. I was not mistaken. I informed Tito and the others of what I had seen. At the plenum Tito did not fail to ask him about it, abruptly and with an air of mystery.

Žujović appealed to our "revolutionary conscience," then pleaded with us to stick close to the Soviet Union and be doubly receptive to the slightest criticism by Stalin. He said nothing of the Soviet leaders' lies and unjust accusations. Even though his disagreement was not unexpected, his words provoked angry, impatient interruptions.

I was sitting one or two seats to the left of Tito. No sooner did Žujović begin his appeals than Tito jumped up and began pacing to and fro. "Treason!" he hissed. "Treason to the people, the state, the party!" Although the conflict with Moscow involved preserving our power, our state, especially where Tito was concerned, the truth is that he, as a patriot, no less than the rest of us, was genuinely enraged. This feeling sprang from a trait of his personality that internalized events so that he felt them personally, and externalized his personal situation so as to view it as a problem for the party and the state.

Tito repeated the word "treason" many times over, then just as quickly sat down, kicking aside his briefcase. But I jumped up in turn, tears of pain and anger filling my eyes. "Crni," I shouted (it was our nickname for Sreten), "you've known me for ten years—do you really think of me as a Trotskyite?" Žujović answered, evasively: "I don't think that, but you know some of your latest statements about the Soviet Union. . . ."

There was an uproar of shouts and heckling: "Show your colors!" "Don't beat around the bush!" "What are you covering up?" "Be honest!"

As Žujović grew confused, Tito interrupted him: "Answer, Crni—are we moving toward capitalism? Are our party principles being watered down in the People's Front? Are there foreign spies in our government?"

Then Vladimir Popović spoke. "What Žujović is saying is neither honorable nor Communist. Our policy toward the Soviet Union—I know this as ambassador to Moscow—has been correct, has been Communist. Stalin himself conceded that the joint ownership companies are not a good thing!"

I had known Vlado since 1937, before he left for Spain, but it was during my last stay in Moscow that we had become close, as "companions in misfortune." Our friendship lasted until my fall from power in 1954. In my judgment, Vladimir Popović was a brilliant and exceptional person, both as a human being and as a politician. He was strikingly handsome, stable, courageous, intellectual. It is a pity that, lacking any inclination to write, he left nothing of lasting memory. As ambassador to Moscow he was in the most sensitive of positions, and might conceivably have been recruited by the Soviet leaders, yet no one ever questioned his loyalty, so clear and firm were his views, so plain and unambiguous his conduct.

In those difficult days the two of us took walks around Dedinje until late at night, exploring Soviet policy toward Yugoslavia, concluding that its roots lay deep in the dictatorial structure of the Soviet state—a painful revelation for us at the time. Vlado's insights and understanding, gained from his years in the U.S.S.R., were crucial in our assessments. "There's no human consideration there, no mercy," he said. Kardelj, Kidrič, and I also engaged in extensive discussions and speculations. Ranković did not join in much when the talk was theoretical, but his detailed reports on meddling, intrigue, and recruiting by the Soviet intelligence services were invaluable.

Amid the bitterness and fury at the plenum, Moša Pijade rose to speak. His opening remark was that what surprised him most of all was the ignorance shown in the Molotov-Stalin letter. This was received with a burst of laughter and applause.

The session recessed around two o'clock for lunch, which was served in the palace. When the session resumed, Tito took the floor. He spoke with more composure, thoughtfulness, and strength, though he could not suppress his bitterness and rage. He blamed Žujović for priding himself on loving the Soviet Union more than anyone else, including Tito. He accused him of wanting to break up the party and the leadership—a leadership which had worked together in harmony for eleven years through the harshest trials, and which was bonded in blood with the people. Rising from his seat, Tito cried out: "Our revolution does not devour its children! We honor the children of our revolution!"

His outcry caused excitement and carried conviction. Yet as Tito was putting distance between himself and the Russian Revolution, whose leaders had so insatiably swallowed its children, the Yugoslav revolution's swallowing of its own children was waiting to happen. Tito further asserted that our sacrifices and our war were also a contribution to world socialism: the contribution was not a matter of being attached to the U.S.S.R. and coming under its yoke, but of brotherly equal collaboration and independent development within the framework of such collaboration.

Pijade demanded that Žujović answer the questions Tito had put to him, but Žujović would not reply. Ranković then asked for the floor. What he had to say was overpowering in its concreteness, and devastating for Žujović. He pointed out that at the Fifth Party Congress, in 1940, it was Tito who had brought Žujović into the Central Committee, despite opposition from the Politburo's other members. Either Ranković's statement or the renewed heckling of Žujović prompted Tito to ask, "Crni, what were you doing at the Soviet ambassador's?"

For a moment Žujović was struck dumb. Then he replied, "I went there to see about getting him a car." At that, I interjected, "A Yugoslav federal minister performing such mundane services for the Soviet ambassador—that's pitiful!"

Žujović divulged that he had reported to the Soviet ambassador on the Politburo session of March 1. "Comrades," he went on, "in the event of an attack from the West, can Yugoslavia defend itself alone?"

He was parroting the generally accepted Soviet premise that the people's democracies stood no chance of survival unless they subordinated themselves to Moscow. But moral revulsion and the conviction that we were contributing to socialism had so overwhelmed us that we lost no sleep over alleged dangers from "imperialists." Even so, Kardelj gave a measured answer: "An attack from the West is not in the cards. And even if it were, we wouldn't be the only target!"

Before the meeting ended, Žujović asked Tito's permission to leave for a session of the National Assembly's finance committee, where, as minister of finance, he was to speak. With a strange look, Tito gave his assent, then adjourned the session to the following day, April 13, in the same location. I believe he had chosen the Old Palace, which was not in regular use, because there was less chance of its being bugged by the Soviets.

The next day's session was relatively tranquil: the battle lines had already been drawn. Yet it was at this session that the important decisions were taken. We agreed to Tito's and Kardelj's letter rejecting the Soviet leaders' charges, and decided that a party congress be held, the fifth, the date to be set later. After the first day's fierce polemics—a process that had gone on late into the night in private conversations and arguments—the members projected a calm, unequivocal resoluteness.

In this spirit, the letter from our Central Committee to the Soviets was slightly amended: an offer was made to let the Soviet party leaders send representatives to Yugoslavia to verify the inaccuracy of their charges. We all felt that Stalin would not take us up on this offer, which would only postpone the day of reckoning and undercut the accusations. But sustaining an illusion can be a good tactic while "consciousness is ripening," as long as the real policy is not endangered. A commission was also formed at the plenum to look into the conduct of Žujović and Hebrang. Our break with Moscow thus initiated the settling of accounts with Soviet supporters in the party and the leadership.

We did not have to wait long for these illusions to be dashed. As early as April 16, Judin, of the Cominform, handed Tito a letter from the Hungarian Central Committee. The Hungarians expressed their solidarity with the "criticism" in the Molotov-Stalin letter. This meant, first, that the Soviets were mobilizing other parties against us before settling outstanding issues with our leadership, and, second, that other parties were swallowing Soviet criticism of our party without giving us a hearing. The Hungarian letter infuriated our top ranks, as was evident in Tito's reply. For years the Hungarian leaders had been courting us, while we for our part had been straining to forget the bestialities committed by Hungarian soldiers and fascists on Yugoslav soil during the war. This policy had not always been popular, but we had pursued it in the name of friendship and co-operation. Now it was as if none of this had ever taken place.

Around that time—I think before the plenum of April 12—a member of the Hungarian Politburo, Mihaly Farkas, arrived in Belgrade. Ostensibly visiting us to learn from our party's experience, he was obviously out to collect information. As I recall a conversation he once had with Ranković and me in the Central Committee headquarters, I can see even now the gloating, malicious joy with which he heard us confirm that our party was not a mass organization, that it was composed of cadres. That difference between us and the other parties of Eastern Europe would be listed among the "sins" of our leadership in Soviet letters and propaganda.

The Politburo had no illusions about other parties not supporting the Soviet leaders. There was, however, a moment when it seemed that our Bulgarian brethren might show us some sympathy—if not open, then disguised—particularly since we all still favored unification, and any weakening of our position vis-à-vis Moscow meant outright subjugation for them.

On April 19, a Bulgarian delegation headed by Dimitrov was passing through Belgrade on its way to Prague. At the Topčider station it was to be greeted by our minister of foreign affairs, Stanoje Simić. As a member of the government and the Central Committee, I was to invite our Bulgarian comrades to stop in Belgrade on their way back for a talk about unification. It was an overcast, damp afternoon. While Simić was looking for his Bulgarian colleague, I spotted Dimitrov at a window and boarded his coach. He was waiting for me in the corridor. Squeezing my hand in both of his, he said, emotionally, "Hold fast, hold fast!"

Passing it off lightly, I replied, "With us Yugoslavs, the danger is in holding fast too much, not too little."

Dimitrov continued with warmth and excitement: "You must remain steadfast. The rest will follow."

I conveyed to him our invitation to stop over for two or three days on the way back from Prague to discuss further collaboration, including the unification of our two countries. At that point Dimitrov's wife, Rose, emerged from their compartment. She was a plump redhead, a friendly and unassuming German woman from the Sudetenland whom Dimitrov had met in Moscow when she was an émigrée. She, too, said, with emotion, "We've been so afraid for you lately."

The rest of the Bulgarian delegation soon appeared, Vulko Chervenkov and Dobrij Terpeshev among them. We gathered in the parlor car. The good-natured, open Terpeshev, who through a liking for Serbs had come to love all Yugoslavs, at once began asking after Tito and the rest. Chervenkov listened sulkily.

Someone asked what was new. From Dimitrov's earlier comments it was clear that the Bulgarian Central Committee was familiar with the Soviet letter, so I said there was nothing important except a letter from Molotov and Stalin consisting of a string of inaccuracies, which we had not accepted. At that, Chervenkov remarked irritably that criticism from our Soviet comrades had to be accepted. And Dimitrov, his expression now downcast, added that "since the Central Committee of the Soviet Communist party says so, there must be some truth to it."

And so the conversation ended. Dimitrov had reminded us that he dared not take issue with the argument that our differences with the Soviets had come at a time when war hysteria was growing stronger and imperialist aggression was being prepared. According to reliable reports, he had to be forced into confronting Yugoslavia. Of all the East European leaders, Dimitrov was the only one to congratulate Tito on May 25, his birthday. Although obedient to Stalin, he knew the Soviet leaders well and saw through their intentions.

I believe, however, that Dimitrov lacked support in his Central Committee, where pro-Soviet functionaries predominated. Nor was he immune to that typically Communist weakness, the fear of "falling away," of separating from the party. Enormously decisive toward the "class enemy," Dimitrov, like all such true-believing Communists, was fainthearted and at a loss when facing Stalin, who, through purges and a personality cult, had come to be the movement incarnate. Yet, since Dimitrov was no careerist, no *apparatchik*, but a self-made man who had risen through turmoil and pain, his vacillation now must have had deeper roots. He belonged to that class of Bulgarians—the best of their race—in whom rebellion and self-confidence fuse in an indestructible essence. He must at least have suspected that the Soviet attack on Yugoslavia would entail the subjugation of Bulgaria, and that the realization of his youthful dream of unification with Serbia would be projected into the misty future, thereby reopening the

190

yawning gulf of Balkan conflicts, and unleashing a tumultuous flood of Balkan claims. Today, after so many years, I still think that even though Dimitrov was ailing and diabetic, he did not die a natural death in the Borvilo clinic outside Moscow. Stalin was wary of self-confident personalities, especially if they were revolutionaries, and he was far more interested in Balkan hatreds than in Balkan reconciliations.

The encouragement offered by Dimitrov and his wife came as bracing news to Tito and my Politburo comrades, given the atmosphere of anger and doubt. But their rejoicing was short-lived: a day or two later we received from our Bulgarian brethren a letter, signed by Chervenkov, which not only supported the criticism of the Molotov-Stalin letter, but also boastfully extended it. Our ambassador in Prague, Stilinović, was immediately directed to inform the Bulgarian delegation that, in view of their unfounded support of the Soviet letter, they need not stay over in Belgrade. On their return trip, they were met according to protocol, but without the presence of a single member of the Central Committee. By making common cause with the Soviets and refusing to hear our defense, the Bulgarian Central Committee had "slipped the fraternal knife in our back." But neither I nor anyone else ever thought Dimitrov's encouragement that morning at the Topčider station to have been insincere or provocative. We held him in good memory. His vision had not matured to the point where he dared get into a scrap with Stalin and the Soviet Union.

In the top echelon, nervousness increased. Also, we were eager to prove, not only in our anti-imperialist and anticapitalist propaganda, but also by our everyday practices, that the Soviet leaders were wrong. Yet all such attempts were futile and harmful to our interests. On April 28 the National Assembly approved the law on nationalization: 3,100 enterprises were nationalized, mostly small ones. Three or four years later even Kidrič took the view that this nationalization had been forced on us by the Soviet charges, and that it was economically damaging. Errors are dearly paid for, especially if they are ideological.

The May Day celebration came and went, observed in much

the same way as in previous years, except that there were more pictures of Tito than of Stalin.

Two episodes of interest occurred at that time. First, Žujović, who was not invited to be on the reviewing stand, protested by attaching himself to a group in the parade, all decked out in his general's uniform and covered with decorations. The second had to do with Vladimir Velebit. On May 2 I drove to Montenegro, taking him with me. The Soviet charge that he was an "English spy" had noticeably depressed him. I suggested that, as an experienced hunter, he might like to try, around Lake Biograd, for partridge. My real intention—I had discussed it with Tito—was to assure him that it had never occurred to anyone on the Central Committee to sacrifice him for the sake of reconciliation with Moscow.

As we passed through Bijelo Polje we were joined by Ilija Bulatović, then secretary of the district committee. The regional committees had informed the district committees about our disputes with the Soviet leadership, and I had already received a letter from Ilija warning me not to "betray socialism," meaning the U.S.S.R. This was a good opportunity to have a talk with him. But in the meantime he had clammed up and, in reply to my initial feeler, said he had written the letter on the spur of the moment, and I should not attach any importance to it. I explained the Soviet charges and their untruthfulness, but he did not yield. I felt he was insincere. No doubt the general atmosphere of suspicion created by the Molotov-Stalin letter helps to explain this, but that feeling was so strong that, while lying in wait for a roebuck, I suddenly imagined that Ilija was after me—Ilija, whom I had known well since my youth. Revolutions and ideological conflicts, overnight, so to speak, can transform comrades in arms and friends into sworn enemies.

On May 4, we received a second letter from the Soviet Central Committee, this one nearly thirty pages long. It breathed new life into old disputes; rounded out criticism of Yugoslav party policy; inspired intrigues among our leaders; quibbled over the number of Central Committee members; defended Hebrang and Žujović; and flattered other parties. Tito and Kardelj were finally named as the chief sinners. In its style and composition, the hand of Stalin was felt.

Clearly, this letter was meant to provide the political basis for judging the Yugoslav leadership and bringing our party into line, all the more because it insisted on a thorough airing of the Soviet-Yugoslav dispute at a session of the Cominform. It abounded in lies and half-truths, but contained some truths as well. The lies and half-truths gave grounds for our resistance, whereas the truths had now forfeited any significance. Who could argue, for example, that the Central Committee had not convened for years, or that the party lacked a proper legal basis? But these were trivial in view of the substance of the confrontation: the independence of party and state. Their criticism of irregularities in the Yugoslav Central Committee and the party implied that Tito was the main culprit.

On May 9 another plenum of the Central Committee convened to reply to this latest letter. The occasion was undramatic, in spite of the document's wide-ranging, more thoroughgoing nature. A brief reply, prepared by Tito, was accepted. Again we rejected the charges, the latest letter having "convinced us of the futility of all our attempts to show, even with the support of facts, that the charges against us are based on distorted information."

Far more significant and crucial, we avoided Moscow's "international fishhook" by refusing to submit the dispute to the Cominform. "We are not running away from criticism on questions of principle, but in this matter we feel so unequal that we cannot agree to have it now decided before the Cominform. Nine parties have already received your first letter without our prior knowledge and have taken their stand in resolutions. To dispose of the matter, we want to prove by our deeds the injustice of the charges against us, prove that we are tenaciously building socialism and remaining true to the Soviet Union, true to the teachings of Marx, Engels, Lenin, and Stalin. The future will show, as the past has, that we shall carry out what we have promised you."

This plenum was concerned more with current party issues

than with the Soviet letter. It was then, I believe, that the agenda and speakers were set for the Fifth Party Congress.

The decision was also reached to expel Žujović and Hebrang from the party. They were already under house arrest, in a villa outside Belgrade. Soon thereafter they were placed in solitary confinement in the old Belgrade prison, the Glavnjača, whose bombed-out remnants were still functioning on the site of today's Chemical Institute. Neither the plenum nor the Politburo, however, made the decision to confine and then arrest Žujović and Hebrang; Tito did it. Or, rather, he gave the order to Ranković, and Ranković expedited it.

Thus both the Politburo and the Central Committee were presented with a *fait accompli*. Had anyone dared suggest a milder solution, he risked being reprimanded, if not actually charged with "opportunism" and bias toward the enemy. I am not saying that certain comrades did not in fact adopt a "milder" or "more reasonable" position, though I myself was for settling accounts with Hebrang and Žujović. Although Tito's autocracy was on the wane, his role was growing. Precisely because of his autocratic power, he exerted more influence over our confrontation with Moscow than did the Central Committee. The Central Committee's makeup and discipline were such that it would undoubtedly have approved without much discussion the measures taken against Hebrang and Žujović. But Tito's decision to act on his own in persecuting officials and Communists was designed to prevent anyone else from sitting on the fence, and, above all, to intimidate high officials and Central Committee members.

Our Politburo sent the second Soviet letter around to the administrations of the various republics and to leading comrades in the party and the federal government. I remember the reaction of the writer Radovan Zogović, who had worked with me in 1944 in the propaganda section attached to the High Command, which later grew into Agitprop. We were at the National Theater, possibly in connection with the celebration of Victory Day. During the intermission Zogović and I began talking about the Soviet letter. He was greatly impressed with it. "An extraordinary composition," he said. "The style is precise and simple. I believe Stalin wrote it, or at least edited it." I agreed with him, and still do, about Stalin's hand in it. But I did not share his opinion of its style, nor could I have, since I did not agree with him about its contents. "There are numerous inaccuracies," I answered. "Take, for example, their equating our party's wartime role with other parties'. Or the charge that we favor the rich peasantry, the village kulaks." Zogović agreed that there were inaccuracies, but felt that several charges were correct. For him, obviously, the inaccuracies were secondary; what mattered was our estrangement from the Soviet Union.

He and I did not finish our conversation at the theater that night, nor did we pick it up later, when we might have explored these questions in depth. All of a sudden we were alienated from each other, as were other Communists at that time and for the same reason: the difference in their positions toward the Soviet Union. A fundamental change in ideology was taking place. The Communist party of Yugoslavia had been trained consistently and tenaciously by Tito's own Central Committee to love and be loyal to the Soviet Union as the first and leading Communist state. Moreover, our party had been consolidated or "Bolshevized" through ideology and the works of Lenin and Stalin. Marx and Engels were of course accepted without question, but as fore-runners of Lenin and Stalin; living Marxism was indeed Lenin-ism. Zogović did not part company with our Central Committee suddenly and forever. But his case was typical of Communist intellectuals caught in the dilemma: whether to declare for the reality of their country and irrefutable facts, or for fixed ideo-logical assumptions and tailored facts.

Once pro-Soviet party functionaries observed with what fury the majority was resisting Soviet pressures and charges, and sensed the threat of persecution—the arrest of Hebrang and Žujović was "instructive"—overnight they became two-faced. There was also the realization that only continued membership in the party offered any prospects, if not for a policy turnabout, at least for continued activity along Soviet lines.

Stefan Mitrović, who had a responsible position in Agitprop, took the same stand as Zogović. The ambiguity of their attitude would be noticed by Vladimir Dedijer—now also working in Agitprop—soon after the Cominform resolution of June 28, 1948. Early one morning Dedijer flew into my office in a fury. "In the Central Committee apparatus, right here in Agitprop, there are Cominform supporters!" he shouted. "Zogović and Mitrović are spreading all kinds of treacherous theories." I agreed with his observations—and still do—but said soothingly that we had to be patient, because everything was still in the discussion stage. In taking this stand I had the support of the Politburo, above all, Ranković. Mitrović and Zogović were rare cases whose attitude was unclear from the beginning and with whom we had to take our time. Veljko Vlahović, too, needed more than a year to make up his mind. Ranković and I, as well as the party, patiently helped, but perhaps more important in his decision was the dark, all-consuming pressure from the Soviet government and the governments and parties under its control.

While Vlahović was in a torment of indecision, Boris Ziherl declared himself for the Soviet leadership. In the summer of 1948 he told me openly—officially, so to speak—in the Central Committee that it did not make sense for the whole country and the party to suffer on account of one man, Tito, no matter how worthy. "Naturally, it doesn't make sense" was my answer. "But dumping that one man would mean selling out a whole policy and subjecting the country and the party to a policy not in their interest."

I informed my comrades of this exchange. But everyone favored caution, believing that Ziherl was suffering from temporary faint-heartedness and ideological confusion. That judgment was confirmed. Still, Kardelj and Kidrič arranged for Ziherl's name to be crossed out by a conspicuous number of delegates at the Slovenian Communist party congress. "Let him feel what could happen," said Kardelj, when I reproached him for using such a method.

Rodoljub Čolaković's irresoluteness took yet another form. At first he came out suddenly and openly for the Soviet leadership, then just as suddenly he withdrew into silence. Čolaković was at the time president of Bosnia and Hercegovina. At a meeting of the regional committee called to discuss the Molotov-Stalin letter, he declared himself—like Žujović at the Central Committee session

—for the Soviet Union and Stalin in the name of "international-ism." Djuro Pucar, then party secretary in Bosnia and Herce-govina, reacted sharply; the Bosnians even voiced the opinion, which Ranković favored, that Čolaković ought to be imprisoned along with Žujović and Hebrang. But Tito rejected the idea. "Let him come talk to me," he said. "I know him well." And Čola-ković came.

I don't know what he and Tito talked about that night, but the next day Čolaković pulled back from his pro-Soviet position. "Comrades, I was demoralized," he explained simply. He was at once pulled out of Bosnia to become federal minister for science and culture, a duty he performed conscientiously and intelligently. He, in that function, and I, as head of Agitprop, often pooled our efforts. We had no disagreements. since Čolaković was tol-erant and flexible.

Until the very end of the Fifth Congress there was no "whip cracking," even over those who openly declared for the Soviet Union and the Cominform. We hoped that the congress would have a positive impact, and that exposure to experience and the truth would bring insight and understanding. In fact, Zogović and Mitrović had been asked to participate actively in prepara-tions for the congress. The two of them put together the Agitprop report, while I edited the party program, which Moša Pijade had written. Consequently, at the congress I would read a report that I had not written but only glanced through and corrected here and there. Even so, I thought it encompassing and clear, but too rigid and detailed, though I cannot deny that I agreed with it.

Recently a certain writer quoted from this report, erroneously linking my name with it but correctly citing the report as a model of consistently formulated socialist realism. Following Soviet pat-terns, "decadents" like Picasso, Sartre, and others were attacked "consistently." Neither its authors nor I was familiar enough with intellectual currents in the West. Even if we had been, our minds were hobbled ideologically: the needs of the day dictated our taking a stand against what we labeled "decadence," to prove both to our membership and to Soviet propaganda that we had not "deviated," that no one was more consistent than we.

Zogović also helped me correct the reports to be delivered by Tito and Kardelj—not only their language and style, but also facts and formulations. Tito's paper was solidly conceived and far-reaching—a history, in fact, of the socialist movement in the South Slavic countries. But as often happens with politicians, it contained a series of inaccuracies.

After the Molotov-Stalin letter, the Soviets continued to apply pressure in accordance with both earlier plans and new opportunities. Moshetov, the Soviet representative responsible for Yugoslav affairs on the Soviet Central Committee, arrived in Belgrade on May 19. Earlier he had been in the habit of appearing in Belgrade in the uniform of an NKVD colonel. Our Moscow returnees recalled how on the eve of the war this youthful but sickly-looking thirty-five-year-old had taken part in the annihilation of the Yugoslav émigré community in the U.S.S.R., whence his "familiarity" with our party. But he gave no outward sign of such familiarity with the party, let alone with our current situation. On prior visits to Belgrade, as in our contacts with him in Moscow, he had displayed a reserved, melancholy attraction to Yugoslavs, but in Belgrade now he was not just reserved but downright cold. He brought a message from the Soviet Central Committee, signed by Mikhail Suslov, enjoining us to participate in the coming meeting of the Cominform. Other Soviet representatives insisted that Tito must attend in person, and spread rumors that Stalin would be there, too. But the very next day our Central Committee affirmed our refusal to attend, as decided at the plenum of May 9.

Soon thereafter came Stalin's personal intervention in, or, more precisely, his protest at, the arrest of Hebrang and Žujović. He accused our Central Committee of intent to murder them (which would have been quite in the spirit of Stalinism), and demanded —no more, no less—the presence of Soviet investigators at the inquiry into their conduct. Pijade and those versed in Serbian history recalled that when Archduke Franz Ferdinand was assassinated in Sarajevo in 1914, Austria-Hungary had made the same demand on Serbia. It was precisely this demand, they said, that the Serbian government had rejected, thus giving the Austrians a pretext to declare war. I drafted a brief reply to this Soviet demand, and the Politburo approved it. The reply read, in part: ". . . the very thought of our leaders being described as 'criminal murderers' is bitterly rejected. . . . The Central Committee of the Communist party of Yugoslavia feels that participation in the investigation of Hebrang and Žujović by the Central Committee of the Soviet Communist party is out of the question."

Reacting quickly, the Soviet leaders had set their apparatus in motion on an international scale. In their letter of May 22 they confirmed that the Cominform would convene "to discuss the state of affairs in the Yugoslav Communist party," paying no attention to our repudiation and directly contradicting the original spirit of voluntary participation and equal rights. Ostensibly bowing to a request from the Czech and Hungarian comrades, their Central Committee agreed to postpone the session until late June.

In late May or early June, a Polish party representative to the Cominform called on me. He brought a message from Gomulka— Moscow did not know about this, he insisted—urging us to attend the Cominform meeting to avoid open confrontation. Gomulka was prepared to come to Belgrade, along with Jakub Berman, to talk matters over in detail—on condition, of course, that we agree to attend the meeting. I promised to consult with the Central Committee and respond in a couple of days. When I met with the Pole at the appointed time, I told him that we would not go to the Cominform meeting, but would see Gomulka. And so the Polish offer came to nothing. I believe Gomulka really was working without the knowledge of the Soviet leaders.

The official invitation from the Cominform came in a telegram on June 19. On June 20 the expanded Politburo met in the Brdo Palace, near Kranj. At the morning session, Tito presented the Cominform's invitation, and we unanimously confirmed the position taken earlier. But then Blagoje Nešković hesitantly took the floor with a proposal for renewed discussion: perhaps our case would be stronger, he said, both within the party and in the world Communist movement if we went to the Cominform meeting and stated our position.

No one agreed with him. But Tito suggested—it was already time for lunch—that we give some thought to the idea and make a decision during the afternoon session. There was no question of second thoughts, but Tito had become more tolerant in discussions and more considerate of his comrades' opinions—and also more careful with Nešković, since we were aware of inconsistency and confusion in his views. Nešković was tough and unequivocal in repudiating lies and in countering the deprecation of our party and its wartime role, but he was rigidly, incurably tied to the Soviet Union and Stalin as the source of socialism's strength. Yet unlike those who were siding with the Soviets and the Cominform, Nešković expressed his position openly.

Once, at the royal villa at Topola, where most of the work on the Fifth Congress was done, Nešković and I had racked our brains late into the night over the Soviet Union, Stalin, socialism, and the like. Would Moscow attack us? Neither of us could believe that would happen, but for different reasons, both ideological. He asserted that it was impossible for one socialist state to attack another, whereas I held that it would mean the disintegration of ideology and Communism as a world movement. We carried our dispute a step further. "We'll fight them," I said, categorically. Nešković backed away. "The Red Army? No, I wouldn't fight the Red Army."

At lunch there was little or no discussion of Nešković's proposal to attend the Cominform meeting in Bucharest, though that would later become the key issue dividing Cominform supporters from those of our Central Committee. After lunch we took a walk around the pond. I was talking with Tito. At one point, when we were on the subject of Soviet intervention, he exclaimed, in bitter exaltation, "To die on one's own soil! At least a memory remains!" I remember that cry because it gave me courage to go on.

At the afternoon session Nešković's proposal was rejected without discussion. Tito remarked gently that "Comrade Blaško ought to concur, since the rest of his comrades are unanimous." And Comrade Blaško silently concurred.

We knew that the Cominform was in session in Bucharest, discussing relations between the Central Committees of Yugoslavia and the U.S.S.R. Leading comrades in Tanjug, the press agency, had been advised to look for any announcements coming out of Eastern Europe and to let me know at once.

On June 28, around 3:30, I had just awakened from an afternoon nap when Tanjug called to say that at 3:00 P.M. Radio Prague had begun announcing a Cominform resolution against the Communist party of Yugoslavia. I immediately went to the Central Committee offices and called my secretary, Dragica Weinberger, and Dedijer, who was at a meeting. The latter went to Tanjug to arrange to have the resolution delivered to us at the Central Committee. He did this promptly, and then my secretary and his, Slavica Fran, typed up the text, in bits and pieces, as it was received from Tanjug, and we sent it on to the Politburo members. The resolution was disseminated by Tanjug so that the world—and, above all, Yugoslavia—would learn about it. Although only Radio Prague was broadcasting it that day, Dedijer and I, like the rest of our comrades, did not doubt its authenticity; we assumed that Radio Prague had acted on impulse and not by any premeditated Soviet plan. The resolution was announced by the rest of the East European countries the next day.

In the late afternoon the Politburo met at Tito's. We decided to call a plenary meeting of the Central Committee for the next day, June 29, to deal with the resolution.

The resolution did not contain anything new or surprising. But its promulgation on the anniversary of the tragic battle in 1389 at Kosovo, which had inaugurated five centuries of Turkish rule over the Serbian people, cut into the minds and hearts of all us Serbs. Though neither religious nor mystical, we noted, with a certain relish almost, this coincidence in dates between ancient calamities and living threats and onslaughts.

I fell asleep as usual around 11:00 but suddenly woke up just after midnight, trembling with anxiety over the Cominform reso-

201

lution. I knew that we would have to respond, although the evening before, when the Politburo met at Tito's, the question had not come up. Without a second thought, driven by cold, measured rage and irrepressible certainty, I locked myself in my study and composed an answer that could serve as a draft for the next day's Central Committee session and, better still, as a release for Tanjug. I was certain that the next day the Soviet and East European radio stations would blast the news, to say nothing of the West, and a statement from Tanjug would be a must. The announcement from Radio Prague was at my fingertips, but I scarcely glanced at it: point by point, the Cominform's charges emerged from my memory as I wrote. I was almost feverish, yet I wrote deliberately, composing and clarifying the formulations. Dawn crept up on me. I didn't go back to bed. Instead, I looked through the newspapers and had a cup of coffee. Work was piling up at the Central Committee, and what I had concocted through the night had to be edited and typed.

The Central Committee meeting on June 29 began in the afternoon. The atmosphere was calm, almost subdued. The confrontation was now public; the rift could not be healed, and there was no end in sight.

After the resolution had been read and briefly discussed—interrupted more than discussed—it was decided, at Tito's suggestion, that an answer should be prepared. I offered the text I had composed overnight. There were no interruptions; everyone listened, solemnly attentive. Everyone, that is, but Tito, who stood up and paced nervously, as he often did when he was deep in thought. When I finished, he exclaimed, "Very good! I think that can serve as a basis."

He at once proposed a committee to edit the reply. His mistrust, his nervous, groundless suspicion, was so great that he chose only those closest to himself—Kardelj, Ranković, and me. Our little group set to work right away, while the Central Committee took up other questions. We kept at it for nearly three hours, wrestling with formulations, though changes were minor and few. Kardelj was responsible for the bulk of the correction. It is interesting to note that he deleted a passage according to which "intentionally citing statements and experiences taken out of the context of our party practice could conceivably be ascribed to other parties, including the Soviet Communist party." The passage could be provocative, as was Tito's reasoning about the relations between socialist states in his reply to the first Molotov-Stalin letter.

The Central Committee accepted our proposed reply in toto. Disagreement arose only over whether to publish the Cominform resolution along with it. Tito was opposed, though not adamantly so; I was adamantly in favor. Kardelj unequivocally supported me, as did the majority. So the next day, June 30, both documents were published. Since the other East European countries did not publicize either our reply or any of our polemics, this publication became a powerful argument in our favor later, when we were settling accounts with domestic and foreign opposition. According to our intelligence service, both Lavrentiev and Judin took a dim view of this double publication. Small wonder: these bureaucrats were used to seeing in print only the views of their own government and Central Committee, whose omnipotence and infallibility they never questioned.

That same day, June 30, also saw the publication of the *Program of the Communist Party of Yugoslavia*, written by a committee I chaired. This program was both inadequate and uninspired. Our Politburo, finding itself under indictment by the Soviet Union—with blockade and armed intervention perhaps in the offing—felt that, as good Leninists, we should subscribe to the Soviet party's program, a program that even in the U.S.S.R. was obsolete. We knew it, but it was what I proposed—with the addition, of course, of certain features pertaining to us—and we all approved. Not even the party membership embraced it wholeheartedly. A year and a half later, we leaders acknowledged that the program was glaringly out of date and unoriginal. But at the time we were spared the frenzied, ruthless "criticism" of Soviet propagandists on this formally important point.

The Cominform resolution was instantly recognized throughout the world as an event of paramount significance, especially for the further development of Communism. No one in the West had foreseen such a conflict, largely because Yugoslavia was characterized there as Satellite Number One. That was quite unfounded in terms of the behind-the-scenes relationship between Yugoslavia and the U.S.S.R., but well founded in relation to Yugoslavs as ideologically intransigent, hard-line revolutionaries. This failure to foresee the conflict seems all the more puzzling given the public differences aired in the press and in the speeches of state officials. A certain high-ranking officer of the American embassy in Belgrade was the exception: he had predicted the confrontation in one of his reports, but Washington thought the idea preposterous.

Such lack of perception on the part of Western statesmen and the media surely cannot be explained away as the result of stupidity and myopia, still less of deficiencies in method and theory. The West had become accustomed to stereotyped notions of Communism, particularly in the throes of the Cold War. It had trained itself to regard the hegemonic role of Moscow as unchanging, and, partly in imitation of Communists themselves, attributed an exaggerated importance to Communism's monolithic ideology.

In retrospect, I am astonished by the West's erroneous predictions about the outcome of the confrontation, not only the forecasts available to everyone through the media, but those emanating from diplomatic sources. To the best of my knowledge, all anticipated the swift fall of the Yugoslav regime, though most observers thought a pro-Soviet team—not monarchists—would then seize power.

I have mentioned these rigid, unrealistic prognoses not to round out my story, but because they represented the antithesis of the confidence then prevalent in Yugoslavia. In the top ranks no one doubted that our regime would hold out—at least no one favoring resistance to Moscow. Nor did we differ, at the time of the resolution and up to the end of 1948, in our appraisal of possible Soviet intervention. This was not likely, we felt, but we knew we had a long, painful struggle ahead of us. True, the dispute led immediately to a worsening of international relations, including threats and provocations. Albania led the way: only two or three days after the resolution, that country began to break its agreements with us and jeopardize our relations. But by and large the argument stayed where it was, on the level of ideology, and not a single party—not even the Soviet—was ideologically prepared for armed intervention against yesterday's acclaimed revolutionary Yugoslavia. Besides, the neighboring Communist countries were militarily inferior to us. We ourselves were poorly armed, but their armies were inadequately organized and plagued by low morale.

So we felt at the time what is widely known today, chiefly from the speeches of Khrushchev at the Twentieth Party Congress: Stalin mistakenly believed that a change would be effected in Yugoslavia from within, by "sound forces" inside the party. As he expressed it to Khrushchev, all he had to do was move his little finger and Tito would come tumbling down.

Our confidence bolstered morale in the party and among the people. The tough resistance on all important levels and in all crucial institutions was indisputable. Our opponents in the party —only there did we have significant opposition—were confused from the start by changes in our living history and the absurdities of the resolution, and driven, by our courage and determination, to cover up and dissemble. Slander and lies had not been unknown before to the Yugoslav party, as to any other, but in the Soviet attack there was clearly something else at issue. This attack was directed against the foundations and the historic heritage from which the new Yugoslav state and the Yugoslav people had grown. At issue was the independence of the state and the autonomy of its internal development. This truth and reality forced Stalin's supporters in Yugoslavia—even those enthralled by internationalism and devoted to the Soviet Union—to cover up their true intentions with shopworn phrases. And this happened all the more readily because the Soviet letters and the Cominform resolution legitimized recourse to hypocrisy and slander in the struggle against Yugoslavia, and thereby in the Communist movement. I do not mean to imply that such methods had been alien to the movement—least of all to Soviet Communism. But now those methods had burst the confines of a single party and of the movement as a whole to slander a victorious revolution, and by attempting to subjugate the Yugoslav state sought to subjugate all the states of Eastern Europe. That was why the Soviet and Cominform lies and calumnies seemed so monstrous, shocking, and therefore utterly unacceptable.

None of this posed a dilemma for non-Communists, ordinary Yugoslav citizens. For them, the whole dispute was natural and altogether supportable, for all the threat of Soviet intervention. The use of force by the great against the small has been a rule rather than an exception for centuries, especially in the Balkans. So among the broad nonparty masses, the confrontation generated enthusiasm. They saw it as a point of departure in the new, healthier, more authentic life of the nation. That popular sentiment did not quite materialize, but neither was it quite betrayed. Even with all its inconsistencies and problems, Yugoslavia was beginning to separate itself from the Soviet center and the other Communist parties and forge ahead on its own. We in the leadership suspected this and foresaw it, though we thought of it less in terms of a "national path" or "national Communism" than as socialism assuming new forms.

Reports from all over the country testified to the unanimity of the people and their support for the Central Committee. I certainly witnessed it on my trips through Montenegro and into villages around Belgrade. Everywhere I found firm, unequivocal support from ordinary, nonideological people, and even from yesterday's adversaries. A Mrs. Gašić came to see me at that time, to ask for my intervention in some matter. She was the wife of Jovan Gašić, in whose villa I had lived at one point, and who had once served as private secretary to the royal premier, Milan Stojadinović. In other words, she represented the Belgrade bourgeoisie and "reactionaries" of the first order. Mrs. Gašić had little feeling for politics—for her, it was a bag of tricks. She said to me: "So long as the Russians don't run the show. At least you are *our* people." Something similar was said to Koča Popović by his mother, also a "reactionary bourgeois." On the other hand, the telegram sent by a mass meeting that took place in Belgrade early in July, expressing love for Stalin but also demanding that he clear our Central Committee of "unjustified charges," did not spring from below, from the people, but, rather, from the head of an official who had not yet rid himself of sentimental illusions about the Soviet Union and Stalin.

The Cominform resolution set the course subsequently taken against us by the other Communist parties and East European governments. The Albanian government and the Albanian Workers' party led the way. The Bulgarian government—though not the Bulgarian party—was still acting with moderation: pro-Soviet Communists headed by Chervenkov obviously now dominated the party, whereas the government was still under Dimitrov's control. But all this is the business of historians. I might mention that in the pages of *Borba* on July 5 I replied to Chervenkov's attack, whereas on July 8 Veljko Vlahović, in an article entitled "Marxist-Leninist Education of Cadres," cited Stalin without a single word about the Cominform attack. Similarly, Zogović, in *Borba* on July 18, praised our OZNA, the former secret police, and the old Soviet Cheka and its organizer, Felix Dzerzhinsky, on the occasion of the arrest of the Ustashi leaders Kavran and Miloš—also without one word about the Soviet and Cominform attack.

Everything was in flux and ideologically confused. But the top leaders and the people had already made their decision and were ready to defend their country. That's how things stood with us on the eve of the Fifth Party Congress.

# 14

The congress, which began on July 21, displayed the customary unanimity, enthusiastic but somewhat strained. The choice of delegates had been determined by the Central Committee, with the regional committees sharing in organization and control. Even so, there were some delegates who secretly supported the Cominform, and others who had not yet decided where they stood.

Thus, despite the show of unanimity, there were nuances in the delegates' speeches. Everyone was still for the Soviet Union and Stalin, but there were differences in how they addressed the main issues. The inner circle took note of these, but did not yet deem them sufficient cause for correction. Particularly with respect to ideology, the leaders themselves had not shifted very far, except on the issue of independence and the truth about the Yugoslav revolution. Among the speeches, the most noted for its firm and unequivocal stand was the one by Ranković's assistant, Veljko Mićunović, later ambassador to Moscow and author of the impressive memoir *Moscow Years*.

But if Mićunović was to be singled out for his courage and

clarity, Blažo Jovanović and Blagoje Nešković, secretaries of the Montenegrin and Serbian regional committees respectively, were notable for their fuzziness, though they were clear enough in their fidelity to the Soviet Union and Stalin. Jovanović: "Our love for and loyalty to the Soviet Union will remain, as always, strong and indestructible." Nešković, to stormy applause: "We have been, are, and shall remain in the socialist front, under the leadership of the U.S.S.R." Nor were the speeches of Boris Ziherl and Stefan Mitrović any more lucid, apart from expressions of loyalty to the U.S.S.R. and Stalin. Though at the time these dissenters all over-emphasized affection for the Soviet Union and Stalin, they later traveled divergent roads, the one leading toward the Yugoslav top echelons, the other toward the U.S.S.R.

Ilija Bulatović, the delegate from Bijelo Polje, also attended the congress. I knew that he was on the fence, and since we were old friends from the same region, I felt particularly sorry that he was drawing away from the party. During the session I invited him for dinner, drove out to Avala with him, and spoke openly. But Bulatović had sealed himself off completely. Though willing to talk, he avoided any argument by concurring with lukewarm enthusiasm. We spoke of the letter he had sent earlier, warning me—and, through me, the Central Committee—against betraying internationalism by breaking away from the Soviet Union. I record this because of the tragic destiny that befell him, one that Bulatović, like so many, chose for himself with a sense of fatalism.

Generally speaking, the broader membership was still infatuated with the Soviet Union and Stalin. But the top leadership was un-clear as to how far the Soviet government and its vassal states would carry their attacks, and even less clear about what social causes or reasons of state impelled them. As late as September 29, 1949, Kardelj, speaking as minister of foreign affairs at a United Nations session, was still supporting the Soviet Union, without ever mentioning the Cominform attacks. This was not prompted simply by the "backward consciousness" of the party rank and file; the leadership itself was slow to recognize Moscow's intentions.

But the confusion and hesitation of prominent officials had a disastrous impact on the stunned and uncertain lower functionaries and regular party members. Reactions varied, depending on the region. Certainly Montenegro's pro-Russian traditions and its patriarchal, preindustrial, half-tribal social structure influenced its delegates—the largest group there—to decide in favor of the Soviets. But there is no doubt in my mind that Blažo Jovanović's fainthearted, equivocal remarks provoked and encouraged this decision. Those who had made up their minds had an intuitive grasp of such vague indecision, as did those who were hestitating to come out for Stalin and the U.S.S.R. Even when, in 1949, Jovanović allied himself with Tito in his public statements, he differed from the leading members of the Central Committee and the Politburo. I vividly recall one occasion, on the reviewing stand in Cetinje that year, during the celebration of the July 13 uprising. Blažo was speaking, expressing sadness over the conflict with Moscow. Mićunović caught my eye and scowled at Blažo.

As time went on, Blažo became noticeably depressed. We were close friends, and I talked it all out with him. That was in 1951 or 1952, when his position had become firm and unambiguous. "I never hesitated in my support for and loyalty to our Central Committee," he explained. "But I took it very hard when loyal, tested comrades fell away, even more because I had personally promoted many and believed in them." Yet when the Security forces purged the party in Montenegro by making arrests, they encountered no resistance from Blažo Jovanović.

Although the top leadership stood united, inevitably there were nuances of opinion among them, too. In my report to the Fifth Congress, for example, I insisted on the truth, and stressed that the struggle with the Cominform would be long and hard. When I reached the little room backstage used by the leadership and the presiding officers, Kardelj's reaction was uneasy: "That cannot stand as is—this is no struggle. We're talking about differences within the Communist movement that sooner or later must be resolved and eliminated." In retrospect one might say that I had correctly grasped that the confrontation would be fierce and prolonged, though Kardelj was right, too, since our differences with Moscow were suppressed, if not eliminated, after Stalin's death and Khrushchev's rise to power. But such an interpretation does not seem right to me: Kardelj hastily reacted to my overly harsh statement, which by no means implied that we would never see an end to our dispute with Moscow.

The congress was held in the Guardhouse—a complex of barracks in the Belgrade suburb of Topčider. The trial of Draža Mihailović had been held in that very hall two years before. There was no other hall large enough in Belgrade then, but this site had also been chosen for security reasons. The surrounding woods, as well as the clearings around the White Palace and the Old Palace, were packed with antiaircraft batteries and machine guns "just in case." None of that was in sight, however, and the delegates, who were served lunch in tents on the lawn, felt relaxed, even carefree.

Nonetheless, the congress did not pass without anger and nervousness, provoked by Soviet propaganda. *Pravda* published a report that a Swiss Trotskyite party delegation had come to the congress. I summoned the *Pravda* correspondent, Barzhenko, and asked him where he had got such information and what it was supposed to mean. Not one whit embarrassed, Barzhenko, rumored to be a Hero of the Soviet Union, asked brazenly, "Do you know that *Pravda* has been edited by Lenin and Stalin?" I did know, I told him, but even so the report was not correct and would have to be denied. He did not want to discuss the matter further.

With the endorsement of my Politburo comrades, I drew up a denial, which was read aloud at the congress and approved amid angry applause. From the Molotov-Stalin letters and the Cominform resolution it was amply clear that Soviet and Soviet-inspired propaganda against Yugoslavia was based on fabrications, provocations, and intimidation. It was therefore all the more important for our reply to be measured and buttressed by facts.

The congress lasted nine days, ending on July 29. The party then had 490,000 members. In the three years since the war, membership had quintupled, but this was seen as a strengthening of socialism, not a reaching out for power and privilege.

Historians will assess the Fifth Congress on their own terms, but for us in the leadership it meant, above all, the final attainment of legitimacy independent of the Soviet Union and international Communist assemblies. It was obvious that Tito's role had been strengthened, and that of his closest colleagues as well. This was particularly true of the Central Committee Secretariat, whose members had now achieved a legitimacy hitherto bestowed on them by the Comintern through its emissary, Tito.

For our adversaries, however—both foreign and domestic—the congress meant change. They interpreted its resolutions as extortion and deception by a "Tito clique," and therefore intensified their pressure and provocation both within and without. Of the pro-Soviet Communists who conspired or emigrated, I shall mention a few with whom I had some indirect connection.

Surely the most notorious was Arso Jovanović, if only because he had headed the High Command during the war and was the top General Staff officer. He had been among the group of high-ranking officers who in 1946 had been sent to attend the best Soviet military institute, the Voroshilov. Koča Popović had taken over as head of the General Staff. Upon completing their studies in the spring of 1948, at the time of the Molotov-Stalin letter to our Central Committee, this group of officers returned to Yugoslavia. The Politburo had already been informed of the differences of opinion and the hostilities that had developed in Moscow among them. The sharpest differences arose between Jovanović and Dapčević. These clashes, however, were not yet perceived as political, pro-Stalin or anti-Tito. In an effort to clarify matters and exert his influence, Tito invited the most prominent officers —four of them, I believe—to visit him at Brdo.

They were there at the time of a Politburo meeting and they attended a joint dinner. Among them was Arso Jovanović. One could tell from the conversation that the generals were abreast of our conflict with the Soviets—Tito had of course informed them— but they, Arso in particular, were reluctant to make their positions known or to look into the heart of the matter.

My close friendship with Arso Jovanović went back to wartime. He was an open man who made friendships easily. Yet, except for

Mitar Bakić, Arso's high-school friend, few were on terms of such intimacy and warmth with him as I. My friendship extended to his wife, Senka, a sensitive, straightforward woman devoted to her husband. But at Brdo I didn't have a chance to speak to him privately—nor would that have been appropriate—about relations with the Soviet leadership, since Tito had already said what was necessary.

During and after the Fifth Congress, Arso and I saw each other a good deal, and once, when he was having lunch at my house, I told him in no uncertain terms what I thought about the Soviet attack. He listened in silent embarrassment, then said: "I don't know what the Russians want."

I conveyed his indecision to Ranković, who had gotten the same impression, though they saw each other rarely and were not close friends. I also discussed it with Tito. But both men, while sharing my impression, felt that the relationship with Arso must not deteriorate, and that we should bide our time while casting about for a way to help him. Yet, upon his return from Moscow, Arso was not returned to duty as head of the General Staff. Instead, he was assigned command of the top military school (still on the drawing boards). This confirms that Tito and Ranković already had their doubts about his loyalty. Subsequent to the lunch at my house, Arso and I still saw each other, but the relationship was under a pall. By pure chance, I dropped in at his house a couple of days prior to his death, but he was not there.

At about 11:00 A.M. on August 12, Ranković phoned me to come see him immediately (our offices were close). There had been a "terrible accident," he said: Arso Jovanović had been killed. "How? Where?" I asked. "On the Rumanian border, while hunting," he replied, in a voice that feigned more shock than his words conveyed. Regaining my composure, I said, "He must have been trying to escape!" He made no reply, simply repeating his request that I come to see him.

With Ranković was Otmar Kreačić, Vukmanović-Tempo's deputy in the army's political administration. He repeated briefly what he had already told Ranković: Arso Jovanović, Colonel Vlado Dapčević, brother of Peko, and General Branko "Kadja"

Petričević, also an assistant to Vukmanović, had gone hunting wild boar on the government estate of Sočica, on the Rumanian border. They ran into a militia patrol at night. In the confusion there was firing, and Arso was killed. The story had come from Petričević, who had returned to the city and was now at the army's political administration headquarters.

The three of us realized that the incident would provoke all sorts of interpretations, especially from pro-Soviet propaganda sources, but not one of us—myself least of all—felt especially upset or grief-stricken. Ranković and I both knew that Arso was not a hunter, and I knew that he possessed no weapons for hunting. I was certain that he and the others had been trying to escape to Rumania. Ranković said that Petričević would be arriving at any moment to give a more detailed report, to which Kreačić asserted, "I'd go through fire for Petričević!"

Just then, Petričević arrived, in a muddy, rumpled uniform. His story contained nothing that we didn't already know. We kept plying him with questions. More upset and uneasy by the minute, he answered that the three of them had agreed to go hunting wild boar, and set off at night with the estate manager so that dawn would find them in position. They had stumbled on a border patrol. In the confusion, people started firing. He fled. In the morning he met State Security patrols, who told him of Arso's death. Arabjac, the estate manager, was also killed. So he returned to Belgrade immediately to report.

He had not even finished his story before I was pressing him with more questions. "How come Arso decided to go hunting, and for wild boar, when he was not a hunter and had no hunting weapons? Did the two of you, you and Dapčević, have such weapons? No, you didn't. Do you know what sorts of weapons are employed in hunting wild boar? A special carbine; not a shotgun. And where is Dapčević, what happened to him?" Petričević: "We had no hunting weapons, only pistols. Well, it was more like a hike. We were bored and we wanted to take a little walk. Dapčević? In all the commotion he disappeared. He's bound to turn up." One question led to another; I would have kept on had I not noticed Ranković frowning. So I concluded by saying,

"You've really put your foot in it!" Petričević agreed. Then Ranković said, "Go get cleaned up, Kadja, take a rest, then we'll talk some more."

He left, and I turned to Kreačić: "Would you go through fire for him now?" He replied quickly, with a smile, that he would not.

Kreačić also departed, leaving Ranković and me to put our own interpretation on the incident. I did most of the talking, carried away by the torrent of my thoughts, while he kept shaking his head and interjecting comments. In the end he picked up the phone and quickly and decisively said to Kreačić: "Listen to me, Kreačić. Send two officers to arrest Petričević at once."

That same day Petričević confessed. Arso, Dapčević, and he had long realized that they shared the same views regarding the dispute with the Soviet Union. After the Fifth Congress, the conflict was exacerbated to such an extent that they saw no possibility for any opposition activity. So they decided to flee to the U.S.S.R. across Rumania. They planned to seize a tank in Vršac and make a run for it with the help of a sympathetic officer, Vukan Božović. But as ill luck would have it, Božović was not in Vršac on the day chosen, so they decided to cross the border on foot, on the pretext that they were hunting boar. Arabjac, the estate manager, suspecting nothing, put himself at their service. Our border with Rumania was not well secured, but since gypsies from both countries traditionally engaged in horse stealing and smuggling, militia patrolled the vicinity. The fugitives stumbled on one of these patrols, and when ordered to halt—had they done so, nothing would have happened—Arso Jovanović opened fire with his pistol. The fire was returned, he was fatally wounded in the head, and the innocent Arabjac also was slain. Petričević and Dapčević ran off. Petričević came back to Belgrade, hoping to get by with his simple-minded cover story. Dapčević hid out in Belgrade, only to be apprehended on the Hungarian border three months later.

One of the most frequent questions posed to me after I was removed from power was: "Why did you people kill Arso Jovanović?" Because of the closed and oppressive nature of our political system, nonparty and even party people took the truth to be a fabrication. A conviction spread that Arso was killed in

Belgrade and that his body was transported to the Rumanian border. The official statement may have contributed to this rumor; it was not announced until several days after Arso's death and it did not explain all the circumstances. Disclosure of the facts at the trial of Dapčević and Petričević also failed to quell doubts and misgivings. I gather from a trustworthy former Cominform émigré that Vlado Dapčević gave an accurate account of the incident later, in exile in the Soviet Union.

I played a greater and more direct share in releasing Sreten Žujović from prison, if planting the idea can be so viewed; as with many others, his fate depended very little on me.

After a brief "friendly" house arrest, Žujović and Hebrang had been transferred to Belgrade's Glavnjača. Žujović—and I believe Hebrang, too—was put in solitary confinement. Pavle Baljević, a high-ranking Security officer and prewar party member, was assigned the sole duty of looking after Žujović. He received no papers or journals, a rule strictly observed. He did get decent medical care, rations, cigarettes, and even "neutral" books printed before his arrest, but he was permanently confined to his cell, which was well lighted, though, and relatively spacious.

He stayed there for two and a half years, during which time no investigation of his case was ever conducted. There were two reasons for this cruel isolation: to preclude any contact with the outside world and to break the prisoner's resistance. State Security exercised here its full power.

But inevitably the time came to settle his case. This was prompted not by Hebrang's sudden death in prison, but by political changes: relations with the U.S.S.R. had improved, pro-Soviet members and sympathizers had been purged; "self-criticisms" were pouring in from prisoners in the camp on Goli Otok; the Yugoslav leadership was gaining prestige; and our ties abroad had grown, above all with the West. In short, conditions were ripe for disposing of the "Žujović-Hebrang myth," which Soviet propaganda incessantly revived and inflated. It was Ranković who set the machinery in motion, upon his return from vacation in September 1950. Yet he did not really know how to go about it. I suggested that Žujović be furnished a book about the trial of Laszlo Rajk in Hungary—the stenographic notes published by the pro-Soviet Russian émigrés. At first Ranković hesitated, but a talk with Kardelj, who went along with my proposal, tipped the balance in favor of it.

I was motivated by my reading of Žujović's character as well as by the Soviet campaign against Yugoslavia. I had always valued Žujović more highly than did Ranković, though more as a fighter and revolutionary than as an intellectual, and concluded that he could not remain indifferent to the mendacious and absurd charges leveled at our leadership and our revolution. After all, this was his life story, too, his sacrifice, his creation. As for the Soviet campaign, by now it stood revealed, not only as ridiculous and dogmatic, but also as bent on subjugation and expansion.

No sooner had Žujović finished the book on the Rajk trial than he asked for a complete run of *Borba* from the day of his arrest, Ranković told me with a hopeful, meaningful smile. A few days later he reported that the prisoner was devouring *Borba* day and night. Ten days later Žujović asked, through Baljević, to talk with someone in the leadership. Ranković, probably after consulting with Tito, decided that he and I would see him. Perhaps I was included because my suggestion to have Žujovic read the Rajk material had proven successful.

As we were driving to the Glavnjača, Ranković wondered whether we should shake hands with Žujović; the thought had crossed my mind as well. "Why not?" I said. "Even enemies shake hands when they negotiate in wartime." But our dilemma was quickly resolved when Žujović was brought into the office: he almost rushed toward us and might have kissed us had we not held ourselves aloof. So first I and then Ranković shook his hand, and we all sat down around a little table. Žujović was plainly excited. He was in good shape both mentally and physically; the only change seemed to be that pale bluish prison cast.

The conversation proceeded as if we had never separated, as if he had not "betrayed" us, and we had not become his jailers. I led the talk for the most part, though we had no set agenda—

217

Ranković simply left it to me. I went straight to the issue: "What are your thoughts about our confrontation with the Russians, now that you know what went on?" Without blinking an eyelash, Žujović replied, "They're imperialists!" "You've discovered America!" I cried. Then Ranković interrupted: "And how do you look on your own case?"

Again without hesitation—Žujović was never the man to hesitate —he said he had made a mistake. We did not pursue the matter, because the conversation quickly turned to how best to resolve the issue. "You'll have to explain your position in public," Ranković and I emphasized, to which he assented without protest. We agreed that this would take the form of an article in *Borba*. Ranković said he would be set free the next day and be transferred to the former Stojadinović villa, which was set aside for foreign guests and properly guarded. He would remain there until his status was cleared up and he wrote his statement. Just before we left we couldn't resist asking Žujović what he had done with his notes from the Central Committee meetings—I don't recall which of us brought it up. He confessed uncomfortably: "I deposited them with Lavrentiev."

Our visit with Žujović had lasted more than two hours and dealt in part with personal matters. The moment he had come out for the Soviet Central Committee in May 1948, his "war bride," Mileva Planojević, left him—she was going along with our party and the Central Committee. Mileva was young, so her action was given a humorous interpretation—a most unfair one, because she had acted from conviction—that she had killed two birds with one stone: displayed party solidarity and rid herself of an old husband. Žujović said that he wanted to return to his former wife, Lepa, who had stayed loyal to him through it all, even though he had deserted her. Neither Ranković nor I had commented, looking on this as his own affair, but also recognizing it as his impatience to begin a new life.

Žujović asked, of course, about his only son, Zoran. Zoran was doing well and already had won distinction on the staff of the newspaper *Politika*. After the Cominform resolution, he had returned from his studies in Moscow, and though his father's fate was obviously hard on him, he had sided with our Central Committee. In the top ranks of State Security there was some question as to the sincerity of his stand, but Ranković and I, insofar as I came into it, insisted on his being left in peace. All doubt was subsequently dispelled by his consistently honorable conduct. We told Žujović that he could re-establish contact with Zoran at once. As a boy, Zoran had spent most of the war with the High Command. He was intelligent, courageous, and witty. Sometimes he jested at the expense of us leaders, which was understandable for someone so young who had experienced "great events" at first hand, rather than through propaganda.

A few days later, I went to see Žujović at the Stojadinović villa and read through the statement he had prepared for *Borba*. It was soon published, virtually as he had written it, with perhaps three or four minor changes I had suggested. Žujović also agreed—that was arranged by Ranković—to hold a press conference.

Žujović had raised the question of re-entering the party when Ranković and I had our talk with him. Ranković made no firm promise, but he didn't close the door. "We'll see, after these problems are settled," he said. Soon after his release, Žujović was received by Tito, who gave his word that he would be taken back into the party. After he started working on the *Borba* staff, Žujović saw me several times at the Central Committee and invariably raised the question. I brought it up at a meeting of the Secretariat, which Tito attended. But Ranković opposed it, and for some reason Tito and Kardelj went along.

Yet Žujović managed to return to the fold, most likely after Ranković's fall in 1966. He died a party member, as was evident from the eulogies delivered at his funeral, though the speaker for the League of Communists did not neglect to mention over the bier his "inconsistency" at the "decisive moment" in 1948. Even so, Žujović was unquestionably a consistent revolutionary and Communist.


Our parting of the ways with Blagoje Nešković took a different form, though for him it had the same painful consequences.

Nešković was secretary of the Serbian Communist party and at the Fifth Congress was voted into the Politburo, even though he was known to have an ambiguous view of the Soviet confrontation. Following the congress, his differences with the Politburo on that issue grew more frequent and more emphatic. The inner circle around Tito concluded that for Nešković to remain at the head of the government and party in Serbia could have unpleasant consequences. Therefore, he was offered—forced into—a new and seemingly more important position, that of chairing the Control Commission, which Kardelj had handled previously. A disciplined party man, he took it on, albeit against his will.

Gradually, Nešković grew isolated. There was so much rumor in the top echelons that leading comrades avoided even the most trivial contact with him. True, he had a share in this himself. He was hard and inflexible, and sometimes gave vent to his own "more moderate" views on our relationship with Moscow. At the beginning of 1949, in an article for the journal *Komunist*, he quoted Stalin—something no one in the top ranks did any more. I pointed this out to him but he insisted that the quotation remain, because it was the best, most succinct formulation of the concept of control.

I had never doubted Stalin's intelligence, but our argument about the quote drove me to think harder about the quotation itself. It was one of those truisms that have come down to us from the Pharaohs, if not Neolithic man, to the effect that control consists of setting a mission, overseeing its execution, and accepting the results. Pointing out to Nešković the banality of this "brilliant" thought of Stalin's, I deleted it. Kardelj agreed. Then, in the summer of 1949, Nešković expressed to Ranković his disagreement both with my speech in Montenegro on the anniversary of the July 13 uprising and with the speech by Moša Pijade in Belgrade in which he said: "Yugoslavia wants to be neither a Russian province nor a Western colony." To make matters worse, Nešković's wife, Brana, was pro-Soviet.

Nešković was tough and alone in his toughness; he was the captive, if not the slave, of his thinking. He had no contact with the

Soviet embassy, nor with Žujović and Hebrang. This intransigence was the rule with him, not an exception. It showed while
he was head of the government of Serbia, for example, in the
carrying out of the compulsory purchase of foodstuffs and the
standardization of prices, the brunt of the burden of which was
borne by Serbia. That episode caused him to be suspected of
nationalism, though he was no more nationalistic than anyone
else.

Bad relations with Nešković—the suspicion and ostracism and
his own defiance and intransigence—continued until just before
the Sixth Congress. At the end of the summer, a party commission
was formed, consisting of Ranković, Moma Marković, and, as
chairman, myself, to investigate Nešković. The outcome was
foreordained. We had two or three prolonged, futile conversations
with him. Ranković kept insisting that he had to be "broken,"
implying no doubt a confession and penitence. I was against it.
But even had I been for it, it would have done no good: Nešković
was driven easily to tears but not to remorse. Our charges against
him were flimsy, and he conceded only that he had a different
approach to the Soviet Union.

On the eve of the Sixth Congress I proposed writing a letter to
Morgan Phillips, secretary of the British Labour party, to acquaint
him with the details of the Nešković case and thus avoid mis-
interpretations that could embroil us in polemics. I was given the
green light. After reading my letter, Phillips asked: "Will this man
be arrested?" Told that he would not be, Phillips accepted the
information without further argument. At the congress, Nešković
was expelled from the party. When I delivered my report at Tito's,
I suggested a government pension for him at the ministerial level.
It was my distinct impression that Tito would have agreed if
Ranković had not objected. So Nešković, who was a doctor, was
sent back to the laboratory where he had worked before the war.


Our differences and squabbles with Radovan Zogović and Stefan
Mitrović in Agitprop and on the Central Committee escalated.

Ranković and I hoped that in time they would overcome their crisis of conscience—Zogović in particular—and see the falsehood in Moscow's accusations, especially as the Soviet campaign daily grew more hysterical and menacing. But that campaign had a twofold effect: those who believed in our cause turned bitter and hard, while those who stuck with Stalin grew frightened and harassed.

Differences of opinion with Zogović and Mitrović arose daily, and personal relations soon became intolerable. Everyone in Agit-prop and the other Central Committee agencies shunned them, and some, like Dedijer, blew up at every opportunity. I remember a quarrel I had with Mitrović soon after the Fifth Congress. I no longer recall how it began, but he tried to prove that the most important struggle now was against imperialism. No one disputed the "struggle against imperialism," but to give priority to this struggle, to bring Agitprop to bear on it, at a time of insane and shameless attacks on us, when our own ranks were wavering, would have dissipated our strength. Furthermore, behind his stand lay a crafty tactic: to catch the leadership (in this case, me) in some inconsistency in our stand on capitalism, and so lead us all onto thin ice. His insistence was groundless; we leaders and the media continued to take a firm and unequivocal stand toward imperialism, and supported the Soviet Union and the other Communist parties. Zogović, on the other hand, behaved more openly, insisting on popularizing "socialist" culture while stamping out and stigmatizing decadent capitalist culture.

Toward the end of 1948, the situation became insufferable, and the Politburo decided that Kardelj, Ranković, and I should have a talk with Zogović and Mitrović. The meeting was held at Kardelj's villa. Neither acknowledged endorsing the Soviet accusations and views, but their positions on individual questions showed that they in effect did accept the bulk of the Soviet criticism, and doubted that their country had the strength and potential to build socialism apart from the "socialist community." In these discussions I kept a low profile, as far as their evasions and inconsistencies and my own temperament permitted. I did so because they justified their deviations from the party—as often happens in such disputes—by alleging that I had "something personal" against them.

Members of the Central Committee Secretariat were especially fond of Zogović and wanted to "save" him. When we had briefed Tito, he wondered if he should speak personally with Zogović. He, too, was interested in "saving" a well-known poet of the revolution and of a wartime poem about him that had become very popular. But it was impossible to save Zogović, because— consistent and doctrinaire as he was—he gave not the slightest hint of wanting to be saved, or even of having reservations.

Zogović and Mitrović were expelled from the party but continued to be friends, and the Security forces continued to follow them. In the summer of 1949, Mitrović was arrested while taking a walk with Zogović. According to Ranković, Zogović pulled off his shoe and defended Mitrović; according to Zogović, he himself was struck by the agents. Zogović was allowed to stay at his villa at Dedinje a while longer, but then had to move into a little apartment, where, in addition to various inconveniences, he had to put up with a female State Security agent as a subtenant. That was his story, at any rate. Mitrović was treated much more brutally. He was thrown into prison on suspicion that his release from the camp at Banjica—where he ended up after he was captured by the Chetniks in late 1941 or early 1942—was engineered by the collaborationist secret police, or, worse still, by the Gestapo. Prolonged investigation did not yield the desired results, so Mitrović was sent to the camp on Goli Otok. Since I was a close friend of the Mitrović family, his father came to see me several times, asking that I intercede for his son. This I did with Ranković, but to no avail. Doubts about Mitrović's past were too strong, and served to prove what sorts of "weaklings" and "traitors" had sided with the Cominform.

In the camp on Goli Otok, Mitrović had a mental breakdown, but he still retained an awareness of political circumstances and was able to take care of himself. Dobrica Ćosić recognized him there and offered him a cigarette, but Mitrović replied that, as a traitor, he was unworthy of having one. At his mother's funeral, Mitrović delivered a speech thanking her for having brought up her children for the party and Tito. Zogović scowled, or so the story goes, and when his wife reminded him that Mitrović was mad, he retorted: "Why can't he be mad in some other way?"

The fate of the Mitrović family is one of the most moving, but also typical of the time: the oldest brother, Niko, was executed during the occupation, though he was feeble-minded; one sister, Vukica, was tortured and executed; another sister, Lepa, was executed; one younger brother, Stefan, was expelled from the party because of his poor conduct when in the hands of the royal police and became deranged in prison under the new regime; another brother, Ratko, became a traitor when in the hands of the police; still another brother, Veljko, vanished during an enemy offensive and was presumed dead; and the parents, Ivanica and Ivo, lived to see it all.

Meanwhile, Zogović had been left at liberty. Members of the Politburo, especially Ranković and I, were partial to him and had faith that in time he would "return to the fold." On one occasion, however, when Zogović had again challenged us arrogantly, I told Ranković that he ought to be arrested. I was rebuffed.

His wife, Vera, came to seek my help when she was fearful that she might be arrested for embezzlement. It turned out that her assistant at the publishing house Kultura had engaged in fraud, sometimes using Vera's name, and the Security forces had it in for Vera, though she was entirely innocent. I intervened with Ranković and State Security, and the investigation was suspended.

When Zogović's apostasy was in the open, but before he was expelled from the party, Krleža stated in my presence that he would continue seeing his friend. I never criticized his intention, but Krleža evidently had second thoughts and did not visit Zogović after all. Nevertheless, he obtained permission—through Tito, naturally—to have Zogović published, after an unofficial but total ban of fifteen years.

At the end of the summer of 1948, after the Fifth Congress, I was at Lake Bled with Tito, Kardelj, and Ranković. Tito told me that Krleža and Josip Vidmar, the Slovenian critic and playwright, had asked if someone from the Politburo would talk over with them the confrontation with Moscow. "Go see what's up. Find out what's cooking in those intellectual minds," said Tito. He was concerned, but also mildly ironic.

So I went to Vidmar's villa, arriving early in the afternoon. I was dazzled by the elegance and refinement of the place, which had belonged to a wealthy man, a Nazi collaborator who had been executed; it was near Tržić, with an open view all the way to Ljubljana. We started our discussion immediately and continued through dinner and late into the night. It was an endless, incredible discussion, a surprise even to me, a Communist intellectual accustomed to long arguments. One hypothesis gave way to the next, and we concluded that the Soviets would not intervene. "But what if they do?" asked Krleža. "We'll fight," I replied. "Yet the prospects for prolonged resistance—successful resistance—are not good, are they? What then?" "We'll withdraw to the sea and the islands." "And after that?" "After that, to the west." "I am going with you," Krleža announced. "I've lived through one occupation too many."

When I returned to Bled the next day, Tito asked, "Well, how was it?" My answer was brief: "They are not wavering. They hate Stalin more than we do!" Tito laughed, and Kardelj said he had thought as much.

In late 1949, a group of Ljubljana intellectuals exploited the tense atmosphere to create a little confusion. From a party given by the actress Sava Severova, they telephoned Vidmar and a number of officials in the name of State Security, and told them that the Russians had invaded us, everybody must be at the airport within an hour. People rushed around, packed frantically, and as they were about to drive out to the airport, they learned that it was a false alarm. This incident would have been brushed off as a crude joke if it had not been for State Security, who ferreted out and locked up the ringleaders, some of whom got several years in prison. Kardelj, I recall, was angry over the "provocation," but he couldn't help laughing. Neither our top leaders nor the times they were living through had room for innocent jokes.

Soon after the Cominform resolution, the Russian wife of Colonel Vinko Švob asked to see me at the Central Committee. I have forgotten her name, but remember her appearance and case. We had met in Moscow in the spring of 1944, when I was there as chief of the military mission. She and another young Russian girl had obtained access to our mission through the daughters of the then royal ambassador, Stanoje Simić, who had declared for Tito and expressed his ardent desire to join the Yugoslav Partisans. She introduced herself as a student, which may or may not have been the case, but she certainly was a beauty, with marked Mongolian features and coloring. She also said she was the daughter of a general on special assignment in China. In one form or another, this story was often encountered among Soviet intelligence agents. Her version was later found to be pure fabrication; she was in fact the daughter of a divorced lower-middle-class couple. We did not enlist her in the Partisans, but Švob fell in love with her and soon they were married. Arriving with her husband in Yugoslavia right after the liberation, she quickly gained access to the White Palace and Tito, on the pretext of setting up a library. But she was later transferred, more because of envy than from political motives.

In any case, she appeared in my office in 1948 to lodge a complaint: pressure was being exerted on her to declare herself against the government of her own country, the Soviet Union. I brought the case up before Tito and other comrades, and Tito reacted with genuine indignation: "No one has the right to demand that of her. It would mean we're anti-Soviet!" The others agreed, even Ranković, who was always suspicious. But Security later turned up the fact that this woman, by now the mother of Švob's children, had been a Soviet agent right from the beginning. That doomed the career of her husband, who had been a loyal, brave, far-sighted officer from the ranks of the workers.

In fact, Russian brides of our officers and officials almost invariably turned out to be Soviet intelligence agents, even those who by birth were not Russians but émigrées or the daughters of our own émigrés in the U.S.S.R.

Pro-Soviet naïveté and ideological blindness lulled our vigilance and impaired our self-awareness. It required time, experience, and bitter knowledge for us to wake up and be ourselves. To recall now those Stalinist frauds and effronteries truly fills one with shame. It takes an extraordinary effort to shake off the natural but irresponsible reaction: this is what Russians are like! Yet Russians are a warm, compassionate, tolerant people. Are not these wonderful, exceptional qualities among the very reasons why this marvelous people yields so easily to despots and pretentious secular messiahs?

Learning comes at a high cost in politics—painfully high. Even we at the top did not immediately grasp what dark, unpredictable dangers lay in wait for us and our nation. Not just from external pressures—propaganda and economic and diplomatic boycott—but also from our routed and suppressed domestic Stalinists. Yet there was no large-scale conspiracy: our leaders enjoyed broad support, and our Security services were efficient, thanks to the stubborn and resourceful vigilance of Ranković and his colleagues.

But even in Tito's proximity, among the employees who worked with him daily, there were Soviet agents, whom we had to remove gradually, without attracting attention. Among his personal bodyguards we found officers who planned to wipe out the Politburo with automatic rifles as they were relaxing over billiards in Tito's villa at 15 Rumunska (later Užička) Street. This was never mentioned in the inner circle, lest it create a sense of insecurity and, worse still, undermine the leadership's cult of invulnerability. Kardelj feared wholesale sedition among the troops, which, he used to say, "would discredit us." Tito also was a little afraid of trouble from that quarter, hence our stricter measures with the military than with the party itself. As for me, I was not afraid of anything, trusting State Security, the people, and most of the party membership. I believe that Ranković felt the same.

But if the Soviet intelligence services had no apparent success in hatching conspiracy, it was not for lack of trying. The case of Brana Marković, wife of the onetime party leader Sima Marković, a victim of the Soviet purges, put us on notice. Before the war, Brana had gone, with her husband, into exile in the Soviet Union.

I don't know whether she had any role in her husband's fate, but after the war she came back to Yugoslavia alive and well. Following our confrontation with the Cominform, she urged a certain highly placed general to declare for the Soviets. He agreed to do so, and then told Ranković the whole story. Brana was arrested and sent to a camp, where she was uncommonly obdurate. After her release, I was told, she hanged herself in Belgrade's New Cemetery. What a self-destructive course, what a horrible destiny!

One day during the busy fall of 1948, Ranković asked me to come to his Central Committee office to attend the interrogation of a pilot, a Partisan veteran, who swore that he was innocent of any wrongdoing with regard to the Cominform. I had known this prisoner from the early days of the uprising in Montenegro. A rather tall, powerfully built man, thirtyish, with a heavy, close-cropped head, light brown hair, and strong features, was ushered in. We lost no time in addressing the issues. He swore he had been falsely accused. Tears welled in his eyes as he angrily vowed: "Comrades, give me a bomber and I'll show Sofia and Budapest and Tirana who is a revisionist, who is a traitor. Let me serve my country and my party! Let me die honorably as a soldier and a revolutionary! Comrades, don't let the shame of betrayal and cowardice fall on me."

I would have been even less prepared than Ranković to believe such an earnest appeal, especially since it came from a Montenegrin —and Montenegrins are prone to pathetics and hysteria—had the wretch not been unusually brave during the war, and had he not himself acknowledged the evidence against him. "That's exactly so, comrades. I did say, 'Our comrades ought to go to the Cominform conference in Bucharest!' But what did I mean by that? I, like all honest, uninformed Communists, meant that there would be a friendly discussion in which our comrades would easily prove that it was all a slander by Rákosi, Hoxha, and the like. Anyone who says anything different about me lies like a dog! Just show me the person, comrades, who lied about me and I'll spit in his face right here in front of you."

Ranković told him he would be set free at once, and I agreed. The tears and the vows had disarmed me, still more his war record.

There was only one flaw: he had been a noncommissioned officer in the former royal army, and we tended to be accommodating toward those with such a past history, not having yet observed that a high proportion of Soviet adherents were to be found precisely among former royal army men.

Tears of joy gushed from the prisoner's eyes on hearing Ranković's dispensation. It was painful and embarrassing to see this seasoned soldier and comrade in arms so agonizingly happy, especially because things ought never to have reached that point. But Ranković and I found solace in the thought that, compared to the greater miseries this man might have endured, we had been reasonable and just. Before saying good-by our airman mentioned, as though seeking permission, that before rejoining his unit he would like to go down to Kosovo to get some rest, and reassure his family. Ranković approved, but I felt a flicker of doubt—doubt so weak that I did not express it openly.

A day or two later we were having dinner at Tito's. Informed by Ranković of the pilot's case, Tito declared in exaltation: "We must not be sectarians. We mustn't allow petty suspicions to lead us, like the Russians, into destroying our comrades. We have to give our comrades a chance to correct their mistaken views. Take this pilot, now—he's ready to fly to his death tomorrow, if need be. And yet we play the narrow sectarians!"

But that flicker of doubt had crossed Ranković's mind, too, and, unlike me, he did express it openly, ordering State Security in Kosovo to keep an eye on the man. Security found out that the pilot was actually visiting relatives in Kosovo on his way to escape to Albania. They staked him out. The desperate man broke through the ambush with hand grenades and an automatic rifle, but a second ambush turned him back. The next day they surrounded him in a forest, there was an exchange of fire, and he was killed.

One day in 1949, Vera Obrenović-Delibašić was announced to me at the Central Committee. She was a left-wing poetess whom I had known before the war through Mitra. As a writer she was insignificant, and as a Partisan undistinguished, but I nevertheless felt impelled to help her. She told me her son had been arrested, though innocent, and that he was not well. I consoled her by promising to make inquiries, but added: "I don't believe he's all that innocent. They don't make arrests without some basis." She was stubborn and categorical about her son's innocence, though she herself did not give the impression of sincerely supporting our Central Committee against Moscow. After clearing it with Ranković, I checked into her son's case with State Security. They said he belonged to a small illegal group of "leafleteers" that was trying to broaden its organizational base. I obtained a copy of the verbatim notes from his interrogation, and handed it to Vera when she returned a few days later. "Now, don't tell me he's innocent!" I said. "I had no idea," she gasped. "Instead of talking about his innocence," I continued, "let's see what we can do for him." I informed Ranković, who had the young man released after three or four months. It is of interest that Vera's sister, Mirjana, who was also arrested as a Cominformist, later became a State Security agent. In 1976, she and another female agent decoyed the Yugoslav Cominformist leader Mileta Perović into a trap in Switzerland. Kidnapped and transported back to Yugoslavia, he was sentenced to twenty years at hard labor.

Yet another Vera came to see me—Vera Bakotić, who before the war had been married to General Koča Popović. Her current husband had been taken into custody and placed under investigation. She wanted to visit him and take along some necessities. In jest I said to her, alluding to the rounds of the jails she had made before the war, when Koča was in trouble, "And for you, Vera, it's just like it was before the war. For you, nothing has changed." "Nothing, it seems," she replied with a sad smile. And so I arranged for her to see her husband, although State Security rarely allowed visits to Cominformists under investigation.

One day early in 1949, Mileva Šćepanović came to see me, a fellow Montenegrin and a soldier, six times wounded, of the First Proletarian Brigade from its creation. Her brother Jovo had been taken into custody. He was a judge on the Supreme Military Tribunal, and a school friend of mine. "I don't know what he's done wrong," said Mileva. "There must be something, or they wouldn't have arrested him. But never mind Jovo . . . what's going to happen to his children?" I took her to see Ranković, who knew all about the case. A number of Cominform supporters, including Jovo, had organized a group within the tribunal. Ranković interceded, and Jovo was released, and even given work, though at a much lower rank and outside the military.

Much later—in 1951, after the conflict with the Soviets had been brought under control—a certain woman, a teacher by profession, was announced at my office. My secretary, Dragica Weinberger, listened to her story, but the visitor did not wish to disclose to her "something very important," so I received her. This woman was aggressive in everything—her speech, gestures, make-up, clothes. A poetess, she at first said she wanted me to read her work and recommend it for publication. I urged her to come to the point, whereupon she made a long, emotional speech about her patriotism, her love of her country, and her duty to reveal something that was not exactly pleasant. In short, her husband, another former royal officer, was the radio operator on a plane making flights to the West; outside our country he used the radio to transmit reports to Soviet intelligence.

All of a sudden it was clear to me that she now wanted to get rid of this husband; otherwise, "as a patriot," she would have revealed his activities in 1948, not in 1951. I felt awkward getting mixed up in this business, but, given my responsibility, I had to pass it all on to Ranković and State Security. They bugged her apartment, got her to talk with her husband about his intelligence activity, recorded everything, and sent him off to hard labor. The crowning touch was that the Security agent in charge was seduced by the woman—for which he got a disciplinary fine.

At the end of 1948, Ivan Gošnjak, a Politburo member and Tito's deputy in the armed forces, phoned to ask if I would talk with Sava Zlatić, a prewar Communist who had come out for the Cominform. I had a long conversation with Zlatić. A mild-mannered man of honest convictions, he simply could not take the ferment in the party or stand up to the savage Soviet propaganda. On the other hand, he was incapable of concealing his dissent from the leadership. He tried to prove to me that we could not preserve our independence and ideology if we left the Communist fold, and that therefore our policy toward Moscow, the mainstay of socialism, was incorrect. In rebuttal, I demonstrated that it was a question of our party's being slandered and our economy dominated. "Was our Albanian policy centered on exploitation and subjugation, as Enver Hoxha claims today?" I asked. "Oh, no! Not true at all, as I well know!" he declared confidently, having been our party representative in Albania. But Zlatić was expelled from the party, removed from his high function, and, needlessly, sent to the camp on Goli Otok.

Apart from being a member of the Politburo, I had nothing to do with pinpointing where Duško Brkić, Rado Žigić, and Ćanica Opačić stood in the Soviet conflict. All three had played a prominent role in Croatia, especially during the uprising, and Brkić was organizational secretary of the party and vice-president of the government—the second in command of that republic.

At the end of 1948, Brkić and I toured Slavonia and those areas where we had fought together in wartime. I could see that he was perplexed and somewhat undecided, more with respect to the U.S.S.R. than the Cominform. But I did not attach much importance to it, interpreting his views as part and parcel of his withdrawn, nonideological temperament. Indeed, the decisions of Brkić, Žigić, and Opačić to side with the Cominform matured only gradually and for different reasons, though the three were in contact with one another. Inasmuch as they were Serbs, their actions also sprang from dissatisfaction with our sluggishness in rebuilding those Serbian regions that had been hotbeds of rebellion throughout the war and as such had suffered the most. We did not necessarily conclude that Brkić and Company had turned into Serbian nationalists, but noticed that the only "rebels" in the Croatian Central Committee were Serbs.

Nor did it go unnoticed that in his report to the congress of the Communist party of Croatia, in late November 1948, Brkić failed to mention the confrontation with the Cominform, which by then had become acute. Since these were high officials, and Serbs from Croatia to boot, Ranković—as a Serb and the organizational secretary of the party—headed a commission to investigate their case. He reported that none of the three approved of the way the confrontation was being handled, which meant they were siding with the Cominform. But neither Ranković nor anyone else, so far as I know, suspected them of being connected with the Soviet ambassador or the Soviet intelligence services.

Brkić, Žigić, and Opačić were expelled from the party and sent to Goli Otok. There, Brkić exhibited a rare tenacity. After he was released from the camp, he was rearrested and sentenced again— the last time, in the 1970s, without real cause, I am convinced, simply for not knuckling under. Žigić died in the camp on a hunger strike, proclaiming his innocence and insisting in vain that someone from the leadership visit him.

I cannot judge how much I influenced the writer Mihailo Lalić. We did have a long, frank talk, at his request, and I urged him to exercise restraint in protesting the confrontation and the arrests of Cominformists.

In 1949, Minister of Foreign Affairs Stanoje Simić was replaced by Edvard Kardelj. As the royal ambassador to Moscow in 1944, Simić had declared himself for Tito. In doing so, he underscored the fact that he was closely connected with the top ranks of the Soviet Commissariat of Foreign Affairs. During the era of cordial relations with the U.S.S.R., he was promoted to minister of foreign affairs. But when relations soured in 1948, Simić, with his prewar "bourgeois" mentality, could not find his bearings; furthermore, because of his intimacy and empathy with Soviet officials, he became a trifle suspect. So we had to entrust this important and sensitive position to a strong, noncontroversial person—Kardelj.

Around that same time Koča Popović was involved in an amusing and characteristic incident. He got lost while driving along the Trieste border, and because of bad telephone connections the border guard detained him for a whole summer's day, until Ranković and I, apprised of his predicament, could get him released. In vain did Koča try to convince the guard that he was chief of the General Staff and a colonel-general. At one point the guard commander scoffed, "I have an easy enough time with the lower ranks; it's the colonel-generals who are a pain!" Though

Koča took offense, later on he would cynically gibe, alluding to Arso Jovanović and Žujović: "That border guard wasn't so wrong, you know. Percentagewise, the most traitors are found among the colonel-generals!"


The confrontation with the U.S.S.R. and with the people's democracies and their parties has not yet been properly described or explained. Numerous mysteries remain, not so much factual as psychological and ideological. Here I have related only what I personally experienced and remembered—a piece of the painful, foolish, heroic reality.

# 15

The camp for Cominformists on Goli Otok ("Bare Island") in the northern Adriatic was organized without a legal basis. At first, Cominformists were simply taken into custody and shipped there. A law was passed later covering obligatory "socially useful labor," as the camp activities were innocently designated for official purposes. Moreover, not even the Politburo, or its inner circle, the Secretariat, ever made any decision about the camp. It was made by Tito himself and implemented through Ranković's State Security apparatus.

It was not unusual for Tito, if he was uncertain of unanimity on some issue, to bypass every forum and deal with the comrade in charge, which in matters like this meant Ranković. It should not be assumed that he would have encountered resistance in the Politburo or the Central Committee. No; he simply feared the possibility. Any opposition at all, in view of the shaky legitimacy of the newly elected Central Committee and Politburo, could create further difficulties. If someone rebelled at decisions reached outside any party assembly, it would be easier to deal with him if he had not first spoken up in a sanctioned forum.

Even though I was one of the four Central Committee secretaries, I learned of the decision to establish a prison camp only when I was in Montenegro in the late summer of 1948. A member of the Montenegrin party leadership, Andro Mugoša, told me an order had come through to round up Cominformists to be shipped off to a camp. *To a camp!* I remember how stunned I was, in part because no one had informed me, though I had been in Belgrade two days earlier; in part, of course, because of the form of punishment, odious and infamous.

Reflecting on it, then and now, I came to the conclusion that harsh, radical measures had to be taken against exponents of a pro-Soviet line. They were increasing in numbers, branching out into illegal activities, and appearing where least expected. Tolerating pro-Soviet Communists and sympathizers in a one-party system like ours would have brought about instability and insecurity. In no respect was ours a democratic society, where contradictions smooth each other's rough edges. Freedom for Cominformists amid general nonfreedom would have been interpreted as capitulating to Moscow and legitimizing the pro-Soviet opposition. Above all else, the propaganda emanating from Moscow and its satellites strongly implied that the "sound forces" within our country would be supported by intervention. In such circumstances, indecision and forbearance would have had disastrous consequences, both for our policy of independent development and for those who created it.

In short, then, we had to cripple the Stalinists and Cominformists—initially, perhaps, by setting up a camp, in order to avoid the appearance of confusion and forestall outside intervention that could link up with domestic inner-party opposition. But the way we dealt with those arrested and their families—that was something else again. There was no need to behave as we did. That conduct sprang from our ideological dogmatism, from our Leninist and Stalinist methods, and, of course, in part from our Balkan traditions of reprisal.

But analyses can be left to historians and philosophers. My business is to get on with the tale, a tale of defeat and disgrace, not only for Yugoslav Communism but also for our times and humankind. If the Yugoslav *gulag*, like the Soviet, is explained purely in terms of the "inhuman" or "antihuman" nature of Communism, that is an oversimplified judgment that in its way is just as ideological. Ideology, I think, was only a motivational expression, the appeal to an ideal, justifying the insane human yearning to be lord and master. Sending people off to camps is neither the invention nor the distinction of Communists. People like those of us at the top of the heap, with our ideals and absolute power, are bound to throw our opponents into a camp. Yet if the treatment of the inmates had come up for discussion—if discussion had not been precluded by Tito's omnipotent will—different views would have emerged among us and more common-sense and humane procedures would have been instituted. Some of us were aware of this paradox: a camp must be established, yet to do so was terrible.

After I returned from Montenegro, I remember saying to Ranković, as we drove around Topčider, "So now we treat Stalin's followers the way he treated his enemies!" To which Ranković replied with horror, "Please don't talk about it now!"

Families, too, were mistreated. People were fired from their jobs, publicly "unmasked," hounded out of the party. Pressure was put on wives—successfully, more often than not—to divorce their "traitor" husbands.

Goli Otok, a small island just south of the town of Senj in the northern Adriatic, had been selected by State Security after careful thought and inspection. It was well adapted for security, sitting there in Siberian isolation, unpopulated, inaccessible to any possible Soviet intervention. These positive aspects outweighed the negative: lack of water, utter barrenness, scorching heat, northeast gales. This was to be no vacation, after all, but a place to work and be re-educated.

The inmates were not only to work off their expenses but also "to make a useful contribution." And since Goli Otok was a rock, and this rock was alleged to contain quality marble, the sculptor Antun Avgustinčić was invited to have a look at it. Marble of some sort was indeed found, but to Avgustinčić's regret it was too brittle for sculpture.

Speaking off the record, top Security officials commented on the ironic fact that the highest peak on the mainland across from Goli Otok was called "Marko's Mountain," and Marko was the pseudonym—the second name, as it were—of Aleksandar-Leka Ranković.

At first, those sent straight to Goli Otok were people who had more or less openly come out for the Cominform and the Soviet Union. Persons whom Soviet intelligence had recruited, whether from among émigrés in the U.S.S.R. or people within our borders, were sentenced first and then shipped off to the camp.

All kinds of motives impelled people to side with the Cominform. Some were purely idealistic. They were dogmatists who neither could nor would renounce internationalism. Their self-denial was the outcome of already set preconceptions, of permanent thinking that was inveterate and unassailable. Even if such persons conceded that Stalin and the other Communist parties might be the tiniest bit wrong about Yugoslavia, they argued that this did not justify abandoning the "mother" and "cradle" of the whole movement. Communism, they insisted, never had been immune to error, but, being "scientific," it was self-correcting: loyalty to the final goal always had, and always would, guarantee that mistakes would be corrected and the true path found again. Such dogmatic idealists were, I think, in the minority, but they included a lot of prewar and wartime party members. Those who served Soviet intelligence, I believe, were also dogmatic idealists, though Yugoslav officials then and now consider them to be "corrupted souls" who deserve no sympathy. Idealism and dogmatism were then strongly in evidence among the country's top leaders. Indeed, how could one get embroiled in such a settling of accounts unless convinced he was defending truth and justice—in other words, authentic socialism?

I believe the largest group of Cominformists were malcontents—people disgruntled over their careers, their lack of recognition, and their treatment. These came in two categories, seniors and juniors. There were, naturally, more of the latter, since those who had joined the party during the war and postwar years were in the majority. With the smell of victory in the air at the end of the war and just afterward, careerists of all kinds came crowding into the party to share the power. For them, the Soviet confrontation at first offered easy prospects. But it is "naïve" to assume that revolutionaries are immune to jealousy. Jealousy exists, jealousy of the darkest, fiercest, most violent kind. Jealousy grows rampant with the prospect of victory and a share in power. Jealousy only appears to be the reverse of, and incompatible with, sacrifice and solidarity. For what true revolutionary acknowledges that his comrade is the greater revolutionary? This would be acknowledging oneself to be less devoted, less trustworthy, even less noble. Among revolutionaries, revolutionism and revolution are the highest values. Any scatterbrain, any numbskull who is otherwise an excellent fighter and revolutionary, is easily seduced by this consideration alone into insanely overestimating his services and rights.

Among the Cominformists there were genuinely dishonest men and manipulators who had simply miscalculated. In the camp, they often turned into stool pigeons and tormentors of their fellow sufferers.

Interestingly enough, siding with the U.S.S.R. took different forms from republic to republic, or from nationality to nationality. Montenegrins constituted the smallest republic and smallest group, but in absolute terms they predominated among adherents of the Cominform and Moscow. Next came the Serbs. Numerically, those from Vojvodina, Croatia, and Bosnia surpassed those from Serbia proper. And if the Montenegrins, for they are a part of the Serbian people, are added to the Serbs, the number of Serbian Cominformists so exceeds all the rest that one might view Cominformism as a Serbian phenomenon. Macedonia was not altogether free of it. In Croatia, Cominformists were mostly in the rebellious provinces of Dalmatia; in Slovenia, there were so few as to be hardly noticeable. Such distribution gives cause for reflection. The conflict with the Soviet Union revealed that when people chose sides, ideology was not the only factor, not even a major one; the primary motives were social, psychological, cultural, and historical.

But regardless of any such factor, there is no question that the vast majority of Cominformists would never have been sent to Goli Otok had the proceedings been the least bit legal, reasonable, and undogmatic. People were arrested and committed to the camp for failure to report intimate "Cominformist" conversations or for reading leaflets and listening to the short-wave radio. Subsequent victims included those who at the time of the resolution said that we ought to have attended the Bucharest meeting at which our party was condemned.

This excessive, uncompromising, barbarous procedure resulted from the belief that Cominformism had to be torn up by the roots. No such position had been adopted by any party forum—Tito adopted it. He was the highest forum, if not the only one, especially in matters of this kind. Both his Soviet, Stalinist experience and his own ambition told him that, once the revolution was over, only internal party opposition would threaten him and the state. In the fall of 1948, he exploded more than once with "Off to jail with him—off to the camp! What else can he expect if he works against his own party?"

The prisoners were often subjected not merely to indifference but also to bureaucratic whim. There was no time limit on investigation. They sometimes languished two years and more before their cases came up. Our new revolutionary regime had preserved the jail system of past generations, and added to this all that it had learned from the torture and suffering of revolutionaries in royalist and wartime prisons.

But on Goli Otok, prison regulations in force elsewhere had no validity. New and foolproof methods were applied to the new intraparty enemy. A task was set, a principle established: the prisoners on Goli Otok were to be "re-educated." Tito took credit for this in public.

In 1949, especially after the trial of Rajk in Budapest, it finally became clear to us at the top that the extermination of the various anti-Stalinist party opposition groups in the U.S.S.R., including the Yugoslav emigration, had taken place under false pretexts. Stalin obviously had intended the fate of Rajk to be ours as well. In this connection Tito said at the time, "The oppositionists needed a few knocks on the head, but why take their heads off?"

This nuance of his—on the head but not off with it—explains why so few Cominformists were killed. But it also became the basis for unimagined, unheard-of coercion, pressure, and torture on the island. There, re-education, or "head-knocking," was made the responsibility of certain inmates—the "reconstructed" ones— who in effect collaborated with Security. The latter involved itself as little as possible, leaving the re-education to "self-managing units" made up of reconstructed inmates, who went to inhuman extremes to ingratiate themselves and win their own release. They were inventive in driving their fellow victims similarly to "reconstruct" themselves. There is no limit to the hatred and meanness of the new convert toward yesterday's coreligionists.

Sentences to Goli Otok were imposed by the Security organs. By law, no term could exceed two years, but there was no limit on its renewal. Inmates who languished there for ten years were not uncommon.

On his passage to the island the prisoner was shoved—in fact, hurled—to the bottom of the boat. Then, when he emerged on Goli Otok, he had to run the gauntlet. This was a double line of inmates, who vied with one another in hitting him. If gouged eyes were a rarity, broken teeth and ribs were not. There were also incorrigibles, who were subjected to lynching, sometimes spontaneous, sometimes not.

The inmates had no visitation rights. They received neither letters nor packages—at least not in the early period. Until word leaked out unofficially, their families had no idea where they were; letters were addressed to a number, as to soldiers in wartime. Their labor was not only hard and compulsory, but often meaningless as well. One of the punishments was carrying heavy stones back and forth. Work went on in all kinds of weather. What stuck in their tormented memories, as I can well understand, was laboring on rocky ground in scorching heat. State Security got carried away with making a productive enterprise out of Goli Otok, for this was the period when the Security bosses were tinkering with our economy and founding export firms; yet nothing came of this "production" but suffering and madness. Then, when finally released, inmates were sworn to silence about the camp and its methods. This could have been taken for granted, yet little by little the truth came out anyway, especially after the fall of Ranković in 1966.

No one at the top level knew about Goli Otok in all its horrible detail, not even Ranković. But no one at that level can be exonerated either, since we all suspected at least part of the truth, if only because we all knew of the treatment of families. Furthermore, public recantations had come flooding in from the camp.

I had been against publishing these testimonials. We had no need of such assistance, I thought, and they reflected badly on us for extracting them. I must admit that my opposition lacked firmness and was inadequately argued. Close as he was to me, Kardelj was all but indifferent to the question, but Ranković—leaning, of course, on Tito—insisted on publishing the recantations, because they would demoralize the Cominformists. And so they were published.

After my return from the United States and a United Nations session in 1949, in a meeting at Tito's I proposed that the Goli Otok camp be closed down and that those who were indictable be turned over to the courts. Kardelj was the first to oppose this: "We need this camp desperately right now." Ranković, too, was opposed: there were far too many Cominformists for us to cope with them through the courts. According to what he said later, around 12,000 passed through the camp. Tito, with a hesitant expression, vetoed my proposal as premature. He had no confidence in our judiciary.

Characteristic both of the time and of the relationships then unfolding was the attitude of the press, Eastern as well as Western, toward the camp. The Western press by and large showed no interest in it, certainly no critical interest. The same could be said of the Western diplomatic corps. Whenever the persecution of Cominformists came up, as if by agreement these diplomats displayed a tacit understanding: our independence and the state were threatened by a combination of external and internal pressures. But there was also a note of ambiguity, of malicious joy behind the Westerners' façade of understanding: let the Communists exterminate one another and so reveal the very nature of Communism. A Parisian organization opposed to concentration camps requested a visit to Goli Otok. I felt they should be allowed to go, and the Security chiefs reluctantly agreed. I believe the visit did take place in 1951 or 1952, not on the island itself but at some highway work site, with the usual prior admonitions to the prisoners.

Both East European propaganda and Cominformist propaganda of our exiles passed over in silence the camp on Goli Otok, while abounding in the most senseless and shameless lies about our country. With the help of Soviet branch offices (*Vidali* in Trieste, *L'Humanité* in Paris, for example), the propaganda of the Communist parties—automatically, without exception—took up Moscow's stereotyped theses and forced them on the parties, with the obligatory promiscuous besmirching of our leadership and country. Not even during the civil war had our class adversaries—counterrevolutionaries!—spoken and written with such distorted, mendacious, murderous invention—invention directed against a Yugoslav leadership composed of yesterday's comrades, who hardly differed from the slanderers themselves. For the wartime counterrevolutionaries we Communists had been "bandits," foolish atheists estranged from our own people, who by premature armed attacks provoked the occupation forces into butchering the populace. They had seen us, too, as "agents of Moscow" who forced people to share everything, including pots, pans, and wives. These class enemies had slaughtered Communists without stint or mercy, even while marveling at our courage and sacrifice.

But for Moscow and the Cominformists, we were transformed overnight into former agents of the Gestapo, hirelings of America, fascists, and warmongers. Our unparalleled four years of fierce resistance to the invader were slandered; a great revolution carried out by a small people was dishonored; a shameful traitor's death was planned for its leaders and for hundreds of thousands of Communists and patriots. I will not say that our own propaganda was untainted by exaggeration, delusion, extravagance, and error—we were cut from the same cloth, forged of the same alloy. But the tone of our leaders' speeches was principled and dignified.

Our own propaganda rapidly became specific and critical. The journalists of *Borba,* which then had the greatest circulation and was regarded as the most competent and reliable newspaper, especially came into their own. Among these were Bogdan Pešić and Jaša Almuli, who managed to find the right ironic tone and the right form, concise and factual. Their writing, avoiding clichés and unencumbered by theorizing, enjoyed an enormous, vital, and impressive influence.

The Cominformist émigrés in Moscow, who were in a privileged position vis-à-vis other émigrés, such as, for instance, the Spaniards, were dismayed that no brochure about Goli Otok was allowed to be published there. But there was a certain logic in Moscow's inconsistency: though the Yugoslav leaders were frequently accused of wicked, repulsive deeds that had never so much as crossed their minds, Goli Otok was so likely to remind the reader of Moscow's own *"gulag* archipelago" that it was best to drown it in silence. Predictably, Moscow called upon the Cominformists only when it could put them to good use.

The first clear and unsettling warning about Goli Otok came from the writer Dobrica Ćosić. In the summer of 1953, spurred partly by his own anxiety and partly by literary curiosity, Ćosić, with help from me, obtained permission to tour the camp. In September, we both found ourselves at Vrnjačka Banja, where he informed me that conditions on the island were horrible beyond belief. As soon as I returned to Belgrade I alerted Ranković. Ćosić was brought to the Central Committee, and in the presence of Ranković and Kardelj reported more or less what he had told me. Kardelj exclaimed acidly, "I knew that we would end up in some such shit out there!" He was not given to cursing, but when infuriated he would blurt out an obscenity. Ranković ordered an investigation, made a few changes, and substantially improved the situation.

And so the camp remained. It went on for years to come—right into the late 1950s and the early 1960s, when rapprochement with

Khrushchev made it an inconvenience for the regime in Belgrade. Nor, so far as I know, has the law authorizing the camp been repealed to this day. When he gave a speech in Novi Sad occasioned by the arrest of those participating in the Cominform Congress of Bar, Tito threatened to reopen it: "We have a place for them!"

Goli Otok was the darkest and most shameful fact in the history of Yugoslav Communism. Goli Otok was worse than that: it was an unimaginable humiliation. No one who put in time on the island returned whole. Nor do I think that those who ran this camp will ever rest easy. Even though their appalling task was assigned them, they will never be able to justify what they did or exonerate themselves.

# 16

With the end of the war, I was oppressed by fear of lying fallow and missing my true inner calling if, instead of getting back to literature, I let mundane political life suck me into its vortex. As I have mentioned, I even discussed the matter with Tito, reminding him of my desire long before the war started to devote myself to literature. It was too early, he replied, the party needed me. "Arrange your affairs so you can do both." I did reschedule my work hours, but it was no use: political tasks by their very nature cannot be put off. Politics, especially if one takes it seriously, is all-absorbing.

In the summer of 1947, I retreated to Pokljuka, in Slovenia, to a little house spared the ravages of war. There, over about a month and a half, I wrote a novel that had long—too long—been gestating within me, a novel about the struggle and disintegration of a certain clan. I destroyed that manuscript, but later, when I was serving a sentence in prison, the seed grew to become my novel *Under the Colors*.

I finally resolved to end these vacillations between love and duty, literature and politics. Then suddenly the unforeseen, fateful menace of the Soviet Union and Stalin loomed over our party and our country. But if our ideological kinship with Moscow had blinded us to the dangers lurking in our devotion, still less did we suspect the energies the confrontation would release, and the heightened awareness it would generate. I experienced the confrontation as a challenge and an inspiration, the culmination of our revolution. I was certainly not alone in this, but I doubt whether anyone in the top circle experienced it with quite the same cathartic intensity as I. Both instinctively and consciously I grasped that my time had come; I must complete my own integration. It is no accident that even now I look back on that period of my political and intellectual activity as the most fruitful, boldest, and most decisive.

My day-to-day work in the Secretariat of the Politburo and in Agitprop spurred rather than hampered my journalistic activity. Looking through *Borba* three or four years ago, I was astonished by its scope. Very few important events slipped by without my making some comment. Most important—for a proper appraisal of the time, the party, and my work in that period—I set forth on theoretical grounds not only the distinctive features of our experience, but also the nature of the Soviet system, which drove it to attack us. These public statements initiated and deepened the real rift with Moscow. My temperament played only a secondary role. Intellectual restlessness and moral revulsion from Soviet behavior were the crucial factors.

Yet it would be immodest and unjust not to mention the considerable role that discussion played in my activity, especially discussion with Kidrič and Kardelj. My original contribution, to the extent that there was one, consisted in my having articulated the scattered currents and spontaneous reflections appearing here and there in the party and my immediate vicinity. Some inner backlash of resistance to lies drove me to do this. The same trait would later show up far more intensely in my clash with Tito and my critical recognition of what Communism is.

Soon after the Fifth Congress, I came to think of it as a hollow enterprise, despite its strong and spontaneous manifestation of unity. We had failed to probe the essential questions, failed to put enough distance between us and the Soviets in ideology and experience. As I lay awake at night, it dawned on me that in trying to prove our oneness with Stalin and the Stalinists and show how true we were to them, we were walking into a trap. For if all that were true, why then were we not obeying them? Why all the argument? At bottom, I now realize, I was groping for national and revolutionary uniqueness and sensing its vague beginnings, as opposed to the borrowed legacy of ideological identity with Moscow.

But on this score confusion reigned in the party, even in its topmost ranks. Thus, on August 24, 1948, *Borba* published a two-page article by Boris Ziherl, a prominent party theoretician, that dealt with our party but breathed not a single word about the Cominform. Yet those were the very days when our government was sending protest notes to Hungary and Rumania; when all across Yugoslavia protest meetings were held against the Cominform; when I delivered a speech to the activists of the Second Proletarian Division that stressed how we were building socialism with our own forces and in our own way.

In the United Nations at the end of September, Kardelj lent his full support to the U.S.S.R. without mentioning our confrontation, for it was our standing policy to be "anti-imperialist." The Serbian Academy formally met to mark the October Revolution. The newspapers celebrated the sixty-ninth birthday of "the great Stalin." I, on the other hand, was just then completing an article called "On Injustice and False Accusations," which was published in *Borba* on October 2–4, 1948. I wrote it with care and inspiration, and it was typed by Štefica Štefanija-Barić, my temporary secretary, to whom I was now drawn by feelings that went beyond party comradeship.

In that article the claim was first advanced—cautiously, amid eulogy, but in a public and unambiguous way—that Stalin was in the wrong. Yugoslavia had undergone a national revolution, I said, which justified our resistance to falsehood and injustice. Earlier, in a 1946 article, with Kardelj's agreement I had made a tentative claim for revolution, but here the fact was stated openly and boldly. Sensing its importance, I submitted the piece to Tito. After he had red-penciled my criticisms of Stalin, I went to see him and persuaded him to let them stand as written; it was surprisingly easy. I argued that everyone knew Stalin was behind all this, and that the party membership was only confused by our silence. "Good," agreed Tito. "Let it stand. We've spared Stalin long enough."

I was in ecstasy over crossing swords with Stalin and affirming the Yugoslav revolution in one and the same article. The very act of undermining the cult of Stalin confirmed our revolution's essence. Up to this point, the imprecise Comintern and Titoist phrase "war of national liberation" had been used in Yugoslavia to designate the revolution. I had never been convinced that this term precisely expressed our revolutionary process—revolution through a national war. Today, too, I believe that a term pointing up not only the national but also the revolutionary character of our uprising would have served better as a rallying cry and call to arms. The premise of my article—that our revolution was at issue—met with unanimous acceptance, and soon was endorsed by Tito as well. At the same time, widespread questioning of Stalin's infallibility deepened and legitimized doubts about the Soviet Union's "pure" brand of socialism. This was the starting point for criticism of the Soviet system, although it developed at a slower pace than awareness of our revolutionary past.

I continued along this line, sometimes with unexpected results. Invited to speak at the plenum of the Central Committee of Montenegro in January 1949, I stressed that bureaucratic deviations and retreats from socialism must be tracked down in ourselves and in the system we championed. Some in the audience looked aghast and others seemed enraptured, as if their intimations of a higher truth had at last been confirmed. In front of the building where the plenum was meeting, mass rallies had been organized by the Cetinje party committee and, with a great display of energy, by militia and government officials. The leadership prevailed on me to greet the demonstrators. Among them I noticed people—and the loudest ones, at that (for instance, the chief of the militia)—whose hoarse voices were distrustful and whose looks radiated fear and hatred. As it turned out later, the rallies had been initiated by Cominformists, of whom many were sent to Goli Otok.

That was only one side of the confrontation with Moscow, the revolutionary-democratic side. For tactical reasons, though, the press supported and popularized the U.S.S.R. and growled at the NATO alliance. Concurrently there was a "re-Stalinization" —stricter administrative measures for the economy, and a strengthening of the party and political police. The Second Plenum of the Central Committee, convened in early February 1949, initiated and prescribed "greater boldness and a faster pace in setting up collective farms." And so began collectivization—less violent, but just as economically unwise as collectivization had been in the U.S.S.R. We thus succumbed to the "bureaucratic element" in the lower and professional party ranks, but it was also an expression of a petty copycat psychology struggling to prove that we had not betrayed socialism, that we were more zealous and braver than the Soviet Communists.

In his report to the plenum Kardelj generalized from experience and instilled eagerness, but privately he had doubts about the whole undertaking. Just as Ranković, once a decision was confirmed, could earnestly carry out what he did not believe in, so Kardelj could talk himself into a policy. This trait was suppressed or less developed in me. But often I, too, did things that privately I did not agree with. It is unavoidable in politics, where discipline and a critical mind constitute twin building blocks of any policy, even more so when it is revolutionary. In Agitprop I did everything necessary to promulgate the collective farms. It was the one rather important issue where I took no separate initiative, feeling that I did not understand the question well enough, whereas others did.

In the fall of 1951, Kardelj held a meeting at which Vladimir

Bakarić, head of the Croatian government, was present, to take up a proposal made by Ivan Buković to reorganize the collectives. By this time I was skeptical about collective farms and of Buković's proposal. Bakarić was enthusiastic (insofar as he was capable of enthusiasm), and even Kardelj, while uncommitted, thought this might be the "sensible course." But Buković's plan—to introduce economic accountability into the collective-farm system—was an immediate failure: the peasants were interested only in private ownership.

Tito was for collective farms but evinced no great enthusiasm. The Central Committee, on the other hand, was solidly in their favor, many members fervently so. It reflected a bureaucratic frame of mind, plus their conviction that on no account must they "turn off the socialist road." Collective farms were created by compulsion: at first the voluntary principle was strongly emphasized, but as the process gained momentum, less so.

In our country collectivization took a different course from that in the U.S.S.R. To say there was less coercion—though true—would be too simple. Our coercion was more psychological than physical. In Montenegro and Macedonia collectives spread like wildfire. While there had been only two such farms in Macedonia in 1945, by the end of March 1949 there were more than four hundred. In Croatia their number doubled during the first quarter of that year. The example of Montenegro and Macedonia, like that of other backward regions, shows that the greater the poverty and backwardness, the more rapidly did collectivization proceed. In such areas the peasants had nothing to lose, and secretly hoped that the more prosperous regions would support them. Why, then, did collectivization also enjoy a huge success in the richer areas, especially Vojvodina and Slavonia? The explanation can lie only in the pressure exerted and in noisy promises that the farms would be mechanized, would get fertilizer, would benefit socially and culturally, and so on. Peasants in the prosperous regions had already had several years of painful and ruinous experience with compulsory selling. In accordance with arbitrary quotas, they had had to surrender, very cheaply, even what was in short supply

(Kidrič called it "plunder"), and had been mistreated and arrested for noncompliance by the thousands. When Kidrič presented a compulsory-selling plan at a Politburo meeting, Ranković, making notes on his memo pad, groaned, "Another 12,000 arrested!" And the violence involved more than just arrests and mistreatment.

Both higher and lower party ranks had their eye on Vojvodina and Slavonia, since there the ground was level and fertile. It was predicted that collective farms would cause a sudden jump in production, thereby not only solving our food problems, but also creating a surplus for export. Kidrič at that time regarded the Slovenian worker, because of his discipline, and the Vojvodina peasant, because he lent himself to the new collectivist practices, as the most progressive social forces. In Serbia, on the other hand, collectivization had no great success, because of a system rooted in small property, which meant peasant resistance.

The year 1949 was decisive. It brought a change not in our conscious, ideological separation, but in our relationship as a state to the U.S.S.R. and its East European vassals. One after another, the top officials throughout Eastern Europe were arrested and put through a show trial: Kochi Xoxe, Traicho Kostov, Laszlo Rajk, Wladislaw Gomulka, and others. We were presented as the main culprit, the evil genius, the diversionist spy center taken over from the Gestapo by the CIA and all the rest of the imperialist intelligence services.

Then came the collapse of the Greek uprising, for which, in my judgment, Stalin deserves the greatest credit. The Soviet and East European governments broke their treaties with Yugoslavia and imposed an economic blockade. That summer, relations with Moscow further deteriorated because of our alleged persecution of "Soviet citizens," Russian émigrés. Along our borders incidents multiplied, and Soviet and pro-Soviet troops carried out threatening maneuvers. The revolution in China achieved its decisive victory, although, despite our secret wishes and cautious hopes, the new Chinese leadership sided with the Soviets against Yugoslavia.

We undertook extensive measures against attack. These included preparations for both guerrilla and conventional warfare; planned dismantling of factories; building up the domestic armaments industry. Our leadership was conscious of real danger and did all it could to ward it off. Tito made two speeches, marking two decisive moments in our recognition of danger and our defense preparations. At the Third Congress of the Popular Front, on March 9, 1949, he broadly and convincingly explained, with documentation, the pressure and blockade to which Yugoslavia was being subjected. Then, on August 2, in Skoplje, he declared unambiguously that Yugoslavia would defend itself if attacked. Those were days when reinforced troop movements were taking place just across our borders—Soviet troops in Hungary, Bulgarian in Bulgaria.

I went with Tito to Skoplje. En route he seemed neither worried nor irascible, but it all collected inside him overnight and poured out at the meeting. Dimitar Vlahov, an old Macedonian party member, was traveling with us, and when I asked him in the parlor car how they had treated him in a Soviet jail during the purge, he replied, "Beatings, brother, beatings!" Vlahov had been saved by Dimitrov, though under torture he had already confessed to being a Turkish spy—simply because he had been a delegate to the Young Turk parliament before World War I.

We took a great interest in the East European trials, but prior to the trial of Rajk we did not react adequately, with reasoned militancy. We at first made only a mild defense of Kochi Xoxe, so as not to damage him further. And because of mistaken judgment on the part of State Security, we faulted the Bulgarian leadership for not completetly unmasking the imprisoned Traicho Kostov and exposing his "noxious activity." Our argument was that he had been "out to get" Yugoslavia. To be sure, I did follow Xoxe's execution with an editorial in *Borba*, on June 14, 1949, but the gist of it was simply moral revulsion: "Every Communist, every honest fighter for truth and justice, ought to examine his conscience over the innocent sacrifice of Kochi Xoxe." Our other leaders felt the same moral revulsion and confidence in the victory of truth.

When, during those summer days of 1949, the Greek uprising collapsed, we got the blame for it, even though we had continued to help the insurgents until the last day. Both we and the Greek rebel leaders were aware of the danger to their uprising from our confrontation with Moscow, inasmuch as most aid to them originated in Yugoslavia and flowed across our country. Soon after the Cominform issued its resolution, Nicholas Zachariades, secretary of their Central Committee, and another member of that body met Ranković and me in Belgrade. As we had anticipated, he let us know, tacitly, that they would be unable to take our side in the dispute. But we hoped that they would at least not say anything or would somehow take a neutral position. With a somber expression, Zachariades beseeched us, "Keep up the help as long as you can!" We did. But Moscow, acting through its agents and retainers, first replaced Markos Vafiades, their commander, and then forced the rebels to abandon their guerrilla tactics for fortifications and entrenched lines, which was most welcome to the technically and organizationally superior enemy. Back in February 1948, Stalin had all but ordered the Bulgarian delegates and us to wrap things up in Greece, in accord with his agreements on postwar spheres of influence with the Western powers. We knew all that—we had heard it with our own ears. Yet now *we* were blamed for the collapse of the Greek uprising. We were angry, and bitter from our new knowledge that the U.S.S.R. was a Great Power "just like all the rest."

Not setting ourselves strictly apart from the Soviet Union and its so-called socialism encumbered us ideologically and caused us to lag behind. Kardelj, Bakarić, Kidrič, Milentije Popović, and I realized it most clearly at the time, each in his own way. Tito still fought shy of settling ideological accounts with Moscow and was even against it. Before leaving for the UN session in New York in 1949, Kardelj and I tried to persuade him that we had to begin making a deeper ideological critique of the Soviet system, lest our resistance become incomprehensible and lead to chaos in the party. He replied: "We'd find it hard to cope with them. They know all the right quotations." "Well, we can quote a thing or two ourselves," I shot back. Tito gave in, and later helped square accounts ideologically with the Soviet system in his own simple, succinct way.

Trying to grasp why the Soviet leaders were behaving as they were, neither I nor the other party theoreticians could be satisfied with what we called "vulgar, bourgeois" explanations: that it all sprang from Russia's backwardness and the totalitarian nature of the Soviet system. An article by Milentije Popović for the periodical *Komunist,* which I helped edit, though the basic ideas and structure were his, showed that relations between socialist states could not be equal if based on the exchange of money and goods. As minister of foreign trade—a trade oriented predominantly toward Eastern Europe—Popović was in an excellent position to observe daily practice in this regard. Reprinted in *Borba,* the article was enormously sobering for the party's leading intellectuals. I turned back to Lenin and plunged into his teachings, still believing them correct. Just as Popović had discovered that inequity was unavoidable in the economic relations of socialist states, so I found that Lenin foresaw both conflict and hegemony among these same states as long as they existed as states. My original intent was simply to cull some Lenin quotations concerning relations between socialist states, but then, with all my citations lined up thematically, a longish article fell into place all by itself. It was reprinted from *Komunist* in *Borba* on September 5–12, 1949.

In that same summer of 1949, the first "self-criticisms" arrived —penitent testimonials by Cominformists who had once been party officials—those of Voja Ljujić and Bane Andrejev. In some mysterious way, they appeared to be linked with the strain in our relations with Moscow and the ideological maturing of our party leaders.

It was also at that time, if memory serves, that we decided—at Agitprop's initiative—to publish documents from the party and military archives. We were impelled less by false Soviet propaganda than by our certainty that, if the Soviets invaded us, these archives would be destroyed so as to stamp out historic awareness among us Communists. We set to work at once, with intensity, our work going all the more smoothly because a lot had been done already to put the archives in order and preserve them. There were some problems, especially with Tito: for example, he was opposed to publishing those documents where his signature appeared beside that of Arso Jovanović. But Kardelj and I convinced him that it all had to be printed. Dedijer also participated in these efforts, whether directly or not I don't now remember.

Tito was still burdened by the Stalinist habit of publishing only what "did no harm." In 1946, for instance, he was against letting *Komunist* print those portions of the resolution from the Fifth Party Conference of 1940 that attacked Great Britain and France and characterized the war as imperialist. He thwarted the publication of passages from that same conference criticizing the writer Miroslav Krleža, who was then working closely with Tito and the Central Committee. Yet in recent years Dedijer has stated more than once that it was Tito who emphasized the necessity of publishing everything. I don't think that Tito changed his mind, but because his absolute power grew as time went by, he became convinced that nothing would in any case be published that would be "harmful" to him.

Soviet threats and provocations, the senseless accusations against the Yugoslav leadership, and the deriding and boycotting of everything Yugoslav, only quickened our leadership's political and ideological activity. Our feverish, heretical tension did not hamper us, but stimulated our search for new ways, new discoveries. The agitation and unanticipated, fateful danger renewed that closeness and warmth which since the war had become eroded by power and hierarchy. We became more direct, more open and

selfless than we had ever been—even when building a revolutionary party before the war, and during the most frightful wartime
suffering.

In contrast to our prewar and wartime intimacy and harmony,
which entailed fitting into the collective by renouncing the personal, the new Moscow-induced strains and the daily revelation
of horrors and betrayals awoke personal energies, talents, and in-
clinations in each of us. A silent, inner reckoning began with that
"alien," acquired experience and with our consciences, which
were both our own and not our own. The confrontation with the
Soviet Union flared up inside each individual, who discovered
within himself his powers, his self-discipline, and his delusions.
Unwilling and unaware, each thereby gained the right to be more
his own self than he had been, and to marshal all his powers
against the disaster looming over the nation, the leadership as a
whole, and each leader down to his most intimate, most essential
self. By such "individualization"—such free, irresistible expression
of our personalities—we leaders became more collective and
democratic. Tito's role both increased and diminished—increased
as the center of opposition, diminished as the expression of
omnipotence, omniscience, and infallibility. Autocracy gradually
gave way to oligarchy.


The most important event in that summer heat of 1949, while we
were searching our souls and making our readjustments, was the
Soviet note of August 18. This note brutally and unambiguously
threatened the "fascist bullies," as it labeled the Yugoslav leadership and system. Prompting it was our expulsion of Czarist Russian
émigrés who had taken Soviet citizenship. As our dispute with
the Soviets progressed, these émigrés, these new-baked Soviet citizens, had been transformed into an intricate propaganda and
intelligence network. Numbering around 20,000, they formed a
solid, cohesive mass, reminiscent of the pro-Hitler German *Volks-
deutsche*. In the process they affiliated themselves strongly and
openly with the Soviet embassy. At a meeting of the Politburo,

Ranković had declared, "We're totally unable to establish any control over them. They've become an invincible fifth column."

The Yugoslav government proposed many times that the Soviet government take these citizens back, but Moscow turned a deaf ear. Furthermore, the Soviet embassy took under its wing those who had been prosecuted for spying or spreading anti-Yugoslav propaganda. Feeling threatened and having no alternative, our government canceled their residence rights and began expelling those who refused to leave. With few exceptions the Soviet government would not take them back, so most of them made their way to the West or Hungary or Czechoslovakia. These events provoked Moscow's threatening note. In those days, diplomatic notes were not transmitted in the ordinary way, to the minister or the ambassador, but were left with the doorman.

I felt we had to respond to the note, if not officially through the government, then quasi-officially through Tanjug. I therefore formulated a response and took it to Kardelj, then our minister of foreign affairs, for approval. He accepted it almost without change as the official note. Here it is, in abbreviated form:

The government of the Federal People's Republic of Yugoslavia [FNRJ] does not intend to get into a dispute with the government of the U.S.S.R. over the character of the regime in Yugoslavia. . . . However, the government of the FNRJ considers it its duty to point out that the Federal People's Republic of Yugoslavia is an independent and sovereign state and that its peoples and its government are under no circumstances willing to let anyone interfere in its internal affairs. Further, the government of the FNRJ wishes to point out that to date no external pressure has had any influence on its internal policy, nor will it in the future. As regards foreign policy . . . the government of the FNRJ likewise considers it necessary to declare that it carries out this policy in accordance with its country's independence and sovereignty; in accordance with progressive principles of peace and cooperation between peoples and states on the basis of equality and mutual respect for sovereignty; and in accordance with international treaties and obligations which have been and remain a public act on the part of the government of the FNRJ. The peoples of the FNRJ are unwilling under any circumstances to renounce these principles under outside pressure.

The note also urged the Soviet government to take back its citizens, former White Guards, and to return our children and war orphans. At the end of the war these children had been shipped off to the U.S.S.R to be educated in the Suvorov military schools, where instruction begins in childhood. They never returned, nor was it ever established, so far as I know, who had sent them to the Soviet Union in the first place.

Not long afterward, Kidrič and I found ourselves discussing the exchange of notes in Kardelj's office. We were tense and apprehensive, but resolute. "The Russians wouldn't have sent such a note if they were not in collusion with the Americans," said Kidrič. "What else should imperialists be doing but manipulating some agreement at the expense of the little fellows? Greece to the Americans, Yugoslavia to the Russians. That's quite possible." I thought so, too, without expressing it as categorically. Kardelj was more cautious, but even he did not entirely exclude the possibility of a Soviet-American agreement at our expense: "That's hardly feasible today, and yet . . ." Certainly our conclusions were premature and unsupported. But even today I don't put it past Moscow to have been ready to "make a deal"—anything to choke off the "Yugoslav heresy." Moscow failed to find a partner, though. The United States was sufficiently strong and sufficiently anti-Soviet, and Yugoslavia was in a strategic position. Relief was in sight. On September 3, U.S. Secretary of State Dean Acheson and Deputy Foreign Secretary Hector McNeil of Great Britain put Moscow on notice that an attack on Yugoslavia would have serious consequences.

Our press published the Acheson-McNeil declaration without commentary, but conspicuously. We were still wary of being stung by Soviet propaganda with regard to "Western imperialists' " support, but we had to acknowledge the importance, perhaps crucial importance, of such support. We found a way to inform and hearten our readers by taking issue with the Soviet press when it distorted Western press accounts of Yugoslavia and of Moscow's threat to our country. Almost overnight, our thesis about a deal between imperialists of the West and the East at Yugoslavia's expense was demolished.

It must have been my ideological activity that led Kardelj to propose that I be included in our UN delegation; his secondary reason was that he preferred not to be our only leader to engage Moscow in polemics in New York—a strategy that had been decided on after open threats, innumerable border provocations, and the economic blockade. Though I had no experience in diplomacy, it pleased me that I would be speaking out against the Soviet government in the world parliament. We sailed on the *Queen Elizabeth*—Tito was not the only one of our leaders to avoid planes. Besides, travel by ship offered a welcome chance for rest.

Rest, however, completely eluded me. With our foreign affairs staff, I worked on a declaration concerning national rights, to which we attached great significance, but which went virtually unnoticed at the United Nations and in the foreign press. My main burden, though, was two sacks of reports and analyses about education produced by an assortment of commissions under Central Committee supervision. I read from morning till late at night, despite the repetitiveness and triviality of the material. But those sacks—real sacks of waterproof canvas—were pretty big, so I continued reading in New York. I never quite finished the final neatly organized, all-encompassing survey, the product of exhaustive labor by many informed people and countless employees working with one end in view: a school system that would be strong administratively, and well forged ideologically. Tired and ever more dubious, I skipped to the proposals and conclusions. They were, indeed, methodical and consistent. At first glance I liked them, though they seemed too sweeping for the Central Committee resolution to be based on them. Then suddenly I had a flash of insight—I think it dawned on me overnight—that such a mountain of work was unnecessary to determine a Central Committee position. From that critical, "heretical" realization my thoughts spiraled onward. Why, I said to myself, these proposals and conclusions are not only too sweeping and too detailed, but also too inflexible, relying too much on injunctions like "we must," "we ought," "we should," "we are obliged," and "all our might and main." It finally struck me that our whole direction, our whole educational methodology needed to be turned around— and that sack of proposals and conclusions along with it. Instead of schools of indoctrination on the Soviet model, we needed gradually to reconstitute schools along traditional, freer lines. I had spoken earlier with Kardelj about the problem, and when I told him of my sudden change of mind, he took a moment to reflect. Then, as if he had figured something out for himself, he agreed: "That's excellent, that's the way to go. Set it up on that basis." In New York I wrote a paper on the school system, and Kardelj endorsed it on the spot, as did Tito and the others later in Belgrade.

The British delegation and part of the Soviet were also on the *Queen Elizabeth.* Contact was quickly established with the British, but the Soviets would not even let their eyes meet ours, and the way they moved about in a herd and dined in a special room prompted ironic comments on our part. At one point, Ernest Hemingway—or someone who looked just like him—appeared on deck, only to vanish as if swallowed up by the ocean.

Despite all my intellectual intensity, both on shipboard and in New York, I was torn by a wild sense of desolation. I had decided to separate from Mitra, but had not yet made up my mind about Štefica. Before leaving I had quarreled with her—what about, I don't really know, unless it was that, on that long and responsible journey, I wanted to feel still lonelier and more self-sacrificing. I remember so distinctly the endless gray-and-blue expanse of the ocean, which merged in my mind with Štefica's grieving, hurt eyes. Kardelj noticed my dejection and was very considerate toward me, very tender. He knew the reason: before our departure Mitra had been to see him to ask that he use his influence on me—a request he had courteously declined.

I was not impressed by America's standard of living and technology, probably because for me human and social relations were far more important. Such priorities went back to my childhood, before Marxism came to dominate my consciousness. But America did strongly influence the direction of my thoughts, and not mine alone, I am sure. Something must be wrong with our Marxist teachings, I thought, if a country so well developed and with so large a proletariat was not socialist, and if that proletariat was actually antisocialist.

At the end of September, Kardelj gave his speech at the United Nations. He had worked on it carefully, consulting his comrades. Our main criticism concerned its length. In balanced, unambiguous terms, he set Soviet conduct toward our country officially before the world for the first time. He emphasized that this was not a question of a superficial ideological argument, but of hegemonic tendencies threatening Yugoslavia's independence. The Soviet delegation, headed by Andrei Vyshinsky, assumed a condescending attitude toward our position, which they were incapable of following through because they could not refrain from profanity. Suddenly, through our own case, Soviet foreign policy stood revealed to us in all its unreality. The performance of Dmitri Manuilsky would have been comic had it not been so pathetic: all that remained of the onetime leader and great orator of the Comintern were trite phrases and cheap theatricality—an old man foaming at the mouth. That must have registered with the Soviet leadership, for after this UN session Manuilsky vanished, like so many others, into the bottomless pit of Stalinist violence.

While we were still on our way to France from Yugoslavia, en route to New York, news reached us that General Peko Dapčević had stated that he wouldn't say no to having an atom bomb in his possession. Anyone who knew Dapčević also knew that the remark was made in jest. But Kardelj flared up. "That's all Vyshinsky needs, to start yelling 'Who would the chief of Yugoslavia's General Staff like to use his atom bomb against?'" That was exactly what happened. Vyshinsky soon repeated word for word what Kardelj had said. We had no trouble slipping into the skin of a Russian and predicting his reaction, but the Russians for their part knew exactly what we were saying to one another, having planted an informer in our midst in the person of our translator, a Russian émigré who passed Kardelj's words on to them.

In mid-November, I gave a speech to the UN political committee that was entirely devoted to Soviet pressures and attacks. Since Soviet delegates, especially Vyshinsky, made generous use of quotations from literature and examples from history, it occurred to me—not without malice, I confess—to read them the fantasies uttered by Nozdrev, the untrammeled liar in Gogol's *Dead Souls*. With a wicked grin, Kardelj went along with my plan. The result was laughter among the delegates and sour looks from the Soviet representatives. Vyshinsky cast me a glance of the most delicious murderous hatred, which all but said aloud, "Just wait till we get our paws on you . . ."

There was no response at all to my speech in the American press, and hardly any to Kardelj's. At one reception I asked an American reporter—from the *New York Times,* I think—why they were not publishing our refutation of the slander that Rajk spied for us and we spied for America. "We write from our own country's point of view" was the answer. It was clear to us that the American press printed the Soviet slanders but suppressed our rebuttal in order to deepen the rift between us and Moscow. They were aiming for a "truer" exposé of the "Communist jungle." But the *Times* did publish my account of my talk with Dimitrov at the Topčider railway station, when he encouraged us to stand fast in our clash with Stalin. That was new and interesting, and fit in with their country's "point of view."

But if the press ignored us, the diplomatic corps did not. We received so many invitations to receptions and meetings that we could just barely handle them. At the opening of the General Assembly—our delegates had already taken their seats—Ernest Bevin, the British foreign secretary, came up to us. He warmly gripped Kardelj by the hand and held on for a long time, so photographers could record the scene and the Soviet representatives get a good look. Like Bevin, Kardelj smiled warmly. I had the impression that Kardelj was not too comfortable with such a sudden, excessively cordial encounter, but that he was conscious of its importance. By now we had learned to live with the Soviet leaders and their criticism, but we were still anxious not to be perceived as "abetting capitalism and imperialism."

The most interesting and striking person we dined with was Canadian Minister of External Affairs Lester Pearson. In UN circles he was considered one of the most intelligent of Western diplomats—and rightly so. Half in jest, he remarked, "I don't suppose I'll ever be a Communist, but if I were, I'd be a Yugoslav Communist!" Regarding the Soviet Union, he said: "The Russians have the atom bomb now, but we Westerners are stronger. We could occupy them, but it would demand enormous sacrifice and who'd know what to do with them? They're such awful nationalists, they'd never simmer down."

The press may have remained indifferent to the Soviet-Yugoslav dispute, but at the United Nations it took center stage, especially after we were put up for membership in the Security Council. Kardelj had raised the idea in Belgrade, in the Secretariat, and Tito had agreed at once. There now began a bitter backstage struggle, the climax to which came after the first vote. The Soviet delegation did everything to block our election, from public accusations about charter violations and a "gentlemen's agreement" to surreptitious blackmail and threats. But our people were backed by the United States, and through the latter (then dominant at the United Nations) got the support of Latin America as well, which, with its large number of votes, tipped the balance in our favor. We realized that this was a victory on a world scale, not just for our little country, but for a great principle. I wrote an article about it in New York, which was immediately published in Yugoslavia.

With Veljko Mićunović, I took a trip to Niagara Falls and to a Ford Motor Company plant. With Kardelj, on the eve of departure, I visited Washington. Kardelj took the opportunity to meet the new American ambassador to Yugoslavia, George V. Allen. "A typical American professional diplomat," reported Kardelj, "self-confident and intelligent." Allen had answered Kardelj's inquiry about loans by suggesting that Yugoslavia seek American aid. Kardelj thought it over and said to us, "That might be the most sensible thing to do. We're in big trouble economically."

On our national holiday, November 29, the Cominform characterized us as "fascists" and "murderers" and accused us of yet another definitive shift into the "imperialist camp." At the beginning of December, they offered yet another resolution which was predictable, after our election to the Security Council—but it only elicited our mockery. Stalin and the Soviet leadership were living in the past.

I wanted to return home by plane, but Kardelj would have none of it. We sailed on the *Ile-de-France*; it was not big and pompous like the *Queen Elizabeth*, but cozier and less formal.

I did not find Mitra at home; taking what she considered essential with her, she had moved to a smaller villa. I went over to Ranković's home with little presents for his wife, Slavka, and their children. There I found Štefica, probably at Slavka's invitation. The visit over, I was going to drive her to her apartment on Vojvoda Dobrnjac Street, but stopped first at my home to present her with a little ring I had bought for her in New York. She was delighted. All this time I had been thinking of her, and now the crucial moment had arrived. The thought of marriage was no longer strange, though we left it unsaid.


Toward the end of December 1949, soon after our return from the United States, a Third Plenum was held; education was the main topic. The majority viewed this plenum as a significant milestone, if not the decisive one, in our departure from Soviet ideology and methods. In my paper I posed the issue thus: "The problem is therefore not so much what kind of person we wish to create as what method will produce the best results." In the adopted resolutions, which I also drafted, Marxism was no longer a special, separate subject. We insisted that instruction be truly scholarly, especially on the topic of Marxism. Russian no longer had priority; there was now freedom of choice between that language and other foreign languages (English, German, French).

It would be grotesquely inaccurate for any one person to claim credit for the success of that plenum. I could not have given such a democratic paper had not Kardelj and, later, Tito supported me.

Nor would such "heretical" thoughts ever have crossed my mind had it not been for Soviet pressures, fierce and terrible, to say nothing of the passionate, sobering, creative discussions among the party leadership. My merit, for what it was worth, lay only in comprehending and formulating the ideas simmering around me.

One need only glance at the election speeches of Tito, Pijade, Kidrič, and others at the beginning of 1950 to realize that our prevailing tendency, though it varied individually, was to discard Soviet methods and reinvestigate our own. Otherwise my speech to our students on March 18, 1950, would have been inconceivable. Given the audience, I made it as learned and complex as possible, expounding the thesis that in the Soviet Union the state's monopoly of production had turned into a monopoly of society, and that we, the Yugoslav party, were the Hegelian antithesis of the Soviet system.

Democratization was neither simple nor easy, nor did it enjoy courageous or unanimous support. Even the watershed of the Third Plenum had its bureaucratic and Stalinist side: "We must strive earnestly," said the economic resolutions, "to consolidate the existing collective farms." This inconsistency of theory and practice was widespread in daily economic life. While still insisting on collectivized agriculture, in industry and trade we had already taken the first radical steps toward decentralizing and strengthening the free marketplace. The most resolute and penetrating advocate of this policy was Kidrič, whose energy was admirable. Perhaps even more than I in matters of ideology, Kidrič had the support of Kardelj, who continued to bear the greatest responsibility for the functioning of our state and our society.

I was drawn to Kidrič less by interest in the economy than by his critical powers of reflection, so akin to my own. This in turn eventually aroused my interest in the economy, though I did not develop any deep, concrete understanding of the subject. Lacking the necessary training, I looked at economic relations (and still do) as one aspect—perhaps the most important one—of human relations generally. My occasional initiatives in shattering Leninist economic dogmatism stemmed from this outlook. With time I came to realize that Marxism is a social philosophy, not a recipe for regulating that delicate, unstable thing, the economy. Busy though Kidrić was, he welcomed my interruptions. One winter evening in 1950, I looked in on him at the Planning Commission. As we chatted, he boasted of getting daily progress reports from all Yugoslav factories, businesses, and building sites. "Not even the Russians have managed that—they get only monthly reports. Two truckloads a day!" he added. "But who reads them?" I asked. "We have comrades for just that purpose." "How many does it take? And who are they? Are they qualified? What happens if one day somebody hasn't met his production quota?" Kidrič, a little uncertain of his ground by now, began to explain. I retreated, but a few days later he phoned me. "You know, those daily reports from every enterprise are the purest bureaucratic idiocy—a hopeless job. The two or three employees assigned to them can't get through even a fraction of the material." His recognition of this folly of the planning mentality was one of the reasons he changed the whole system. We began instead planning for a balanced economy. With droll cynicism, he greeted every new "free market" decision with the remark, "Fine—one more capitalist measure!"

Kidrič had a wide-ranging intelligence and, for one with a technological background, a broad education. Once he adopted a certain plan, he carried it through with passionate, tempestuous energy, overlooking what was secondary or brushing it aside. This trait, bad for a statesman in peacetime, could be precious and decisive for a revolutionary, and we were still operating under revolutionary conditions. These characteristics of Kidrič—his intelligence and energy—laid the foundations on which the Yugoslav system rests to this day.

By late 1949 and early 1950, theoretical thinking among our top people not only had abandoned Stalin, but also was working its way back to the roots, from Lenin to Marx. Kardelj maintained that one could prove anything with quotations, but that it was impossible to separate Lenin from Stalin completely. After all, Stalin was an outgrowth of Lenin.

As we made our way back to Marx, we often paused in our critical ponderings on the Leninist type of party. It was not only the source and instrument of victory, but a means of moving on after power had been seized. In accepting Marx's theory of the withering away of the state—and the more decisively we broke away from Stalinism, the more firmly we believed Marx on that point—we realized that such withering away required a change in the role of the party. Yet in the domain of party problems, progress was minimal and slow. We kept running up against a solid wall of ossified functionaries and a layer of party bureaucracy already formed and consolidated.

Once again I began working through *Das Kapital*, intent on finding the source of truth, namely, the "heterodoxy and errors" of Stalin and Lenin. My social interest in the economy merged with my study of Marx. In my ruminations, no small role was played by keen discussions with Kidrič and Kardelj, and by the bureaucratic impasse in which our economy found itself.

And so, as I perused in Marx those passages dealing with a future "association of immediate producers" as a form of the transition to communism, it occurred to me that our whole economic mechanism might be simplified by leaving administration to those who worked in the enterprises, the state only securing for itself the tax. One rainy day in late spring, while we sat talking in a car in front of my villa, I presented this idea to Kardelj and Kidrič. Both thought it premature. At the same time, trade union officials meeting with Kardelj proposed, among other things, discontinuing the workers' councils, which had long existed as anemic, purely advisory forms. Kardelj, however, urged that the councils be strengthened. Then one day Kidrič phoned me: "You know that idea of yours—now might be the moment to introduce it." Kardelj was to link my idea to the workers' councils.

In the ensuing discussion on self-management, Kardelj played the crucial role, both creative and practical. We believed that at last we had discovered the definitive path to the withering away of the state and a classless society. When we presented this in the National Assembly's Hall of Ministers, Tito at first was opposed: "Our workers aren't mature enough yet." But Kardelj and I would not give in; work on the legal structure had already begun. Tito generally kept out of the discussions of theory, because he was preoccupied with other matters, elevated in rank, and not given to theorizing. But on this occasion, after pacing about for a bit, he exclaimed excitedly, "But this is Marxist—factories to the workers!"

Kardelj and the rest of us attached great importance to the Fundamental Law on Management (that is, self-management); we thought it a historic turning point. Tito adopted it and then, as the most responsible leader, defended it in the Assembly on June 26, 1950. He emphasized that it could have been worked out earlier had we attuned Marxism-Leninism more to our own conditions and been less receptive to obsolete Soviet formulas.

The day we began our discussion of the law on self-management, war broke out in Korea. We were sure that Stalin and his government stood behind this adventure. In our press we took the side of North Korea, but also carried reports from the American side and long hesitated to define our official position. Meanwhile, Bulgarian troops began building up along our borders, and incidents multiplied. These did not, however, cause as much fear or concern as they had the previous summer. Quite by chance I heard the chief of military intelligence, General Srećko Manola, say that the Cominform armies massing on our borders fell far short of the number required for intervention in Yugoslavia. Our army's intelligence reports on the troop movements, strength, and disposition proved amazingly accurate.

Even so, the chief of the General Staff, Koča Popović, was in a ticklish position. Although he bore enormous responsibility, he lacked reliable official evaluation of the situation. I suspect he felt uncomfortable going to see Tito, expecting to be told that he, Koča, should worry about his own business, and others would worry about intelligence. He and I were close, so he invited me over to headquarters one afternoon for a talk. "The responsibility is mine; yet I don't know how our leadership evaluates the situation. Is the Politburo aware that our army is so ill-equipped that if the Soviets attacked, it would disintegrate into guerrilla units within a few days?" The Politburo had not discussed the matter,

I told him, but the prevailing opinion was that it would not come to an attack, which didn't mean we should not bend every effort toward preparing a defense.

To clarify our propaganda, I urged that we take an official stand on the war in Korea, but the question was put off to the fall, partly because Kardelj was on vacation. On September 6, he at last issued a statement, bearing the marks of our collaboration. The aggressor might have been defined more precisely, but Moscow was labeled a direct instigator with no interest in the freedom of the Korean people, which was enough for propaganda purposes and party orientation. Incidentally, General Dapčević made a forecast—right on target—that the Americans would hold a bridgehead in the south while launching a counteroffensive from the flank.

We had now made a complete turnabout and were publishing news and information from the West, along with speeches of their statesmen. A similar turnabout had also occurred in contacts with Western representatives, particularly socialists. I remember attending (Kardelj being out of Belgrade) the Bastille Day reception at the French embassy in 1950, and how the diplomats listened, and with what sharp curiosity and approval, to my report on self-management and further democratization. Yugoslavia was setting out on a new democratic path, or so it seemed to most people, and certainly to the majority in the top ranks. Many were our illusions and self-deceptions—which is inevitable in any idealization of one's own experience, particularly of revolutionary experience. The party bureaucracy, pressed from without and within, took cover in ideological anonymity, but it remained pigheaded and tough whenever it found its material and social privileges encroached upon.

Especially violent was the reaction to Branko Ćopić's satire *A Heretical Story*, which laid bare the torpid and voracious character of the political bureaucracy. Security officials openly threatened to beat him up, and Tito himself blew up, as much from personal as from party pique. "He lies. What he's written is false," he declared at a Women's Congress on October 29, naturally to their enthusiastic approval. Pijade hastened to write an unsolicited article against the author, "The Heroism of Branko Ćopić." I edited the article for him, commenting cynically that I was behaving just like a district committee member. From the island of Brioni, where Tito had a residence, thunderbolts were hurled at Ćopić, to be deflected only with great difficulty when I proposed that he and I have a talk. I explained to him that by being overhasty he was hamstringing democratization. "I see now, Comrade Djido, just what I did wrong," he said. Knowing that Branko was a joker, I said, "Don't give me that! As soon as you're out in the corridor you'll be snickering up your sleeve, thinking, 'Did I put one over on him!' " Though Branko and his fellow satirists were silenced for some time to come, things turned out better for him than they might have.

I myself was not silent, nor was I willing to silence myself. At the same time that Pijade was attacking Ćopić, my article "Contemporary Themes" came out. It analyzed the Soviet system as state capitalism and concluded that the contradiction between us and the Soviet Union was greater than that between the Soviet Union and the United States. My thesis about state capitalism in the U.S.S.R. was later taken up by the leadership, including Kardelj and Tito—only to be dropped overnight after my removal in 1954 and the reconciliation with Khrushchev.

My article, along with similar articles and speeches by other leaders, triggered a new and significant decision by the Politburo: theoretical discussions were now permitted at party cell meetings, breaking with the practice of Politburo approval of all public statements. The decision was announced by Tito in a speech delivered before the Guards officers on November 29, 1951, but only after Kardelj and I had warned him that the problem was acute. An unpleasant incident had occurred, which was reflected in Tito's words. A certain officer, pressed to the wall and accused of "Cominformist fence-sitting" by his party organization or some other party forum because he did not accept the thesis of state capitalism in the U.S.S.R., had committed suicide. This had painful repercussions at the top. Not one good intention, not one new step, could be taken without sacrificing the innocent—such was the ideological intolerance and compartmentalization in the top reaches of our party. Tito had shouted in anger, "My officers are killing themselves because someone says the Soviet Union isn't socialist!" But that assertion had its roots in top-level discussions to which Tito was no stranger, and to which he himself subscribed as soon as he got over his shock.

In his speech to the Guards, Tito concluded that such public statements by leaders were becoming so numerous and so widely disseminated that requiring official approval for them would not stop them, and, moreover, would be impractical from a time standpoint. Tito grasped the problem all the more rapidly for having himself observed the new, democratic climate in the party:

Regardless of whether or not such articles are basically accurate, none of us can always give a one-hundred-percent correct assessment and analysis before grasping the causes of certain phenomena, and before those causes have had a chance to filter down into the consciousness of the majority. Theoretical articles should not be discussed at party cell meetings as something prescribed and definitive; accordingly, party members should feel free to talk them over—not as the party line, not as something given and axiomatic, but as material that must make its impact on the mass development of theoretical thought. . . . Accordingly, it is a mistake to confuse free discussion about questions of theory within a party organization with decisions already adopted on individual issues. . . . In such discussions we dare not, we cannot judge people or make hasty decisions. Therefore, before bringing in a definitive judgment, it is quite correct to have discussions along democratic lines. Disciplined acceptance of a position taken by the majority on individual issues can come later.

The year 1951 saw the climax, and in many respects the winding down, of our confrontation with the Soviet Union. For me, it began with a visit to London—at the formal invitation of Chatham House (the Institute for International Affairs), to lecture on Soviet-Yugoslav relations, but actually at the invitation of the British government. Dedijer went along, not simply as a responsible official, but also as my interpreter on a concurrent and most confidential mission.

We had already received aid in food and raw materials from the Western powers—mainly the United States, but also from Britain and France. However, aid in arms and equipment—even more necessary and more valuable than food—we had not yet sought, because of the "backwardness" of our Communists, because, they claimed, right here in our party ranks Soviet propaganda would find fertile soil for the Cominformist claim that the "Tito clique" had gone over to the imperialist camp.

In the Politburo, our need for weapons and our inability to do anything about it had been discussed since 1950. Tito and the military command felt the problem acutely and voiced it more than anyone. By the end of 1950, the Soviet bloc's conduct and the aggressive intentions of the Soviet government had become so widely known that, in the judgment of Tito and the Politburo, the first steps might now be taken toward acquiring military aid from the West, meaning the United States. First, in a United Press interview early in January 1951, Tito pointed out the need for arms from abroad, stressing that we had sought nothing till now, "so as not to furnish material for hostile propaganda." A meeting of the Secretariat was held at Tito's before I left for London, and I was instructed to request such aid .

It was no accident that London, meaning among the Labour party, was chosen as the place to do it. A representative Labour delegation, headed by Morgan Phillips and Hugh Seton-Watson, had spent some time in Yugoslavia in 1950, holding candid talks with our leadership. These talks, which I conducted in large measure, had done much to bring us closer. Official relations with the Labour government also grew more open and cordial. Thus the British Labourites, along with other European socialists, provided a bridge toward collaboration with the West, while also freeing us from our ideological prejudice that only Communists truly represent the working class and socialism.

By 1949, our leadership, as opposed to the political apparatus, had quickly rid itself of any illusions that rifts would show up in other Communist parties over the Soviet-Yugoslav dispute. Only certain individuals turned to us—people who had broken with their own parties anyway because of disillusionment with Moscow —for instance, the Spaniards Felix Montiel and José del Bario. (The Italians Aldo Cucchi and Valdo Magnani quit their party much later, because of disagreement with their own leadership.) A department to handle relations with socialist movements was set up and attached to the Central Committee; I headed it, with Dedijer as my assistant. Some German dissidents also showed up, with whom I had a clandestine meeting in Switzerland. I judged them to be limited, unresourceful, and without influence, which was later confirmed. Co-operation proceeded smoothly with the Spaniards and the Italians, but without much impact on the questions at issue. These parties were Stalinized as well as preoccupied with their own problems. Only the socialist parties thought and acted undogmatically in the light of the realignments brought about by the Soviet-Yugoslav dispute.

To preserve the secrecy of our London arms mission even from the code clerk, Ranković and I had agreed to use pseudonyms for both Prime Minister Clement Attlee and the mission. We arrived on January 28, 1951; two days later we were received by Ernest Davis, replacing Foreign Secretary Ernest Bevin, who had been taken ill. On January 31, we were told Churchill wished to see us. That same day the British government arranged a dinner in our honor that was attended by the most prominent Labour leaders as well as the prime minister. Dedijer and I took Attlee aside for a moment to ask his government's views on possible Western arms aid. He said he would call and give us an answer. In two or three days we were invited to No. 10 Downing Street and taken into the room set aside for cabinet sessions. Attlee at once sat us at a long table, extracted a sheet of paper, and read off a one-sentence announcement: The British government looks with sympathy upon your request for military assistance.

My Chatham House lecture seemed to be well received and my answers to often provocative questions went especially well. Dedijer and I took a trip to the city of Durham. During the day we crawled through mine shafts and in the evening had supper at

Seton-Watson's, which was all the more pleasant because it was modest and unofficial. Even the Conservatives, headed by Harold Macmillan, who impressed me with his composed and unassuming geniality, had a reception for us at the Houses of Parliament. The English would not have been true to their refined, centuries-old political experience had they not seated me at dinner next to Seton-Watson, so he could intervene with me, in Serbian, on behalf of our prisoner Dragoljub Jovanović. Our hosts also tried to arrange a meeting between me and the émigré Vjećeslav Vilder, my acquaintance from schooldays. In addition, at a dinner given by our ambassador, Joža Brilej, I made the acquaintance of Aneurin Bevan, leader of the left-wing Labourites, who impressed me as a dynamic personality with a lively, unconventional mind.

Filled with curiosity and joyous anticipation, we went to see Churchill at his London house, an establishment no larger or more luxurious than the average middle-class villa at Dedinje— the type that our top Yugoslav officials acquired after the war. We found him in his bedroom, in bed. He begged our pardon for receiving us thus and at once invited us to dinner. We had a prior engagement for dinner with the British government, and so had to decline, with genuine regret. Churchill then said, "I have a feeling that you and we are on the same side of the barricade." We confirmed his feeling, whereupon he inquired with delight, "And how is my old friend Tito?"

On the way to his house I had entertained the thought of reproaching him for having once offended Tito, so when Brilej or Dedijer replied that Tito felt fine, I added, "But you said he had deceived you." "When? Where?" Churchill asked in surprise. "In your speech at Fulton, Missouri, in 1946." With an expression of discomfort Churchill replied, "Oh, I've said a lot of silly things in my life." I then added, with a smile, "But we took no offense at your words. We understood them as a sort of acknowledgment." He gave a sardonic laugh.

Churchill then said to me: "You're a member of the Politburo, you've got a feeling for the Soviet mentality. If you belonged to the Soviet Politburo, would you invade Europe?" I replied that

I would not. "But *I* would, you see!" he said. "What's Europe—disarmed, disunited? In two weeks the Russians would push right through to the English Channel. This island would defend itself one way or another, but Europe . . . ? If it weren't for atomic weapons, the Russians might have made their move already." One of us pointed out that the Russians were exhausted and had not yet recovered from the war. "The fact the Russians haven't invaded by now shows they don't intend to invade Europe," I observed. "Yes," said Churchill, "they're held in check because Stalin is smart enough to shun adventures. And old—he's got no stomach for running around Siberia dodging atom bombs!"

At one point Churchill became quite carried away by strategic considerations. "Yes, the Russians are held back by their fear of atom bombs. They're a centralized empire. If atom bombs were dropped on their communications centers—which wouldn't cause heavy civilian casualties—the periphery would loosen up and start to fall away. Stalin knows that well." Here Churchill reared up in bed, toothless, in his nightcap, and with fingers spread and pointed down, began to imitate the falling of bombs—a specter in whom the spirit of battle blazed on undiminished.

Our talk with Churchill lasted about half an hour and ended with an almost compassionate plea: "Don't be too hard on the peasants—they're innocent, they're not to blame for anything!"

Negotiations to acquire weaponry from the West developed quickly and smoothly. Preoccupied with my own affairs, I did not follow them. In an interview with Reuters at the beginning of March, Tito announced publicly that we might get weapons from the West. From our generals—especially Dapčević, with whom I was on close terms—I heard that the American arms arrived beautifully packed and brand new, the artillery even with its own cleaning devices. Nevertheless, if I understood correctly, these arms were technically of World War II vintage, not the latest models. But we were content: our hypothetical adversaries were no better armed, and military technology had still not advanced significantly except in jet aircraft and atomic weaponry, neither of which we had asked for.

Subsequently I had a small share in obtaining arms from the United States. When General J. Lawton Collins, U.S. army chief of staff, paid us a visit in October 1951, I represented my government at a dinner given in his honor by the American ambassador. As we drove there, Generals Koča Popović and Dapčević suggested that I ask Collins for jet aircraft. When I made the request, Collins begged off, saying that this was not exclusively his responsibility, and that the United States had to provide for its allies first. I replied: "We don't understand why we shouldn't be given jet aircraft. The one reason we can see is your ideological prejudice—we are Communists." I had a feeling that Collins, who impressed us not least because he looked like a civilian in uniform, was struck by this view of the matter. Be that as it may, we soon got our jet aircraft—trainers, to be sure, but fit for combat.

As if reborn, all our powers surged into action. Our grasp of ideology, our tragic past, our nation's changed status now bore fruit in domestic reforms. Early February 1951 saw the adoption of a new criminal code, followed by a new criminal procedure. Both were the result of dogged, passionate work by Moša Pijade, helped by specialists, under Kardelj's supervision. Pijade thought these laws among the best and most democratic on earth. Indeed, they did betoken a sudden turn for the better, in contrast to the judicial arbitrariness and police omnipotence previously characteristic of our system.

While these measures were being discussed and adopted, the Secretary-General of the United Nations, Trygve Lie, visited Yugoslavia, on April 12, 1951. Our own self-confident enthusiasm was thus reflected in the growth of our prestige in the world. After a series of acute gallbladder attacks. Tito was soon to be operated on, and Kardelj was recuperating from a spinal operation. So I played host to the Secretary-General. The visit proceeded with more cordiality than his actual function demanded. While I was taking him to the airport, he asked me, "Why did you help the rebels in Greece?" "Revolutionary idealism," I replied. "And how

277

much help did you give them?" I answered in round numbers, convinced that he would not abuse the confidence. "Rather a lot of help," he commented.

Tito's operation, at Lake Bled, at a time of resistance to Moscow and of reform within, brought the leadership closer together. Not since the war had we felt our bond with him to be so close and warm, and I, for one, felt it to be permanent and unbreakable. Now Jovanka Budisavljević, in her role as Tito's nurse, emerged into public view from the position of secret mistress. We leaders accepted her warmly and trustfully.

The May 1 proclamation was usually written by Tito, but because he was ill, the task fell to me that year. Its central passage is worth quoting as an illustration of the aspirations and illusions of our political thinking:

The further consolidation and extension of the personal rights of citizens, the further involvement of the broad masses in administering the state and the economy, the further development of brotherhood and unity among all our peoples, the further struggle against bureaucratic tendencies and all instances of the violation of our socialist legality—these are the tasks that confront our national groups, our party, the People's Front, and social organizations.

And so our country raises high the banner of democracy and of socialism—a banner that today's rulers of the Soviet Union have trampled upon after depriving the working masses of all rights and freedoms, and adopting a policy of spheres of interest, of wars of conquest, of subjugating other peoples. All this they do to feed the exploitative, insatiable appetites of a bureaucratic caste that assumes the right—allegedly in the name of the struggle against capitalism—to plunder and squander the work of laborers in its "own" country and the countries of others.

I thought then, and still do today, that the most important public statements were the paper read by Ranković at the Fourth Plenum of the Central Committee, on June 3, 1951, and the

278

article by Kardelj entitled "In the Struggle for Socialism and Independence," which appeared in *Borba* on July 1–3, 1951.

Ranković's paper was concerned with the police and the judiciary, though its title had the innocent ring of a slogan: "Toward the Further Strengthening of the Judiciary and the Rule of Law." The fact that he administered or oversaw these services might have lessened the objectivity of his judgment. But with the precision that came naturally to him, and the consistency of a Communist bent on a change in course, Ranković presented the "real" state of affairs and thereby, if indirectly, showed that the whole system was shot through with lawlessness. The weight and credibility of this shattering criticism were greatly enhanced by the fact that they came from the chief of the entire police force, who was simultaneously organizational secretary of the party. Here is a portion of what he said:

There are courts that turn specific acts of disobedience toward individual state agencies or officials into counterrevolutionary activity. Thus one court declared that a certain local committee chairman and his wife were guilty of criminal activity against the people and the state and for their offense sentenced them to three years in prison. . . . Some courts openly flout the law. For one and the same criminal act they apply punishments that are too lenient or else too severe. . . . The internal affairs agencies, including the State Security Administration, likewise display major deficiencies, above all in respecting and carrying out the law. . . . There are instances of rash deprivation of civil rights by certain agencies. . . . Criminal charges that have been unjustifiably pressed, according to the reports of prosecutors' offices, are as follows, by republic: Serbia, 40 percent; Slovenia, 39 percent; Bosnia and Hercegovnia, 51 percent; Macedonia, 36 percent; Montenegro, 47 percent. . . . There are instances of "directives" being given as to how judgment is to be passed in a given case, and even of specific prior instructions regarding the severity of punishment.

Ranković emphasized that there were even judges sitting on the bench illegally. The unprofessionalism of the courts that he cited was all the more shocking in that the kingdom of Yugoslavia had had an organized and professional judiciary, and the new Yugoslavia's law faculties were graduating hundreds of students every year. In Croatia—formerly a judicially autonomous province of Austria-Hungary—20 judges out of 324 had no legal training; in Serbia, two judges of a district court had finished only elementary school; in Bosnia and Hercegovina, 110 out of 184 judges were without legal training, and three district court judges had only elementary education; and in the Kosovo Region, 65 judges —practically the entire judiciary—had had only elementary schooling. Citizens not only complained in vain, but were sometimes even punished for doing so.

Thus in the territory under the jurisdiction of the district and municipal people's councils in Trebinje, citizens rarely lodged a grievance because council functionaries would talk them out of it. The executive committee of the district people's council in Stara Pazova decided to penalize all who complained of the way prices had been set on corn, and even entered its illegal resolution in the minutes of an executive committee session.*

Ranković also furnished the number of arrested Cominformists since 1948: 8,403 sentenced to "socially useful labor via administrative proceedings," of whom 3,718 were released and 12 percent of these rearrested. His paper at that Fourth Plenum was a turning point for the introduction of law and order into the daily lives of ordinary citizens. But the status of political opponents did not change, nor was the power of the secret police essentially diminished.

I, too, spoke at the plenum, on "Certain Questions of Party Theoretical Work." Criticizing the Soviet Union for making theory the monopoly not of a party forum but of a single person (Stalin was still alive then), I pointed out that we, too, tended to monopolize theory. Without doubt my conclusion was overly optimistic, a reflection more of hope than of the real state of affairs:

---

* Trebinje is an old city in Bosnia; Stara Pazova is near Belgrade.—Trans.

Our Central Committee and our party are struggling against every form of monopolism. In the domain of opinion, not only is monopoly harmful to the progress of human thought, but it represents the beginning and closing phases in the struggle of reactionary forces to create that other monopoly—a monopoly of material and social life— which takes the form of lording it over men and the fruits of their labor. Without the monopoly of ideology, that other monopoly and its reactionary and despotic domination cannot be firmly established or long sustained.

But this was not just the expression of my own hopes: a plenum resolution on questions of theory confirmed that party cell approval of public statements was not obligatory unless a Politburo directive was anticipated. It is at this point that the Tito cult began to abate: no one disputed his services or leadership, but the idolatry of him as a person began to decline.

Kardelj's article focused on the danger to socialism arising from "the bureaucracy of one's own socialist state." He saw a way out by letting power trickle down from above to the factories, the institutions, and the local governments—in short, to the sort of commune that Marx had foreseen. Kardelj believed in the evolution of his own awareness and that of one part of the leadership:

The principle of gradually entrusting administrative "management" to the grass roots in our country is already a living reality. This speaks eloquently to the fact that the tendencies of state capitalist bureaucracy have suffered a defeat among us. . . . Consequently, there is no reason to fear in the future for the fate of our socialism, as long as our working people possess greater rights than any other people in history.

Kardelj's article may seem romantic from today's perspective, but at the time it served as a source of encouragement to democratic currents in the party leadership, in the state administration, and in the lower ranks.

Finally, in early September 1951, I published a rather long article, "Thoughts on Various Questions," which, with its unconventional, noncommittal title and, still more, its upsetting content, revealed further rejection of dogmatic clichés and acceptance of more liberal interpretations.

That summer, following a suggestion by Kardelj, it was decided to seek UN condemnation of the Soviet Union for threatening Yugoslavia. He proposed that I present our case to the Special Political Committee, which that year met in Paris. Our delegation went by train. In Switzerland one of our parlor cars—the very one in which Kardelj and other high officials were riding—caught fire because it could not sustain the speed of European trains. The fire did no harm, but until it was put out we were detached from the rest of the train. Kardelj was angry and upset, whereas I treated it as something of a joke.

In Belgrade I had prepared my speech with the help of Ministry of Foreign Affairs officials and had submitted it to Kardelj for his review at the end of October. He had found no fault with it the first time around: "All right, good," he agreed. But in Paris Dedijer burst into Kardelj's hotel room with a flood of adverse comments. My speech was not documented from the legal standpoint, he said; I had enumerated incidents without furnishing the legal basis establishing each case individually, which was the only criterion acceptable to the United Nations; we would be in a very awkward situation if someone asked for legal documentation and we could not provide it, and the like. He had no criticism of the political or stylistic aspects of my speech. Kardelj agreed with Dedijer, and I accepted his comments, to this day believing that they were justified and that they contributed to the substance and plausibility of my speech in its final form.

However, there are inaccuracies in Dedijer's description of the incident in *The Battle Stalin Lost*. This is what he says:

I saw the text of Djilas' statement a few days before he was scheduled to give it to the Special Political Committee. Reading it carefully, I thought it would be inappropriate for what we wanted to achieve in the U.N. Instead of laying stress on relations between states, on violations of international law, this was a Marxist disputation on philosophy, with theological overtones as to who was right and who wrong, and falling just short of discussing how many angels could fit on the head of a pin. . . .

Djilas and I went to Kardelj's room for Turkish coffee and I said what I thought of Djilas' statement. . . . Again I had made my usual mistake: my criticism was sound, but I had put it so clumsily that Djilas was furious. . . .

Bad luck dogged me the whole day. That evening President Vincent Auriol was giving a reception for the delegations at the Elysée Palace. Djilas and I had been invited. . . . In our car on the way to the reception Djilas and I continued our quarrel. I refused to shut up. Even as we were entering the palace and a footman in livery announced "His Excellency Milovan Djilas and M. Vladimir Dedijer," I said something nasty and Djilas turned on his heel and left, just as we were approaching Auriol. Flustered, I stood before the silver-haired M. Auriol, who shook my hand saying, "I am happy to see you, M. Djilas."

The next day Kardelj summoned me to his room. Djilas was also there. Kardelj told me he did not agree with the way I had put things, but that he did agree with the substance of my criticism. He had read the report and found it inappropriate; it would have to be rewritten. Djilas took this good-naturedly. We slept on it, and the next day I begged his pardon for being so clumsy. This ended the incident between us. He never mentioned it again, nor did he ever try to "get even." We continued working together—he as president and I as secretary of the Central Committee's International Commission. (Upon returning to Belgrade he even proposed that I become president, which I immediately turned down, not being interested in formalities.)

Working day and night with Kardelj, [Milan] Bartoš and Veljko Mićunović, we made a new outline. We had to get fresh material from Belgrade by messenger. Bartoš, Mićunović and I got no sleep for twenty-eight hours, until the statement was ready.*

---

* Vladimir Dedijer, *The Battle Stalin Lost: Memoirs of Yugoslavia, 1948–1953*, New York: Viking, 1971, pp. 285–86.

I shall not go into the question of whether my speech was a "Marxist disputation on philosophy, with theological overtones . . . falling just short of discussing how many angels could fit on the head of a pin"; the text can probably be found in some archive. But this was not my first public appearance on the "international scene," whether with Dedijer or without him, as he well knows. I turned back in front of the Elysée Palace, and not after we were announced. And the "silver-haired" Vincent Auriol knew me from our recent hunt at the Rambouillet château, so he could have addressed Dedijer as Djilas only by mechanical reflex, something I don't exclude. As I recall, Dedijer and I didn't make peace until we returned to Belgrade.

None of this was important. People react as temperament dictates, including Dedijer and me. But from his account it appears that I took no part in composing the report: ". . . with Kardelj, Bartoš and Veljko Mićunović, we made a new outline. . . . Bartoš, Mićunović and I got no sleep for twenty-eight hours, until the statement was ready." It is true that these comrades—and I as well, not just Dedijer—worked on the topics and issues to be covered, and that it lasted well into the night. But I carried on from there, with the assistance of Security and Ministry of Foreign Affairs staff and, most of all, my secretary, Dragica Weinberger, in collecting and organizing materials and retyping them. We sent written messages, telegrams, and couriers to Belgrade for hastily gathered documentation. For fifteen days the staff and I worked round the clock so as not to lose our turn before the Special Political Committee. This was a speech of close to a hundred pages, one of the longest ever delivered in the United Nations. It could not possibly have been put together by Bartoš, Mićunović, and Dedijer in twenty-eight wakeful hours. I will add one fact more: the speech was published over my signature in 1951. Why didn't Dedijer dispute its authorship then?

At some point during my stay in Paris the well-known American journalist Cyrus L. Sulzberger dropped by the residence of our ambassador, Marko Ristić, with his wife, a slender brunette. I don't remember the exact occasion now. Sulzberger and I had long been antagonistic. On my part, it stemmed from his anti-

Communism in the press; on his part, probably from my supposedly having said that, because of this, he deserved to be hanged. Up to that point we had had no contact at all, but here we were chatting in Paris like old friends, while his wife cast curious and somewhat ironic glances at us. I remember that we dwelt the longest on the Stepinac question. Sulzberger said that aid to Yugoslavia was encountering resistance in the U.S. Senate because of the archbishop's continued imprisonment, and asked why we did not send him into exile. I explained that our constitution prohibits expelling our citizens from the country, and that altering it for the sake of Stepinac would not make sense or be acceptable. Today Sulzberger and I are the best of friends. We look forward to fishing for trout together every summer, and to the rambling conversations shared by intellectuals who have grown old, each with a distinctly different experience.

By now our position toward the U.S.S.R. and our conflict with it had completely changed—a circumstance to which the UN session gave final, formal definition. Speaking to the General Assembly on November 15, Kardelj touched on current world problems, but dealt mostly with the Soviet bloc's aggression against Yugoslavia as a threat to peace. I lodged our written grievance on November 26 and 27. For the delegates this was a long and rather boring document, but it was packed with facts. The Soviets responded with confused and false arguments. Our warmest support came from the Brazilian delegate and the one from Belgium. The resolution condemning the Soviet bloc was put together by our diplomat Aleš Bebler, with citations from the UN Charter. The vote to condemn the U.S.S.R. was 50 yeas and 5 Soviet-bloc nays, with Afghanistan and Iran abstaining. The Belgian delegate could not resist a rhetorical comment in open session: "How can anyone be a member of the United Nations and yet vote against a resolution comprising portions of the charter?"

These events marked Yugoslavia's departure from the protected sanctuary of party and ideology, to venture at last out into the world at large as its own sovereign agent. On our side, polemics lost their hysterical edge and took on a quieter tone, more self-confident and nonideological. Tito, in his New Year's

285

speech for 1952, did not even mention the Soviet Union and the Soviet bloc's campaign, but was content to note the growth of our country's reputation as the truth about us spread throughout the world in 1951.

We stayed almost two months in Paris, attending the session. Whenever I was free I made the rounds of the museums, most often the Louvre, and took walks at night, generally along the Champes-Elysées and the Rue de Rivoli. Rodin's *Balzac* and the Sainte-Chapelle pleased me most, the latter's exquisite harmony moving me in a way I felt only one other time, at the Taj Mahal. One night friends from the embassy took us to a night club, but since I couldn't bear watching women strip for money, I left.

Back in Belgrade, I settled down to writing *Njegoš*, in addition to my other work. This was a polemic against the writer and scholar Isidora Sekulić, specifically against her book about the nineteenth-century Montenegrin poet Petar Petrović Njegoš. Though I had read her book earlier, it was the fervor of a Marxist intellectual and Communist that now spurred me to polemics.

Soon after *Njegoš* came out, Mitra, my former wife, showed me her copy, with many passages underlined and the margins cluttered with question and exclamation marks. "The book is dogmatic!" she said. Indeed it is. But at the same time it attempts to take the dogma out of Marxism and is, in any case, my highest attainment as an orthodox Marxist. (*The New Class* is also Marxist, but unorthodox.) I gave Tito one of three finely bound copies of *Njegoš*. A couple of weeks later he said, "I've read your book and like it. It's very good." I was glad of the praise but marveled that he had managed to read such a queer, moody work. "It caught my interest," he continued. "I completely agree with your criticism of the national mystique."

In the course of 1952, I made a fair number of public statements in the form of articles and talks. I shall mention only one, the article "Class or Caste," in which I defined the ruling stratum of Soviet society as a caste, and two other writers tried to prove me wrong, arguing that it was not a caste but a class. The argument strikes me today as doctrinaire, but in that article lie the roots of my book *The New Class*. In my mind ideas would crop up haphazardly, the old interpenetrating the new, and one blotting out another. Then they would all gradually fade as distinct entities and fuse into a unified whole.

Kardelj and I tried to give Tito's 1952 birthday celebration less pomp and idolatry, more affection and simplicity. This was his sixtieth, and we decided that the Central Committee should present him with a formal written address. I wrote the address and also a piece called "The Homeland," in which I avoided mentioning Tito's name, but which was published in conjunction with the address. The first version of the address was bombastic and forced, a fact that dawned on me overnight. I called Kardelj in the morning and asked if he had read it and how he liked it. "Well, it's all right," he said, but I could tell by his voice that he wasn't too excited. "It's lousy!" I yelled. "Cold, artificial!" "Yes, it is," Kardelj agreed. "You'll have to write another with more warmth to it." So I did. We decided to present the address in a silver-and-gold box designed by the painter Krsto Hegedušić. With the Central Committee members looking on, I made the presentation to Tito, who said as he took the box, "Now here, by God, is a piece of real art!"

As preparations for the upcoming Sixth Congress, scheduled for the fall of 1952, proceeded, the Agitprop and *Literary News* staffs hit on the idea of starting a new, broadly based journal in which writers and scholars would analyze our inherited stock of ideas. It was, of course, conceived to be Marxist in spirit, but a Marxism to be postulated in the most general, philosophical, and antidogmatic sense. While we were talking about it on a stroll through Topčider, the writer Oskar Davičo remarked, with a sly little smile, "This reminds me of those illegal meetings we used to have before the war." No one concealed a thing or had any reason to do so, but there was indeed something "illegal" in the concept, in the spontaneous yearning to put our theoretical thinking on a footing independent of the party apparatus and political forums. I reported to the Secretariat on the project, and Tito was present. I also mentioned three or four names that had been proposed for the journal. Like most of the future editorial board, I favored *Nova misao* (New Thought). Tito remarked, "That's the best title!" and Kardelj and Ranković agreed.

My article "Is Stalin Going in Circles?"—published in *Borba* on October 11–13, 1952—was a polemic against Stalin's new economic theses. More specifically, it took an outspoken stand against the "workers' collectives" (collective farms), meaning our "quasi-collectivized theoreticians." So far as I am aware, this was the first public stand against them within the party, though it lacked firmness and clear perspective. Either then or maybe a little later, Kardelj and I proposed dissolving the collectives, but Tito, with the nostalgic support of some party "agricultural experts" (Petar Stambolić, Mijalko Todorović), was opposed. Nonetheless, they did get dissolved a year later, because of irreparable agricultural losses.

I would not mention here my article "Anti-Semitism" (*Borba*, December 14, 1952), written in response to news of the arrest of the Jewish doctors (the "white coats") in the U.S.S.R., had not Davičo recently accused me—on top of all my other "misdeeds"— of anti-Semitism. Here are the main points from his indictment:

... After the London edition* in Serbo-Croatian of Djilas's ineptitudes and untruths about Tito, I cannot help but recall publicly some of his actions which reveal that neither a renegade nor a traitor comes into being overnight. ...

He mounts so brazen an attack that I am sure a legion of foreign lawyers stands behind him from the various psychological services. ... ["Psychological services" means intelligence services which conduct psychological warfare.]

... Arrested in 1933 and beaten, Djilas betrayed Pirika and Beška Bembas, two excellent comrades, two sisters. ...

---

* Cf. Djilas's *Tito.*—Trans.

. . . He told me, "You don't know Serbian and you never will. It's not your language. You're a Jew." That was during preparations for the trial of the "white coats."

. . . And come to think of it, wasn't it he who in December 1940 informed me that, by a resolution of the Central Committee of the Communist party of Yugoslavia, I had been expelled from the party for collaborating with Krleža's journal *Pečat* [The Seal]? . . . Which means that Djilas arrogated to himself the right to make decisions in the name of the whole Central Committee.*

In lieu of a defense against Davičo's accusations, here are the facts.

Like other writers, I write books out of my knowledge and experience, but since the Yugoslav government does not permit their publication in Yugoslavia, I am under no moral obligation to take into account what anyone will say or think about my writing. If in the beginning of my conflict with Tito I was obsessed with spies ("psychological services"), my reason taught me to go my own way, as did Tito's lawless sentencing of me, without appeal, to political and spiritual death—and I was only one extreme case among many. If Davičo considers it his Communist and patriotic duty to conform to the Yugoslav "psychological services," let him. I do not have to conform to anyone or anything.

Davičo cannot know who sold whom down the river in a case he was not involved in, but he is ethically bound not to cast blame on the innocent. I did not inform on the Bembas sisters; I didn't know them. They belonged to a so-called wildcat group that had no connection with the party. For Davičo's information, they were betrayed by a barber, Dimitrije Jovanović. (His Macedonian last name had been Serbianized against his will; what it is today I don't know.)

Oskar Davičo was not expelled for collaborating with Krleša's *Pečat*, but for refusing to return to his party duties in Belgrade, and for joining the antiparty group then associated with the journal. Prior to that, there had been prolonged, fruitless attempts

---

* *Svijet,* Sarajevo, March 3, 1981.

to convince him. Ognjen Prica, who was very close to Daviĉo and upset by his break with the party, was especially active in this regard. I took no part in the Politburo session that expelled him, though I was not against the decision. Daviĉo's case was too well known in the top echelons, and the duties and rights of a party member were too well known to the man himself—if only because he had spent five years in prison—for me to have been able to "lie" about his expulsion. Where was he and what was he doing from 1940 to 1943? Why didn't he return to the party that today he defends so zealously against a "renegade" and a "traitor"?

At the very time when I allegedly criticized Daviĉo for not knowing Serbian because he was a Jew, he and I were close and worked together in complete harmony. I may have criticized him for doing violence to the Serbian language, for insensitivity to its nature—I don't recall—but that had nothing to do with his Jewishness. Indeed, Daviĉo always said he felt like a Serb. Above all, it had nothing to do with the "white coats" affair. Daviĉo sees something sinister in this coincidence only now, twenty-nine years later, "after the London edition in Serbo-Croatian of Djilas's ineptitudes and untruths about Tito. . . ."

Here, finally, is the citation from my article "Anti-Semitism":

. . . persecutions of Jews . . . are a sure sign of the blackest social reaction. . . . Anti-Semitism besmirches and consumes all that is human in man and all that is democratic in a people. The historic stigma of shame that it imprints can never be wiped out. The violence of anti-Semitism is the measure by which a reactionary regime succeeds in enslaving its own people. But by the same token anti-Semitism marks the beginning of the end for those who make use of it, even if their powers are still on the rise.

On December 18, 1952, prompted by our break in relations with the Vatican, Kardelj gave a speech in the National Assembly which I liked for its composition and its persuasiveness. It was not the custom for us leaders to congratulate one another on our speeches or articles, but I could not resist telling Kardelj that this had been one of his best speeches, if not the best. Reading it over now, I see that it is the kind of speech a politician makes to force some urgent issue—in this case, our dispute with the Italians over Trieste—into conformity with a theoretical framework. "One of the most important vehicles for Italian expansionist tendencies is the Vatican." Such was his basic thesis, incorrect but understandable at the time.

Friends of Krleža like to treat his paper at the Ljubljana Writers' Congress on October 5, 1952, as decisive in freeing South Slavic culture, especially literature, from the grip of Stalinist dogmas. There are even those who regard this paper as proof of some special Croatian sense of democracy and progressivism. Certainly Krleža's paper was important, and in our resistance to Moscow he played a major role on the broader cultural scene, such as his initiation of the Paris Exhibition of Medieval Yugoslav Art and the Lexicographic Institute. But it is exaggerated and wrong to separate his activity from that of the party's top leadership in creating our hard-won liberal climate. Nor does such an approach reflect the facts. His speech at the congress was agreed upon in advance with the Central Committee: I checked it out, and Kardelj probably did, too. This does not detract from his initiative, but shows that he did not turn any new corner, since that corner had been turned earlier—during three and a half years of political and ideological struggle—by the top party ranks, among whom Krleža worked with discipline and zeal. After all, less than a month after the Writers' Congress and Krleža's paper, the party's Sixth Congress convened in Zagreb and our fight against dogmatism reached its culmination. I saw in Krleža then and still do—regardless of all the arguments I had with him—the most significant cultural phenomenon in modern South Slav history.

Our preparations for the Sixth Congress were less intensive, better organized than for the Fifth. In the Secretariat or the Politburo I proposed that it convene in Zagreb, on the principle that, in the future, party congresses should be held in turn in each republic's capital, and not in Belgrade alone. The proposal to rename the party a "league" was also mine. Only after the idea first occurred to me did Kardelj remember that the original Marxist organization had been called the League of Communists. He took up my suggestion. The change was meant to point up the reformed, democratic character of our party as opposed to the Leninist, Soviet type of organization, and signaled a shift toward a more democratic society. When we next saw Tito he concurred, after brief reflection. Ranković was against the change of name but accepted it with disciplined silence. Turning to him, Tito said, "It's not the name that's important, but what you mean by it." Another suggestion was Kardelj's: instead of having the leaders address individual topics with the usual long, boring papers, let only Tito speak programatically, and have committees of the delegates pick up the burden of the work. I was in charge of the political and ideological side. I drafted all resolutions, had them approved by Tito and Kardelj, and then submitted them for further comment to the relevant congress committees.

During the session, members of the Secretariat and Kidrič—who was already seriously, fatally ill—were put up in a block of villas at Tito's disposal which Pavelić had seized from their Jewish owners during the war, so that over meals we could exchange thoughts about the congress and other current issues.

Just as the Sixth Congress convened, Ljubodrag Djurić, secretary of the federal government, publicly accused Petar Stambolić, president of the Republic of Serbia, of having seduced his wife. Confusion arose in the hall and on the platform. As members of State Security (themselves delegates) hustled Djurić out, I stepped up to the rostrum to announce that the matter was already under investigation by a party committee, so the congress need not be concerned with it. Western correspondents promptly rechristened the Sixth Congress the "Sex Congress."

Over lunch—despite attempts by Ranković and me to dissuade him—Tito angrily accused Djurić of Cominformist motives, of a desire to compromise the congress. When the afternoon session began, he stated that "the enemy's hand" lay behind the deed. As it turned out, Djurić was imprisoned only briefly. Having broken no law, he was soon released and sent to administer an agricultural property somewhere.

A bizarre incident took place in Slavonski Brod apropos of the Djurić episode. That district's representative happened to be Djuro Salaj, president of the Yugoslav Federation of Labor Unions. Someone listening to the radio got the last name Djurić mixed up with the first name Djuro and informed the local committee that Djuro Salaj had come out against Tito and the Central Committee at the congress. Preparations began at once to unmask Salaj as a "Soviet agent" (he had long lived in exile in the U.S.S.R.) and an "old opportunist" (he had once leaned toward the rightist faction). Fortunately, the facts were clarified before the campaign assumed unmanageable proportions.

To this day I believe that Tito dominated the Sixth Congress politically and that his leading role was never in dispute. That role was most eloquently expressed in the opening speech, though I confess I had expected him to say less than he did. It was the peak of his criticism of Moscow and Leninist autocratic power. I shall quote several passages that have stayed with me all these many years.

. . . The roots of the present state of affairs in the world go back to the imperialist method applied at Teheran, Yalta, Moscow, and Berlin during the war, when an attempt was first made to solve international problems. . . .

No one in this country or in the world was surprised when at Teheran, Yalta, Moscow, and Berlin the Western powers approached the solution of world problems in their accustomed way. But for all who credited the rumor that the U.S.S.R. was the protector of little peoples, this came as a real moral blow, as the first strong doubts about the Soviet Union and the correctness of Moscow's policy. From Teheran to this day, Moscow has flaunted its imperialist majesty. Today we can boldly assert that the whole of Soviet foreign policy—setting aside ordinary propaganda tricks like their alleged struggle for peace and the rest—has been such as to contribute eminently to present international tension.

. . . It was Moscow, was it not, who created colonies in the heart of

Europe where there had once been independent states like Czechoslovakia, Poland, Hungary, Rumania, Bulgaria, and so on. Not to
mention the enslavement of the Baltic countries back before the war.
. . . The U.S.S.R. has pushed North Korea into an aggressive war,
so as to bring South Korea under its sway while letting others get their
hands dirty. In saying this I do not in the least diminish the responsibility of the Western powers. They are just as responsible for
the situation in Korea since the war began in 1950. This Korean war
—which could turn into a world conflict—results from a division into
spheres of interest.

Defending Marx, Tito criticized Stalin's recent articles on the
economy. Nor did he neglect to mention how national groups
had been uprooted in the U.S.S.R.—"and in the harshest possible
way at that, which even Hitler might well have envied." Stubbornly, he took issue with the West's unfounded criticism of our
country for having socialized the means of production, since precisely that socialization, he said, makes "real democracy" possible.
He formulated in his own way, but forthrightly, our striving for
a corrective, as opposed to a prescriptive, role for the party.

Once we are reconciled to the idea that the Communist party of
Yugoslavia is not exclusively in charge here—that it does not have
total dominion over all things as if it were a supreme arbiter imposing
its immutable, infallible judgment on all the various problems of social
life—then it is clear that the party's role consists in educating, in
ideological management, in taking care that our socialist society
develops normally and correctly. That is the most important task of
all. In other words, the role of the Communist consists in re-educating
our country and raising it in the socialist spirit.

The idea of changing the party's role from command to teaching was expressed at the congress still more lucidly by Kardelj,
who presented the Socialist Alliance, formerly called the People's
Front, as a broad organization gathering under its wing all who
followed socialism, regardless of ideological differences. "The
League of Communists," he said, "needs to be the most aware

part of the Socialist Alliance of Working People." At that time there was talk in the top leadership of letting the Socialist Alliance itself become the main political organization. Until socialism reached its lasting consolidation and social relations changed for good, we argued, Communists in this alliance represented only socialism's most energetic, "most conscious" core. I think it was at this time that Tito stated one evening, while taking leave of the Secretariat in his office at 15 Užička Street, "We will not have a multiparty, but a multigroup system."

I spoke at the congress of introducing a new party program, since the one adopted at the Fifth Congress was already outmoded. In urging democratization I was even then farther out front than anyone else, if only because my formulations were the most pointed and the least restrained.

If we are to deal with these new forms of the class struggle, we must shake off bureaucratic clichés and methods, we must stand up and fight for political and moral arguments—and soon—for there can be no talk of democracy if administrative measures replace political arguments based on ideas.

It is not to please the West or the East that we advocate democracy, and certainly not to please the vestiges of the bourgeoisie. We favor democracy for our own sake; for the sake of our own working class and our own people; for socialism's sake (for without democracy there can be no socialism); and for the purity of our socialist and Communist being and our final goals.

Delegates at this congress were far less reticent than at the Fifth Congress or similar party gatherings. The same was true of the press. Foreign correspondents were also present. I held two press conferences for them, at which I was subjected to some awkward questions. But the most dramatic, stormiest moment came with my October Revolution speech, which I gave almost by accident. It was November 7, the anniversary of the Russian Revolution, and until recently we had put our hearts into its solemn celebration. But we and the Soviets were by now so estranged, and our relations so poisoned, that while the congress was under way no leader so much as remembered the date. Even in 1949, portraits of Stalin had no longer been displayed at the celebrations, and only here and there could ones of Lenin be seen. Both the Yugoslavia-U.S.S.R. Friendship Society and the Pan-Slavic Committee had stopped functioning. Over lunch with Tito, I remembered the date and suggested that we mark it at the start of the afternoon session. I thought Tito, or at least Kardelj, should do this. But they said they were tired, so I did it.

The assignment made me so nervous that I omitted the after-lunch nap that had been my habit since early youth, and sketched the speech out on slips of paper. I did not stick to those jottings, however, but, for the most part, improvised. The gist of my short speech was that the Soviet leaders had abandoned the promises of the October Revolution, and new forces were taking them in hand. Appropriately enough, the speech was an outcry and an ecstasy, a verdict and a conviction. The hall and the platform erupted into one continuous round of applause. It carried me away. One delegate—I forget who, but someone close to the top—later said to me, "I suddenly felt that the banner of the revolution had passed from the hands of the Soviets into ours!" In Belgrade, my mother was listening with my wife to a broadcast of the congress meeting. Once the hubbub had died away, the ancient, eternal wisdom spoke through her lips: "It's not good for Djido when they clap more for him than for Tito."

# Part Three

# REBELLION

# 17

Man, while a part of the world, is a world unto himself. He is no more capable of fully knowing himself than he is of fully knowing the world. But as I take stock of what I do know of myself and my past, now at seventy-one, I understand that the crucial periods in my career were closely connected with my private life, including my loves. In *Land Without Justice* and *Memoir of a Revolutionary* I depicted my childhood and youth as cheerless and austere, just like the world around me—or as I understood my place in this scheme of things and acted upon it. With only minor discrepancies, I could interpret my political activity and intellectual transformations as reflections of my emotional life. The periods of my personal life and my professional activity are separate entities, though not sharply marked. That, at least, is how I see myself and my past.

The poetic revolutionary ecstasies of my youth bore the stamp of my bond with Mitra Mitrović and my love for her. Similarly, my break with Leninist dogmatism and with the Yugoslav party bureaucracy, and my turning to literature and independent thinking were closely linked to my attachment and love for Štefica Barić, my present wife.

I must have seen Štefica, who had been assigned to work at the Central Committee of the Yugoslav Communist party in 1946, many times. But the first encounter preserved in my memory is one that took on symbolic, even mystical, meaning for me. It was in the autumn of 1946. On some business or other I had to go to the department where Štefica worked, on the third floor. Walking into an office where there were three or four people, I saw her in profile at a desk, leafing through something and explaining it. As I made my inquiry, my attention was riveted by that profile: high forehead, straight nose, chiseled lips, gray-blue eyes, ash-blond hair, pale skin sprinkled here and there with freckles, cheekbones flushed with nervous pink. In the face, which was almost nunlike, and the downcast, watchful eyes, I discerned an air of devotion—devotion that seemed capable of encompassing not simply the party, but also the man with whom she might share her life. Though we didn't exchange a word and she hardly gave me a glance, a new and strange thought entered my mind: here might be the woman for me, with whom I could have a family, maybe three children. That was the first time I had wanted children, and a wife who would be not just a friend but also a devoted being inseparable from me.

For days and weeks I did not see Štefica, but her face hovered in my mind's eye and I couldn't shake loose that thought, that yearning for her devotion. It persisted with a sad hopelessness. It was significant that she attracted me not so much physically as by the womanly devotion she radiated. My mind and my feelings had been so identified with party norms and with Mitra—jestingly I used to call her my "Marxist-Leninist wife"—that I rejected the very thought of intimacy with another woman, especially a party member, even if divorce and bitterness would not have been the inevitable result. In my story "The Bird and the Girl" I described with fair accuracy the amorous feelings I experienced in those days. "Woman is destiny," goes the saying. I had always liked dark women, but I had fallen in love first with a fair-skinned woman and the second time with a blonde.

Several months went by before I got to know Štefica better. The occasion was the opening ceremonies for work on the "young people's" railroad from Šamac to Sarajevo on April 1, 1947, where I was asked to speak in the name of the Central Committee. Several staff members, including Štefica, came along, and we shared a compartment on the train heading for Šamac. Grown thin and pale, but with a bewitching smile enhanced by her shining teeth, she did her share of storytelling and small talk. For all my efforts to resist and be nonchalant, I was overwhelmed by tender affection and an irresistible sense of our closeness.

But more than a year passed before we spoke again, not simply as good acquaintances, but as man and woman, with repressed desires and dreams. All loves are accidental; I apologize to the reader for going into my private experiences in so much detail, and do so only because they illustrate my inner transformation, or, more precisely, my development as a revolutionary and my emancipation from dogmatic rigor.

It was in July 1948 that Štefica and I had a direct encounter. The occasion was the Fifth Congress, which convened after several months of surreptitious conflict and a month of open clash with Moscow. She was on the congress's planning committee. In the flower of womanhood at twenty-seven, with a nice figure, which her pastel silk dress softened and highlighted, Štefica had been nicknamed "Miss Fifth Congress." I was not aware of that at the time, but amid the tension of the sessions she was constantly on my mind. At the end of the congress, as we sat awaiting the results of the voting, I asked her if she would temporarily replace my secretary, Dragica Weinberger. With a look of dumbfounded hope, she replied that she would.

A few days later, before Štefica joined me for a two-month tour of duty and before I had said anything to her about my feelings, on returning home from work I confessed to Mitra in my study that I loved another woman. Her face contracted spasmodically, like a child's, and tears burst from her large, dark eyes. That very evening I moved into my study, lock, stock, and barrel.

My relationship with Štefica went through vicissitudes and crises, only to be reborn every time with new devotion and strength. For too long I was torn between love and duty. I was aware that breaking up with Mitra would be badly received in party circles, where our marriage was regarded as exemplary—as indeed it had been, while it lasted. But at the same time I was driven toward separation no less by love for Štefica than by the impulse to break with a now traditional party morality that imposed its own rigid mold. Later, when I parted ways with the Central Committee, there was gossip in these same upper circles that Štefica had had a fatal influence on me and my decision. That was not true, though in her own way she agreed with my course of action. But my separation from Mitra, or, rather, my attachment to Štefica, was the incentive as well as the symptom of my heresy: my search for a way out of the icy, ironclad darkness of Marxist and Leninist dogmas.

The bond between Mitra and me had lasted fourteen years, not counting the three I spent in prison. During all those years from 1931 to 1948, from the time I fell in love with Mitra to my love for Štefica, I had no connection with or even desire for any other woman. I would not even speak of this had not Vladimir Dedijer misrepresented this aspect of my personality. In his book, he writes as follows:

In several of his memoirs Milovan Djilas, carried away by his own vanity, tries to insinuate that he was the main subjective factor influencing Yugoslav Communists to take up revolutionary asceticism.

I regard his approach as too subjective. He takes no account of tradition, nor of the mood prevailing among young Communists on the eve of the war. I should like to add, too, in the interests of historic truth, that, lacking the courage to be straight with himself, Djilas is applying a double standard. It is true that on more than one occasion he preached a ban on free love; he even hounded to his death the young Bosnian militant, Paternoster, who loved two girls at once. But as his closest friend of that period, who never left his side, I must tell the truth: that was the time when Djilas himself was having several so-called "healthy" love affairs.*

---

* Vladimir Dedijer, *Novi prilozi za biografiju druga Tita* (New Contributions toward a Biography of Comrade Tito), Rijeka: Liburnija; Zagreb: Mladost, 1981, p. 627.

It is hardly enough to state that Dedijer's claims are untrue. Disastrously characteristic of him is the conscious, almost congenital ease with which he fabricates and perverts reality. But let me take things in order. First and foremost, Dedijer was never my "closest friend," least of all before the war, nor was he a man who "never left" my side. He and I never could have been that close for the simple reason that we lived and worked in different circumstances: I served in the two highest councils of an illegal party, whereas Dedijer was a journalist, a sympathizer who only later became a party member. I moved almost exclusively in the circle of party officials and illegal operatives; Dedijer, in the intellectual and bourgeois milieu of a newsman. I don't mean that we were not on good terms or never saw each other: we were close, but saw each other off and on as party requirements dictated. Weeks would pass, even months, without our meeting.

Dedijer offers no proof apart from our alleged intimacy for my "double standard" and "healthy" affairs. Such a standard and such affairs not only were not sanctioned, but could not have been kept secret in the narrow, puritanical environment in which I lived. Other comrades with whom I was close personally and in party life would have known of it. To list only those still alive: Moma Marković, Zogović, Ranković, Vukmanović-Tempo, Koča Popović, and others, including my first wife, Mitra. And if Dedijer knew about my "double standard" and " 'healthy' love affairs," in the name of what moral standard and party ethic did he, as a party member during that period of "revolutionary asceticism," conceal these things from the party?

It is also untrue that I have wished to present myself to the reader as "the main subjective factor influencing Yugoslav Communists to take up revolutionary asceticism." In this respect—in this perhaps more than in anything else—I was only one of the leaders. I do not regard asceticism as a virtue or as my own particular merit, but as necessary to the process whereby our revolutionary movement matured, purified itself, and became homogeneous. Without self-denial, without austerities of all kinds, there is no revolutionary movement, or any revolution either, regardless of opinion today. As for Dedijer's assertion that I "even hounded to his death . . . Paternoster," how could that be, when I was not the "main factor"? How could that be, when I did not even belong to the student organization with whose ascetic revolutionary morality Paternoster came into tragic conflict?

As I said earlier, Mitra moved out at the end of 1949, when I was at the United Nations in New York. During that painful, devastating separation I had the understanding of my comrades: Kardelj, indirectly Tito, more directly Ranković, the last perhaps not only because of his own closeness to me but because his wife, Slavka, was a good friend of Štefica. But two and a half years passed before I made up my mind to marry Štefica. The ambivalence in my private life was one component—who knows how decisive?—of the ambivalence in my ideas, the transition from one intellectual world to another. Is this not indicated by my passionate absorption just then, not only in Marx and *Das Kapital*, but also in Aristotle, Plato, Hume, Diderot, and Hegel?

# 18

In midsummer of 1952 a Dr. Bulić from Dragiša Mišović Hospital came to see me in my apartment at 6 Banjičkih žrtava Street, to inform me that Boris Kidrič had leukemia and would die in six to nine months.

Kidrič had been complaining of physical discomfort—nausea, loss of appetite, exhaustion—and had had some checkups. The final diagnosis had now been made by Bulić. He showed me the evidence under a microscope: Kidrič's white blood cells, their edges nibbled all around, "like the lid of a tin can," as he expressed it. He had no particular reason to convey this finding to me, though I had the impression that he was prompted by intellectual affinity, and certainly by the fact that I was the only person not away on annual holiday. Later he reported to me regularly, as the illness progressed.

I immediately informed the Secretariat. Word had spread of Kidrič's illness simply because he was no longer able to administer the entire economy—a burdensome job under any circumstances. Even so, Kidrič kept at it practically to his dying breath, communicating to his subordinates his own inexhaustible energy. And, though already gravely ill and noticeably turned inward, he could not resist speaking at the Sixth Congress.

Kidrič's would be the first unavoidable peacetime death in the uppermost ranks of our leadership; somber knowledge, a dull sense of foreboding, penetrated our circle, weighing upon each man individually. I felt shaken, also a little isolated. I had been very close to Kidrič, especially after the struggle with Moscow. We used to see each other whenever we could snatch a moment of free time. Most often this was in the summer, since neither of us took any vacation except for a couple of days at a time—Kidrič hunting, I fishing, or the two of us hunting together. His devotion to his work was such that he could not tear himself away. As for me, I was cutting myself off intellectually and emotionally and no longer fit into the Brioni vacations others took. But in those post-Cominform years, Kidrič, Kardelj, and I by turns and by pairs had such lively discussions about even the most trifling points of ideology—were they really so trifling for us then?—that we eagerly anticipated every get-together. In our memos and public statements it is difficult to say which idea was whose, no matter how we differed otherwise in style and approach.

The most dramatic moment in Kidrič's illness was when he went into shock following a transfusion. Whose fault it was I cannot say; according to one of the doctors, a blood subgroup had not been checked. Kidrič lost his hearing completely as a result and could have gone blind, but for some luck in the midst of misfortune. Dr. Bulić again notified me, and I sent word to members of the Politburo and rushed off to the hospital. There I found Kidrič's wife, Zdenka, who never left his side. While nervous staff members hovered about, he lay with flushed cheeks and wandering glance. But he recognized me and said, "Well, Djido, here I am." I went out into the hall to wipe away my tears in silence.

Soon the other Politburo members arrived, then Tito. We spent the whole afternoon in the hall, talking to Kidrič's doctors. It was not until late that evening, after we were assured that his condition had stabilized, that we began to disperse. We felt the sudden release from tension and dull foreboding, but Bulić warned us not to be overly optimistic. Ranković, carried away by hope and popular mistrust of doctors, whispered in my ear, "They don't know everything, do they?"

It was no longer possible to conceal Kidrič's illness. The next day a press release identified it as leukemia. Yet before long he had so collected his intellectual strength as to follow the newspapers regularly, even asking for the back issues. The issue of *Borba* containing the release was withheld, but he insisted on having it. His wife, who had hidden from him the nature of his illness, sounded the alarm: with the help of the *Borba* staff, I had the press put together a copy omitting the release. Yet Kidrič suspected the truth, judging by what his wife told us. He got hold of an encyclopedia, buried himself in the article on blood diseases, and, intelligent and brave as he was, realized what the problem was.

British doctors—famous specialists—were called in, not because we lacked confidence in our own physicians, but so we could show the public we had done all that we could. In a chance encounter at the hospital I spoke with the head British doctor, a stiff, bent old man. He told me that our doctors had done just what they, the British, would have done.

I visited Kidrič often, perhaps more often than anyone but Kardelj, with whom he had always worked closely. We communicated in writing. To my surprise, he continued to sense quickly and easily what was on another's mind. If I correctly understand a remark made by Zdenka, he had thoughts of an afterlife shortly before his death. Doesn't that speak of human hope, which cuts through whatever philosophy one espouses?

I was with Kidrič on the eve of his death, just before my departure for Montenegro to attend a congress of the People's Front. He did not seem in bad shape or look any worse than on other days. In our exchange of notes there was talk about death and "comforting" materialist rationalizations from me about the imperishability of matter, which, Zdenka later told me in mild reproach, led Kidrič to thoughts of his own imminent death.

It was past noon on April 12, and I was occupying the chair

at the congress in Titograd. Suddenly a courier approached and whispered that Štefica was on the telephone. Vukmanović-Tempo, sitting next to me, overheard and asked what was the matter. I replied that maybe our little son, Aleksa, was not feeling well and Štefica was upset. "Hardly likely!" said Vukmanović. "She's a serious, tested comrade."

In agitated tones my wife said, "Boris is dead! Dr. Bulić just called." Returning, I told Blažo Jovanović and Vukmanović. In a whisper, we decided that I should communicate the sad news to the congress. While waiting for the speaker to finish, I had the sudden sensation that, as my folded hands rested on the table, my fingers had detached themselves. There was a moment of shock before I came to myself. I did not even have time to ask what was happening to me before my fingers joined themselves again to my hands.

As I informed the delegates of Kidrič's death, the tears flowed down my face, but I neither sobbed nor lost control. Sobs could be heard from the hall. I spoke of him as "one of the wisest men of our revolution."

Gathering like a bereaved family in the Hotel Montenegro lobby that evening, we officials spent hours exchanging memories of the revolution and visions of the socialist future. No one mentioned Kidrič, but he was with us the whole time.

The next day we "Belgrade Montenegrins" returned by plane to the capital, where I drove to the Central Committee to join forces with the commission in charge of funeral arrangements. It was chaired by Ranković with a precision that overlooked not the tiniest detail. This would be a funeral such as the new Yugoslavia had never before witnessed.

Tito's train transported the coffin and the mourners to Ljubljana, where Kidrič was to be buried. On the way we had one of those conversations about life and death that come naturally in such circumstances. Again I expounded my materialistic beliefs. Half facetiously, Tito observed that one ought not to talk about life beyond the grave, inasmuch as no one knew anything about it.

At the funeral Kardelj spoke with the sadness of a true friend, and Tito as though he had lost an irreplaceable comrade in the war. As the procession wound through the streets of Ljubljana in the rain, someone offered an umbrella to Kardelj, who wanted to shelter me, too, so that neither of us was really protected. It gave me a strange pleasure to be putting up with this trifling inconvenience for Kidrič's sake. We had a plaster of Paris death mask made of Kidrič and kept it in a cabinet in my Central Committee building office. I did not have a chance to recast it in bronze before I was expelled from the Central Committee a few months after his death. But I well recall that ironic smile, that withered, wise forehead.

# 19

After 1949 the Yugoslav Communist party broadened its ties with the European socialists, and they in turn paid more frequent visits to Belgrade. In other quarters, too—Asia and Latin America —interest grew in the "Yugoslav experiment" as a socialist phenomenon distinct from that of the Soviet Union. Naturally our leadership tried to consolidate this interest by establishing direct and more lasting links with socialist movements outside Europe, and with national movements in former and existing colonies. Wider and more dependable contacts were developed than Moscow and its satellite parties could ever offer.

Such were our motives and perceptions in sending a party delegation to Asia at the beginning of 1953 to attend the conference of Asian socialists. Aleš Bebler and I were chosen, he as an experienced diplomat, with languages, I as a member of the top leadership. We set out by train from Belgrade on December 25, 1952, and continued by plane from Rome via Cairo and New Delhi to Rangoon, where the conference was held in the first half of January. We returned to Belgrade on February 4, 1953.

We were the only Communist guests at the conference. Behind us lay a twofold rebellion, against Hitler and against Stalin. The second, with its fresh, antibureaucratic ideas for self-management and its fusion of socialism with freedom, heralded the democratic way out of Communism. So we leaders—or at least a significant portion of us—believed. Why would anyone else believe, if we didn't? For that reason our delegation enjoyed, in my judgment, a reputation and a role at the conference greater than that of the British Labourites led by Clement Attlee. We were consulted by the two leading delegations, the Indian and the Burmese.

A hodgepodge of views characterized that conference, but there was common ground: the wish to be delivered from poverty while preserving democracy, and to resist exploitation by the West and hegemony by the U.S.S.R. The views of the Egyptian and Israeli representatives stood out by contrast, the former for relying on the Koran and a military regime, the latter because of their excessively Europeanized socialist ideas. To us it was obvious and, more important, instructive that socialism was not and could not be monolithic, that its theoretical foundations and stages could not be uniform. There were a few Marxists there, but their views differed from both ours and the Soviets'. Life and reality turned out to be more socialist than socialist doctrines themselves. As Communist heretics, we felt we belonged in this ferment and were quite comfortable. Our one weakness was taking aid from the United States, which we justified by the Soviet blockade and the need for self-defense.

My speech at the conference, which owed much to Bebler, was not limited to mere greetings. Attlee, too, gave a short speech on matters of principle; the point of it—that only the parliamentary system was worthy of humanity—left Bebler and me resentful. Though we no longer denied the value of the parliamentary system, especially its historic value, I thought Attlee's assumption old-fashioned and dogmatic. The majority of humanity is not "parliamentary" and seeks different, nonparliamentary, paths. Moreover, I myself was persuaded that we Yugoslavs had found in self-management a form more democratic than any parliament, including the British. Even today I find Attlee's assumption one-sided, no longer because I regard our "invented" form as worthier than a parliament, but because many human beings, blinded by doctrines and smothered by violence, cannot grasp what human dignity is all about.

We saw incredible regions and marvelous monuments on this trip. I presented my impressions in a travel essay, "The Eastern Sky," whose title was suggested by journalist Bora Drenovac. It was published in *Nova misao*.

Bebler's knowledge of the outside world was incomparably richer than mine, and he took a greater interest in historic monuments. But I think I was more deeply, more permanently, affected by this journey. Above all, by the poverty—the thousands and hundreds of thousands of homeless sleeping on the sidewalks and squares of Calcutta; the crowds of leprous beggars in the bazaars of Karachi; the thousands of refugee families in bamboo shelters along the streets of Rangoon. Bebler shuddered, but his shuddering was mixed with the curiosity of a worldly tourist. I felt a painful shock of recognition, as though witnessing a part of my own world. And while he, a jet-age diplomat and a revolutionary by both instinct and knowledge, was preoccupied with political nuances, I felt ideas crystallizing in my mind out of the chaos of impressions: human survival had no bounds; the forms taken by society and human thought cannot be ordained. Hitherto indistinct, my awareness of this broadened and consolidated. No science, no scientific view can possibly anticipate, let alone regulate, human existence. Science and scientific views that pretend to do so at best only mask violence and privilege, if not naked force. Why do the peoples of Asia endure such poverty, such suffering? Is it because of their belief in higher, permanent values of the spirit? Or are those qualities cultivated simply to make poverty and suffering more tolerable and exalted? Is the life of the individual—or, for that matter, the nation—any more than a link in the chain of eternal suffering and searching?

As we approached Rangoon from the air, we were dazzled by the golden pagoda rising gently upward from the deep green landscape. Later, the harmonious splendor of the Taj Mahal took our breath away; I was shivering. But human beings, human circumstances riveted our attention and stimulated our thinking.

Burma was in the throes of civil war. The war was felt through the refugees on the streets of Rangoon and the timorous, indecisive reactions of Burma's leaders. Generally modest and well intentioned, they were deeply unhappy over the misfortunes that had come to their idyllic but undeveloped and war-torn land. From us Communist heretics they expected more than we could offer: an end to their civil war.

Our ambassador, Dobrivoje Vidić, had not yet settled in, but already enjoyed close and interesting contacts with Burmese leaders. Like us, he was living in a comfortable hotel in the midst of disease, filth, want, and overpopulation. The worst problem our embassy faced was how to secure hygienic living conditions. Talking with Vidić, I could do no better than ask, "What can be done here? Your responsibility must be thought of as war duty." I think he saw it just that way, but this was no comfort to his wife, fearful for her little son's health.

We had given a dinner for Attlee, and the British ambassador reciprocated by inviting Bebler and me to a meal. Naturally, this ambassador had no problems with housing. He lived in a luxurious villa surrounded by lawns and a park filled with Burmese evergreens. He remarked complacently, "If there was ever a paradise, it must have been in Burma." After dinner, over cognac and coffee, he asked casually, "What are you exporting to Burma? What are you interested in here?" Bebler explained that we were interested in ideological collaboration. "So it's ideas you're exporting," observed the ambassador, with gentle but unconcealed irony.

In New Delhi, Ambassador Jože Vilfan was comfortably installed in a villa, with a dozen servants. Vilfan's wife, Marija, a striking-looking intellectual, had had trouble co-ordinating the work of these servants, but then her Slovene cook had arrived, whose orders all were glad to obey. We were told of ambassadorial residences—for instance, the Canadian—that had up to one hundred servants, who were underpaid by European standards.

According to the caste system, every servant does only one job. Indian servants are esteemed all over southern Asia as perfection itself, and we could well believe it. Preparing for some reception, at just the right hour we would find the prescribed clothing all ironed, the trousers neatly laid out on the bed, so that one had only to pull them on.

Vilfan and the embassy officers maintained close relations with both the government and the socialist opposition. He drew our attention to something we had already noticed: the vast, untried possibilities for co-operation and affirmation among Third World nations. In this liberated world, swayed by modern ideas and ripe for the unimaginable potential of industrialization, we could see a role for Yugoslavia.

We were invited to lunch by Nehru, architect and exponent of collaboration and friendship among the uncommitted countries. His daughter Indira was also present at the lunch, which was served on a lawn beside the residence of the head of state. Indira was restrained in all things, from her personal beauty to the elegant sari she wore. Nehru was more watchful than talkative, expressing his views concisely and listening carefully. His way of thinking was European—logical and rational—but its substance was rooted in the reality of India and the Indian cultural heritage. Though he seemed more thinker than politician, he did combine the two. He observed Indian customs, eating vegetarian food with his fingers and abstaining from alcohol. I do not recall anything significant from our encounter with him, apart from his critical attitude toward blocs and, especially, the U.S.S.R. Moscow's policy had been a disappointment to him, more so when his hopes of establishing close relations with Czechoslovakia—a "harmless" industrial country—were dashed. I also remember his playing with a Himalayan panda after our lunch.

In New Delhi we met with the socialists. All the Indian socialists were consistent, even doctrinaire, in their democratic beliefs and egalitarianism, though they differed in much else. Not one of them was a Marxist. Among the most dynamic and original was Ram Manohar Lohia, who gave a dinner for us in Calcutta. He headed a movement within the Socialist party that was almost autonomous, and published his own journal. A small, stocky, loquacious man, he seemed steady and principled in his views. He was particularly concerned with the socialist transformation of the villages, which, he realized, could not be accomplished without modern machinery. He was obsessed with the idea of building a small, all-purpose agricultural machine, which he thought feasible at the present level of technology.

We, however, were of a different opinion. We felt that the way out lay in large-scale collective holdings, some sort of truly voluntary collective farms. Lohia was against collective farms, feeling that villagers must own their own property and engage in both labor and trade. As for the little all-purpose machine, I remarked that that should be the concern, not of politicians and social reformers, but of technicians and agronomists. As we talked, ideas flashed and dreams merged; who would have thought we were from opposite ends of the earth with different cultures and circumstances? Although our discussions with Lohia were heated and marked by irreconcilable differences, they did no damage to friendly relations, nor did anyone bear a grudge.

A year later, when I was ousted for "revisionism," at Lohia's invitation I wrote an article for his journal. However, as I was about to mail my article, registered, from the main post office in Belgrade, one of the two agents accompanying me ordered the clerk to withhold it. I no longer recall how I got the article to Lohia, but I did and he published it. At the same time he initiated a search for the letter, established that it had not left Belgrade, and published an account of the proceedings. I went to the post office with the confirmation and was recompensed for the "lost" letter in the amount of five hundred dinars. While I was in prison, though, Lohia died. I cannot judge how much India and socialism lost by his death, but I experienced it in prison as the death of a comrade in arms who placed principle above personal advantage.

With the Indian socialist Jaya Prakash Narayan we did not have such heated and wide-ranging discussions, but in Rangoon we reached an agreement about the tactics of the conference and its final resolution. In a special meeting he suggested we co-operate with Nehru and the Congress party in an effort to bring together reformist and socialist forces. In principle, we agreed. Later Narayan started a new movement and played an important role in the overthrow of Indira Gandhi. Without question he was an extraordinary person: wise, patient, immune to fame and titles, sure of the superiority of ideas, tolerant in all things.

On one of his trips to Europe he stopped in Yugoslavia. I was enormously surprised and deeply moved when he told me in his room at the Hotel Metropole that he had come to Belgrade specifically to see me after I was released from prison. Our talk on that occasion was open, colored by his compassion and my resignation. His interest lay less in Yugoslavia's economic and political prospects than in the methods and character of power. We touched on questions of party pluralism. He spoke out against a multiparty system in principle, because parties become corrupted and tend toward monopoly. The agents of political life, he felt, should be communal associations. I commented that European tradition and the complexity of European social life demanded parties, adding that a nonparty political system without a free press leads to dictatorship. Narayan agreed wholeheartedly; in the basic units of society and in modest, simple forms of human existence he sought freedom as the greatest value. When the government of Indira Gandhi arrested Narayan, some Indians in London asked that I join in signing a demand for his release. I did so gladly, only regretting that I could do nothing more.

Asoka Mehta, the socialist closest to Nehru, whom I had met on that visit to India, also visited me in Belgrade upon my release from prison. Though Mehta's political views were for me more understandable and closer to my own, Narayan left a deeper trace in my memory, by virtue of his personality and his utopianism.

From New Delhi we flew to Bombay to visit socialists in that city. We were put up in the sumptuous apartment of a most considerate couple, the Trikumdas. After three or four days there we flew on to Karachi, the capital of Pakistan, at the invitation of the government. We were not particularly enthusiastic, but there was no reason not to go. We agreed in advance to avoid giving our views about the disputed province of Kashmir, lest we offend the

Indians who had received us so handsomely and with whose government Yugoslavia was on cordial terms.

But though the Pakistani government could not induce us to take an open stand on the Kashmir issue, it tried to create the impression that we sympathized with its position. Our ambassador, Obrad Cicmil, did not see through this gambit and accepted the arrangements proposed by the Pakistanis.

We were put up in a second-class hotel—perhaps there was no better in Karachi. Since we were not a formal state delegation but more of a good-will mission, and since Pakistan was a backward country, we lodged no complaint. But an argument arose over the order of visits. The Pakistanis had arranged for us to call on the minister for Kashmir first thing the next morning, which would suggest that we took a strong interest in Kashmir, or that we had traveled to Karachi precisely for that reason. We immediately registered a complaint with the Pakistani Ministry of Foreign Affairs, and a clerk from the ministry kept coming and going through the day with fresh excuses. Our ambassador, who found himself in a sticky situation, but who was by nature friendly and patient, gave us his full support. Finally we decided to take a plane the next day without seeing a single official. Late that evening we were told that the Pakistanis had accepted our proposal, which was to be received first by the president of the government and only then by other officials, including the minister for Kashmir.

Kashmir, as it turned out, was not even brought up in talks the next day, except once, in passing, by its minister, a dignified gentleman in an elaborate costume who reminded me of a Montenegrin tribal chief, all the more so because he bore the title *serdar*. But the disagreement and tension threw a pall over the talks and the receptions given in our honor.

From Karachi we flew to Beirut, intending to go from there to Israel: the Israeli delegate at the Rangoon conference, Moshe Sharett, had invited us and we had tentatively agreed. In Beirut we got into discussions with Lebanese socialists, who combined a reformist, democratic outlook with nationalist hostility to Israel.

These encounters made us somewhat hesitant about going to Israel, so we queried Belgrade, which did not support the visit. Regretfully, we abandoned the idea, and I sent Sharett a letter explaining our change of plans. I later heard that he was active on my behalf when I was in prison, but I don't know the details. Sharett was wise and moderate; his ideas were those of European socialists. He, too, has died, so I will never meet him again, even if my desire to see Israel should be granted. Nor will I ever see Beirut again, since insane hatreds and armed ideologies have butchered that city of Mediterranean warmth and Roman harmony. No pacifist, I am convinced that wars and revolutions are humanly unavoidable, but I know, too, that life and beauty cannot be resurrected.

From Beirut we went to Damascus. Our stay there was pleasant but without consequence, as was true of our stopover in Athens, whence we flew back to Belgrade. Before leaving Damascus, I bought, with the balance of my travel money, enough camel's-hair cloth to make a coat for Tito. He had asked me to do this before we left on the trip. This trivial detail would hardly be worth mentioning, except that it indicates the closeness of our friendship, which in less than two years would be transformed into intolerance, bitterness, and persecution.

Waiting at the Belgrade airport were Ranković and Štefica. He was there for reasons of protocol since, to my surprise, while I was in Asia I had been named one of the three vice-presidents of the republic. I was flattered and pleased by his presence: it seemed as though nothing could spoil a tested friendship of many years. I made a short statement, sentimental but political.

# 20

Stalin's death in March 1953 was greeted with relief and even re-joicing by the Yugoslav leadership, but there were distinctions among us, apparently minor, in anticipating changes in the Soviet Union. Tito did not look for change in the system, but he did expect a less aggressive foreign policy, especially toward Yugo-slavia. Ranković predicted great, if not decisive, change in the Soviet power structure, which he saw as based on the cult and role of Stalin. I saw privilege and expansionism as so ingrained in the Soviet party bureaucracy that even the disappearance of Stalin would have little impact. My assessment was based on the Marxist premise that the system is more important than the leader. Kardelj's position was somewhere between Tito's and Ranković's and mine: Stalin's death would not lead to anything radical, but it would force the Soviet leaders toward gradual change.

No one in or out of the inner circle was aware of the depth of the divergences triggered by the death of Stalin.

About this time Tito began to stress the need for dispensing with American aid as quickly as possible. "Without an independent foreign policy there is no true independence," he would say. We all agreed to end such aid, and so end our dependence on the West. But the way he harped on it hinted of the coming reversal in domestic policy, whereby democratization would be halted— especially on the intellectual front, where we had advanced the farthest. That was the sphere where incipient differences would first be detected. Tito was now talking of the West's "negative influences" on culture and youth, whereas I, in my thoughts, no longer distinguished between Western and Eastern, or even between "decadent" and "progressive."

Differences also began to emerge in the way we viewed the League of Communists. Tito was now publicly concerned about the league, claiming that it was fading into ineffectiveness, that it was, above all, losing its ideological unity. A number of us, including Kardelj, Bakarić, Vukmanović, and me, believed that the league should exercise leadership ideologically but not tactically, that it should function through free discussion rather than by giving orders, imposing interdictions, and applying labels. Kardelj and I even dreamed of founding another league, a league of socialists: a broad, nonideological organization in which Communists would be only the most militant and conscious core. There in embryo lay the idea of breaking the monopoly of the Communist party and of assimilating it to a mass democratic and socialist movement.

Tito sometimes wavered on specific issues, putting the stress now here, now there. But always he betrayed an urge to strengthen ideological conformity and return the party to its hallowed "leading role" in all things. This came out more frequently and strongly in small meetings and private talks than in public. In Tito's insistence there was conservatism, and fear that his personal power would be weakened—which didn't go unnoticed in the top echelon. He associated—almost identified—himself and his personal power with ideological uniformity and an obedient, indivisible party. There was still unity among us, though now perhaps a little forced. We procrastinated over important decisions, then carried them out in a dispirited, mechanical fashion. Within the party there appeared the first differentiation along national lines. The administrative machinery grew lax, officials were taking it easy. In this respect Tito's observations and apprehensions could not be faulted. What I questioned were the means he used to resolve these problems.

Certain reformist, democratic tendencies were still too powerful to be stopped. Soon after Stalin's death, we abolished voluntary mass physical labor for youth and disbanded the collective farms. The initiative for the first came from the youth leadership at its congress of March 6 and was promoted by economists: youth labor was too costly and inefficient. I supported their initiative, though more for political than for economic reasons. I felt that voluntary mass labor was an outmoded form that encouraged quasi-military, monolithic thinking among our young people—thinking more akin to slogans than to freedom. I know that some members of the Politburo, Kardelj, for one, shared my opinion, but the decision to repeal could be taken only by the Politburo as a whole. After my fall, when mass youth labor was revived, Tito blamed its earlier abolition entirely on "that traitor Djilas." My motives are partly revealed in my welcoming speech in the name of the Politburo at the March youth congress.

Mass youth labor action was necessary and heroic, but it can no longer be justified economically or politically. As we continue to strive for socialist education, let me point out that we should beware of dogmatism and fixed forms. . . . In a country where socialism has triumphed . . . a socialist education is not just the study of pure socialist theory, pure socialist principles; it is cultural achievement, it is raising the level of general education, it is attainment of literacy. Our country, our peoples, and especially our young are in a position where everything that moves man ahead and in any way lifts his cultural level constitutes socialist education.

The Decree on Property Relations and Reorganization of Peasant Workers' Co-operatives, promulgated on March 30, 1953, marked the de facto dissolution of our collective farms, a year later than originally planned because of Tito's rejection of Kardelj's and my proposal. Workers' co-operatives and compulsory selling had not only proved wasteful and illogical, but also kept the country excessively dependent on Western aid. This did not mean, however, that deception and self-delusion lost any of their attraction. At the Congress of the League of Communists held in Ljubljana on April 6, even Kardelj, who had sponsored the new measure, justified it as a way of strengthening socialism in the villages, where workers' co-operatives in "new forms of partnership" would play an important role.

In the army, meanwhile, the post of political commissar was abolished. Tito had long resisted this step. Two months earlier he had caustically characterized my suggestion that we do away with the commissars as "wrecking the army."

Yugoslavia's reputation was on the rise. Tito visited London in March, and Chief of the General Staff Peko Dapčević traveled to Washington. As for me, I attended the coronation of Queen Elizabeth II on June 1, 1953, with Dapčević and Minister of Foreign Affairs Koča Popović. Tito and the government valued this opportunity to emphasize what good terms we were on with the West while waiting for our relations with Moscow to normalize, as was indicated by the extravagant size of our delegation. We marveled at the pomp and ceremony of the coronation and envied the royalist unanimity of the British people and the elegant courtesy of the upper classes. But we felt uncomfortable at a luncheon with editors of the most respected British newspapers. Although by now we had become accustomed to informal information gathering, on this occasion we were subjected to such "interrogation" that we might just as well have been in the hands of the political police. Yet we, too, gathered intelligence. It was made clear to us that the Western powers paid only lip service to German unification, and that the division of Europe was a consequence not only of superior Soviet strength and Soviet ex-

pansionism, but also of self-seeking imperial interests and the
aspirations of the Western Great Powers.

The critical juncture in putting the brakes on democratization—
in other words, in returning to Leninist norms and a dictatorship
of the proletariat—came at the Second Plenum, held in late June
1953 at Tito's residence on Brioni. The plenum's setting and its
most important agenda item—the status of ideology in the party—
were strictly Tito's ideas. This does not mean that he lacked the
support of many Central Committee members; he was sure of a
majority, especially if the fence-sitters were included. But since
he wished to avoid friction and divisiveness, the plenum named
no names in citing channels of "deviation" and "weakness."

I had a feeling at the time that this plenum had set its sights
on our "democratic currents," and, moreover, I suspected Tito of
"factionalist" activity in relation to individual comrades. Too
much was being written and spoken, he was heard to say, against
the bureaucracy.

The very fact that we were meeting on Brioni provoked my
disapproval—something I neither could nor would conceal. It
had always been our custom to hold plenums of the Central
Committee in Belgrade, seat of that committee and of the government. I felt that to convene the plenum on Brioni, Tito's best-
known residence, was to subordinate the Central Committee to
Tito, instead of subordinating Tito to the leading body. I debated
with myself whether to place this before the plenum, but I
dropped the idea, sensing that I would find no support. In Belgrade, on the eve of my departure for Brioni, I mentioned to
Kardelj, and possibly to Ranković and Vukmanović-Tempo, that
collecting Central Committee members from all over Yugoslavia
for a meeting at Brioni was tantamount to depreciating our
highest forum. I don't recall how they reacted, but I remember
that Kardelj shrugged it off. Even so, I had the impression he
agreed with me.

Guards officers were conspicuously stationed everywhere in the hotel where we were staying and even in Tito's villa, though there were no grounds for such security measures; the island was guarded by both the army and the navy. I believe I was not the only one oppressed by the sensation of having been enticed to some secret conclave in a conspirator's stronghold.

My impressions were confirmed by the behavior toward me of certain Central Committee members, to say nothing of Tito. During a break on the terrace of the spacious villa, we were looking over a sculpture by Avgustinčić of a swimming maiden. Jovan Veselinov, the Serbian Central Committee secretary, asked me what I thought of it. "Charming," I said. "And there are five thousand others in the world just like it." He replied, challengingly, "Tito likes it." "That's his taste," I retorted. An insignificant encounter, one might think, but it did not stand alone. I knew Veselinov from prison days as a Communist who attuned his thinking to that of the powers that be, though otherwise he was pleasant and cordial.

I had to give some weight to my brush with Veselinov because of a remark of Tito's early in the session, as we were taking our places. Motioning me to sit on his left, he said in a soft, loaded tone of voice, "You must speak, too, so they won't think we aren't united." I had always assumed that any differences ought to be aired, if not at a plenum, then in the Central Committee Secretariat or the Politburo. Now, suddenly, one had to rise and speak lest Central Committee members suspect differences among the top leaders, with me in particular.

This was not merely factionalist recruitment—to which I had never before submitted—but pressure to speak as Tito wished, even though that might be contrary to my convictions. So I did speak, though irresolute and confused, reconciling my private views with those I believed—in fact knew—to be Tito's. I remember, for instance, criticizing the introduction of "Mr." and "Mrs." into public discourse.

But I pulled myself together overnight and came to my senses. My convictions hardened. On our way back to Belgrade in a convertible, I suggested to Kardelj that we go trout fishing in the river Gacka, in the Lika region. It was a warm summer day. As we were driving up the serpentine road above the town of Senj, I told him that I could not support the new "Brioni" line. With a look of dejection, he replied that I was exaggerating, after which we lapsed into silence. Kardelj loved the fishing. Our luck was superb, perhaps because we were on a reserved stretch of the river, not the open stream. I was mulling over what had happened on Brioni and what I had inadvertently conveyed to Kardelj.

# 21

Tito seemed satisfied with the results of the Second Plenum. On August 1, when we met by chance along the river Una, he poked fun at me for having spent the night in the hay. I had gone there with Major Nedić for some trout fishing, and Tito was touring Lika and Dalmatia. Nedić and I, and our escort, had found no better lodging than a tumble-down haystack, since the people in that area, including Nedić's mother, were still living in shacks next to the skeletons of burned houses. Tito's train had halted on the embankment, its bright glare in sharp contrast to the dilapidated settlement and rocky landscape. We dined together, and I was invited to join him as his tour continued. Perhaps even then there was a touch of coldness in our relationship, a certain stiffness, but it was hard to notice, since even in the most cordial situations Tito kept his closest comrades at arm's length. My hopes of keeping our friendship intact were, if anything, reinforced, but so was my "heretical" thinking.

I had to rush back to Belgrade, because the next day I was to welcome the leader of the left wing of the British Labour party,

Aneurin Bevan, and his wife, Jennie Lee. My driver, Tomo, and I left Tito late that afternoon but lost our way on the bad roads and drove all night, alternating at the wheel, and arrived in Belgrade at dawn, so the Bevans' reception proceeded on schedule. The leader of the Labour party, Clement Attlee, was visiting in Yugoslavia at the same time. He and Bevan were at swords' points, but Bevan avoided casting aspersions on his party's leader, and Dedijer and I saw to it that their paths never crossed.

Bevan and Jennie Lee stayed with us in Belgrade for a day or two. Štefica and I let them have our bedroom. Then Dedijer and I, acting as escorts, drove them to Bosnia and Montenegro, because Bevan wanted to see backward areas and "the real people." In Sarajevo we dined with Djuro Pucar, the Bosnian Central Committee secretary, whose unforced simplicity made a nice impression on Bevan. We took a turn around the old bazaar, of course, and also the indoor market, which was swarming with flies. Bevan commented that DDT was called for. Jennie incautiously exposed herself to the sun and her tender white skin was mildly sunburned. We lingered longest in Montenegro, at Durmitor and on Lake Biograd, spending the night in a peasant cottage near Plevlje. The Bevans and I parted at Cetinje; Dedijer took them on to meet Tito. Little did I know that this would be my last glimpse of Aneurin, and the end of a selfless common search within the socialist movement from two corners of Europe, two different cultures and types of experience.

Plump, with a florid face and light blue "Welsh" eyes, prematurely gray, Bevan expounded his views slowly and patiently. But along with that went an inquiring mind, quick response, and sparkling wit. The qualities I most liked in him were the unconventionality of his sharp intelligence and a faith in socialism that was that of a man of the people, primordial, unshakable.

Between Bevan and me there was a curious affinity in our perception of the crisis into which both variants of socialism, Western and Eastern, were plunging. We both believed in moral boundaries in politics, though politics as such neither can nor need be moral. Those boundaries do not coincide with the striving for truth, but they are not totally distinct from it either. The later conjectures and charges that Bevan influenced me are untrue. Those charges were officially denied in Tito's letter to Bevan after accounts with me had been settled.

To the end, Bevan and Jennie Lee stubbornly protested against the pressures brought to bear on me, and he turned for help to the Socialist International. His death in 1960, while I was in prison, hit me like the loss of a very close friend. Other friends had long since abandoned me, and I had been anathematized by many. With me, affinities in viewpoint always blend with personal affection. When I first left prison, I dedicated my book *Conversations with Stalin* to Bevan, repaying as best I could the debt I owed this faithful and constant fighter.

Jennie Lee differed from her husband, not so much in the principles she stood for as in her way of interpreting them. More reserved, not as rhetorical, she was sharper and harder than her husband, who in his early youth had been a miner, whereas she had had a university education. For her, principles were the main thing; for him, testing them was equally important.

Jennie Lee came twice to Belgrade on my account, first when I was arrested in 1956 and again when I was released in 1961. The 1956 trip was without question a solace to Štefica and our small circle of sympathizers, but its impact on officials was probably limited to their meting out a "gentler" penalty. Her second trip reinforced our friendship and brought sad memories of Aneurin. We have continued corresponding—infrequently but warmly— to this day. When Štefica and I visited London in 1969, we were in effect guests of hers and under her constant care.


No sooner did I return to Belgrade, after leaving the Bevans in Cetinje, than I got down to work on our periodical, *Nova misao* (New Thought). In the Soviet Union change was in the wind, stirring our top leadership with secret hopes, no less for a change in their system than for a normalization of our relations—if not a radical change, at least one that, like our own, would open new horizons. I, however, did not believe that any radical change was in store there. In the spirit of this theme and the style of the times,

I therefore wrote an extensive and complicated article entitled "The Beginning of the End and of the Beginning." It met with a mixed reaction in leading circles. "Democrats" were enthusiastic about it, but "bureaucrats" were not so sure, since it might impede normalizing our relations with Moscow. The bureaucrats were to some extent justified, but they entertained doubts chiefly because I criticized Yugoslav parallels with the Soviet system. One Soviet diplomat, visiting our Ministry of Foreign Affairs, remarked that such articles did not encourage normalization.

Around this time I published an article in *Nova misao* congratulating Miroslav Krleža on his sixtieth birthday, and another about Oscar Davičo and his novel *Song*. Krleža's birthday had passed unnoticed in both the press and official circles. After my article he was given a decoration. Davičo's novel, which even now I think of as in many respects a remarkable achievement, I overpraised, because of the criticism it had generated in purist and dogmatic top circles.

Work on *Nova misao* and everything related to it was becoming more and more dynamic and varied. Ad hoc groups of eminent writers and scholars were brought together to debate various questions. I remember discussions of a history of the Yugoslav peoples and of modern physics. Krleža joined the editorial board, at his own wish but to a warm reception. The board included Dobrica Ćosić, Milan Bogdanović, Oskar Davičo, Mihailo Lalić, Mitra Mitrović, Milentije Popović, Dušan Kostić, Bora Drenovac, and, later, Jože Vilfan. It held meetings frequently. Coming out once a month in twelve thousand copies, *Nova misao* was financed entirely by subscriptions and paid its contributors. As far as I know, to the present day it is the only Yugoslav cultural monthly not subsidized. It had two salaried staff members, the managing editor, Skender Kulenović, and a secretary. Administrative tasks were handled by *Borba*.

As the new journal matured and the circle around it strengthened and diversified, Agitprop faded away as a bureaucratic party organization. I and the other leading Agitprop comrades devoted most of our time to *Nova misao,* leaving only a few minor administrators to plod through informational tasks. This weakening of Agitprop was made possible not only by the formation of an intellectual democratic-socialist nucleus around our journal, but also by the improved organization and liberalization of the news media.

Neither *Nova misao* nor its associated groups set out to be a parallel or opposition center, nor did they become such. They were, together, an informal party grouping, arising from democratic trends, concerned with the rejuvenation of socialist ideas and a critique of Leninist-Stalinist dogmatism.

# 22

New elections were set for November 22, 1953, while at the same time a fresh and this time decisive crisis broke out over Trieste. Far from abating, the intellectual and ideological ferment associated with *Nova misao*—at least as far as I was involved—was stimulated all the more by these events. No matter how elaborate and responsible a task our elections were, they were no more than a symbolic, routine chore. So it is in every one-party system, and so it always had been with us. A new element, however, had entered the picture: the United States and Great Britain had decided to hand over the disputed Zone A of Trieste, which was occupied by their troops, to Italy. This invested the election campaign with a certain liveliness, supplanting the litanies about our glorious past and bright future with exasperation and anger.

The decision was reported on October 9; the very next day demonstrations broke out in Belgrade and spread throughout the country. In the new Yugoslavia these were the first demonstrations to outstrip official intent, even though they began under official auspices. The worst excesses took place in Belgrade.

The Western decision had in face been made several days before its official publication, and already, on September 6, Tito had given a speech at the Italian border declaring that Yugoslavia would never permit Italy to occupy Zone A, meaning Trieste itself. Others took his lead, and the information media joined in. The atmosphere heated up, and maneuvers were held opposite Trieste. In Leskovac, on October 10, Tito delivered so fierce a speech as to leave no doubt that if Italian troops entered Zone A, our troops would march in also. He gave a similar speech the next day in Skoplje.

Our combined party-state leadership found itself in a predicament. It favored demonstrations as an expression of indignation at the Americans and the British, but their unpredictable nature could make things awkward. With Tito present, the Central Committee Secretariat endorsed them, but resolved to strengthen organizational control. This was no simple matter, since the demonstrations enjoyed the backing of our top echelons, and many party members felt the urge to let themselves go. Our militia and State Security were ordered to treat people gently but to curb them from "running wild." Two such contradictory missions presented Ranković with a dilemma. He was obliged to send a troop of cavalry to Knez Mihailova Street, where the libraries of the Western nations were located, and to throw protective cordons around the Western embassies.

That same evening, as demonstrations raged through the city, I drove from a conference at Tito's to make an on-the-spot survey. The libraries on Knez Mihailova Street were wrecked. Windows at the British embassy were broken, but the militia, helped by a strong iron fence, had prevented greater destruction. Held in check, mobs were still chanting "Trieste is ours!" and "Pela's a mongrel!" (Pela džukela). (Giuseppe Pela was the Italian minister for foreign affairs; "džukela" was a spur-of-the-moment inspiration for the sake of rhyme.) I consulted briefly with those in charge, who recognized me, then returned to Tito's villa, where my appraisal was accepted: the demonstrations had exceeded the desired limits, but there was nothing hostile in them, nothing requiring more than organizational and propaganda measures.

On October 11, a mass meeting was held at the Hotel Slavija, followed by a great gathering on Republic Square. Both were called by social organizations, but were unruly even so. Joining the speakers at the hotel, I told the crowd that I, too, would have demonstrated were I not a high official, but warned them not to smash American and British property, since we would have to pay for it later. After the speeches the crowd moved from the Slavija to the mass meeting in Republic Square. I was at the head of the procession. Some young people hoisted me up on their shoulders, and the following day a picture of it was published in the papers. I found the picture distasteful, for it provoked malicious remarks in top circles about my demagoguery, but also because I had qualms about the glorification of leaders.

On that same day, October 11, *Borba* printed the first in a series of articles I had written, which were to result in my being driven off the Central Committee by January and were eventually to lead me to adopt a critical stance toward Marxism. The initiative for these articles came from *Politika*. I don't remember specifically from whom—perhaps Vladislav Ribnikar. Comrades from *Politika* felt that a number of ideological problems needed analysis and reformulation. Modeled on a practice of newspapers in the West, my articles were to be always of the same length and place in the same prominent spot. But as soon as the comrades from *Borba,* then edited by Veljko Vlahović, found out, there was a chorus of protests: as the party organ, *Borba* had priority in publishing articles of this nature. I yielded to their demand, but because I had already given my word to *Politika,* a compromise was worked out: Moša Pijade would write for it. And so he did, though in a different way from the way I would have.

The articles in *Borba* at first came out every Sunday. After December 22, at the suggestion of the *Borba* staff and because of rising interest, they appeared on Tuesdays, Thursdays, and Sundays. I wrote them carefully and simply, avoiding "dialectics" and other such artifice, since my expository manner was changing along with my views. The first article was entitled "New Content"; the gist of it was as follows:

Revolution cannot be saved by its past. Revolution has to find new ideas, new forms, new challenges, different from its everyday self; a new style and language. The bourgeoisie and the bureaucracy have already found new forms and slogans. Democracy seeks them, too, and it will find them—in order for Yugoslavia and that spark of opposition in today's world to move ahead. . . .

I cite this to illustrate my concept of democracy as an extension of revolution, and my view of Yugoslavia as a focal point where socialism and freedom converge. In a meeting with Tito to discuss ways of dealing with the Trieste crisis, I said that what most pleased me was the fact that we were still revolutionaries. "You bet!" he replied. Even though my hopes for democracy as the continuation of revolution have been dashed (Yugoslavia, it seems, was not destined to resolve the problem of freedom as the condition of socialism), even though my own views have since evolved, to this day I think of myself as a revolutionary, a democratic revolutionary. What else could I be? What else could anyone be who consistently espouses pluralism in one-party dictatorships?

In my last published article in the *Borba* series—my last piece to be published in Yugoslavia—the final sentence read as follows: "The main objective strength of socialism can arise only from the true freedom of truly socialist forces." Without any doubt I knew the "error" of my ideas by this time and had some inkling of what my fate was to be. Since then, nearly thirty years have passed, but this fundamental problem of Eastern Europe, and of Yugoslavia in particular, remains unarticulated except in "heretical" disputes: freedom for oneself is both the precondition and condition of freedom for others, and the other way around.

Eighteen of my articles were published, the next to last one on December 29. The last, already set in type, was suspended by Kardelj, which is to say the executive arm of the Central Committee. Those articles, I believe, form a single whole; there was talk at *Borba*—the suggestion came from Milo Vitorović—of having them published as a brochure entitled "Ideas." This never came about because of the ban.

Were my articles in *Borba* an accident? What would have happened if I hadn't written them? I think I would have encountered the opposition of Tito and the Titoists in any case, though maybe a month or two later. *Nova misao* and its associated activity were more than enough to provoke the conservative forces in the party bureaucracy. Nor could I stop myself any longer. I would have gone on writing, giving lectures, promoting the convictions that had taken root in me. Not all was crystal clear in my thinking, but there was no intellectual ambivalence. It was my psyche—my sense of right and wrong—that wavered and was torn two ways. It was hard to part from comrades with whom I had borne historic responsibilities, shared the good and the bad.

Those uncertainties and inner conflicts drove me to seek an audience with Tito after he returned from Skoplje. I wanted to know what he thought of my articles. I found him at the White Palace, with General Staff maps pinned on the walls. To my direct question, he reflected for a moment and then said that what I had written was good, but that I ought to write more about young people and the danger from the bourgeoisie. I could see that the young were important and the bourgeoisie a danger, but by now he and I were living in different worlds. My visit with him was brief, less than half an hour.

Tito's demeanor on this occasion was that of a general at his command post. From the "front" outside Trieste they were transmitting reports and requesting instructions. I think it was to General Kosta Nadj that Tito gave orders to send in Soviet, not American, tanks, "otherwise it will be awkward." I asked questions, unable to picture the entry of our troops into Zone A with British and American troops present. "We will go in!" Tito declared. "But what if they open fire?" "They won't. And if the Italians start firing, we'll fire back." I approved of our troops entering Zone A, though I thought then and still do that the whole campaign was too abrupt, too violent. Once the British and

Americans backed down from their decision and the atmosphere had relaxed, I had the impression that Tito saw how sudden and drastic our actions had been. As if to justify himself a little to his close colleagues, he said, "It's not a question just of Zone A. They'll be after Zone B, too, if we don't show some spunk."

The vehemence of the campaign was of a piece with our newly emphasized independence from the West, which implied a normalization of relations with the U.S.S.R. To the best of my knowledge, there is no proof that the United States and Great Britain supported Italian claims to Zone A. My understanding is that they simply wanted to get that zone off their own backs and thus break the deadlock. Such a conclusion is favored, it seems to me, by the successful negotiations carried out in London in 1954 by our ambassador, Vladimir Velebit, and representatives of the United States, Great Britain, and Italy, whereby Zone A went to Italy and Zone B to Yugoslavia, plus some insignificant territorial and financial concessions to us.

The Trieste crisis postponed and obscured the differences— now to be surmised, if not directly observed—that separated me from Tito and from those who, like him, advocated a monolithic party and ideological unity. The top echelon's unity endured, because differences had not yet arisen on specific questions. The façade of the ideological monolith had cracked only a little; it seemed that political unity could coexist with nuances in ideology. Otherwise there would have been no dinner party at my house on October 20, attended by Tito, Kardelj, Ranković, Vukmanović-Tempo, Pijade, and Koča Popović, all with their wives.

This dinner had come about when Štefica, who was friends with Jovanka, once found herself at Tito's at dinnertime. She declined to join them, because she felt awkward about constantly dining there when Tito and Jovanka never ate at our house. "No one invites me!" joked Tito, whereupon Štefica invited them to dinner and they accepted. This was the first top-level dinner attended by Tito, which says something about the change to a more direct and "equal" relationship among us. The atmosphere was warm and friendly, as well it should have been among comrades in arms far removed from the revolutionary fray. "We ought to have dinners like this more often," said Kardelj in the course of the evening.

Along with my intensive writing and my work on *Nova misao,* I managed to take part in the election campaign. I spoke at a rally in Titograd, where I was nominated. From there I rushed to Belgrade, and from Belgrade to another rally, in Maribor, and from Maribor to Banja Luka. We were "criss-crossing the country like a telegram," as my Security escort, Petar Vojvodić, quipped. I also spoke at a rally in Požarevac, driving there with Ranković's deputy, Svetislav Stefanović-Ćeća. It struck me that the two of us were already separated by so many differences in viewpoint, and, above all, in our general approach to problems, that we might as well have come from two different worlds. In Titograd I felt the malicious, childish urge to shout out that, being the only candidate, I would be elected no matter what. Out of respect for my listeners I squelched that urge—were they to blame for participating in such "elections"? I did insist that there be no official dinner in Požarevac, and so we dined in the apartment of a local party official, without fanfare or state expense.

Before leaving for Maribor I consulted with Kardelj about the topic of my speech. He suggested the working class in the revolution, because it had not received the attention it deserved. I agreed to do so, partly out of doctrinaire identification of the "historic role" of the workers with that of the Communists, and partly to forestall any accusation of underrating the working class. In my speeches I also made sharp attacks on the West—attacks motivated both by the Trieste crisis, which was still acute, and by a hunch that I might also be accused of favoring "Western ideology."

# 23

Once I had set out along a new path, my unimpeded thoughts assumed ever clearer and firmer shape. Around me clouds of disapproval were gathering, though on occasion I won enthusiastic support. I myself was torn between existing relationships, which were real and structured, and my own knowledge and conceptions. By the end of November I realized that confrontation was inevitable, but still hoped for some mutually acceptable solution. Even if removed from the highest forum, I might be allowed to express my views independently.

This conclusion reflected the intellectual atmosphere in which I moved and the democratic atmosphere prevalent in the party itself. That atmosphere was evident from the positive response to my articles. According to Vlahović, *Borba* was receiving more letters with each article; their number was nearing 30,000. At the end of December, I was invited to dinner by someone with whom I had never been close, Osman Karabegović, a Bosnian official holding a high position in Belgrade. The other guests were also Bosnian officials, friends of his. We talked into the night about democratization and new approaches to socialism. Then, however, came the decision to convene a Third Plenum, to discuss "the case of Comrade M. Djilas." How abruptly the climate changed can be illustrated by the fact that this same Karabegović did not even respond to my greeting when I happened to sit next to him at the plenum.

My hopes were also fed by the attitudes of officials. A substantial number encouraged and praised me, while as many acted suspicious and were darkly silent. I well knew the proclivity of Communists to change their minds the moment they sense a change of course at the top, but in this case I felt it less likely because of democratization.

It was clear to me from the start that my side was the weaker; therefore I would be pushed out. But this was not why I refrained from organizing a faction or group. I wished to answer for my actions and ideas all alone. During that entire period of my "heretical" intellectual and journalistic activity, I did not attempt by a single word or act to win anyone over to my views. To the end, I remained loyal to the leadership of which I was a member. I regarded my articles as a seed, was a slave to my own ideas, and felt myself to be blameless, having taken no action contrary to party rules and my conscience.

Except for a little more tension, my life proceeded routinely. One day might bring a premonition of the bureaucracy's inevitable reckoning with me, but the next would restore my faith in the permanence of my relationships with my comrades.

Working with a team of legal experts and leading party members, Kardelj had completed a constitutional ordinance which was, in effect, a new constitution. Tito, however, did not agree to a government composed of professionals, with party leaders relegated to the National Assembly as representatives. Kardelj meant this to be a significant step toward democratization—one that would invigorate the Assembly. But Tito saw this as isolating him and probably suspected that his functions would come under the Assembly's control. Early in September 1953, he summoned Kardelj to Belje, where he was deer hunting. It offended me that Tito could so readily and arbitrarily alter a draft labored over with diligence and trust—still more, that he should order Kardelj to come and hear his objections on the hunting grounds. Stifling his indignation, Kardelj returned from Belje prepared to carry out Tito's instructions. I expressed open disapproval: "So even you knuckle under!" Later I told Kardelj that Tito was on the side of bureaucracy—a statement he would divulge at the Third Plenum in January.

Just before Kardelj left for Belje, he, Ranković, and I strolled down Užička Street, where all our villas, including Tito's, were located. In recent years thick walls had gone up around Tito's residence, and as we passed them I remarked that these walls symbolized the bureaucratic way of looking at things, or words to that effect. Kardelj said: "Everything has changed or is changing, except for the Old Man and all that relates to him." I then observed that Tito should somehow be brought to realize the impropriety of his style and all this pomp. But Ranković interrupted. "Let's not talk about it here." Kardelj and I took that to mean that even the street was bugged.

Never again would the three of us have such a conversation. Later on, at the Third Plenum, that exchange, through some indiscretion by Kardelj or Ranković, gave rise to the story that I had wanted them to join me in a faction. There is no truth to it, if only because our thoughts were voiced spontaneously. None of us showed any inclination to form a "faction" against Tito. I myself never, not even privately, envisioned more than a gradual diminution of Tito's ostentation and autocratic conduct. However, on the basis of that unpremeditated conversation, I concluded that, although there were no essential differences among the three of us, I would get no support from Kardelj, still less from Ranković.

Even the least significant events of the revolution were widely commemorated in Yugoslavia. That year, 1953, was the tenth anniversary of the Second Session of AVNOJ. The session's date, November 29, was already a national holiday, but the tenth anniversary had to be celebrated in a special way. Orders went out for all surviving AVNOJ participants to attend a formal reunion at Jajce, the site of that Second Session. The diplomatic corps was transported there, and a reception was organized.

On the eve of the festivities I took a walk around Jajce with Koča Popović, reviving wartime memories and talking about the future. I remarked in jest: "It's curious how much heavier our council members are today than they were in 1943." He glanced at a wartime photograph of me, part of a nearby display. "A religious fanatic!" he remarked.

We all continued in easy harmony, with "heretical" gibes at the system, but the usual warmth was missing. At the fortress, before going into the underground shrine, which had once been Tito's shelter, he, Kardelj, Ranković, and I were photographed in various combinations. These were the last pictures ever taken of us together.

During the formal session Tito sulked. Kardelj had mentioned to me beforehand that on this most important of commemorations we had forgotten to give Tito some mark of our esteem. Kardelj had talked of awarding him the marshal's badge, which Avgustinčić had designed earlier in consultation with Tito, and which was supposed to be worn like a pendant. But Tito may have been in a bad mood because of our forgetfulness; I don't know. Or there might have been some other reason.

I sat on Tito's right. Recalling what Kardelj had said, I whispered to him: "That marshal's badge that Avgustinčić made ought to be passed down to future presidents of the republic, since the president is supreme commander." I thought that the idea of continuity of his leadership would please him, but he took offense. "That's right—so some good-for-nothing can wear it!" Tito had not changed. He neither could nor would make any distinction between the state and his personal prestige.

I left Jajce by car with Generals Peko Dapčević and Veljko Kovačević. With Dapčević I was then on close terms. Though our conversation on the road was pleasant enough, I felt depressed and hemmed in. I avoided broaching the ideas expressed in my articles, although the two men themselves touched on such themes in passing, unaware of dissent at the top. Still, for all my gloomy uncertainty, I had resolved to continue expressing myself and was confused only about future ways and means of doing so.

Upon my return to Belgrade both my trepidation and my resolve intensified. Ideas, once ingrained, have a way of becoming invincible, as if they were eternal. No weakness, no hesitation, can bring them to a halt. Though I continued writing for *Nova misao,* the bond with my comrades remained strong, as did my hope for a solution that would guarantee my intellectual existence.

Inside me, however, thoughts and conclusions ripened of their own accord. On the night of December 7–8, I suddenly awoke with the sure knowledge that I had to part with my comrades— that I had already done it. It was a piercing, irrevocable sensation. I have written about it in *The Unperfect Society* and mention it here for the sake of continuity. This knowledge would not go away, although I didn't want to escalate conflict with my comrades and shunned any hint of faction.

In mid-December, I called on Ranković one Sunday morning, when visits were not customary, having sensed that my articles had caused division between us. We sat in his study and talked randomly. He was reserved but very kind. I felt that he was troubled by our obvious estrangement. To my question about what he thought of my articles, he replied briefly and categorically that they "damaged the party." He pressed me to take as a gift a double-barreled shotgun that I had admired, but I declined. To accept a gift from someone with whom one foresees breaking off wouldn't be right, I thought, our long friendship notwithstanding.

In his *Novi prilozi za biografiju druga Tita,* Vladimir Dedijer writes: "But when the time came for drastic erosion in that original partisan ethic, when Ranković and Djilas tore at each other's throats in the struggle for power—not simply over who would be the heir to Tito but who would wrest his power from him—all that friendship begotten in blood burst like a bubble on the water." This claim of Dedijer's has no basis in fact. Ranković and I were close to the very end. There were no quarrels between us, no intrigues, no jealousies. As for some sort of "power struggle," with me a thirst for power could be no more than a reflex, if only because I knew I was dealing from a weak hand and wished to remain pure, a lonely rebel supporting an idea.

Sometime after seeing Ranković, I went to visit Kardelj at his home—on December 22, I think. I don't recall what led up to it—whether at his or my initiative, or even on some business matter—but it was not out of any sentimentality on my part, as with Ranković. I believed all along that Kardelj and I were basically in agreement. Even today I think so, although we differed in certain nuances—nuances that shortly thereafter, at the Third Plenum, he would develop into differences rooted in principle. This conversation, too, was random, though he made reference to my "exaggerating" and being "premature." When I said that we were fundamentally in agreement, he declared, "No, we are not. You are against the party, and I am for it." I was not against the party, I said, only against a Leninist party. I wanted a party that was reformed and democratic. But it was now clear to me that I could expect no support from this quarter either—not even to the extent of not being ostracized.

I was alone with Štefica. She drew her strength and devotion from two unfailing sources: the sacred marriage bond, and our tragic shared experience of seeing an ideal betrayed and of consenting to solitude and damnation.

# 24

Kardelj informed me that I had to assume the office of president of the National Assembly—a decision reached with Tito. The Secretariat of the Central Committee had had nothing to do with this, so it came to me as a surprise. And an unpleasant one, for two reasons. First, it was tactless to go over the head of Moša Pijade, who had been passionately involved with the Assembly's business. Second, I took this to be a backstage move to keep me quiet and soak up my time with a purely ceremonial duty that would prevent me from writing. Kardelj probably detected the unhappiness behind my overhearty acquiescence in every duty the party entrusted to me, including this. As for my objection regarding Pijade, he said that, under the new constitutional system, it was necessary that a younger man—someone from the inner circle —take over the Assembly.

I was elected to the presidency on December 25, only fifteen days prior to the decision to dismiss me. This indicates some hesitation in the inner circle—Tito, Ranković, and Kardelj. It was not just an evasion of political difficulty and embarrassment;

our friendship of many years surely played a role. Besides, it was clear to them that I was no "enemy," no adversary or factionalist, only a comrade with divergent opinions.

The motion to elect me president of the Assembly was made by Vladimir Bakarić on behalf of a group of representatives. That was not accidental: he was selected not only as a respected leader but as one of the exponents of democratic reform. Although I was now well involved with my own heresies, I took up my new duties with dispatch. I had the support of Pijade, despite his justified offense at not having been given the position himself. Vladimir Simić, the onetime leader of the Republicans, proposed at a meeting of the Assembly leadership that a special office be set up in the Assembly building for Tito. I rejected this, and Pijade agreed, because the government already had its own offices and Tito only rarely attended. This detail would not be worth mentioning had Simić not added it to the accusations and mudslinging that followed the Third Plenum. Fellow travelers are often more zealous than Communists themselves.

Doubts and pressures from party functionaries and the party apparatus, and probably also from the police and the military, pushed Tito and the leadership toward their decision. The top echelon daily received confidential reports from all districts about even the most trivial occurrences—what this or that person said on a particular level of society or in a given coterie, and especially what was said within the party. Besides, comrades from the leadership probably tipped their hand while with Tito. I know for certain that Kardelj warned him of the negative impact of my articles and the confusion they were creating, in that party cadres took them as official. Indeed, he practically boasted of it to me in one of our conversations at the time. Ranković may have felt duty-bound to do the same, though I cannot say for certain.

The reticence and ill will around me began to hit home. At an Assembly meeting, Petar Stambolić with unconcealed resentment flung in my face, "When a person reads your articles, he gets the impression that it would be best to throw everything to the devil." At a reception, Cana Babović was so deviously sweet with me that I realized she knew about my "deviations" and the reckoning to come. And Miroslav Krleža, dropping in on me at the Central Committee, asked, "Do you show your articles to the Old Man before publication?" When I answered that I didn't show them to Tito because they were not official positions, Krleža's face stiffened with worry. His eyes downcast, he said, "You should. Without the Old Man's imprimatur, who knows how people may interpret them?"

But the note of approval was still mounting; people even encouraged me. I used to see Vukmanović-Tempo often in those days, despite what he says in his memoirs. For a year or more I had been taking walks around Belgrade. One day in late December we arranged to meet on Knez Mihailova Street, in front of the Glogovac shoe shop. He praised my writing, and I said only half in jest, "Tempo, don't praise me so much. What will you do tomorrow if judgment comes from on high?" "Who—me?" he exclaimed. "I'd always say openly what I thought." Then there was Vlahović, who, partly because he was following the response to my articles from his vantage point at *Borba*, sang praises of my writing. "You know," he told me once, "you're saying what we've all been saying. But you say it so much more deftly!" Dapčević and Koča Popović also agreed, though Dapčević lacked conviction and Popović said so only in passing when we happened to meet.

I also remember distinctly a conversation I had with Vladimir Bakarić in November 1953. In Zagreb on business, I was staying at the Villa Weiss, the guest house of the Croatian government. Bakarić gave a dinner, which Štefica attended as well as Zvonko Brkić, organizational secretary of the Croatian Central Committee. Our rambling conversation on politics and theory continued till midnight. In many ways Bakarić had gone farther than I. Needless to say, he did not question socialism or the Yugoslav system, but was more radical than I in criticizing Leninism and the legacies that so burdened us.

I would not take note of that conversation with Bakarić were it not illustrative of the way in which I was called to account. At the Third Plenum, in January 1954, Bakarić headed the commission that weighed my case and proposed measures against me.

This was no accident, I am convinced. Since Zvonko Brkić, also present at the dinner, kept his thoughts to himself and later was fanatically opposed to me, I suspect that he informed Tito or someone else in the inner circle about Bakarić's views. This would explain why Bakarić was chosen to chair the commission, even though in the Assembly some ten days earlier—clearly, before the decision to censure me had been reached—he had nominated me to be its president.

I don't mean that Bakarić betrayed me, but rather that, like so many high officials, he changed his mind, or pretended to change it. He submitted and consented to be manipulated. This is confirmed by Marijan Stilinović, who was thrown off the Croatian Central Committee (one member of which committed suicide) because he opposed further ideological reckonings of the kind imposed on me. In October 1956, in a conversation at Dedijer's apartment, Stilinović told me this during a break in the Croatian Central Committee meeting that was called to drop Stilinović. Bakarić said he would like to submit his resignation and withdraw into intellectual pursuits.

New Year's Eve finally convinced me that Tito and the leadership would soon call me to account. There were plenty of facts to go on, though I still nourished false hopes as to the method and its degree of harshness. That night Štefica and I went from one New Year's Eve celebration to another with Dapčević and his wife. There were all kinds of rumors about my situation. First, Dapčević told me that two or three days earlier, when he and a group of generals—he was then chief of the General Staff—had met with Tito at Brdo, in Slovenia, Tito had been fuming over the views I had expressed in print. Dapčević did not consider it serious, or else wanted to soothe me: "Tito flies off the handle, then changes his mind." But I saw deeper meaning in his story— decisive meaning—and was not a bit soothed.

That night I also met Koča Popović. When I asked his opinion of my writing and my prospects, he replied, "You know what I think, but I'll act as the powers that be decide!" I ran into Jovan Veselinov, the Serbian Central Committee secretary. Usually cordial, Veselinov hardly spoke to me. The film critic

Zija Adamović, though remote from top party echelons, said to me that evening in the journalists' club, "I marvel at your courage, making statements like this!" I don't recall my answer, but his "marveling" was one more confirmation that my position was well undermined. The trial had yet to begin, but the verdict had been reached.

# 25

Štefica and I now withdrew into deliberate isolation, in an effort not to implicate our friends. We proceeded to organize a lonely life for ourselves—long walks, reading, movies. Three or four days after the new year began—maybe it was January 5, 1954— we went to see Orson Welles's *Citizen Kane*. Suddenly Security agents came up to me in the darkness and said softly that I was to step outside. Thinking my arrest imminent, Štefica came out, too. I was told to go and see Kardelj at once at his home on Užička Street.

Kardelj and Ranković were waiting for me in the study. I have described this meeting in my book on Tito, but I will repeat some details here.

The conversation, which lasted more than an hour, skipped around and was ambiguous: they asked nothing of me, they told me nothing. Ranković was silent by and large, but there was a sadness about him, perhaps for the long-standing friendship between us no less than for the breaking up of the party's central core.

Kardelj wanted me to know that Tito was extremely angry, nor did he conceal the fact that he had warned Tito of my "revisionism." At one point Ranković stressed that reports from the district committees indicated that my articles were provoking consternation and disarray in the ranks. Kardelj labeled my revisionist positions "Bernsteinism." I had not read Bernstein, I replied, except as quoted by Lenin. "But *I* have—here he is, right here!" was the rejoinder. The defense I put up was only half-hearted, for I sensed that the decision to settle accounts with me had already been reached. And so it had. When, at the conclusion of our meeting, I asked Kardelj in friendly fashion what he was doing— was he writing anything?—"Oh, yes," he replied with a chuckle. "I'm doing some writing, all right." I took this to mean writing something against me. It was his speech to be delivered at the Third Plenum, though nothing was said then to me about either plenum or speech.

No, nothing then and nothing later about this plenary meeting of the Central Committee, called "the case of Comrade Djilas." It was contrary to party rules but completely in the spirit of the factionalism and behind-the-scenes mobilization practiced in Leninist parties against "deviationists" and "renegades." It was through the newspapers several days later that I found out such a plenum had been called. So it is not true that my essay "Anatomy of a Moral"—published around this time in *Nova misao*—precipitated the plenum and the settling of accounts. Not a word had been said at Kardelj's about "Anatomy," obviously because neither he nor Ranković had read it, that edition having just been run off. But obviously "Anatomy" poured oil on the flames later and served as a convenient pretext to mobilize the top ranks. Wives of the top officials were especially chagrined by this essay, because, under the guise of invented but recognizable characters, they were mocked for boycotting a young actress, the wife of General Dapčević.

Ranković left on some business a little before our meeting ended. With genuine, sober resignation, Kardelj said in the hall as we parted, "Nothing in my life has ever been more difficult." He gestured, as if to say, "But what can you do?" I remain convinced that he was not eager to take on the role of public prosecutor against me at the plenum. Probably he was selected by Tito because we were so close in our views. This way Tito and his heavy-handed cohorts flushed Kardelj into the open and rendered him harmless as a vehicle for democratic ideas. It is sufficient to read what Kardelj was writing at that time to realize that settling accounts with me was the same as settling accounts with himself, with his own barely conceived, stillborn views and democratic aspirations.

It was clear to me especially. In my presence two or three months earlier, Kardelj had gone even farther than I. "Maybe that's how we'll arrive at an opposition," he had said. "As for this party"—he meant the League of Communists—"so far as I'm concerned"—he hesitated—"it would be better if it didn't exist." In the last analysis, however, I have no doubt that Kardelj, taking note of the growing hostility toward me on the part of Tito and the Titoists, began to disassociate himself from me. Such was his personality: penetrating, analytic, patient, but too cautious, his ideas lacking constancy. There was something unresolved about his character. Relations between Tito and Kardelj were more professional than friendly. Tito knew him well and had a feel for his potential.

The meeting at Kardelj's had been a prologue to a drama that in a few days absorbed many Communists and many intellectuals, even many ordinary citizens. With the announcement of the Third Plenum, on January 17, the democratic movement set in motion by our struggle against Stalin was brought to a halt: the party bureaucracy had again gained the upper hand.

Even though the press announcement on January 17 threw me overnight into solitary confinement, as it were, I carried on with my duties for *Nova misao*. But I walked around without feeling my own body. City and people seemed alien, as in a dream. To the extent that people addressed me at all, they looked unnatural and could not find the right words, as if communicating with a man coming down from the scaffold or about to be forced up onto it. Štefica often accompanied me on my walks. We would move along snow-heaped sidewalks and icy footpaths, stiff with cold and apprehension. At home we lost our appetite and insomnia tightened its grip. In the bedroom we did not turn on the heat, anticipating hard times. Yet it was not from the cold, but from the need for closeness, that Štefica shared my bed. Whenever, anxious and sleepless, I turned over and asked some question, I at once got a wakeful, reassuring answer. A suicide pact crossed our minds; Štefica was readier for it than I. Did we have the right to die? Could we live like this? But how could we abandon Aleksa, our son of barely a year, to such a world? What was it that held us back? Not so much desire for life as the thought of leaving our son to strangers and discrediting ourselves and our convictions.

We heard the rumor—was it planted, or a whisper born of panic?—that UBDA, the secret police, was preparing lists of "Djilasites." The shadow of Goli Otok, that camp for pro-Soviets, loomed over us, too, and with it the terrible knowledge—ever suspected, ever dismissed—that there was a secret, inconceivable place of torment for "separatists" and "turncoats." Across my mind flashed the thought that remaining a Communist led not just to defeat but to hopeless, boundless shame. Was it not precisely for that reason that Trotsky, Bukharin, and so many thousands of Communist heretics had not simply been defeated but had vanished altogether from the world?

My whole past, my work in the party, my long years of sacrifice and struggle for it, rose before me in all its unimagined, appalling truth. I thought of writing it all down for some truth-loving future generation. But those ideas I had been trying to formulate seemed timid now, cautious and only half-baked. A meeting of the editorial board of *Nova misao* had been called before the plenum was announced. It was held—after the announcement—in the offices of *Borba*, our headquarters. We ran through the agenda, morose and despondent. Everyone's mind and face registered what convening a plenum of the Central Committee to discuss Milovan Djilas meant, not only for the future of the journal, but also for continuing democratization. They kept looking at me with compassion. Only Jože Vilfan—a kind of general secretary to Tito who had recently been made a member of the board, I think at

Dedijer's suggestion and with the concurrence of Kardelj—remarked that this board meeting could be construed as factionalist. All present dismissed the idea out of hand, and it had not the slightest impact.

The meeting was attended by Krleža, who was unusually silent and depressed. In answer to some remark by Dedijer, he said: "You don't know what it's like to be sixty. You're worn out and don't feel like fighting." We took these words to mean that he was withdrawing into himself, choosing not to participate in the reckoning that hung over me and the journal. On the way out, he kissed me. Others, too, kissed me, as a sign of sympathy and farewell.

After that meeting, as I recall, Dobrica Ćosić, Antonije Isaković, and I went to Isaković's apartment. We sat around for a while, then dispersed. The atmosphere was oppressive, the talk disconnected and anxious.

With the exception of Štefica, Bora Drenovac was the person I saw most in those days; he worked both in Agitprop and on *Nova misao*. Brave, reserved, darkly foreboding, he stood staunchly by me and our democratic ideas. He was conscientious on the job, straightforward in his opinions, firm and unafraid when carrying out policies. Though he had worked with me a long time, I hadn't got to know him well until now. In public, he gave the impression of being a rigid, dogmatic, hard-driving cultural executive. And so he was, to the extent that every *apparatchik* is saddled with such a role. But gradually Bora came to acquire democratic convictions that he stuck to throughout the heyday of *Nova misao* and later disappointment. He never capitulated, though he did beat a tactical retreat. I cannot explain his aloofness a year and a half later other than by an intellectual and emotional crisis of his own, a radical disillusionment with Communism and its prospects. He withdrew into linguistic research, which was all the easier for him after he had been cast out of the party and suffered a long period of unemployment. I called on him with the lawyer Jovan Barović in 1967 after my second term in prison. He was the same Bora Drenovac, though now engrossed in different, nonpolitical work.

In those days our most frequent visitor was Milena, the wife of Peko Dapčević. Too young to grasp my hopeless position, she was obliged to Štefica as a friend and to me as a writer who had taken her under his wing. To my surprise, Dedijer also kept coming to call; he bubbled with rumors and suggestions. By now distrustful and reclusive, I had no confidence in the man. When, in my apartment, he tried to read me the speech he would make at the plenum, I refused to listen, suspecting that he was under instructions to draw me into factionalism.

I don't remember how I found out that Tito had returned to Belgrade—perhaps from the papers—obviously to attend the plenum. Nor do I remember who proposed that I write to him—perhaps both Dapčević and Dedijer. This idea had taken root in the narrow circle in which I moved. I met it halfway; in order not to have my letter interpreted as weakness, I phrased it as a wish to say farewell to Tito after seventeen years of collaboration, stressing that I was not disputing his leadership or his role, nor was I accepting any precedence for Kardelj and Ranković.

After two or three days I was asked to come to the White Palace, where I found Kardelj and Ranković waiting with Tito. In *Tito: The Story from Inside* I have told of that last encounter with comrades of many years' standing, so here I shall add some details omitted there. As I sat down, I asked for coffee, complaining of lack of sleep. As Tito got up to order it, he snapped at me, "We aren't sleeping either." At one point I said to him, "You, I can understand. You've accomplished a lot and so you're protecting it. I've begun something and am defending it. But I wonder at these two [I meant Kardelj and Ranković]. Why are they so stubborn?"

Tito remarked that there seemed to be no movement organized around me, as indeed there was not. My only intention, I said, was to develop socialism further. Tito's rebuttal consisted of trying to point out that the "reaction"—the bourgeoisie—was very strong still in our country and that all sorts of critics could hardly wait to attack us. As an example he cited *Socrates*, a satire, just published, by Branko Ćopić, in which voters elect a dog by the name of Socrates, quite unconcerned with the object of their choice because they are convinced that this has been mandated "from on high." I maintained that Ćopić's satire was an innocent joke, but no one agreed. Kardelj added that a few days earlier the funeral of a politician from the old regime—I forget who— had been attended by several hundred citizens! Ranković sat the whole time in somber silence. His only comment, when my resignation as president of the National Assembly came up, was that I ought to see to that myself, so that it wouldn't look as if it had been extracted under pressure or by administrative methods. Finally Tito asked me to submit my resignation, adding decisively, "What must be, must be." As we said good-by he held out his hand, but with a look of hatred and vindictiveness.

As soon as I returned home, I wrote out my resignation, in bitterness. At the same time I asked my driver, Tomo, to deliver my cars to the White Palace. I had two—a Mercedes and a Jeep, which I used in isolated areas. Two days later Luka Leskošek, my escort, came looking for the suitcases that belonged to the Mercedes. In my haste I had forgotten them, and now I felt awkward because my initials had been engraved on them.

In the course of our conversation, Tito had remarked that my "case" was having the greatest world repercussion since our confrontation with the Soviet Union. I had replied that I didn't read the reports from Tanjug any more; they were no longer sent to me. "Get hold of them and see for yourself," Tito had said. That same day I went to Tanjug to look over the foreign press reports regarding my case. Reluctantly the news agency people obliged me. The volume and variety of reports had a twofold effect: I was impressed and encouraged but at the same time embarrassed and bothered that Western "capitalist" propaganda was so obviously biased in my favor.

Business matters connected with *Nova misao* took me to the *Borba* offices, where I used to go anyway to see Veljko Vlahović, the editor-in-chief. He had views similar to mine, but was also concerned about the consequences that the reckoning with me would entail. On one of these brief visits he said, "You know, your role in the Cominform fight was enormous, and a judgment against you will have very negative consequences: it will be interpreted both inside the party and out as an end to democratization."

A couple of days before the plenum, I dropped in on Vlahović again and found him a changed man, both in his outlook and in his behavior toward me, which showed calculated compassion. He said he, too, would speak at the plenum, but didn't say what the thrust would be. I assumed he would speak from his previous convictions, but did not care to verify this, lest it be interpreted as "factionalizing," recruiting supporters among Central Committee members. Finally Vlahović offered some advice: "Give in to Tito! What else can you do?" He didn't say that he had been to see Tito, which would account for the change in him, but I was told as much by Dedijer, who had also been summoned by Tito. One by one Tito called in the "doubtfuls," those members of the Central Committee who had expressed views similar to mine. In this way he guaranteed "unity" and prepared the plenum's contrite yet aggressive atmosphere. All surrendered with the exception of Dedijer, who devised a formula by which he opposed this kind of settling of accounts by the Central Committee without getting on the wrong side of Tito.

Mitra Mitrović, my former wife, did not approve of the whipped-up unity against me and, so far as I know, was not "granted the honor" of a talk with Tito. Later, Dedijer held me responsible for Vlahović's not having sided with us. To this day I haven't been able to understand why I was responsible. Some months after the plenum, Vlahović wrote of both Dedijer and me as "internal émigrés," a term used by the Soviets when dealing with "deviationists" and "foreign elements."

The day before the plenum convened, I went to the Central Committee building to put my office in order and return some documents. There I ran into Stana Tomašević, an Agitprop official; dejected and speechless, she burst into tears. A Central Committee comrade who was also there reproached me for rashness and justified the reckoning in these words: "Only the end counts; all the rest is secondary."

That evening a terrible restlessness came over me. Štefica and

I had agreed to meet Dapčević and his wife in front of the National Theater. His brother-in-law came, but no Dapčević. Štefica and Milena disappeared somewhere and I was left to wait with Milena's brother. It was cold, and we spent a long time walking back and forth. I thought Dapčević had been arrested. From moral obligation I'd have to take some desperate step, I thought. Finally Dapčević turned up, changed just as Vlahović had changed. He, too, had been to see Tito, though he did not tell me so. He, too, would attack me at the plenum.

# 26

Even the most fearful dream gets forgotten, but this was no dream. The Third Plenum was reality, a vain and shameful reality for all who took part. My main accusers, Tito and Kardelj, though seemingly concerned for party unity, were in fact concerned for their own prestige and power. To inflate the peril, they fabricated guilt. After they had had their say, it was the turn of the tough, sharp-sighted powermongers—among them Minić and Stambolić, Pucar and Marinko, Blažo Jovanović and Maslarić; then came the party weaklings, like Čolaković, and the hysterically penitent "self-critics," like Vukmanović, Dapčević, Vlahović, Crvenkovski, and even Pijade—yes, Pijade, too, who until the day the plenum was scheduled had been sweetly smacking his lips over my articles. It could all have been foreseen. I had foreseen it. But reality is always different, either better or worse. This reality was more horrible, more shameless.

I was more prepared intellectually than emotionally for that plenum and its verdict, sure that I was in the right, yet sentimentally tied to my comrades. But that, too, is an oversimplification; the inner reality was more complex. My aloofness, my indifference to functions and honors—to power itself—helped account for my intellectual readiness, the ripeness of my understanding. What is more, having often in the previous months felt altogether sick of power, I had been relinquishing functions and plunging into reading and writing.

I knew at the time the importance of power, especially for carrying out political ideas, and know it even more clearly today. But at the time, I was repelled by that power, which was more an end in itself than the means to an end, and my disgust grew in proportion as I gazed into its "unsocialist," undemocratic nature. I couldn't say which came first, disgust or insight; they seemed mutually complementary and interchangeable. Even before the plenum was scheduled, I wanted to be "an ordinary person," I wanted to withdraw from power into intellectual and moral independence. Obviously I was deluding myself. This was only in part because the top leadership of a totalitarian party is incapable of releasing a member from its ranks except for "betrayal." My delusion owed just as much to my own intransigence, to my perceptions, which continued to mature, and to my sense of moral obligation to make them known.

The Third Plenum was held in the Central Committee building, which gave it an all-party character. (All plenary sessions of the Central Committee had previously been held at Tito's, in the White Palace.) The proceedings were also carried by radio, to give them a public and national character. I walked there with Štefica by my side; Dedijer accompanied us part of the way.

I arrived feeling numb, bodiless. A heretic, beyond doubt. One who was to be burned at the stake by yesterday's closest comrades, veterans who had fought decisive, momentous battles together. In the conference hall no one showed me to a seat, so I found a place for myself off at one corner of a square table. Nor did anyone exchange so much as a word with me, except when officially required to do so. To pass the time and record the facts, I took notes of the speeches. These I burned once the verbatim notes from the plenum were published.

Though I knew that the verdict had already been reached, I

had no way of knowing the nature or severity of my punishment. Secretly, I hoped that, even while repudiating and dissociating itself from my opinions, the Central Committee would not expel me from the party, perhaps not even from the plenum. But all my democratic and comradely hopes were dashed once the contest was joined. Tito's speech was a piece of bitingly intolerant demogoguery. The reckoning it defined and articulated was not with an adversary who had simply gone astray or been disloyal in their eyes, but with one who had betrayed principle itself.

As Tito was speaking, the respect and fondness I had once felt for him turned to alienation and repulsion. That corpulent, carefully uniformed body with its pudgy, shaven neck filled me with disgust. I saw Kardelj as a petty and inconsistent man who disparaged ideas that till yesterday had been his as well, who employed antirevisionist tirades dating from the turn of the century, and who quoted alleged anti-Tito and anti-party remarks of mine from private conversations and out of context.

But I hated no one, not even these two, whose ideological and political rationalizations were so resolute, so bigoted, that the rest of my self-styled critics took their cue to be rabidly abusive—the Titoists aggressively and the penitents hysterically. Instead of requiting them with hatred and fury of my own, I withdrew into empty desolation behind my moral defenses.

The longer the plenum went on with its monotonous drumbeat of dogma, hatred, and resentment, the more conscious I became of the utter lack of open-minded, principled argument. It was a Stalinist show trial pure and simple. Bloodless it may have been, but no less Stalinist in every other dimension—intellectual, moral, and political.

Nonetheless, it had to be lived through, for surmise demands its own confirmation. The experience was bound to be depressing and demoralizing. In my mental perceptions and style of life I had struck out along my own path, yet I felt bound to my prosecutors and judges by some ancient, still-unbroken cord. Was this, perhaps, because of the suddenness with which I had been made a model victim of the Stalinism of yesterday's anti-Stalinist comrades in arms? In my rational and moral self I was now sundered; in my memory and sensibility I was a slave in bonds. In short, I was still a Communist. Revolutionary ideals and comrades held me fast. At the plenum I would pay for that bondage with a half-hearted show of remorse; but speeches of my comrades combined with the harassment that followed would complete the path of deliverance.

Tito probably sensed that the atmosphere was fast turning into the sort of badgering and provocation that had characterized the Moscow trials. That is why, before the afternoon session on the first day, he said to me, "We are going to behave humanely toward you, not vindictively." But the speeches strung out, each more frenzied and bloodthirsty than the last. Tito's own brutal intransigence and Kardelj's theoretical underpinning had burgeoned to a level of savagery that perhaps even they had not wanted. Whether for this reason or, more likely, because of the repercussions in the Western news media, the next day, in the corridor during the morning-session break, Kardelj, half in confidence, told me that "the Old Man says this is the way it has to be now, but afterward we'll change your position." I don't believe Kardelj had in mind inducing me to repent, but, rather, giving me some meaningless function to show that they were treating me not as Stalin would have, but in a humane and comradely way. They were being forced to shun Stalinist conduct for reasons of state and their own self-respect. But I was neither suited nor inclined to take on a formal role, still less so now that, through the Third Plenum, my estrangement from the party and my intellectual perceptions had found their way into independent channels.

That night, day number one over and done with, I slept as if I had been drugged. It was my first sleep of any kind for some time. The tension had been replaced by indifference. At the next morning's session I heard the same rabidly abusive speeches, but it was as if they had to do with someone else, not me.

Sometime that morning I came up with a notion—no, not a notion, but a malicious way of punishing myself and the comrades who had been closest to me—of beating a retreat. I was still in thrall to the doctrine that ideas are without value if not corroborated in practice, and still equated "practice" with what the party did.

Over lunch in the Šumadija restaurant I told Štefica that I ought to yield a little so as not to break with the party. The thought of Goli Otok oppressed me like a leaden weight. That's where they will send people who take my side, I thought, and in no small numbers at that. Out there they will torment them worse than any Cominformist. There's no organization to defend them, to fight for my ideas and these spontaneous supporters. I dare not drag the innocent into suffering and misery. If I retreat, they will have a chance to take cover and calm down. Then we'll see. . . .

My wife was adamantly opposed to any self-criticism on my part, but at the same time was thoughtful and tender. "I don't think you should do that. It would be a mistake. But I won't keep after you. Do as you think best. You could tell them, 'I'm tired, I want some time to think it over.' "

In *The Unperfect Society* I wrote about that last retreat. Here I will only add that my retraction put the plenum's participants to shame and dampened their spirits. The heavy-handed were overjoyed to have shot me down; the penitent were smug because they were not the only ones to capitulate; and the silent ones were absorbed in their own gloomy torment. But no one—Tito and Ranković least of all—believed that my self-criticism was sincere or final. That was confirmed by the campaign begun against me in the party—my "Bernsteinism" was condemned even in the most forlorn little villages—and even more drastically by the attitude of the top party and government leaders, who turned threatening and hostile virtually the next day.

At the plenum I had a premonition that my last rendering of dues to Communism would cost me dear: for years to come the realization of error and weakness would drive me to prove myself and to correct my views, to look into myself and Communism. It was Tito who prompted this insight, by his concluding remarks, in which he said that they would have to see how sincere I was.

That meant I had no choice: the hounding and harassing would go on until I either turned into a cipher or broke with these people once and for all and stood on my own two feet.

Vladimir Bakarić chaired the committee that was to propose my punishment, and, as mentioned earlier, this was surely done by design. But neither he nor the committee acted independently. They did not hide even from me—why should they?—their consultations with Tito and the other leaders in a special office. Bakarić proposed a final warning (one step short of expulsion) and dismissal from all functions. Later, people said, in public statements made against me, that I had been expelled. Formally, this was not so, but it was not far from the truth.

When I returned with Dedijer for the afternoon session, there was a large crowd waiting in front of the Central Committee building. Just then Tito drove up with a cavalcade of cars. The public applauded him. They applauded me, too.

It was an awkward moment. There was nothing I could do, since there was no organization of any kind. For me to have said a few words to them as an isolated member of the Central Committee would hardly have been proper. What was the size of that spontaneous gathering? My friend Borislav Mihailović-Mihiz thinks 50,000; I estimate closer to 20,000.

Mihiz, a non-Communist intellectual and critic, also thought that my "self-criticism" was the greatest mistake of my life. He would be right were he not losing sight of what it is to be a Communist psychologically, and forgetting that at that time—if only emotionally and pragmatically—I still was one.

The plenum greeted the committee's proposal with a rumble of discontent, so that Tito had to step in: "He should not be expelled, or the foreign press will write that we are behaving like Stalinists!" Here was a new blow, driving home the mistake I had made with my lukewarm self-criticism. My party membership, my allegiance to an idea, depended not on party or idea any longer, but on the Western press! Henceforth, reasons of state and Tito's judgment would govern my destiny. With this I could never be reconciled, and I knew it in my bones as the Third Plenum concluded.

One stage of my life was over; I had to begin another or die. The plenum unanimously adopted the committee's—Tito's—proposal. "All followed the devil's trail" goes the saying: neither Dedijer nor Mitra nor I voted nay. When I emerged from the building, it was already dark. Snow, frost, dim streetlights. I had to wait to cross the street, since the militia and the Guards had blocked it off until Tito was driven away. I saw Tito settling himself comfortably in a limousine. Kardelj was with him. Bitterly I imagined them congratulating each other on a job well done.

The moment the crush of official limousines had thinned out, Dedijer joined me. "I still agree with your ideas," he said. I replied that now we would have to collect our wits and see what next.

Štefica was waiting for me, as I knew she would be, on the path in our snow-covered garden. She was depressed but unwavering. Indoors I found my mother, concerned but constant as ever: "You shouldn't have come out with that last bit, but now it doesn't matter. You know best."

There was no support from anywhere; all was in ruins. We had no savings, no food supplies. We huddled in my mother's room, the only one we kept heated. I was now forty-three years old. The most important, perhaps most vital, part of my life had passed. Perhaps my whole life. Was another one possible? A new one? Hope and confidence broke through: you can always start from scratch.

# 27

Three or four days after the plenum I was at my writing again, taking refuge in a new, more exalted reality, indulging a great desire to express myself in my own way. Bruised and alone but unbroken and free, I continued to think ever more intensively and to put my thoughts down painstakingly on paper.

In two or three days that January, I wrote an essay called "Nordic Dream." In it I expressed regret at being unable to visit Sweden and Norway, to which I had been invited before the plenum, but also took a critical look at myself and at the reality of my refusal to be reconciled with the fate thrust upon me. In February, I wrote a drama, "The Legacy," which dealt with the property motif in human and ideological terms—a theme that had long preoccupied me. Mihiz read both. He liked the essay but not the drama. I burned the drama, a decision I have never regretted.

For some time I had been haunted by the idea of writing my memoirs, telling the story of the Communist movement from the inside, from personal recollection and experience. In the spring and summer of 1954, I wrote *Land Without Justice*, as the first volume of my memoirs. That manuscript, too, still unrevised, was read by Mihiz. His advice was to arrange the material into three basic thematic groups. Though no large change was required, this improved the form of the book and also elevated its tone. The title was suggested by the writer Živorad Stojković, from Njegoš's characterization of Montenegro as a "land without justice."

During those first weeks, we experienced shortages of all kinds, but then the Nikšić Communists, with their grotesque and hysterical party-mindedness, came to our rescue. I had sent my fee for the "revisionist" articles in *Borba* to the library in Nikšić. After the plenum had passed its judgment, I was deemed unworthy of making them a gift, so they sent it back. We rejoiced like children, Štefica and I because now we could afford a typewriter. "By God, that's good!" said my mother, adding the time-honored curse "And may the dog eat their flesh!"

Štefica found work at the beginning of March. We were far from prosperous, but we would not go hungry. About that time Ranković received the English journalist Eric Bourne and his then wife, Desa Pavlović, a *New York Times* correspondent. They asked how I and my family were getting along. Ranković said that, with my mother's annuity, Štefica's salary, and my veteran's pension as a Partisan, we were better off than the average Yugoslav. Although at that time and especially the following year (1955–56) I had to sell things, like my hunting weapons and books, we did not go hungry for a single day and could assure an adequate diet for our child. But we did let go the girl who was taking care of Aleksa, and my niece, who was living with us while finishing school, had to return to her mother in Montenegro. Ranković told the Bournes that he was surprised they took an interest in a person who "represents nobody." From his police/party perspective, he had a point.

At the beginning, in January, I maintained frequent and close relations with Dedijer, his brother Steva, and Bora Drenovac. But early in February, Dedijer and I began to draw apart. Alternating intimacy and estrangement would characterize our relationship until my arrest in November 1956. My relations with Steva, on the other hand, though less close, remained stable. I am not sure just what was the cause of the cooling off of my relationship with Dedijer, but the problem did not arise with me. At any rate, I took it pretty well, although I was sorry that it happened.

When all is said and done, I believe that the primary cause lay in certain traits of Dedijer's character and his undue pragmatism in politics. In February, according to what he himself told me, Dedijer met with Ranković more than once and was told that the highest leadership would receive me if I personally requested it. Immediately after the plenum, Tito and his closest circle looked on Dedijer differently, as is seen in Tito's letter of February 22, 1954—exactly a month after the plenum—to Aneurin Bevan.

On February 1, Bevan had written Tito to protest, among other things, the fact that he, Bevan, had been mentioned at the plenum as having exerted an influence on me. Tito replied that my "case" did not mean Yugoslavia was turning away from democratization, and certainly not from collaboration with the Western socialists. Among other things, he said the following:

In the course of this discussion [at the plenum] your name came up only on one occasion and I have to say that we all regret the publicity it received, for we do not believe you exerted any kind of influence on Djilas regarding the direction in which he was moving, i.e., the direction of anarchist conceptions: we recognize you as a realistic politician. Therefore we beg you not to take this in the least tragically.

As for the present fates of Comrades Djilas and Dedijer, I think one has to make a distinction between them, for Dedijer was not fully informed when he defended Djilas. I believe he has now modified his views to a certain degree as far as Djilas' actions are concerned and, from our general standpoint, positively.*

Tito's letter does not, I think, confirm that Dedijer really joined forces with the regime, but, rather, that he chose to follow a

---

* Michael Foot, *Aneurin Bevan*, London: Davis-Poynter, 1973, pp. 420–22.

different course from mine. Since the plenum my behavior had foreshadowed a critical investigation and final break.

The plenum had brought home to me this tragic but precious—indeed crucial—realization: a superficial, pragmatic, sentimental relationship not only to a leadership but also to an ideology brings denial of the self and destruction of the self, which lets that same leadership treat the "guilty party" as its own needs dictate. I could not but think there had to be something fallacious in the principle, and in the structure it inspired, when its tried-and-true champions could so easily, and with such conscious mendacity, be destroyed merely for misgivings concerning totalitarian and autocratic methods.

Soon, Dedijer began to dissociate himself publicly from me, allegedly for my lack of realism, or, as he put it to Sulzberger of the *New York Times*, for having "flown off like a balloon." It may sound absurd, but the fact is I had no opportunity to be realistic; in addition to which, to be realistic under a dictatorial, still largely totalitarian regime would have undermined my integrity and my views. I remembered that being "realistic" and conciliatory had made Stalin's task easier when he set out to destroy Trotsky, Bukharin, and the other party oppositionists, not just physically but mentally, as marginal figures in the struggle for power. I recalled the maxim "Better to be an honorable man than a minister of state." Moral rebellion is the beginning of all rebellion. But there was more to it than that. Implicit in this maxim is the assumption that it is possible to survive only in negation, in criticism of the given state of affairs. By this I do not mean criticism that reverts to the old, prerevolutionary relationships—here I was a realist—but criticism that seeks to create something new. New! Yes, even when "new" is but the intimation of newness. Consistent, rational, selfless criticism of the status quo opens up a vista of the new. To stick with one's idea, one's creativity—however insanely—in sacrifice and self-criticism means to survive, if only for generations yet unborn.

With moving, irrefutable finality it dawned on me that there was no other way out of bondage to the whims of dictators and oligarchs than by the existence of another party, socialist or

Communist. At the same time, and no less unavoidably, there had to be criticism of Leninism and Leninist Communism, all the way to its Marxist roots. Immediately, I set to work on theoretical texts, side by side with my memoirs. An essay called "The Omniscience of Stupidity," a critique of all-knowing ideology and an all-knowing dictator, was sketched out in 1954. I also began drafting and writing portions of "Freedom and Ownership," from which, in the second half of 1956, *The New Class* would emerge.

We lived an ever more solitary existence, I with my speculations and conclusions, which at one and the same time intoxicated and alarmed me. With Dedijer, I could not talk about ideas. He came less often, systematically avoiding conversation about politics and making the point that his visits were for sentimental and moral reasons. With Drenovac, on the other hand, conversations were almost exclusively about politics.

In March, I resigned from the party. Before doing so I attended a meeting of the local party organization, to avoid reproach for not having made an attempt to adapt to that level of party activity. All was as I had foreseen: around Štefica and me a circle of empty seats like a halo. No one said a word to us; either they dared not or cared not to do so. To remain a party member in such circumstances would have been ignominious, so I asked Štefica to take my membership card to the next meeting with a short statement saying that I was resigning. The news of my resignation spread fast, and Tito was reported to have said that this was a unique case in the history of our party.

The poetess Desanka Maksimović unexpectedly turned up one day, bearing gifts of candy and fruit, as one does when visiting the sick. One couldn't talk to her about politics, still less about political theory, for her interests were those of a writer and friend. Yet her visit cemented our relationship. Anxious to have someone of flawless taste and reputation evaluate my *Land Without Justice* before I offered it to the publishing house Srpska književna zadruga, the Serbian Literary Guild, through Desanka, in 1956, I asked the writer Ivo Andrić to read it. The suggestion actually came from Desanka, who liked the work. But Andrić refused: "It's awkward for me, Desanka. I'm a party member."

Another unexpected but welcome visitor was the critic Borislav Mihailović-Mihiz. We used to see each other on occasion, but had never been close. His wife, Milica, had given me English lessons for a short time. In her instruction she had been conscientious and rigorous, and treated me as if I were a little boy and not an adult and an official. I continued my study of English in prison on my own and so I cannot claim to know it well.

Mihiz explained his visit simply and candidly: "I know you're lonely. I'm not joining the boycott, and I think a visit from me will not be unwelcome." My friendship with him had special significance for me. Quite apart from the intensified ostracism and pressure, he introduced me to a different, non-Communist, world, unlimited not in numbers but in its ways. It was an intellectual, bohemian crowd, to which I could not really adapt, though I enjoyed its spirit and freedom from convention. I think that it was at Mihiz's initiative, in April or May of 1954, that Yugoslavia's most famous actress, Mira Stupica, gave a dinner party for Štefica and me. Stupica asked me on that occasion, "How will it end? What will happen to you?" "I don't know what will happen," I replied, "but I do know that this is not the end." Such socializing quickly ceased, however, under pressure from the authorities, but also, in all fairness, because of the absence of any real affinity.

Mihiz himself is one of the most intelligent people I have ever known. He is frank to the point of impertinence and he carries his honesty to the point of sacrifice. A man of impressions, of momentary inspiration, precipitous in his thinking, he fastens on a point with fierce and dazzling conviction. Though he is not strong on political theory or the history of Communism—he has never been a Communist—we had many useful discussions. Once, I brought up the question of discrimination as not typical of Communism. Mihiz urged me to devote more attention—an entire chapter—in *The New Class* to ideological discrimination as in fact typical of Communism. When he turns to generalizations, on the other hand, Mihiz is not nearly as impressive. His learning, while not systematic, is voluminous. Though no dogmatist, either as a person or in his ideas, he is inflexible in his nationalism. I have often asked myself to what extent his Serbianism is a reaction to ideological dictatorship, and to what extent it is triggered by senseless anti-Serbianism.

Essentially, Mihiz is a national democrat in the tradition of Serbian liberalism. To what degree is a consistent democrat like Mihiz at the same time a nationalist and not merely a patriot? I consider that nationalism does not and cannot exist in itself as ideology, but that every political movement, every social group, draws upon national sources. Nationalism as an ideology can exist only in times of national emergency: then all are patriots and nationalists, or at least the most militant are.

A born conversationalist and gifted critic, Mihiz lives by force of political circumstance in an age not his own, condemned to salon rhetoric and intermittent, nonpolitical criticism. He is not alone in this, but few possess his gifts to such a degree; his tragedy is thus the more profound and irreparable.

Through him I met, among others, the painter Mića Popović and the author Živorad Stojković. Although I felt closer to Mihiz, I saw Stojković more often. He lived not far from the apartment at 8 Palmotićeva Street where the authorities had moved my family from Dedinje in May 1954. Mihiz and I remained in touch, however. He even came by the evening before I went on trial in January 1955. We left the apartment "to take a walk" (as the phrase goes), so he could make some suggestions for my speech in court.

In 1956, the authorities again increased their pressure. Agents openly followed me around, photographing and checking out everyone entering my building. Stojković stopped coming, alleging that my seeing American newsmen compromised him.

Mihiz took a different approach. In the fall of 1956, he came to my apartment to say that he could not afford to be seen with me. "You they write about in the Western press, but I can be liquidated over the telephone." No doubt through the efforts of Stevan Doronsky, a party official and Mihiz's old school friend, the authorities were "saving" him from me—in other words, punishing me with total isolation. Mihiz was sent to Novi Sad to live, and I was soon arrested. Yet during my first imprisonment, from 1956 to 1961, only Mihiz offered Štefica financial assistance.

This she declined, for somehow she was making ends meet. After my final release, at the end of 1966, he and I renewed our friendship, picking up where we left off.

In May 1954, two foreign journalists had come to visit me. One mentioned the official claim that I had not requested a pension for reasons of demagoguery, though it would gladly have been given me. I then applied for and got my pension immediately, and a relatively high one. It guaranteed our existence—for six months. In January 1955, this pension was discontinued, when Dedijer and I were conditionally sentenced for making statements to the foreign press. The signature on the order canceling it was the same as the one granting it: Slobodan Penezić, head of the Serbian government.

Late in the summer of 1954, Jovan Barović and his wife, Dušanka, came to see me. Barović, a high-ranking officer, had been discharged from the army for dissenting from the official party position in a discussion of my case. From that time on the bond between us was never broken, and it continued with his family after Barović died in an auto accident in 1979. He was very close to me in his views and always remained so, though we differed on some details. Like me, he was a Montenegrin and had been a revolutionary from early youth, yet it was not that bond, but, rather, a creative disillusionment with Leninism that held us together. In this unity of views, Barović and I were the exception; other oppositionists criticized the handling of my case, only to go each his own way. The main reason, of course, for the splitting up of "Djilasites" was the authorities' total control and systematic intimidation. But there were other reasons as well. The phenomenon called "Djilasism" represented the disintegration of official consciousness more than a consciously defined program. The same, after all, has been true of other opposition movements in Eastern Europe, where every man saves himself as best he can. Between Barović and me, though, if serious disagreements ever existed, they had no deep or lasting political roots. He always stood ready to help, even though his means, like my needs, were not great. I have written an article about him, first published in the émigré periodical *Kontinent,* and so will say no more, though as an oppositionist from within the party he perhaps deserves more attention than anyone else.

One day at the end of the summer, I ran into the writer Oskar Davičo on Revolution Boulevard. At the time of the Third Plenum, he had been abroad, but no sooner was it over than he, too, had been attacked in the press. I don't know how he looked upon his relationship with the party, but he neither sought me out nor took any interest in me after he returned. Nor did he linger at that chance encounter, except to ask gloomily how I was and give me a pitying embrace as we said good-by. Never again did we speak, though at times we met on the street.

The prominent British Labourite Ernest Davis came to Belgrade at the end of that same summer and asked to see me in order to inform himself about my case and the further measures to be taken by the Yugoslav leadership. We met in the Hotel Excelsior and talked through an interpreter from the British embassy. I presented my views candidly but diplomatically. Finally he asked what he might do for me. Make it possible, I replied, for me to publish my views in the Labour paper, the *Daily Herald*. He gave me his word, and I prepared three articles, pending an invitation. It never came and they went unpublished. That unsuccessful attempt to publish my work—and in a socialist newspaper at that—reveals my position from the very beginning. It also reveals how solicitous, if not downright opportunistic, the Labour leadership was toward Tito and the Yugoslav government.

Also at the end of that summer of 1954, a group of foreign students—Americans, I think—asked to meet me. Our conversation, held in front of the café on Kosovo Street, was disconnected and lacking in substance because of my poor English and their nonexistent Serbian. Yet this was more than enough to make the authorities unhappy. They accelerated pressure by planting informers and following me. Nothing, though, could stop me from writing, taking walks with Štefica, and playing with my son. It looked as if one could go on living like this. But I didn't believe in such a life.

# 28

It seemed for a while there that I would welcome in the year
1955 without major incident. But then, late in the fall, the Central Committee began to settle accounts with Dedijer. They had
obviously been waiting for the party's dogmatic, antidemocratic
course to stabilize after the "Djilas affair" had faded in the
Western press. Judging by the method—to wait until the dust had
settled in the party—I would say that the initiative came from
Ranković. He of course had the support of the other major officials.

The reckoning apparently involved Mitra and Dapčević, too,
since both made statements against me. Mitra, I know, was
pressured into it. She and I had been in touch intermittently,
mainly because of our daughter, Vukica, who lived with her
mother. But with Dapčević I had been out of touch since the
plenum, when he came out against me. Over the summer of 1954,
his wife kept in occasional touch with Štefica and me through her
sister.

Dedijer, however, rebelled: refusing to respond to a party commission, he took his case to foreign correspondents. The whole affair flared up afresh in the Western media. I was not involved at the beginning, because Dedijer had shunned me since the summer; we merely nodded to each other in chance encounters on the street. But foreign newsmen now turned to me as well, and I was soon pulled into the affair. I was glad of the chance, not only from feelings of solidarity with Dedijer, but also because at last I could draw the line publicly between myself and the party leadership and the regime.

Apparently the leadership, too, was surprised that this business flared up again. The police reacted sluggishly and observed normal procedures. The fact that Tito and Ranković were on their way to India must have accounted for it. Their trip was used against Dedijer and me both in the press and in court: allegedly acting upon foreign instructions, we had made our statements in order to compromise Tito's peacemaking mission to India. An article appeared in *Borba* entitled "The Obedient Pawn"—from its style, I detected the hand of Pijade—which portrayed me as a treacherous puppet set in motion from abroad at the push of a button.

More journalists arrived. I can remember an interview with Catherine and Edward Clark, of Reuters, I think, and another with Jack Raymond, the *New York Times*'s Belgrade correspondent, and his secretary, Mirjana Komarecki, who translated. Though my knowledge of English had broadened, it was not adequate for precise expression.

Dedijer and I had not worked out a common approach. At the beginning of the affair we were not in touch, so he proceeded on his own. It was Catherine Clark, I believe, who told me that Dedijer maintained that the regime wanted to kill him. She asked if they had any such plans for me. I said that was out of the question. But in attempting to shed some light on his claim, I remarked that Dedijer was unjustly attacked. He took this remark of mine amiss. I met with Jack Raymond at the Union Hotel, which was in my neighborhood, and gave him a statement characterizing the present order in Yugoslavia as totalitarian. This was the first time I suggested that the way out of our impasse might be the creation of a second party. I also made a prediction: that the regime in Yugoslavia would change in twelve to fifteen years. The regime did not change, but the country did.

The regime obviously could not remain indifferent to the statements made by Dedijer and me, for that would suggest indecision regarding the new socialist oppositionists. Almost a year after my sentencing at the Central Committee plenum, criminal charges were lodged against us for "hostile propaganda." The investigation was so undramatic, so routine, that I cannot recall any details. But Dedijer and I prepared ourselves thoroughly for the trial, each in his own way. He hired a famous old lawyer, Ivo Politeo, who had defended Tito in 1928; I worked up a long speech.

At first it was my intention to let the court appoint a lawyer. I told everybody freely in my apartment, which was bugged, and elsewhere that I would take any lawyer who got in touch with me. Sure enough, a few days later one did, and I accepted his offer. But I soon realized that this lawyer was planted by the secret police. I withdrew my authorization, with thanks. Then I encountered Desanka Maksimović, or perhaps I dropped in on her, and she suggested I turn to Veljko Kovačević, a lawyer and a socialist whom I had known before the war. He was happy to take my case. He worked very hard and prepared an excellent defense statement. With courage and intelligence, he also defended me at my two subsequent trials: in 1956, for my statement concerning the Hungarian uprising, and in 1957, when *The New Class* was published. Relations between us continued to be friendly and warm right down to his death in 1981.

Waiting for us in front of the court was a crowd of students and police agents, among whom I recognized a high officer of the Guards. Foreign newsmen were present, too. The crowd was chanting "Traitors! Revisionists!" I paid them back in kind. Toward evening our sympathizers stood scattered in the streets near the courthouse.

The trial lasted one day. Since it was held behind closed doors, neither my testimony nor my speech and Kovačević's defense had any significance outside the court and its records. Štefica was present, but my mother was not allowed to attend. Dedijer had not even prepared a speech; his replies were brief and despondent, interspersed with complaints about his illness. We were conditionally sentenced—Dedijer to six months, I up to a year and a half. Dedijer told me later that Kardelj had proposed to Tito, who was still in India, that I be given twenty years and he, if I recall correctly, twelve. I have never believed that story, because political circumstances did not call for such sentences, and, moreover, Kardelj could not have been so senseless.

The day after the trial Dedijer gave a dinner for the lawyers and me, though the friendship thus revived was not to last long. On a stroll through Topčider that spring he suggested that I put my ideas into a book. My response was that any book I wrote could only be critical of Communism. He also told me that he was eager to write my biography, and I proposed that we jointly work on a history of the Yugoslav revolution. Thereafter, Dedijer and I saw each other less often. From the start, I had made a policy of visiting no one unless invited, and of greeting no one on the street unless they first greeted me; too often I would say hello only to see a head turning away. In 1955 or 1956, I don't recall exactly, Dedijer told me he had seen Tito and had told him they had made a mistake with regard to me, attacking a man who was defending the principle of freedom, which is always unpopular.

With his large family, Dedijer had trouble making ends meet. But so did Barović, Drenovac, and I. Still, as time went on, we all managed. In my own family, though, two sisters, a brother-in-law, all with numerous children, and even more distant relatives were fired from their jobs and exposed to misery and blackmail.

My last sight of Dedijer, on the eve of my arrest, reaffirmed our differences both in behavior and in point of view. Marijan Stilinović had come to Belgrade. He was an old Communist and member of the Croatian Central Committee, who had been expelled from the party for objecting to the way accounts had been settled with me. He dropped in on Dedijer, who then invited me to dinner as well. After the meal we had a discussion about how to proceed: what was to be done? Stilinović, who was very critical of Kardelj's lengthy "speechifying," as he called it, proposed that we write a letter to Tito. "You know, the Old Man can change his mind, once he grasps what's going on."

I was opposed. "They'll get that letter up there," I said, "and send an order back down: 'You first, Comrades—say you're sorry!' " Stilinović agreed. "You are right," he said; "nothing would come of that!" I continued: "We don't agree on what should be done, but we do agree on the assessment that the party and the country are moving toward bureaucracy, violence, and stagnation." Dedijer interrupted: "We don't agree even on that. You see things too negatively. We have to wait a while. I expect a great deal from the communes Kardelj is espousing." I turned to him. "Communes! Communes are a euphemism for administrative reorganization!" Not long after, Tito used the same phrase— administrative reorganization—in warning the party bureaucracy against any illusions that might arise from Kardelj's "theory of communalism" as a democratic change and democratic solution.

That was in effect where our efforts to reach an understanding ended. I never saw Stilinović again. He died in dignified disillusionment while I was in prison. Dedijer I saw once more, in the winter of 1967, after my second release, following a written invitation to dinner at the Two Stags restaurant. Our relationship had been hurt by his disparagement of me and my wife to the British Labourites and mutual Yugoslav friends, but I went in hopes of smoothing over old enmities. Nothing of the sort—he was interested in the High Command's negotiations with the Germans in March 1943. I told him what I could remember, and he made notes. He also asked indirectly whether I thought some political scheme was behind my release from prison, but I assured him that was not the case. Ranković's recent removal came up, and Dedijer commented, "When all is said and done, Ranković is an honorable man." While not disputing the claim, I added, "But in politics, the difference between what one wants to do and what one does is important."

I have not seen Dedijer since, nor had any contact with him aside from declining an invitation to be his guest at Bohinje, in Slovenia, in 1967. Actually, he and I had parted company long before, over the differences in our views and methods—differences apparent from the very beginning of my confrontation with the party leadership, and which the years had only deepened.

In a statement in *Politika* of March 13, 1982, Dedijer said: "A big squabble between Djilas and me erupted at the time of the Vietnam war. While he was praising the morale of the American troops in Vietnam, I was condemning them before the Bertrand Russell court."

His claim is untrue on two counts. First, there could have been no squabble over Vietnam, big or little, since he and I never engaged in any discussion, public or private, over that war. Second, only once did I make a public statement on the Vietnam war—and against American intervention at that—in an article published in the U.S. and Latin American press. I have always been of one mind about the lack of justification and good sense in the American involvement in Indochina—this despite the fact that the victorious Vietnamese Communists have since shackled their own people with a system that does not lag far behind the most oppressive of our era, an era so prodigal with violence. And despite the fact that their country's unification had scarcely been achieved before they overran their Cambodian neighbors, forcing on them a puppet government and a ruinous war!

After my arrest on November 19, 1956, Dedijer, speaking to foreign journalists, publicly decried it. Even so, he was allowed to travel abroad—under what conditions I don't know. Permission was granted, it is true, after the tragic suicide of his son Branko, a calamity for Dedijer that I took very hard when I heard about it in prison.

When I was arrested again on April 7, 1962, Dedijer was still abroad. Never after that did he support me, declaring—I quote from memory—that his country was so small and in such difficulties that he did not wish to cause it more problems. But Dedijer then critically dissociated himself from me in the foreign press, and slandered me to leading Labourites and other democrats abroad who sympathized with my resistance and my views. The fact is that for almost thirty years, attacks on me have been a reliable, indeed the most recommended, means of advancement for Yugoslav leaders and major journalists. One way or another, the same applies to Dedijer.

Yet I was taken aback when in 1980, after Tito's death, Dedijer began a noisy, obstreperous, calculated campaign against me through the Yugoslav information media. It took place simultaneously and was synchronized with a campaign led by a group of writers paid by the secret police—boulevard newsmen and obscure café scribblers. It did astonish me; I didn't know what was behind it, but I did know that at one time Dedijer and I had been friends and colleagues. Today, however, I know more. Dedijer struck a deal with Tito—as reported by many Yugoslav publications, including *Politika* on December 18, 1981—to refute so-called inaccuracies in my book *Wartime* in his own forthcoming work, *Djilas Against Djilas*. At Tito's behest, the archives and the hearts of otherwise distrustful functionaries were opened to him.

I am not entering into the man's deeper, private motives, where I could be of only incidental significance—that is the business of historians and of Dedijer himself. But for some two years he carried on a campaign against me, although he knew from his own experience and suffering that I could not defend myself. In Yugoslavia no one wants or dares to publish anything of mine, and abroad they take no interest in such domestic altercations. Later, when both officials and historians began to attack his new book on Tito,* Dedijer, trying to vindicate himself, carried his attacks on me to the foreign news services in Germany, Sweden, and elsewhere. A truly pathetic epilogue to our friendship. Of all the campaigns conducted against me in more than twenty-eight years in Yugoslavia, his has been the most untruthful, and therefore the most arbitrary and ruthless.

It was my original intention to devote an entire chapter to a point-by-point rebuttal of Dedijer's inaccuracies concerning me in his book about Tito and in his numerous statements. But I shall not do so, even though all that Dedijer has written or said

---

* *Novi prilozi za biografiju druga Tita.*

about me is untrue, distorted, misinterpreted, or torn from the context of war and revolution—the actual positions and directives of the party and military leadership of which I was a member. I have never been ashamed of my party and revolutionary past. I have never denied it. In my writings I have described the past and tried to explain it. From today's perspective, that past might have been more beautiful and just had the stage and the actors not been what they were.

And so I abandon the idea of refuting Dedijer because the object of this memoir is not to refute someone else's lies but to narrate truths of my own. I have made exceptions only of certain moral questions and in matters that do not touch on me alone. Future investigators interested in delving more deeply into my shifting relationship with Dedijer will confirm the facts one way or another and evaluate us more justly.

However, I cannot refrain from speaking up for my father, whom Dedijer's *Novi prilozi* depicts as an oppressor of Albanians. No one else may ever come to his defense, leaving Dedijer's claim to be taken at face value. On page 589 he says the following:

After Macedonia and Kosovo were set free in 1912, the bourgeois Serbian state failed to apply the provisions of its own democratic constitution to these areas. Macedonians and Albanians were treated as second-class citizens. An insurrection broke out in Kosovo in 1913 which royalist Serbian troops smothered in blood. Invoking the persecution of Serbs in Kosovo under the Ottomans and carried away by hatred and vengeance, the Serbian bourgeoisie applied the most drastic measures to the Albanian population. [Serbian Socialist leader] Dimitrije Tucović sent to Kosovo his young colleague Kosta Novaković, who published in the periodical *Borba* and in *Workers' News* many accounts of the violence inflicted on the Albanians. Novaković warned Serbia that these bourgeois atrocities would be paid for when propertied Albanians wreaked their vengeance on the Serbs. This came to pass in Kosovo in 1914, with a mass expulsion of Serbs and Montenegrins, as well as many murders. Murdered along with others one night was the father of Milovan Djilas, Nikola Djilas.

There is not one word of truth in the above except that Kosta Novaković reported from Kosovo. The "Serbs and Montenegrins" were not subjected to mass expulsion in 1914, since in 1914 they still retained power in both Kosovo and Metohija. My father was killed by Albanians, but not in 1914 and not by vengeful propertied classes, but by Albanian fascists in 1943, as an old and respected Montenegrin and the father of several Communists. And not "one night," but in broad daylight. Doubtless it is of little concern to history that nothing said here about my father is true either—though it is no minor matter for Dedijer and his relationship to me!

It is inconceivable to me why Dedijer had to have my father meet his death in this way, if not to imply some genetic connection between my so-called misdeeds and my father's alleged crimes as a tool of the "Serbian bourgeoisie" (see page 725 of his book). Furthermore, Dedijer extends that "genetic connection" to my son, Aleksa, associating him (page 77) with the Chetnik counterrevolutionaries, even though Aleksa was not born until 1953. Dedijer knew my mother well, and also my brother and two sisters, who were born between the wars. He knew that my mother was not married twice. Above all, he should have known from my memoirs—which he so often refutes and which impelled Tito to open up the archives to him—that in the first and second volumes my father is spoken of in twenty-one places as alive and well between the wars. Some of those passages go into considerable detail about him. And in the third volume I expressly state that "my father had been killed by Albanian fascists," and go on to cite the killing of two of my brothers and a sister (*Wartime*, pages 417–18). What is the matter with Dedijer? Slovenly research? Malice? Madness? Or all three at once?

# 29

Early in the summer of 1956, I took *Land Without Justice,* a book about my childhood in Montenegro, to Srpska Književna Zadruga in hopes they would publish it. I chose this house more because of its relatively unofficial status than because of its traditional good name, though the latter was not unimportant to me. I was received politely, almost enthusiastically, by Milan Živanović. (Živanović, incidentally, was the nephew of Colonel Dragutin Dimitrijević Apis, who organized the assassinations of King Aleksandar Obrenović and Archduke Franz Ferdinand.)

But when I returned a couple of weeks later to inquire about the manuscript, Živanović testily put me off, telling me that my work had been rejected on the basis of reports by two members of their board of editors, Milorad Panić-Surep and Tanasije Mladenović. Contacts in the circle around my friend Mihiz said afterward that Panić-Surep, a party member with Serbian national-ist leanings, had consulted Ranković and been ordered to reject the manuscript on an appropriate pretext. So instead of being rejected simply because it was mine, the manuscript was declared to be below standard. When I saw Mladenović in 1967 at a memorial for the painter Lazar Vozarević, he remarked, as if in passing, that *Land Without Justice* had been rejected as too "cerebral"—the very word used in his and Panić-Surep's report. He made no mention of Ranković or any order from above. Professor Djurić has told me that as a member of the editorial board he had sought to have his fellow members read my work, but that the opinion of Panić-Surep and Mladenović was pronounced sufficient. He also said that Ivo Andrić had not come to the board meeting, begging off with a headache.

Foreign journalists reported at the time that, though I was writing, I had no prospect of getting anything published. When a certain New York publisher approached me, I mailed him *Land Without Justice,* but soon heard that the work did not fit their publishing program. Shortly thereafter a favorable opinion came from the American Academy of Sciences, which recommended that it be published. The manuscript was given to Harcourt, Brace and Company, which published it in 1958, while I was in prison. *Land Without Justice* has been printed in some ten languages; some critics—I do not share their opinion—regard it as my best work.

The rejection of *Land Without Justice* by Srpska Književna Zadruga had great, not to say paramount, significance for me. I felt the sting and shock of resentment. Here was bitter, painful confirmation that the powers that be, after overthrowing me politically and blackening my name, had resolved to finish me off spiritually, as a writer, unless I submitted and repented. I didn't know how to submit and I couldn't repent without destroying myself. Meanwhile, we were in dire financial straits at home. Some American trade unions wrote me through an American institution in Belgrade, offering aid, but I politely refused.

Only a few days after my rejection by Srpska Književna Zadruga, I set to work on *The New Class.* I had a manuscript to work from, entitled "Freedom and Ownership," but it had not been thought through and lacked organization. Stunned by the rejection, I was now bent on creating a work with broader and more devastating impact. My knowledge, inspiration, and thought all converged into clear, finished thematic units, or chapters. Taking the existing material in hand, I gave it more depth and refinement and welded it into a harmonious, cohesive whole. The book was rewritten from the start in one go.

*The New Class* was completed in three months. Štefica was retyping the final pages in early November 1956, just before my arrest. I cannot claim that *The New Class* would not have been written had the authorities let me publish literary works: the fate of *Land Without Justice* and the organized boycott against me only confirmed a process already under way. But unquestionably that rejection hastened my decision to seek publishers abroad for what I knew would be of interest to them. And, like the boycott and the general campaign, the rejection contributed to the sharpness evident in those new pages.

So while I was writing, I also looked for a publisher. I had one offer, from Praeger in New York, and a vague one at that: for something that might be suitable for them. Keeping quiet about *The New Class* lest the police confiscate it, I made inquiries about Praeger of Catherine Clark and the American library in Belgrade, and was told that in the United States Praeger was considered leftist, which suited my ingrained ideological prejudices. It was my own puritanism that made me shy away from solid "capitalist" firms and conservative newspapers, however respectable, and not the regime's inevitable charges that I had "placed myself in the service of reaction." As it turned out, this proved a mistake: the "leftist" Praeger did not play fair with me.

As soon as half *The New Class* was finished, I sent it off to Praeger. Not through the mail, however, since I knew the police could hardly wait to get their hands on such a manuscript. I had a feeling—I even said as much to Catherine Clark—that the book would be a great success. The other half Štefica sent on after my arrest.

No one knew about the book except my wife and my lawyer, Veljko Kovačević. And not even to him did I give the whole work to read, but only the first half, after it had already been sent to the United States.

As I worked on the book I realized that its original title, "Freedom and Ownership," would not do. I was still undecided when the manuscript was all but completed. Taking a walk with Kovačević near the apartment, I mentioned the problem. Suddenly he said, "Why not call it 'The New Class'?" That was it. How obvious! That was the title of one of the chapters, and it certainly highlighted the work's real thesis. Kovačević gave the manuscript to Nedeljko Divac, the aged head of an insignificant social-democratic group, to read. Divac didn't understand it—for him, it contained little that was new. Kovačević himself thought much more highly of the book, though even he did not foresee its success and acclaim.

Following the Hungarian uprising in October 1956, I made a statement to Agence France Presse opposing the Yugoslav abstention in the UN vote condemning Soviet intervention in Hungary, and published an article in the *New Leader* about the uprising. I allowed for the possibility of arrest. But one evening, as I was walking around Kalemegdan with Barović, a powerful sensation came over me, a certainty, almost, that I would be arrested. Today we know from Veljko Mićunović's *Moscow Years* that Tito and the Soviet leadership were in secret collusion regarding the intervention in Hungary, so it followed logically that I would have to be arrested. But back then I could only have intuited it—and I did.

From my account the reader may get the impression that my ideas were formed simply, step by deliberate step, without any wavering. Not so. To be sure, I did not hesitate when it came to ideas and knowledge. But arriving at the realization that there was no way to publish my views other than in the capitalist West was a long and painful struggle. I needed no special intelligence to understand that I was opening myself to attacks from the Yugoslav leadership because I had betrayed socialism, served as a tool of reaction and who knows of what else besides!

I did not want to go to prison. I remembered the royal prisons and felt that the socialist ones were even more detrimental to mind and soul. I worried about my three-year-old son and young wife—a son who was growing and learning through me, a wife who was sharing my sufferings with all too much devotion. Did I have the right to leave them? Could any idea justify such sacrifices? But my only alternative was to vegetate and rot in shame.

I was arrested on November 19, 1956, but not before the police had searched the apartment so thoroughly that they found some long-lost nail scissors and several stray cartridges. But they paid no attention to a copy of *The New Class* I had purposely left lying around, assuming that it was more of my well-known but rejected and harmless "theorizing." A cold drizzle was falling as they hustled me off between two agents into a car. Štefica, standing in the rain without coat or umbrella, called after me: "Come back! Come back! We'll be waiting for you!"

Before a judge late that afternoon, I was put through the formalities of arrest and opening of an investigation, and then was taken to a spacious cell on the top floor of the Central Jail. Guards were posted outside the door. They took turns sitting there, peering in through the peephole. I lay down in my winter overcoat— I was given a mattress but no bedding—and fell asleep right away. When I looked at *Politika* the next day, Donald Duck caught my eye. I thought of Aleksa climbing into my lap every morning to look at the cartoons with me, and tears came to my eyes. I cried silently, uncontrollably.

The investigation was formal and routine: did you say this, send that, when, and to whom? I confessed to everything, having nothing to hide, apart from what they didn't know and didn't ask. There was nothing of consequence in that interrogation, except the sparks that flew between the judge and me. The judge: "You defend the reactionary rebels in Hungary, yet anyone wearing yellow shoes there is hanged!" (The papers reported that police agents in Budapest wore yellow shoes in order to recognize each other, so now anyone else wearing yellow shoes was also suspect.) I noticed the judge's shoes, and broke in: "You're wearing yellow shoes, too!" At this he smiled in confusion. Judge: "You make statements to the reactionary Western press!" Djilas: "You're using a double standard: when the *New York Times* publishes a statement of mine, it's reactionary, but when it publishes one by Tito, it's reputable." Judge: "You're not the state. You seem unaware of the damage you've done to the party." Djilas:

"What party did you belong to before the war?" The judge turned crimson, for he had once belonged to the Yugoslav Radical Union, which had backed the prewar royalist regime.

I was permitted newspapers and writing materials and weekly visits. Štefica and Aleksa came regularly, with packages from which nothing was missing, as if they themselves were not in want. At my first meeting with my wife, the judge pretended he had other business to attend to and left us alone. We were not fooled, however, and said only what was absolutely necessary. She crossed her forefingers and then gave a flip of her hand, meaning that the second half of *The New Class* had been sent off.

I was in that cell of the Central Jail for about four months, until my sentencing. Sentencing was done in secret, so my voluminous notes and defense preparations came to nothing. Kovačević had engaged two more defense lawyers, Vojislav Grol and Nikola Djonović. This was done to give us political depth, not because he believed any defense would be effective. All three spoke intelligently and persuasively—for the court records, as long as they are preserved. During a recess, while Štefica, Kovačević, and I were consulting in whispers, the question of *The New Class* arose. They were for going ahead with publication, but left the decision to me. Jennie Lee had come to Belgrade in connection with my arrest and, when Štefica told her about the book, had suggested that we not go ahead. "This is for me to decide," I said to my wife and to my lawyer. "The book must be published, come what may."

I didn't have to wait long for the verdict—the authorities were in a hurry to get my case over with. I myself could barely wait to see the last of that monstrous structure in Belgrade, erected against light and life, where all I could glimpse on my exercise walks were the blackbirds flying across a patch of gray sky framed in concrete. The verdict—three years' imprisonment—rendered, I was taken to Sremska Mitrovica Prison, where I had served time before the war with many of the comrades who were now sending me back to prison. Mitrovica, I recalled, at least had some honest-to-goodness criminals and trees, flower beds, and the spacious sky. But that was not for me. For me, a grim cell had been set aside, close to the one in which before the war I had served the first three months of my sentence.

They kept me for sixteen months in cell number 32, building number 2. And there they would have forgotten me, had I not rebelled by threatening a hunger strike. Some democratic international organization, if I remember correctly, was to hold a conference in Yugoslavia, and the moment seemed right to end my isolation, which had grown tiresome.

Two cells down from me, Tibor Vaško was in his eighth year of solitary confinement. Vaško was the Ustashi policeman who had interrogated Hebrang in 1942; so when Hebrang was taken into custody in 1948, Vaško had been dug up from some prison or other and, as an eyewitness valued by the secret police, had been isolated in this cell. He incessantly talked to himself and, fearing poison, kept peeling the crust off his bread—as if they could not have got rid of him in a hundred other ways. In Vaško's fate I saw my own, and that drove me to demand an end to my isolation. He and I were supervised by the same guard when we took our exercise. As we passed each other we had time to exchange a few words. He thought that I knew who he was and why he was in isolation. Once, he said, "They wanted me to testify that Hebrang served the Ustashi. I couldn't do that; I had no knowledge of it."

Approximately two years into my confinement in Mitrovica, I spoke to Marković, the head of prison security, when he was making his rounds, about the illegal and inhumane treatment of Vaško. "You are driving him mad. He's harmless, paying for something he's not guilty of." A month or two later, Vaško was taken away—most likely to another prison.

In my cell I wrote intensively, producing the biography of Njegoš, the novel *Montenegro,* and a collection of short stories. Nothing could come between me and my work, not even a family quarrel in which I severed relations with my brother and younger sister over their unbecoming treatment of Štefica.

One morning in the late summer of 1957, I read in the papers an attack on me triggered by publication of *The New Class.* No one, not even Štefica, had known when the book would come out. The prison authorities were uneasy because the foreign press reported that I had smuggled the manuscript out of prison; Marković lost no time in coming to see me the next day. He always treated me courteously and correctly. I told him that the manuscript had been sent abroad while I was still at liberty. "Will you confirm that in court, if this goes to court?" I said I would, and he left feeling reassured and convinced that I would not let him down.

From the newspaper reports I gathered that a new sentence was in store for me. And, indeed, a few days later, the Mitrovica court began an inquiry. In contrast to the Belgrade judge, who bristled with energy and shrewdness, the Mitrovica judge was a quiet, reasonable man; we had no disagreements or verbal matches.

While waiting to be sentenced again, I was working on Part Two of *Montenegro,* "The Gallows," which describes three men condemned to die. Loneliness and the anticipation of severe punishment left their mark on my text.

On the eve of the trial I was summoned by the prison warden, who asked what penalty I expected. "Ten or twelve years" was my reply. "You can influence the severity of your punishment," he continued. "There are differences between the original and the printed text. Isn't it possible that reactionary circles who have no love for our country have perverted it to suit their own ends? Now, if you were not to recognize the printed text as your own . . ." I cut him off: "The judge warned me of discrepancies in the printed text. But they're trivial. They don't overstep the bounds of a translator's discretion. Even if they did, I wouldn't disown my text."

It was on the basis of this administrative "advice," and before my trial was closed to the public, that I made a statement to foreign journalists that *The New Class* was mine exactly as it had been printed.

Early next day, they took me away to be tried, driving along back roads—policemen love to be vigilant and farsighted—through stands of corn whose yellow tassels breathed wisps of morning mist. As I went on trial, Soviet cosmonaut Yuri Gagarin was beginning man's exploration through the vastness of space.

I refused to answer questions in court, because the trial was held in secret. Kovačević's defense was brilliant, though altogether futile. The prosecutor addressed some compassionate remark to me, and I shot back that I would rather be sitting in the dock than in his chair. I was sentenced to seven years for *The New Class,* or ten in all, taking into account my previous term. I was also stripped of my decorations.

It was now cold between the thick walls of my cell. The prison was poorly heated, and my own cell was not heated at all during the entire nine years I spent in the new Yugoslavia's prisons.

The next summer, 1958, as mentioned already, my solitary confinement ended. To me, this was an indication that the police higher-ups had finally recognized that I was not to be broken by such methods. The change was made by moving selected prisoners to the ground floor. There were about thirty of them, and, as some confided to me, the head of prison security or his assistant had spoken to each individually. They were told to behave decently toward me but to report what I said and did. As before, the forty rooms on the ground floor, which, just prior to my arrival, had been emptied and cut off from an otherwise overcrowded prison, remained sequestered. The only men left in their cells were Tibor Vaško and the witless Šišmanović, a murderer. I served my whole term on this damp ground floor, to make sure I did not send signals through the walls.

Yet from that ground floor, isolated as it was, convicts went out to the prison workshops bearing word of me, and the word then filtered out to their visiting families. The prison administration responded quickly to this error in judgment. After two months, the ground-floor convicts fit for work suddenly left, and old men unfit for work were moved in. There were around twenty of them, all hard-core murderers except for those assigned to my room, who had been convicted of embezzlement and now worked in the ground-floor office. All these men were isolated from the rest of the prisoners and prison areas, but we would all take our "Djilas walk" together. We also went together to the bathhouse and the movies.

In prison as nowhere else, people get to know one another

quickly, or think they do. Every story seems twice told, every response predictable to the point of banality, every temper quick and capricious, every character stereotyped and incorrigible. Avoiding intimacy with anyone, I behaved correctly toward all. Most of these murderers were semiliterate and illiterate peasants. Yet they were human beings with life stories, homes, personalities, and experiences of their own. "It's not the prison that's rough, but the prisoners," goes a prison saying. Still, life with prisoners is easier than life with no human beings at all. Semiliterate or illiterate peasants they may have been, but among them there were honest, intelligent, striking men. I will regret it if I fail to leave a record of some of those lives.

In the fall of 1959, I began to experience nervous spasms—just as my prison discipline had been eased and I relaxed a little. The first symptoms had occurred while I was still at liberty, but discomforts and diseases multiply in prison because one is so self-absorbed. One of the convicts told me that his rheumatism had been relieved by injections. Since the pains I was feeling were similar, I went to the doctor. He prescribed a series of injections, to be administered by a convict on his staff, who went into the next room to fill a syringe. I was afraid he might fill it with a drug to weaken my will, but then I said to myself: "Let's give it a try. They're wrong—I can resist this, too." The rheumatic pains actually went away, although they have not completely ceased to this day. After two or three weeks, however, I began to experience something like a vacuum in parts of my brain, predominantly the left side, and had spasms across my face and temples. Then I really became suspicious that I had been injected with drugs to weaken my will.

I experienced an appalling, unimaginable fear that my will power was indeed weakening. My sleep was racked with terrifying dreams. I even stopped writing, my thoughts broken up by fear. I went to a doctor, who gave me some medicine. It did no good. In the winter of 1959–60 I saw another doctor, the neurologist M., who was brought in from Belgrade. M. recommended that I resolve my "inner conflict," a conflict between "myself and others." He suggested that I write down everything I felt. This I did meticulously, but only the symptoms of my illness, suspicious that any diagnosis based on so-called inner conflict would be police-inspired. The next day I was told that I had not described "what I should do." I ought to have bared the unresolved conflict of my relations to my comrades. I answered that I had written my sensations down and had nothing more to tell. He was in a quandary, even embarrassed. With this, the examination came to an end. In Belgrade later, I learned that this doctor had once been arrested as a reactionary and thereafter had been close to secret police officials.

Far from weakening, my resistance to the authorities grew stronger. But my fears became deeper and more varied. There was fear of madness, fear of doing something unworthy of myself, fear of remorse and submission—all fears worse than the fear of death. I felt no suicidal impulses, but hoped and reassured myself that death or suicide would save me from doing "what I should *not* do."

Thus the days and nights dragged on. In the late winter of 1960, I suffered an attack of appendicitis and was taken to the hospital at the Central Jail in Belgrade. There was a long wait for an examination, so Štefica sounded the alarm abroad. Professor Bukurov concluded that an operation was necessary and arranged to do it himself, with the help of his own assistants and in his own hospital, the Second Surgical Clinic. Kindly inclined toward me, he operated conscientiously and well. A nun named Heribalda took over my nursing care. My wife came to the hospital daily and then issued bulletins to the foreign press. I knew nothing of that, because I was totally isolated: militia from the prison stood guard outside my door, and in my room slept another "patient," a man called Raka, assistant to the head of prison security. Raka was a Partisan from Šumadija, a man broken by dark memories from wartime and after. We talked little, though now and then a friendly "hmm" or word passed between us.

Just after the operation, my nervous affliction almost ceased, leading me to ask Doctor K., a party member who otherwise took no interest in me, whether the illness had perhaps been brought on by the infection in my appendix. He conceded the possibility. But as the wound healed, the spasms reappeared. Yet my senseless conjecture was not wholly irrelevant: the spasms weakened when I concentrated on something else and stopped altogether when my body was in pain.

Upon returning to prison life, I gradually resumed my writing. All too often I lost faith in the logic of my text. Again and again I checked my sentences to make sure they had clarity and cohesion.

In the fall of 1960, the commander of building number 2, where I was in custody, was replaced by the deputy commander of the guard, Šućak. He was a Partisan from the Srem region, open and easygoing. He took only a perfunctory interest in his duties, but quickly displayed a real concern for me, often calling me in for a talk. Realizing that he was there for a purpose, I held myself aloof. Finally, after three months of maneuvering, Šućak tried to talk me into writing a letter to the "comrades up there," asking to be released from prison. "You don't have to cover your head with ashes," he said. "Just say you see the error of your ways, and promise . . ." I stated flatly that I would not write any such petition. Šućak persisted, as one does under orders. Slowly, the price came down: "Go ahead and write—it doesn't matter what. Let's just get the thing off dead center."

Clearly, I thought, Tito and Ranković want to let me go because of pressure from abroad, but not at the price of their own prestige. I began to think. Should I stay in prison when offered a chance—even if not entirely to my liking—to leave? My position had not changed one bit. I understood that this was a game of wits, and I decided to play that game, primarily because of my commitment to writing—my only alternative after leaving prison. Having noticed differences between Ranković's and Kardelj's reports in the press, I wrote to Kardelj. Without pleading or acknowledging any error, I told him I had gathered from my conversations with the prison staff that they wanted to set me free. I also chose Kardelj because he was a man of broader, if not more democratic, views. Besides, I felt then—and still do—that my case had provoked a moral crisis in the top leadership, had created distrust. Tito must have harbored doubts about Kardelj as a "revisionist," and Kardelj, doubts about Tito as a "bureaucrat." Some days later, Šućak told me that I should not have written to Kardelj, who had no authority in this regard. I then composed a letter to Ranković, similar to the one I had sent to Kardelj. But no answer came for some time. They were playing a game with me. Šućak avoided me, and made no overtures.

Finally, in December 1960, there arrived one Vojkan Lukić, the secretary or deputy secretary for Serbian internal affairs. He tried to draw me into conversation, but I remained extremely reserved. His concentration and precision were impressive, but he left without our having come to an agreement.

At the beginning of January came Slobodan Penezić, now the head of the Serbian government, one of the ablest officials in the secret police and the Serbian party. Sentimental and cynical, cruel and intelligent, he was all the harder on me because he had once favored my critical views, only to recant overnight. With calculated hostility toward me, he proceeded to settle accounts with his own onetime "weaknesses." When I reproached him for having signed both the granting and the revoking of my pension, he retorted: "I should say so! You want us to give you a pension and the freedom to work against us."

Penezić presented me with a prepared text for signature. Ranković must have realized that the tug-of-war with me might never end. The petition was skillfully composed, consisting chiefly of passages from my letters to Kardelj and Ranković. The one part I did not like was a promise never to publish *The New Class* again. But I decided not to make an issue of it, since the book had by now been printed in over forty languages. Besides, it was best, I thought, not to change anything in the petition—let "them" be its authors, down to the last word. I signed it.

Back in my cell, when I was handed a copy of "my" petition, there was a sentence at the top I did not recognize and would not have agreed to then, still less now:

In view of the fact that our entire postwar practice and developments in domestic as in foreign policy have refuted everything that led to my provoking criminal proceedings and the pronouncement of a judicial sentence upon me, I expect that the Federal Executive Council will approve my petition to be released from prison.

It was obvious to me that the political leadership and the secret police would use this sentence, if I did not behave, as proof of my wishy-washiness and general instability. But it was too late to change anything; the petition had already gone off. So what? I rationalized. As long as I have not really capitulated, this confused, pusillanimous preamble will not be worth the paper it is written on.

On January 20, 1961, I was conditionally released, and subjected to blackmail and humiliation. The prison warden even read me a short lecture, strained and official in tone. But Štefica and Aleksa were waiting for me in a rented car. The day was cold and gloomy.

My family's financial situation had improved considerably in 1959, when, through the good offices of the Austrian socialist Dr. Christian Brod, we began to receive royalties from *Land Without Justice*, which had recently been published in the United States. That spring, the president of the publishing firm, William Jovanovich, who is Montenegrin on his father's side, stopped off in Belgrade while on a trip to Europe. We struck up a friendship immediately, and his publishing house, Harcourt Brace Jovanovich, undertook to represent my works abroad. We also agreed at that time to publish *Conversations with Stalin*, a work that had long been on my mind though it was not yet written. My professional collaboration with Jovanovich has continued smoothly ever since, and our friendship was strengthened by his testifying before a U.S. Senate subcommittee on my behalf when I was arrested in 1962, and when he was my host in the United States in 1968.

On my release from prison my nervous spasms did not go away, but they became less frequent and proved easier to bear in the company of my wife and son, or when I was working. Through a friend I consulted a Professor R., who prescribed medicines. At first they were ineffective, then they worked. From time to time he would receive me, encourage me, and give me more medicine.

But just before my arrest in the spring of 1962, he extended the intervals between office visits, then missed an appointment and left no message. No Communist, Professor R. was even critical of Communism, but he prudently adapted his medical ethics to the requirements of the authorities. It was then, in February 1962, that I realized I dared not rely on medicines or physicians. As I was returning home from Professor R.'s office, my anger congealed and a decision crystallized: no more medicines—not even what I had left—and no more doctors. Thereafter I followed my own advice. The illness persisted, but I knew that I was stronger than it, and that nothing could ever make me act contrary to my conscience.

Now and then Western journalists and an occasional scholar from the West came to visit. This happened even on the island of Hvar, where Štefica, Aleksa, and I spent our summer vacation. Patrol boats were stationed on the island's little bays—boats that had not been there before we arrived—and the police dogged our every step.

Upon returning to Belgrade in September 1961, I was summoned by Vojkan Lukić to the Serbian Ministry of Internal Affairs. He rebuked me for not holding to the terms of my conditional discharge, then took up my habit of meeting with foreign journalists: "We can easily work your talks with foreigners into a criminal case. I warn you to stop, or you will be sent back to jail." "I'm not going to padlock my lips to suit you," I replied. "You'll have to do that yourself. Furthermore, there is no law that prohibits meetings with foreigners, and even if there were, I wouldn't think twice about breaking it."

But Lukić persisted. "These foreign journalists are intelligence agents. They don't come to you because they're friends of yours but to use you for their own ends." "Some of them may well be agents," I replied, "but that's not stamped on their foreheads, and it has nothing to do with me. I've never been and never will be anyone's agent. I only want to present my social and philosophical views." "We'll publish your petition for mercy. In it you retract your previous beliefs and express regret." "I didn't retract a thing," I said, "and I expressed no regret. It was you who wrote the petition, and you can go ahead and publish it." Thus Lukić, though he kept within proper bounds, persisted in making threats, while I, so recently a prisoner, remained obdurate.

In those days I was working hard on *Conversations with Stalin*, but I was overwhelmed by doubts. Half in jest, I asked my wife to look through the text and judge whether it was logical and coherent. In the opinion of many critics, it is my most harmonious and cleanest piece of work.

I mailed *Conversations with Stalin* to Jovanovich, who received it in late autumn and immediately had it translated. By early February he was in Belgrade to discuss with me obscure passages, of which there were few. By the end of February, a column by C. L. Sulzberger in the *New York Times* announced my forthcoming work. Other papers picked it up, thus alerting the Yugoslav leaders.

Once more I was called in by Lukić. He was politely businesslike: they had been informed about my book, so would I please give them the text. I took a moment to reflect: they'll get their hands on it sooner or later, even if it's in some foreign language; these UDBA chiefs are in a tight spot with Tito—how come they didn't get their hands on the original in time? "Let me think it over till tomorrow," I said. Lukić smiled. "Why put it off? Give it to us now." Well, I thought, I'm not at odds with UDBA— they're simply obeying Tito and Ranković. My quarrel is with Tito and the Central Committee. "All right," I said, "I'll give it to you." Lukić picked up from the table an official receipt for my manuscript, already typed and stamped. I signed—one copy for him, one for me. Then he ordered his secretary, a handsome, pleasant young man, to go with me by car to fetch the manuscript. Štefica was not overjoyed with what I had done but, like me, she did not attach much importance to it. To this day I believe I did the right thing.

Around that time a new paragraph in the Criminal Code was submitted to the National Assembly, whereby former officials could be convicted if they revealed state secrets dating from their earlier employment. As if I had seen it coming, in *Conversations with Stalin* I did not mention anything that others had not already revealed, above all, Tito. It was clear that this paragraph was intended for me. And it was clear to others as well—one Swiss journalist called it the *lex Djilas*.

Several days after my talk with Lukić, Slobodan Penezić called me in. Dispensing with courtesies, he gestured me to a seat and immediately went on the attack. "There you go again! It means nothing to you that you've already been in jail. You won't get out of it this time! You're tied in with Belgrade reactionaries and foreign spies." No less heatedly, I let him have it right back. "What connections can I possibly have? You've isolated me! What reactionaries are you talking about? No one goes around wearing a label 'Spy!'" "Shut up," he hissed, "I am doing the talking." Tit for tat, I gave as good as I got. "Why don't you shut up when I am talking?" That brought the man back to his senses, but hardly mollified him.

Penezić continued, with irony. "Who are your friends? Veljko Kovačević and Voja Grol." "When Veljko Kovačević was in the People's Front," I retorted, "he wasn't your despised reactionary. As for Voja Grol—so what if he's the son of his father? You're the son of a coffeehouse keeper—does anyone hold that against you?" Penezić was silent, then he said scornfully, "You're conceited." To which I replied, "And why not? Talented and famous—first as a Communist, and now as a critic of Communism."

He subsided, then summoned up his fury anew. "I didn't call you in here to fight. Either you retract that book, or else . . ." "I'm not about to retract anything. It's all typeset and announced for publication." ". . . or else this time you'll get ten or twelve years. Being a revisionist isn't enough for you; now you're betraying state secrets." "None that aren't already known." "Even so, that bit about Albania is embarrassing, most embarrassing." And again, getting up steam: "I've told you what I had to say. Think about it. You have a child, a son. Don't think you'll slip out of it easily this time." "I'm not fooling myself one bit," I answered. "And what is there to think over? I'm ready for jail right now." Penezić dismissed me. "You can go. You've heard what you need to know."

That exchange is not accurate down to the last word, nor could it be, after so many years. But I have retained the essence of it in my memory, and a good many details and words, because of its exceptional, dramatic quality. Penezić and I were like members of an estranged family. My brother had received him into the party, and there was a time, according to a mutual friend, when Penezić had been drawn to me and my ideas.

Štefica was waiting for me in front of the Serbian government building. She saw me coming out pale and angry. I told her they would arrest me. On a walk that evening, I complained that I didn't feel like going back to prison, that I was still having problems with my nerves. She was consoling. "Aleksa and I will come see you. We'll take care of you. You'll survive this, too." I felt fairly strong, then, strong enough for another term. But has anyone ever written about the sacrifice, patience, and humiliation of prisoners' wives?

Two days later, on April 7, 1962, police officers and a judge entered my apartment. There was no search. The judge was looking for *Conversations with Stalin*, a copy of which I had placed on the table, though Lukić already had one. The judge then asked for my remaining manuscripts. There were many, so the inventory took a long time. They suggested taking everything in a bundle, making a list, and returning what was not controversial. I agreed, and stuffed a leather suitcase full of manuscripts. The judge was casual and even said that this was a mere formality, that I'd be home again that very day. Even so, I took along necessities: a blanket, warm underwear, books, toilet articles, writing materials. He was a crafty fellow, more cunning than any policeman, this judge under the wing of the secret police. They took me straight to the Central Jail, where my writing materials were taken away. As for my manuscripts, they were not returned to me until five years later, 1967, and then at my request. I got them back bound in small bundles; only the suitcase was missing.

A day or two later, in the evening, I was brought before this same judge. I assumed it to be an official inquiry, but instead he initiated a conversation in which he displayed understanding, even sympathy, and wondered at my unreasonableness, at my failure to grasp realities. "A man of your intelligence, to behave in such a way!" He kept insisting that certain passages in the book made me liable to criminal prosecution, and I kept denying it. "You don't understand—we lawyers look at it differently." I blurted out, "It's been read by lawyers, and not one of them found anything illegal." This was true: I had given *Conversations with Stalin* to my lawyers—Kovačević, Grol, and Barović—waiting, of course, until my New York publisher had it safely in hand. I gave it to them more as friends than as lawyers, but not one of them found any legal problems. The judge seized on that at once. "Who are these lawyers? And what kind of lawyers are they? There are lawyers and lawyers! Who gave you such bad advice?" I drew back. "The names are not important. They're excellent lawyers." "But *who*? I have to know their names." I refused to disclose them, adding, "In the last analysis, the opinions of lawyers aren't important. This is a political matter. You yourself can verify that there's nothing in the book that Tito, Vukmanović, and the others haven't said already."

A few days later the judge was replaced as investigator by an UDBA official. I took that to mean increased pressure on me, but the UDBA man turned out to be, unlike the judge, straightforward and not treacherous. As the investigation proceeded, I was read the judge's statement that I had told him lawyers had seen my manuscript. I did not deny having said this, but now declared, "No lawyers read my manuscript. The judge and I wanted to impress each other." The investigator then asked me straight out if I had given my manuscript to Kovačević, Grol, and Barović. I said I had not. He then handed me their testimony to read, in which they came to my defense but also confirmed that I had let them read the manuscript. I stuck to my story. If they arrest these men, my only friends, I thought, I don't want to put an additional burden on their shoulders. They can then do as they think best.

Four months later came the trial—secret, as before. Again, I refused to answer questions. A court-appointed lawyer defended me, since my defenders had been tricked into becoming witnesses for the prosecution. This official lawyer, a former prison administrator, hung up the phone on Štefica and refused to give her the bill of indictment—lest she pass it on to the foreign press. At the trial he uttered a few sentences, more supportive of the indictment than of me. Stefanović, the judge, was impressive in his efficiency and dignity. The prosecutor, flapping his arms, overturned a carafe of water, which shattered right in front of the bench. When it came the turn of the witnesses for the prosecution, each acted in character, not just in testifying but also in dealing with the broken glass on the floor: Grol took no notice, Kovačević pushed it aside to clear a place to stand, Barović kicked it furiously.

I was sentenced to five years. Added to the earlier punishments, this now came to fifteen. An innocent man was put away in order to silence him on the eve of a visit by Gromyko.

I felt stronger and calmer than ever, because even by the strictest legal standards in Yugoslavia, I was innocent. I did not intend to appeal to a higher court, just as I had not before, but reports reached Štefica—planted, perhaps—that they might revoke the sentence and intern me somewhere, so she insisted. The lawyer Slobodan Subotić, engaged by Veljko Kovačević, visited me in prison and agreed to make the appeal. Before the war Subotić had belonged to the Radical party and the Yugoslav Radical Association, and had been close to the head of the government, Milan Stojadinović. Only among followers of the old parties could I find a lawyer who would voluntarily take on my defense. Subotić composed an appeal to the higher court that I remember as a masterpiece of compression and destructive logic. Naturally it had no effect: courts and judges are only a channel for verdicts that party circles have already determined.

It was a hot July day, and exhaust fumes filled the car taking me once again to Mitrovica Prison. But this time I was steady and calm. I could go on like this to the end of my life. Regularly and without fail Štefica and Aleksa came to see me, she in her best years, he growing up. That all passed with my imprisonment, with my years as a convict.

For more than two years I was given no paper and ink. Ink I did get hold of somehow, but the writing had to be done on toilet paper. It was on toilet paper that I wrote my novel *Under the Colors*, about half of the novel *Worlds and Bridges*, and the beginning of my translation of Milton's *Paradise Lost*. Then it was announced that Yugoslavia would host some congress—the International P.E.N. Club, I think it was. I was fed up with writing on toilet paper, which someone higher up was obviously tolerating. Presenting myself before the prison doctor, I announced that I would go on a hunger strike if writing materials were not given me. He defended himself. "You straighten that out with the administration. I have nothing to do with it." "What do you mean, nothing?" I replied. "As I lie dying here, then you will have something to do with it!" Two or three hours later the head of prison security came to me, meticulously correct and solicitous. "Why go to the doctor about this?" he asked reproachfully. "We're here, the prison administration, if you need anything. I had no idea that you were not allowed writing materials. That happened before I took over." Two days later I was given permission to have writing materials.

At the end of November or the beginning of December 1966, after nine cold winters, an electric heater was installed in my cell. The fall of Ranković in the summer of 1966 served some purpose, after all.

After supper on December 30, my cellmate B. and I were suddenly ordered to take our bedding and move into a room on the floor above. We wondered what this could possibly mean. It occurred to B., a former UDBA man sentenced for taking bribes, that there might have been a coup d'état and they were emptying the cells for new prisoners. Such thinking perhaps stemmed from his "professional deformation," but I easily talked him out of it. After all, the rest of our things—food, my manuscripts, other articles—were staying in the cell. It had to do with us. But why? Perhaps they wanted to know what I was writing. We listened hard: not a sound from down below, in a building whose acoustics were otherwise excellent. It flashed across my mind that I might be set free, but I put the thought behind me. That would be no reason to move us out overnight.

In the morning they sent us back to the cell. Carefully we examined the room. Everything was in its place, but as B. observed, "That doesn't mean anything. You're not supposed to leave a trace when you break into someone's apartment." After the exercise walk I was summoned by the building commander, Petrović, a moderate and conscientious civil servant. "I have good news for you," he said tersely. "You've been amnestied. Get ready to go home." I was freed unconditionally, but neither my decorations nor my civil rights were restored.

Surprised and flustered, I began to pack, not knowing where to begin. B. helped me pull myself together. I had food in reserve; not long before, Štefica had brought me a sizable package. By prison tradition you left your food to your fellow inmates. Scarcely five minutes passed before they had divided it all. Prisoner C., a soldier from Šumadija who had been in the Salonika campaign in World War I, got my sheepskin jacket, which he had long been eyeing. Now it was clear to B. and me: last night we were moved from our cell so they could look through my manuscripts. They kept none of them, however.

I had to wait for Štefica to come from Belgrade with clothes. This time the warden did not preach the usual homily. Handing me my certificate of release, he said in a strained tone that he hoped we would not see each other again soon. Out front were my wife and son, and a handful of foreign correspondents. Passionate hugs, affectionate words.

Everything was better and worse than it might have been. The hour was late, but the road I was on was of my own choosing.

# Biographical Notes

Ivo Andrić (1892–1975)
Serbian writer from Bosnia. His novel *The Bridge on the Drina* is his best-known work. In 1961 he was awarded the Nobel Prize for Literature.

Vladimir Bakarić (1912–1982)
A leading Croatian Communist who helped organize Partisan resistance in Croatia during World War II. He later held high government and party posts in Croatia.

Vulko Chervenkov (1900–    )
Bulgarian Communist leader. He lived in the Soviet Union from 1925 to 1944, when he returned to Bulgaria to become secretary of the Communist party. He became Prime Minister in 1950. After Stalin's death he served in lesser posts.

Dobrica Ćosić (1921–    )
Serbian novelist who fought with the Partisans during World War II. From 1945 to 1968 he served in the Yugoslav Assembly. He is best known for his tetralogy *This Land, This Time*.

# Biographical Notes

### Peko Dapčević (1913–    )
Montenegrin Communist who fought in the Spanish Civil War, joined the Partisan uprising in Montenegro, and became commander of the First Army. In 1953 he was named chief of the Yugoslav General Staff, but was demoted as a result of being indirectly involved in Djilas's troubles with the party.

### Vladimir Dedijer (1914–    )
An editor of the Communist party newspaper *Borba* and a member of the agitprop section during the war. He later became a member of the party's Central Committee. He wrote two important accounts of Partisan history: *Diary* and *Tito,* both of which have been published in English. He broke with the party in 1954, and has since devoted himself to writing history and teaching.

### Georgi Dimitrov (1882–1949)
Prominent Bulgarian Communist and a high-ranking official of the Comintern who lived in the Soviet Union for many years. He returned to Bulgaria at the end of World War II to lead the Communist party there, and became premier in 1946.

### Mitra Mitrović Djilas (1912–    )
Serbian-born first wife of Milovan Djilas. She joined the Partisans in 1941 and did party organization work. After the war, she held important education posts in Serbia.

### Andrija Hebrang (1899–1948)
Prominent Croatian Communist and leader of the Partisan movement in Croatia during the war. In 1946 he was found guilty of wartime cowardice and collaboration with the Ustashi, and was relieved of all his posts. After being arrested while allegedly fleeing to Rumania in 1948, he committed suicide; some sources claim he was murdered.

### Enver Hoxha (1908–    )
Top Albanian Communist leader. He was a founder of the Albanian Communist Party (1941) and of the Albanian National Liberation Movement (1942). He became head of the Albanian party in 1943 and retained that post while also holding various government positions.

### Arso Jovanović (    –1948)
Officer in the prewar Royal Army who joined the Partisans in 1941 and helped organize their army, serving as chief of the General Staff through 1946. When Tito broke with Moscow in 1948, he sided openly with the Soviet Union. He was killed by border guards while trying to escape to Rumania.

Blažo Jovanović (1907–1976)
One of the organizers of the Partisan uprising in Montenegro in 1941. He held high Communist political posts during and after the war. Proclaimed a National Hero.

Edvard Kardelj (1910–1979)
A leading Slovenian Communist who received prewar training in Moscow and was an organizer of the Partisan uprising in Slovenia in 1941. He later became a member of the party's Central Committee and in 1945 vice-premier of the new Yugoslav government. For many years he was Tito's second-in-command and a leading party ideologist.

Boris Kidrič (1912–1953)
A leading Slovenian Communist who, with Kardelj, organized the Partisan uprising in Slovenia in 1941. He held high political posts in Slovenia during and after the war, became a Politburo member in 1948, and was in charge of the Yugoslav economy from 1946 until his death.

Traicho Kostov (1897–1949)
Bulgarian Communist leader, a member of the Politburo and Deputy Prime Minister. Though an anti-Titoist, he was associated with a "Bulgaria-first" outlook. Stripped of power and indicted in 1949, he created a sensation by repudiating his confession at the trial. He was condemned and executed.

Miroslav Krleža (1893–1982)
Croatian dramatist and writer who edited a series of literary and political journals between the two world wars. His progressive views made him a magnet for the interwar intelligentsia.

Veljko Mićunović (1916–1983)
Montenegrin Communist, became a member of the Central Committee in 1952 and a Presidium member in 1972. He was Yugoslav ambassador to the Soviet Union from 1956 to 1958 (an experience he described in *Moscow Years*) and to the United States from 1962 to 1967.

Draža Mihailović (1893–1946)
Colonel in the prewar Royal Army who organized the Chetnik resistance to the German occupation in 1941. He was promoted to general and named minister of war by the royal government-in-exile. When fighting broke out between the Chetniks and the Partisans, he collaborated with the Italians and later with the Germans. The British supported him until 1944. Reluctantly dismissed by King Peter, he was tracked down by the Partisans, captured in 1946, tried as a traitor, and executed.

## Biographical Notes

### Blagoje Nešković (1907–1984)
Serbian Communist who fought in the Spanish Civil War and jointed Tito's Partisans in 1941. In 1945 he was Premier of Serbia. A member of the Central Committee of the Yugoslav Communist Party, he was accused of deviation in 1952 and stripped of his posts.

### Ante Pavelić (1889–1959)
Croatian fascist leader who in 1941, under Axis sponsorship, became head of the puppet Independent State of Croatia. His special troops, the Ustashi, massacred hundreds of thousands of Serbs, Jews, and Gypsies, and fought both Partisans and Chetniks. At the end of the war he escaped from Yugoslavia and took refuge in Argentina and Spain. Allegedly, he died in Madrid in 1959.

### Moša Pijade (1890–1957)
Prominent Yugoslav Communist of Serbian Jewish origin. With Djilas, he led the Partisan uprising in Montenegro in 1941. He held high political posts during and after the war and was a member of the Central Committee and the Politburo. Proclaimed a National Hero.

### Koča Popović (1908–     )
Communist volunteer in the Spanish Civil War who was interned in France. He joined the Partisans in 1941, commanded various units, and was chief of the General Staff from 1946–1953. He became foreign minister of Yugoslavia in 1946. Proclaimed a National Hero.

### Aleksandar-Leka Ranković (1909–1982)
A leading Yugoslav Communist of Serbian origin who was a member of the Politburo from 1940. Captured and tortured by the Gestapo in 1941, he was rescued by a daring Communist raid. He served on the Supreme Staff throughout the war. After the war, he was minister of the interior and head of the military and secret police. He fell from power in 1964, ostensibly for abusing his authority, and was expelled from the party in 1966.

### Ivan Šubašić (1892–1955)
A prewar Croatian political leader who was a member of the Croatian Peasant party and became governor of Croatia in 1939. He fled Yugoslavia in 1941, served the royal government-in-exile, and in June 1944 became its prime minister. In this capacity he concluded two agreements with Tito, which led to a coalition government, with Tito as premier and himself as foreign minister. He resigned in 1945 for political reasons and reasons of health.

### (Josip Broz) Tito (1892–1980)
Wartime and postwar leader of Yugoslavia. Born in Croatia, he was a locksmith and metalworker. Arrested for antiwar propaganda during World War I, he was sent to the front with the Austrian army, was wounded and captured by

the Russians. He joined the Red International Guard during the October Revolution in 1917. Back in Yugoslavia, he joined the Communist party and rose in its ranks. He became secretary-general of the Yugoslav party and reorganized it. He led the Partisan movement from 1941. In 1945 he became premier of a coalition government, then head of the new People's Republic of Yugoslavia. He remained head of the state and the party until his death.

### Vladimit Velebit (1907– )
Croatian Communist who joined the Partisans in 1941. He served on the Supreme Staff. In 1943 he headed a military mission to Great Britian. After the war, he served as ambassador to Italy and to Great Britain. He was a delegate to the United Nations in the 1960's.

### Veljko Vlahović (1914–1975)
Montenegrin member of the Yugoslav Communist Party from 1935. He fought in the Spanish Civil War and was active in organizing the Communist Youth League of Yugoslavia. During World War II he directed the Free Yugoslavia radio. In 1944 he became editor of the Communist daily, *Borba*. He also served as deputy Foreign Minister.

### Svetozar Vukmanović-Tempo (1912– )
A leading Montenegrin Communist and member of the Central Committee. During the war he served on the Supreme Staff, went on missions to Bulgaria, Greece, and Albania, and became Tito's personal representative in Macedonia. He held high positions in the postwar government. Proclaimed a National Hero.

### Kochi Xoxe ( –1948)
Albanian Communist leader, Minister of Interior and head of the secret police, for a brief period the most powerful man in Albania, thanks to Yugoslav backing. He was executed for alleged Trotskyite and Titoist activities at the time of the Tito-Cominform break.

### Radovan Zogović (1907– )
Montenegrin Communist, journalist, and author. He did propaganda work for the party during and after the war.

### Sreten Žujović (1899–1976)
Serbian veteran of World War I and long-time Communist. He was a member of the Central Committee and the Politburo before World War II. He helped organize the Partisan uprising in Serbia in 1941 and became a member of the Supreme Staff. Finance minister in the postwar government, he lost his party membership and high office when he sided with Stalin against Tito in 1948.

# Index

Index

# Index

# Index

Index

# Index

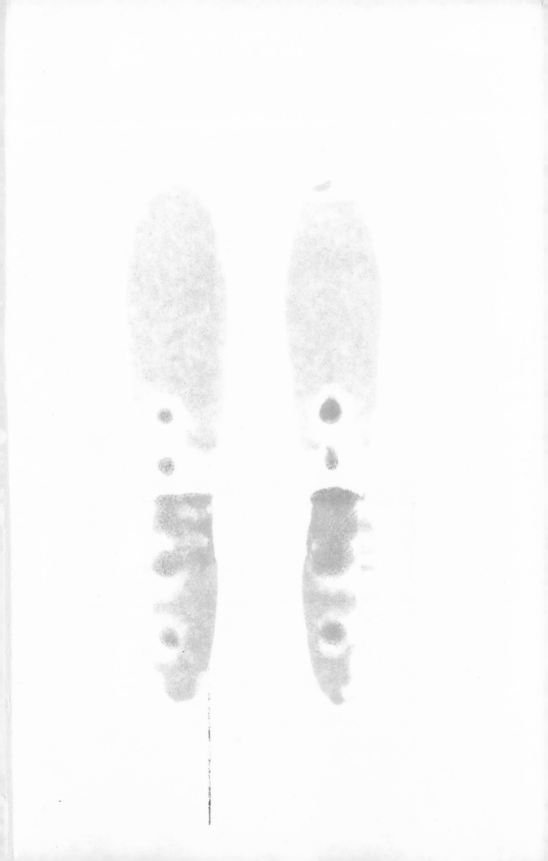